Hannah Arendt

Twenty Years Later

Hannah Arendt

Twenty Years Later

edited by Larry May and Jerome Kohn

The MIT Press
Cambridge, Massachusetts
London, England

First MIT Press paperback edition, 1997

This book was set in Baskerville by Asco Trade Typesetting Ltd., Hong Kong and printed and bound in the United States of America.

Library of Congress Cataloging-in-Publication Data

Hannah Arendt : twenty years later / edited by Larry May and Jerome Kohn.
p. cm. — (Studies in contemporary German social thought)
Includes bibliographical references and index.

ISBN 0-262-13319-9 (HB), 0-262-63182-2 (PB)

1. Arendt, Hannah—Contributions in political science. 2. Arendt, Hannah. I. May, Larry. II. Kohn, Jerome. III. Series.
JC251.A74H39 1996
320.5'092—dc20 95-51067
CIP

Contents

Contributors

Annette Baier, a past president of the American Philosophical Association (Eastern Division), is professor of philosophy at the University of Pittsburgh. She is the author of *Postures of the Mind* (University of Minnesota Press, 1985), *A Progress of Sentiments* (Harvard University Press, 1991) and *Moral Prejudices* (Harvard University Press, 1994).

Bat-Ami Bar On is professor of philosophy and women's studies at the State University of New York in Binghamton. She is the editor of *Engendering Origins: Critical Feminist Readings in Plato and Aristotle* (SUNY Press, 1993) and *Modern Engendering: Critical Feminist Readings in Modern Western Philosophy* (SUNY Press, 1993). She is currently completing a book on Arendt and Jewish identity.

Jeffrey Andrew Barash has taught at the University of Chicago and at Columbia University and is currently professor of philosophy at the University of Picardie in Amiens, France. He is the author of *Martin Heidegger and the Problem of Historical Meaning* (Martinus Nijhoff, 1988) and *Heidegger et son siècle: Temps de l'Être, temps de l'histoire* (1995).

Ronald Beiner is professor of political science at the University of Toronto. He is the author of *Political Judgment* (University of Chicago Press, 1983), *Democratic Theory and Technological Society* (M. E. Sharpe, 1988), and *What's the Matter with Liberalism?* (University of California Press, 1992) and the editor of *Hannah Arendt's Lectures on Kant's Political Philosophy* (University of Chicago Press, 1982).

Richard Bernstein, a past president of the American Philosophical Association (Eastern Division), is professor and chair of philosophy at the New School for Social Research. He is the author of *John Dewey* (Washington Square Press, 1966), *Praxis and Action* (University of Pennsylvania Press, 1971), *Restructuring of Social and Political Theory* (Harcourt Brace, 1976), *Beyond Objectivism and Relativism* (University of Pennsylvania Press, 1983), *Political Profiles* (University of Pennsylvania Press, 1986), and *The New Constellation* (MIT Press, 1992).

James Bohman is associate professor of philosophy at St. Louis University. He is the author of *The New Philosophy of Social Science* (MIT Press, 1991) and has just completed *Public Deliberation* (MIT Press, 1996).

Margaret Canovan, a reader in politics at the University of Keele, has written two books on Arendt, the most recent of which is *Hannah Arendt: A Reinterpretation of Her Political Thought* (Cambridge University Press, 1992).

David Ingram is professor of philosophy at Loyola University of Chicago. He is the author of *Habermas and the Dialectic of Reason* (Yale University Press, 1987) *Critical Theory and Philosophy* (Paragon, 1990), and *Reason, History, and Politics* (State University of New York Press, 1995).

Suzanne Jacobitti is associate professor of political science at Southern Illinois University in Edwardsville.

Jerome Kohn is adjunct professor of philosophy at Cooper Union and lecturer in humanities at the Graduate Faculty of the New School for Social Research. He is currently editing what is projected to be a three-volume set of Hannah Arendt's papers, the first volume of which has been published as *Essays in Understanding 1930–1954* (Harcourt Brace, 1994).

Larry May is professor of philosophy at Washington University in St. Louis. He is the author of *The Morality of Groups* (University of Notre Dame Press, 1987) *Sharing Responsibility* (University of Chicago Press, 1992), and *The Socially Responsive Self* (University of Chicago Press, 1996).

Elizabeth Meade teaches philosophy at Cedar Crest College in Pennsylvania. Her doctoral dissertation at Boston College was on the moral dimension of Hannah Arendt's philosophy.

Dana Villa is associate professor of political science at Amherst College.

Albrecht Wellmer is professor of philosophy at the Free University of Berlin. He is the author of *Critical Theory of Society* (Herder and Herder, 1971) and *The Persistence of Modernity* (MIT Press, 1991).

Elisabeth Young-Bruehl is University Professor of Humanities at Haverford College. She is the author of *Freedom and Karl Jaspers's Philosophy* (Yale University Press, 1981), *Hannah Arendt: For Love of the World* (Yale University Press, 1982), *Anna Freud: A Biography* (Summit, 1988), *Mind and the Body Politic* (Routledge, 1988), and *Creative Characters* (Routledge, 1991).

Introduction

"I don't fit," Hannah Arendt once said of herself. She meant that she was neither "left" nor "right," neither liberal nor conservative, neither progressive nor reactionary. Her political ideal was a stable world that would also be open to novelty. Without question she was a thinker, yet she rejected the calling of philosophy, despite the fact that she had been an exceptionally gifted student of two of the most important German philosophers of the twentieth century. She was also a Jew who was forced to flee her homeland in 1933 and who remained stateless until she became an American citizen in 1951. What she learned from this period of statelessness was the importance of contingency as a factor in human history, and thereafter her thought was indissolubly tied to this experiential insight.

Born in 1906 into a well-established, nonreligious German Jewish family, Arendt grew up in Königsberg, the ancient capital of East Prussia. This was the city of Immanuel Kant, whose work she discovered when she was fourteen years old and continued to read throughout her life. (She used to say that whenever she sat down to write she had the sense that Kant was looking over her shoulder.) She was initially drawn to philosophy, theology, and classical Greek literature, and in her early years, according to her own testimony, politics held no interest for her at all. At Marburg, she studied with Martin Heidegger, whose influence on her, both positive and negative, can hardly be overestimated. At Heidelberg, she studied with Karl Jaspers, writing her dissertation on Saint Augustine's concept of love. Her relationship to Heidegger, controversial in many respects, is treated in more than one of the essays in this collection.[1] Her relationship to Jaspers developed from that of student and teacher into a lasting friendship that would, in time, become a sort of model for Arendt's conception of the realm of the political.[2]

Arendt saw the rise of the National Socialist movement first hand, and the "shock of reality" this experience induced would be crucial for her intellectual development. The world destructiveness of a movement that relied on terror to realize an ideology—what she would come to label "totalitarianism"—lies behind Arendt's distinctive understanding of the world as a fragile human artifact. We believe that it was her intense mental activity—the life of her mind—in conjunction with her experience of unprecedented evil that made her into a unique, conventionally unclassifiable political thinker.

Hannah Arendt died in New York City in December 1975. The two decades that have passed since then have seen profound political changes and many new intellectual fashions, but these events in the political and intellectual worlds have only brought into sharper relief the profound uniqueness of her thought.

The contributors to this volume have located in Arendt's work a variety of new ways to understand current debates in political philosophy and ethics, questions concerning the concepts of self and world, and issues of gender and identity. Arendt enjoyed the role of controversial thinker, and it is only with the passage of time that we can now hear what her very controversiality often prevented being heard when she wrote. Her essays on Little Rock and the Eichmann trial are cases in point, but this is not less true of her reflections on modernity, which are especially illuminating in view of the recent debates between postmodernists and the defenders of modernity.

Arendt's writings not only have a timeless appeal but have also been used as framing discussions in many disparate fields. The political theorist Michael Sandel, for example, chose to end his influential 1984 anthology, *Liberalism and Its Critics*, with a selection from Arendt's *On Revolution*, even though most of the other selections were of more recent vintage. And in the 1980s, Yale Law School devoted a popular course to Arendt's writings, even though she had made no formal contributions to legal theory or philosophy of law. These are the models for our authors, who have each used Arendt's work as a framing mechanism or a point of departure for reconsidering enduring problems in moral, political, and legal philosophy.

Nearly all of the major themes of Arendt's political and moral philosophy are captured in these pages. There are essays on Arendt's doctoral dissertation, on her book on Rahel Varnhagen and the early essays on Zionism, and on the infamous "Reflections on Little Rock." There are essays on the concepts of forgiveness, socialization, political pluralism, and virtue as well as her better-known concepts of the banality of evil, totalitarianism, revolution, political judgment, and moral thinking. Indeed, if we had tried to circumnavigate the world of Arendt's thought, we could not have done better than our authors, left largely to their own devices, have collectively done.

The first set of essays provides a thorough treatment of Arendt's political philosophy and locates Arendt's views in contemporary disputes about reason, radicalism, pluralism, and the public sphere. Margaret Canovan starts off by suggesting interesting parallels as well as "crucial" differences between Arendt's thought and that of Michael Oakeshott, arguably the most important conservative political philosopher of the latter half of the twentieth century. The parallels include their "intellectual style and manner," the independence of their thought and "breadth" of their concerns, and their grasp of the limitations of theory in relation to politics. Yet Canovan finds in Oakeshott little sense of what Arendt means by "world" and "plurality," and they differ fundamentally in their views of the importance for politics of the role played by "tradition." Albrecht Wellmer's essay cuts a different way, attempting a rapprochement between Arendt and Jürgen Habermas. Habermas has argued for an understanding of judgment that is deeply procedural and discourse oriented, and hence firmly planted in the liberal tradition. Wellmer argues that although Arendt recognized these liberal dimensions of judgment, she did not develop them sufficiently to see their liberationist potential. Finally, James Bohman shows how both the liberal and conservative interpretations of Arendt's work could be correct by focusing on the divergent strands of her views that led her to support the civil rights movement but condemn the Little Rock desegregation plan. Arendt's blend of leftist views on liberation and conservative views on the value of family and community are one of the most important undercurrents in this volume, and it stands as a challenge to us all that Arendt felt so comfortable bridging these camps.

The second set of essays takes up Arendt's writings on ethics, which are not nearly as well known as her writings on politics. Exceptional in this respect is the concept of "the banality of evil," which functioned as the lens through which she viewed ethics. Larry May analyzes Arendt's thesis about the way some institutions increase the likelihood that evil will result in the world. He then contrasts her views with those of Habermas, arguing that Habermas places too much faith in large-scale, anonymous, bureaucratic institutions. It is crucial, he argues, that ethical socialization occur in small, face-to-face settings in order to offset this tendency of bureaucracies. Elizabeth Meade argues that ethics should be conceived not as a matter of rule-following but as a matter of personal courage and thoughtfulness in the face of evil. Meade sees Arendt criticizing traditional conceptions of ethics in the same way that she criticized bureaucratic socialization. In both cases, the personal involvement with values and virtues is lacking.

Richard Bernstein, Jerome Kohn, and Dana Villa extend the analysis of the banality of evil. Bernstein wants to show that Arendt is consistent in her understanding of evil. In her writings on totalitarianism, she is struck primarily by the ways in which Nazi ideology rendered human beings superfluous. Later, in writing on Adolf Eichmann, she focuses on his thoughtlessness, the fact that he did not realize the consequences of his deeds. Evil, whether radical or banal, is seen as the eradication of human uniqueness. It is an ever-present possibility that cannot be grasped in terms of evil motives or traditional morality. Kohn is also concerned with radical and banal evil, but he sees the difference between the terms as significant in the development of Arendt's thought. Drawing on lectures from 1965–1966, he argues that Arendt's late concern with mental faculties began as an attempt to come to terms with the concept of the banality of evil by differentiating inner experiences of plurality. He stresses Arendt's reading of Kant as providing the philosophical background of modern "worldlessness," as revealing the self-relatedness of the moral subject, and as discovering, in the autonomy of judgment (here in contrast to Wellmer), intersubjectivity as the condition sine qua non of secular communities. Villa compares Arendt's views with those of Heidegger, focusing specifically on the "world-disclosive character of language" in Heidegger and the dialogic role of thinking in Arendt. In both cases, a withdrawal from the world is necessary, but for Arendt, unlike Heidegger, the withdrawal prepares the way for moral judgment.

The third set of essays explores the relationship between self and world. Suzanne Jacobitti starts by locating Arendt's work in contemporary debates between liberals and communitarians on the importance of a conception of the self for social and political theory. She claims that, for Arendt, the self is "neither fully situated nor fully autonomous. It is an embodied self, with a variety of particular, both inherited and culturally acquired, traits; but this self is also, because of its capacity for freedom, able partially to transcend its situation." Such a conception of the self is communitarian but avoids many of the problems with the contemporary forms of communitarianism. David Ingram is also concerned with Arendt's treatment of freedom, especially in her discussions of revolution and the problem of founding a republic. Ingram locates Arendt's work within the context of recent postmodernist writings on the question of how the obligation to obey a new political and legal authority can arise ex nihilo. On Ingram's reading of Arendt, the problem of initial legitimacy can be circumvented by showing that political freedom is enhanced rather than diminished by the founding of a republic and the ensuing obligation to obey that republic.

Both Jeffrey Barash and Ronald Beiner are interested in the philosophical roots of Arendt's conceptions of self and world. Barash contends that, on Arendt's view, one cannot comprehend the concept of truth except through political reflection on the public world. He provides an extended commentary on Arendt's reading of Heidegger's claim that "the light of the public obscures everything." Out of a political reflection on such obscurity comes an understanding of "common sense" that is used to establish an "authentic" although by no means absolute truth. Beiner goes back to Arendt's dissertation on St. Augustine, in which he finds the beginnings of many of her more mature views, especially those expressed in *The Human Condition.* Beiner argues that already in the dissertation Arendt was concerned with the fact that things do not abide and with the human quest to create a public world that will survive the vicissitudes of natural destruction. Love provides the grounding for such a durable public world.

The final set of essays addresses issues of gender and identity. Bat-Ami Bar On reflects on Arendt's writings about Rahel Varnhagen and Rosa Luxemburg, asking why Arendt was so concerned about Jewish identity and yet so little concerned about sexual identity. She concludes that, for Arendt, Jewishness was urgent in a way that gender was not. Elisabeth Young-Bruehl argues that it is a mistake to regard Arendt as a feminist or even a precursor of feminism. She claims, however, that Arendt provides theoretical frameworks, especially concerning identity and difference, that could give feminists a basis for a critical examination of the state of contemporary feminism. Annette Baier argues, conversely, that Arendt was an important precursor of feminism, especially in her style and the subjects, such as forgiveness and natality, that she chose to emphasize. In the end, Baier contends, Arendt should be seen as someone who attempted to "transfigure old ideas" in light of her experiences as a woman. Arendt, like contemporary feminist philosophers, indulged in "a bit of philosophical transvestitism," by speaking of traditionally masculinist notions in a distinctly woman's voice.

Both editors of this volume were students of Hannah Arendt quite late in her life, and in gathering this anthology our intention has been to highlight some of the ways in which aspects of her thought have continued to influence us and our contemporaries. In soliciting essays on practical and theoretical issues that seem urgent today, we have sought to create a tribute to our teacher that would have been impossible at the time of her death. We first had to traverse the terrain of contemporary political and moral thought in order to return to Arendt with something that might have truly interested her. The authors of these essays frequently employ terms of discourse other than hers, but Arendt would not have objected to that. In fact, she would not have wanted it any other way, for her own mode of thinking simply and consistently precluded anything that even remotely resembled discipleship.

Most important, this collection shows that Arendt's example as an independent thinker still matters to the current generation of scholars. Writing at the end of Arendt's century, we find it fitting to dedicate the volume to the next generation of students, with the hope that they in turn, following their own ways, will take her legacy into a renewed and-changed world. We wish to thank Larry Cohen and Melissa Vaughn from MIT Press for their valuable assistance in producing this volume. We also wish to thank Adam Massie for preparing the index. We are also grateful to Harvard University Press for permission to reprint the essay by Annette Baier.

Notes

1. We are happy to report that the Arendt-Heidegger correspondence, which contrary to Arendt's wishes has heretofore been withheld from the public, is scheduled for publication in the near future.

2. See Lotte Kohler and Hans Saner, eds., *Hannah Arendt-Karl Jaspers: Correspondence 1926–1969.* New York: Harcourt Brace Jovanovich, 1992.

I

Political Action and Judgment

1

Hannah Arendt as a Conservative Thinker

Margaret Canovan

I A Question of Definition

Hans Morganthau: What are you? Are you a conservative? Are you a liberal? Where is your position within the contemporary possibilities?

Hannah Arendt: I don't know. I really don't know and I've never known. And I suppose I never had any such position. You know the left think that I am conservative, and the conservatives sometimes think I am left or I am a maverick or God knows what. And I must say I couldn't care less.[1]

This freedom from conventional labels is one of the sources of Hannah Arendt's enduring fascination as a political thinker. From her stance outside the familiar political spectrum she was able to challenge established assumptions and to think about politics in strikingly original ways. All the same, it is possible to find points of contact between her ideas and positions and preoccupations that are more widely shared. In recent years, in spite of the suspicions indicated in the discussion quoted above, it seems to have been the Left who have been most anxious to claim her, in that a good deal of recent work on her thought has been motivated at least in part by interest in the radical potential of her ideas. She was, after all, a fierce critic of capitalism and the bourgeoisie, a supporter of the student radicalism of the 1960s, a celebrator of revolution as a manifestation of the quasi-miraculous capacity of human beings to make a new beginning, and an enthusiast for participatory democracy. Since the collapse of communism and widespread disillusionment with state socialism, some of those for whom being on the Left has come to mean essentially a commitment to radical democracy are finding in Arendt a strain of radicalism that is all the more congenial for being untainted by materialism, Leninism, or historicism.[2]

There is much in Arendt's work that justifies such an interpretation. Nevertheless, it would be a mistake to view her simply as a radical for our time, for earlier suspicions of her conservatism were not just expressions of Marxist prejudice. Interwoven with the radical elements in her thought are strands that are indeed deeply conservative, and that have tended to be less explored by her interpreters. In what follows I shall try to trace some of those strands and to consider Arendt's affinities with and differences from other versions of conservative thought.

"Conservatism" means and has meant many things, and it will save us some confusion if we clear the ground a little by eliminating a few of the kinds of conservative thinking with which Arendt did not have affinities. For instance, many conservatives—from de Maistre to the "Moral Majority"—have held views that subordinated politics to the dictates of dogmatic religion. Conservatism of this kind has no points of contact with Arendt, whose political thought (whatever her private religious beliefs may have been) was decidedly secular and humanist. Neither had she anything in common with the neoliberal worship of the free market that has been such a strident presence in conservative parties in the last couple of decades. As we shall see, one of the elements in her own brand of conservatism was fear of the destructive effects of unbridled market forces. During the discussion cited earlier she observed, "I do not share Marx's great enthusiasm about capitalism,"[3] and pointed out that at the time when Marx was celebrating the radical achievements of capitalism in the opening pages of *The Communist Manifesto*, the cruelties of the new system were already attracting condemnation from the Right.

This is not to say, however, that the romantic conservatism that sprang from revulsion against the disruptions of modernity is a school to which Arendt belonged. Romantic conservatism is a multifarious phenomenon, but at its core lies an essentially nostalgic contrast between tradition and modernity, nature and artificiality, community and society, *Gemeinschaft* and *Gesellschaft*. The story told by romantic conservatives is one of a fall from grace. Once upon a time human beings lived close to nature and in harmony with one another, leading fulfilling lives in surroundings of natural beauty. Modernization is the process of decline whereby the natural was destroyed in favor of the artificial, agriculture and handicrafts replaced by factories and machines, landscapes by urban wasteland, face-to-face communities by anonymous cities, and rootedness by alienation. So familiar is this story that we are inclined to understand any critic of modernity in its terms—unless, that is, she is sustained by the Marxist faith that once the "labor of the negative" is complete and capitalism has finished its work of destruction, community and harmony with nature will be reconstituted at a higher level. For this reason it is important to stress that Arendt's own criticisms of modernity have as little in common with the views of romantic conservatives as with those of Marxists, and that *Gemeinschaft* and harmony with nature were not ideals to which she looked forward or back.

It is true that "the quest for community"[4] to cure the ills of atomized modern societies is a prominent theme not only in the writings of romantic conservatives but also among the participatory democrats of the 1970s who found Arendt's more radical ideas congenial. Nevertheless, it is not one with which she sympathized. When she looked back to the Greek polis, she regretted the loss not of communal warmth but of the fierce light of the agora; when she deplored the advent of "society" in modern times what she had in mind was the collective life process of a herd of human animals suffering too much togetherness rather than too little.[5]

Romantic communal ideals (right or left) seemed to her to get in the way of a firm grip on political reality. Her own independence from what many of her fellow Jews saw as the duty of loyalty to "the Jewish community" was bound up with her sense that in politics, warmth and light are often mutually exclusive. She argued in her essay "On Humanity in Dark Times" that the desire for communal warmth, although entirely understandable among persecuted people in "dark times," generated a stultifying conformity that made it impossible for individuals to take up different points of view, to talk about their common affairs, and thereby to gain a many-sided understanding of them. Political realism and political freedom alike required that what unites people should not be a "natural" community but a human "world" within which there is space for people to move about and share different perspectives.[6]

If nostalgia for a lost *Gemeinschaft* was not the basis for Arendt's critique of modernity or of the rise of "society," which (she claimed) was characteristic of it, neither was she motivated (as romantic conservatives have been) by the desire to recover a lost harmony with nature in the face of artificial modern structures and practices. On the contrary, what makes her own diagnosis of the ills of modernity so distinctive is her claim that recent times have seen too great a surrender to nature on the part of human beings, and that what has endangered or destroyed the human world is precisely an "unnatural growth of the natural."[7] In her view, phenomena as diverse as imperialism, economic growth, totalitarianism, and nuclear technology illustrate the pernicious tendency of human beings in modern times to let loose or speed up destructive natural processes, instead of using their freedom to limit such processes and to guard the human world of civilization against them. In particular, the advent of "society" meant to her not a departure from natural community but, on the contrary, a move to "liberate the life process" that threatened to engulf the human world.[8]

II A Politics of Limits

Conservative ideology . . . may be defined as a philosophy of imperfection, committed to the idea of limits, and directed towards the defense of a limited style of politics."
—*Noel O'Sullivan*[9]

Arendt's analysis of modernity in terms of processes that are running out of control gives us a clue to the kind of conservatism that is to be found in her thought, a conservatism that is concerned with *limits*: limits to natural processes and to human hubris. The idea of observing limits has often been placed at the center of avowedly conservative thought, particularly in the British tradition coming down from Hume and Burke to Michael Oakeshott and those influenced by him in recent times. One of those Oakeshottian conservatives, Noel O'Sullivan, begins his study of conservatism by observing that it was first defined as an ideology in opposition to the animating idea of the French Revolution, which was that "man's reason and will were powerful enough to regenerate human nature by creating a completely new social order." In opposition to this hubristic faith in infinite possibility, conservative thinkers set out to show that the conditions under which we live are neither so simple to understand nor so easy to remold as the revolutionaries supposed, and that "the world imposes limitations upon what either the individual or the state can hope to achieve without destroying the stability of society."[10] Given these limitations, only a limited style of politics makes sense.

Now, an attempt to link Arendt with conservatism of that kind may on the face of it seem implausible. Indeed, if attitudes toward the French Revolution are to be taken as the test, then surely the project must fall at the first fence? In *The Origins of Totalitarianism* Arendt was prepared to praise the Jacobins, and although in *On Revolution* she depicted them as men driven off course by their unavailing attempts to solve "the social question,"[11] her attitude to revolution in general remained very different from what one might expect from a British conservative. In view of her stress on action, on new beginnings, on the quasi-miraculous human capacity to make a fresh start, should we not see her instead as one of the most notorious recent defenders of *un*limited politics? That is certainly the appearance she has presented to a number of critics.[12]

It is not my purpose here to underestimate the complexity of Arendt's ideas and sympathies. On the contrary, my contention is that the conspicuously radical aspects of her thought have tended to distract our attention from the fact that she is indeed centrally concerned with a politics of limits, and that this concern brings her close to conservatism of a more skeptical kind. I shall argue that the differences that nevertheless remain between her positions and those of more familiar conservative thinkers shed light on some of the problems of trying to be a skeptical conservative in the twentieth century.

The first sense in which Arendt's political thought is a theory of limits has to do with her understanding of civilization as a human world that human beings have built by setting limits to natural processes. Arendt's view of the "world" (as distinct from the "earth") as something built by human work is easily misunderstood as a radical position, because our thinking in these matters tends to be dominated by images bequeathed to us by romantic conservatism: we assume that the alternatives before us are either a romantic conservative view of political and social structures as organic growths (which we did not direct and cannot control) or else a radical humanist view that *we* made them, so we can start again and make them better. In fact this familiar contrast is misleading not only in Arendt's case but in the case of indisputably conservative thinkers.

Burke, for instance, often referred to as an "organic" conservative, described political institutions throughout the *Reflections on the French Revolution* as *buildings* rather than growths, and drew the conclusion that, like ancient houses, they are much more easily destroyed than restored.[13]

Understanding the world of structures and institutions as something built by human hands leads to radical prescriptions only if we can make a number of assumptions that are not often spelled out: for example, that we have firm ground on which to rebuild; that our site is safe and the weather calm; that "we" are agreed about the structure to be built and are all working together; and that we have reason to suppose that what we build will be an improvement on what we have inherited. Linking these tacit assumptions at the back of many humanist minds is a faith in progress—a sense that in building anew, we are working with, not against, the grain of events. One of the aspects of Arendt's thought that most obviously links her with conservatism is her freedom from that most deeply rooted of modern dogmas. There was in her view nothing natural, inevitable, or irreversible about civilization.[14]

A familiar theme in Arendt's thought is that where human beings have managed to build civilized structures, these have been built not with but against the forces of nature, by stopping or setting limits to natural processes. Nature is a perpetual motion of growth and decay, and to give "the human artifice the stability and solidity without which it could not be relied upon to house the unstable and mortal creature which is man,"[15] those processes have to be interrupted or limited. To make a table, the life-process of a tree must be interrupted. To stop the wood from reentering the cycle of decay and rebirth, we have to treat it with preservatives and keep it out of the rain. And if the physical components of the human artifice are fragile and in need of protection against the ravages of nature, the same applies to the cultural and institutional aspects of the human world.[16] The danger here comes from humanity itself—from the natural condition of natality and from the quasi-natural processes that human beings let loose.

We usually think of Arendt's stress on "natality" as a celebration of new beginnings, and so indeed it was, especially in the context of totalitarianism, where it was for her a talisman against despair.[17] But this is not the whole story, for Arendt was also very well aware that human beings are born barbarians and that each new generation represents a potential barbarian invasion of civilization. She wrote about this most explicitly in a neglected essay on "The Crisis in Education" in which she maintained that the proper goal of education was not to instruct the young in the art of living, but to hand on to them the human world:

Conservatism, in the sense of conservation, is of the essence of the educational activity, whose task is always to cherish and protect something—the child against the world, the world against the child, the new against the old, the old against the new.

She hastened to say, it is true, that,

In politics this conservative attitude—which accepts the world as it is, striving only to preserve the status quo—can only lead to destruction, because the world, in gross and in detail, is irrevocably delivered up to the ruin of time unless human beings are determined to intervene, to alter, to create what is new.[18]

As we shall see later, the quietist conservatism to which some British thinkers have inclined was never an option for her. What is striking, however, is that at the same time as cherishing the possibility of new beginnings, she was acutely sensitive to the disruptive potential of human actions and to the need for limits to hedge them in. The proper function of laws was, she believed, not only to protect rights but to act as fences to guard the stability of the human world against the anarchic initiatives of the new people continually appearing in it.[19] For human action sets off processes, the results of which cannot be foreseen or controlled by the actor. Above all, she believed that the greatest threats to the world of civilization came from a series of quasi-natural processes that modern men had set off or accelerated.

It is this (rather than any romantic concern to get back from artificiality to nature) that forms the basis of her critique of modernity:

Today we have begun ... to unchain natural processes of our own which would never have happened without us, and instead of carefully surrounding the human artifice with defenses against nature's elementary forces, keeping them as far as possible outside the man-made world, we have channeled these forces, along with their elementary power, into the world itself.[20]

The most dramatic examples are of course to be found in the realm of technology, from nuclear power to genetic engineering, but Arendt interprets economic growth and totalitarianism in analogous terms. Economic growth, which destroys all stability, forcing more and more of mankind into a perpetual process of change, was in her view set off by the massive expropriations of the age of the Reformation, when stable property was turned on a large scale into fluid wealth.[21] Once started, the trickle became a torrent sweeping away all landmarks and spreading across the globe in the form of imperialism, setting the scene for yet more fundamental surrenders to pseudonatural forces in the shape of totalitarianism. Whereas in a constitutional polity "the stability of the laws corresponds to the constant motion of all human affairs," totalitarian "terror seeks to 'stabilize' men in order to liberate the forces of nature or history."[22] One of the most persistent themes in all Arendt's analyses of modernity is that the human world is at the mercy of dynamic processes which threaten all stable structures.

For our present purposes, what is interesting is the stress that Arendt puts on the role of worldly institutions as limits protecting human civilization against the ravages of natural and pseudonatural forces. Although she has often been read as a supporter of the near-anarchist student radicalism of the 1960s, a persistent theme of her writings concerns the vital importance of laws, property, constitutions, and states, all of which she sees as devices for establishing islands of human stability among the destructive currents of nature and history. The institutions of civilization are largely concerned to *stop* things happening by setting limits, for "the real pride of Western man" consists in "giving laws to the world." Arendt blames both Marxism and capitalism for undermining those stable structures and helping to bring about, in totalitarianism, a politics of perpetual motion from which human beings found no barriers to protect them.[23]

If Arendt's emphasis on the vital importance of stable institutional structures like laws and property sounds decidedly conservative, so do her continual warnings against the dangers of hubris. Totalitarianism in her view was characterized by the belief that "everything is possible"[24]: not just a disregard for *moral* limits, but the conviction that there are no limits at all to what we can do, so long as we understand the dynamic processes of nature or history and go along with them. "Until now the totalitarian belief that everything is possible seems to have proved only that everything can be destroyed,"[25] but this totalitarian extreme of hubris seemed to Arendt to present a recurrent danger because it fed on a much more general refusal on the part of modern human beings to accept anything as given. In her conclusion to the first edition of *The Origins of Totalitarianism* she remarked on "modern man's deep-rooted suspicion of everything he did not make himself,"[26] and at the start of *The Human Condition*, meditating on the launch of the first space satellite, which was being hailed as the start of man's escape from the earth, she suggested that the kind of human being that was emerging wanted "to escape the human condition" and appeared "to be possessed by a rebellion against human existence as it has been given."[27]

It is an ironic comment on the presuppositions of her readers that a work concerned as much with the limits as with the possibilities of the human condition has often been read as an invitation to unlimited action. As she pointed out, however, action means starting processes over which the actor cannot retain control. Precisely because human beings can perform miracles in the sense of making new beginnings, it is vital that they should retain a sense of moderation.[28] In spite of her admiration for the glory of Athens, Arendt recognized the shortcomings of Pericles, who was possessed by "the hubris of power," and compared him unfavorably with Solon the lawgiver. The difference between them was, she says, between "the striving for excellence at any price or putting this within limits."[29]

In trying to communicate her sense of the possibilities and limits of the human condition, Arendt was aware of being hampered by ideological stereotypes. As she pointed out, revolution even in its purely political aspect had two sides, so that "the exhilarating awareness of the human capacity for beginning" was the complement of the foundation of a new body politic, which "involves the grave concern with the stability and durability of the new structure." She lamented the way in which "the concern with stability and the spirit of the new, have become opposites in political thought and terminology."[30] Much of the point of her contrast between the American and the French Revolutions was her insistence on the vital importance of "lasting institutions" such as the American had managed to build and the French had not. There is in all her writings a profound concern with durable institutions, partly because of her deep and thoroughly conservative distrust of the "darkness of the human heart."[31] Her response to the persistent radical illusion that human beings would spontaneously become good if only traditional institutions were scrapped can be found in her comments on the behavior of the pre-totalitarian imperialist adventurers in Africa, who had escaped from the world of civilization into an environment of "'natural' human beings," and who promptly discovered "infinite possibilities for crimes committed in the spirit of play."[32] Only human laws and conventions, not nature or "human nature," can establish and preserve civilized standards and bestow "human rights" upon us. "It is human worldliness that will save men from the pitfalls of human nature."[33]

This is a humanist message, but one quite lacking in the hubristic insouciance of much modern radicalism. If one of Arendt's purposes was to remind modern human beings of their ability and responsibility to take action, another was to warn them against attempting too much, and endangering such civilized institutions as existed by overburdening them with excessive demands. Many of the utterances that have embarrassed Arendt's radical admirers and have led others to apply the label "conservative" to her as a reproach are of this kind. Faced with the liberal assumption (almost universally accepted in Western political discourse, popular and academic) that the whole of mankind is on an escalator that leads to freedom and equality for all, her strong sense of the limits of the human condition led her not only to utter "the old and terrible truth that only violence and rule over others could make some men free" in the absence of material abundance, but also to doubt whether political freedom is feasible in many areas of the world in the foreseeable future.[34] Where equality was concerned, too, she pointed out that equality of rights and status is not a natural datum but a political achievement, and one that can easily be put at risk by hubristic attempts to get rid of all differences. Hence her notorious "Reflections on Little Rock," in which she argued that the unrealistic project of enforcing social uniformity between the races in America could endanger the vital and more feasible equality of constitutional rights.[35]

Many of these "conservative" positions stem from a characteristically conservative concern for realism. She was impatient of sentimental illusions and moralistic simplifications.[36] In spite of her reputation for utopianism, she was in fact a relentless critic of political delusions, whether those being criticized were Israelis who failed to notice the Arabs they were living among, student radicals who evaded hard political issues, or U.S. policy makers deafened by their own Newspeak.[37] She was particularly critical of attempts to avoid having to exercise political judgment by using rationalistic formulas, and her suspicion of ideology, of the incursions of philosophers into politics, and of attempts by political, theorists to direct political actors are all reminiscent of Burke and Oakeshott.[38]

As I hope I have shown, some prominent features of Arendt's political thought bring her into quite close proximity to the more skeptical thinkers in the British conservative tradition, even though in other respects she is a world away from them. A brief comparison with the thought of Michael Oakeshott, her contemporary and the most notable of recent conservative thinkers, may shed some light on her own blend of radical and conservative themes.

III Arendt and Oakeshott

Oakeshott's thought cannot be reduced to a series of hard-edged, quasi-mathematical formulae. It is not a calculus, a method, or an ideology. It promises no shortcuts to wisdom or right action.... Oakeshott's thought is less a self-conscious theoretic edifice than a slowly unfolding imaginative world minutely responsive to the contours of the collective human experience it purports to chart."

—*Robert Grant*[39]

Grant's description could just as well be applied to Arendt, for one obvious connection between the two thinkers is an elusive similarity of intellectual style and manner. On the face of it, their philosophical backgrounds could not have been more different, for Oakeshott's idealism seems utterly at odds with Arendt's roots in existentialism. But they are at one in the justified confidence with which both were able (paying a good deal of attention to the views of their great predecessors and very little to those of their contemporaries) to think their own thoughts on topics of awe-inspiring breadth.[40]

For all their intellectual ambition, both were equally convinced that it was in no sense the business of philosophers to provide guides to political action. Both emphasized the gulf between philosophy and practice, and Arendt would have heartily endorsed Oakeshott's dictum, "What is farthest from our needs is that kings should be philosophers."[41] Oakeshott is best known to political theorists for his critique of "rationalism" in politics, "the politics of the book" and "of the politically inexperienced,"[42] which supposes that the only kind of knowledge that matters is the kind that can be made explicit, that the only worthwhile actions and institutions are those that deliberately follow explicit theories, and therefore that the job of the political theorist is to provide an instruction book. Arendt was equally suspicious of attempts to apply ready-made formulae to politics, and equally convinced that political thinkers were in no position to tell anyone what to do. A distinctive feature of her account of the gap between theory and practice is her insistence that whereas thinking is solitary, both action and the practical judgment that must inform it need the company of others.[43] No doubt there is implicit in Oakeshott's notion of practical activity as participating in a "tradition" or "practice" a similar sense of being joined with others rather than (to quote Burke) putting men "to live and trade each on his own private stock of reason,"[44] but the difference of emphasis is significant, as we shall see.

Another respect in which both were equally at odds with the trend of the times was in deploring the growing tendency for politics to be regarded as a collective enterprise in promoting wealth and welfare, and viewing this tendency with concern for reasons that have nothing to do with neoliberalism. In recent decades there have of course been a great many politicians and political thinkers who have opposed socialism and wanted to "roll back the frontiers of the state," but many of them have done so on the grounds that laissez-faire is a more effective method than state control for achieving what is assumed to be the goal of politics, namely economic growth. Oakeshott and Arendt differ from these and are at one in dissenting from this whole outlook. Paul Franco observes that Arendt resembles Oakeshott in seeing "European history largely in terms of the incursion of the private 'household' into the public realm and the replacement of genuine politics by the 'economy' and the 'administration of things.' "[45] There are differences, of course, not least in terminology. Confusingly, where Arendt speaks of the displacement of pluralistic politics by "society," meaning "national housekeeping" or the monolithic management of a collective life process,[46] "societas" in Oakeshott's terminology refers to the opposite of this sort of thing. "Universitas" is the term he uses to refer to a collective entity with a common purpose,[47] such as the modern state is often understood to be, whereas what he means by societas (the other, competing model for understanding "the character of a modern European state") is an association held together not by a common purpose but by acceptance of shared rules or laws.

For both, the concentration of modern politics on the collective management of economic goals is connected with the political emancipation of the "masses," about whom both write in tones that betray a familiar conservative fear that the freedom of those who have the courage to act as individuals is threatened by the fears and material cravings of those who have not. Oakeshott speaks of how the circumstances that aided the development of individuality in European history also produced "masses" characterized by "their incapacity to sustain an individual life and their longing for the shelter of a community,"[48] whose craving for protection and resentment against difference could easily be manipulated by power-hungry leaders. Echoing Nietzsche, he speaks also of "therapeutic" understandings of the modern state as a kind of hospital for the diseased.[49] There are some affinities here with Arendt's account of the "masses," who (she claimed) supported totalitarian movements, and of "the poor" who threatened republican freedom with their dreams of "abundance and endless consumption."[50] Although one crucial difference is that for Arendt, such tendencies are a threat not just to the freedom of the elite, but to the world of civilization itself.

There is a corresponding difference of focus in the shared concerns of the two writers for individuality and a political order that leaves room for people to be different from one another. Speaking of the two alternative understandings of the state available in Western traditions, societas and universitas, Oakeshott asks about those brought together in the state, "Are they persons joined in keeping 'troth' with one another, a fidelity articulated in a 'law of the land'; or are they united in the recognition of a 'truth' articulated in a common substantive purpose?,"[51] and he makes clear his preference for the former bond of union. The contrast between "troth" and "truth" is very reminiscent of Arendt's reflections on the incompatibility between single truth and plural politics and her stress on the role of promises in holding together plural human beings, but what is lacking in Oakeshott is Arendt's notion of the world as something that appears in the space between human beings, something that is threatened by the quest for unanimity and by the conformist fictions of totalitarian ideology.[52]

A corresponding mix of striking similarities and significant differences can be found in the two writers' discussions of "action." Like Arendt, Oakeshott speaks of the freedom and contingency of action, of the courage necessary to embark on the "adventure" of acting, even of the "self-disclosure" and "self-enactment" of the actor, who "has a 'history' but no 'nature'; he is what in conduct he becomes."[53] Like her, he says that understanding action means putting it into a story, and like her he refers to Isak Dinesen's saying "that all sorrows may be redeemed by putting them into a story."[54] The great difference, and it is a crucial one, concerns relations between agents. Idealist or not, Oakeshott sounds quite classically existentialist as he speaks of "the agent" or "the individual" as if the man in question (always "he") is on his own. By contrast, the very center of Arendt's political thought is the insight that no agent in the world of politics, not even the most heroic or charismatic, ever does or can act on his own: action is always undertaken with and in relation to others. We are reminded that whereas Oakeshott's individual can take for granted the resources of a civilized tradition, Arendt's inhabits a howling post-totalitarian wilderness in which the only source of remedy lies in "the tremendous bliss ... that not a single man but Men inhabit the earth."[55]

It is when we come to compare Oakeshott's view of tradition with Arendt's that the most fundamental differences between them emerge, and it is also at this point that we can see why Arendt not only was able to combine radical positions with conservative ones, but actually found this unavoidable. Famously, in his inaugural lecture on "Political Education," Oakeshott defined politics as "the activity of attending to the general arrangements of a set of people"[56] and stressed that such an activity never starts from scratch. Any such arrangements incorporate a tradition of behavior, and radical ideologies that purport to teach us how to make a fresh start are always just meager "abridgments" of such traditions. Political activity consists, therefore, in "the amendment of existing arrangements by exploring and pursuing what is intimated in them." Apparent breaks or fresh starts are illusory: the course taken by the Russian Revolution, for example, "was not the implementation of an abstract design worked out by Lenin and others in Switzerland: it was a modification of *Russian* circumstances." Oakeshott does admit the theoretical possibility of "serious political crisis," "a genuine cataclysm" that stops politics completely for the time being "by altogether obliterating a current tradition of behaviour," but he excludes it from consideration, apparently not considering that any contemporary crisis qualifies.

In short, political crisis (even when it seems to be imposed upon a society by changes beyond its control) always appears *within* a tradition of political activity; and "salvation" comes from the unimpaired resources of the tradition itself.[57]

This is an account of politics that has worried a great many commentators, and space does not permit serious critical examination of it here. For our present purposes, what is most striking is the apparent message (uttered in 1951, the same year that Arendt published *The Origins of Totalitarianism*) that nothing *very* drastic can happen in politics.[58] The sense of insularity, as if Oakeshott had somehow failed to notice the dramas of the twentieth century going on around him, is reinforced by another essay, "On Being Conservative," in which he speaks of "the conservative disposition" as being "averse from change" and mentions a list of examples of disturbing changes that includes "involuntary exile" alongside "the retirement of a favourite clown."[59] Addressed to an academic world that included so many who had suffered involuntary exile in the most traumatic circumstances, this seems to show (at best) a curious failure of sensitivity.[60] At any rate, it is not surprising that Arendt, being one of those involuntary exiles, should have seen tradition rather differently.

To Arendt, totalitarianism as practiced by the Nazis in Germany was new and unprecedented, and tradition had shown no power to stand in its way.

Totalitarian domination as an established fact ... has broken the continuity of Occidental history. The break in our tradition is now an accomplished fact.[61]

What was particularly shocking was the ease with which the practices and moral conventions of a highly civilized society had adapted themselves to this new barbarism. In her 1953 essay on "Understanding and Politics," Arendt reflected on the relation between morals and *mores*, or customs, and on Montesquieu's observations on the fragility of societies where the authority of law had collapsed, the people were not citizens, and the only barriers to political evil were customs and traditions.

> Tradition can be trusted to prevent the worst for only a limited time. Every incident can destroy customs and morality which no longer have their foundation in lawfulness, every contingency must threaten a society which is no longer guaranteed by citizens.[62]

Where the implication of Oakeshott's understanding of politics seems to be (to put it crudely) that the tradition can take care of itself and the least damage will be done if most of us avoid meddling and get on with our own lives, Arendt's message is that whether we want to conserve or to rebuild, we cannot avoid responsibility for the world or the duty to act together as citizens.

In criticism of Arendt it could perhaps be said that, after all, postwar repair and rebuilding in Germany were made possible by "the unimpaired resources of the tradition"[63]—not the German tradition, perhaps, but the Anglo-Saxon one, which had not been broken. But in criticism of Oakeshott it must be said that this involved much more of a deliberate foundation and fresh start, much more by way of political action in Arendt's sense, than his account of politics seems to allow for.[64] Conservation in this case involved revolution: military defeat to stop the inexorable march of Nazism, followed by the foundation of a new republic. It was paradoxes of this sort that made Arendt so preoccupied with the problem of foundation, of how free people can act to bind themselves and create "lasting institutions" that will gather authority with the years. Conservation and action are inseparable.[65] As Ronald Beiner has rightly said, "The impetus behind Arendt's affirmation of politics and active citizenship was neither romanticism nor utopianism, but *fear* and *dread*."[66]

IV The Dilemma of Contemporary Conservatism

> Political life is not a project of world improvement in which are invested the transcendental hopes of an age without faith. It is instead an almost desperately humble task of endless improvisation, in which one good is compromised for the sake of others, a balance is sought among the necessary evils of human life, and the ever-present prospect of disaster is staved off for another day.
>
> —*John Gray*[67]

I have tried to show not only that Arendt's thought contains significant strands of conservatism as well as radicalism, but that given Arendt's analysis of the circumstances in which she found herself, the radicalism actually gained impetus from the conservatism. In the wake of a catastrophic collapse of traditional institutions, practices, and ideas a fresh start seemed unavoidable; even where, as in the United States, there was still a sound political structure to be conserved, there was the need for a kind of Machiavellian return to the foundations; more generally, modernity was characterized by processes started by human beings but running out of control, so that radical action was needed to set limits to the damage they could do.

Paradoxical as the link between conservatism and radicalism may seem, it is in fact nothing new. We can find analogous paradoxes at the very beginning of the modern conservative tradition if we look beyond Burke (who was, like Oakeshott, in the happy position of being able to defend an unbroken tradition against radicalism) to the European counterrevolutionary thinkers, who had no option but to take to radicalism themselves in an effort to set limits to the processes the revolutionaries had set in motion. Interestingly, a conservative case for radicalism has recently been argued by a British conservative who has some affinities with Hannah Arendt and more with Oakeshott. In *Beyond the New Right* John Gray argues for limited government, but distances himself from many of the ideas and policies of the neoliberal New Right, which seem to him to suffer from the same "ideological hubris" as most versions of modern politics. Gray believes in progress as little as Arendt, and he questions "such dogmas of modernism" as the received wisdom "that incessant growth in goods and services is a feasible, and desirable, object of policy."[68] His distrust of runaway technology has a strong Green tinge, and he argues that many of the preoccupations of the Green movement have more affinity with skeptical conservatism than with the radical Left.

Nevertheless, Gray is forced to admit that stopping what he sees as the drift to ruin requires radical action, and he recognizes "an ancient paradox ... that conservatives cannot help becoming radicals, when current practice embodies the hubristic and careless projects of recent generations, or has been distorted by technological innovations whose consequences for human well-being we have not weighed."[69] Is this, then, a kind of conservatism Arendt could endorse? Up to a point, but I suspect that Gray's apparent confidence in the ability of conservatives to reverse processes and carry this program to a successful conclusion would have seemed to her to partake of the "progressive" hubris that Gray thinks he has repudiated. The difficulty is that those who take radical action for conservative reasons are themselves inexorably setting off new processes, the outcome of which they cannot predict or control. This is not to say, however, that one can escape these dilemmas by refraining from political action. There are no safe or simple answers. Action is always dangerous, but in circumstances like those of Germany during the Nazis' rise to power, *in*action is culpable.

In the end, Arendt's kind of conservatism (but also her kind of radicalism) is the rare kind marked by a sense of tragedy—a sense, that is, of the ultimate futility of human endeavors, but nevertheless of the possibility of greatness in failure. A tragic view of life is profoundly alien to the modern outlook, for which every ill has become a "problem" to be solved through the acquisition of more power, and it is assumed (in defiance of experience) that increased human powers will in future be used for good. In contrast to this characteristically modern confidence (which shows little sign so far of being dented by the much-trumpeted advent of post modernism), Arendt's tragic vision echoes classical themes in seeing human beings as free indeed, but frail, pitted against overwhelming odds and liable to cause catastrophes when they use their freedom to act. Ultimate success in human endeavors is therefore impossible. Human dignity consists in conducting oneself well under the blows of fate, and in contemplating and preserving the memory of that defiance and endurance in others.

On Revolution, the book that contains the most vivid expressions of Arendt's radicalism and of her conservatism, has baffled many readers precisely because it is pervaded by this tragic note. Karl Jaspers, to whom the book was dedicated, delighted her by recognizing immediately that she had presented a vision of tragedy but not of despair. Whereas Burke saw the French Revolution as an avoidable disaster resulting from hubristic rationalism, and de Maistre as God's punishment for sin, for Arendt revolution was a stage on which were displayed the tragedy but also the heroism inherent in the project of human civilization. The distinctiveness of her view of politics, which does not, in the end, consort comfortably with any of the versions of radicalism or conservatism currently on offer, is particularly well expressed in the conclusion of *On*

Revolution, which counterposes Sophocles' lines on the utter futility of human life with the message represented by Athens of "what it was that enabled ordinary men ... to bear life's burden: it was the polis, the space of men's free deeds and living words, which could endow life with splendor."[70]

Notes

1. "Hannah Arendt on Hannah Arendt," in M. A. Hill, ed., *Hannah Arendt: The Recovery of the Public World* (New York: St. Martin's Press, 1979), 333.

2. See, e.g., J. C. Isaac, *Arendt, Camus, and Modern Rebellion* (New Haven: Yale University Press, 1992), 18, 256–259; M. P. D'Entreves, *The Political Philosophy of Hannah Arendt* (London: Routledge, 1994), 2.

3. "Hannah Arendt on Hannah Arendt," 334.

4. R. A. Nisbet, *A Quest for Community* (New York: Oxford University Press, 1953).

5. H. Arendt, *The Human Condition* (Chicago: University of Chicago Press, 1958, referred to below as *HC*), 33, 44–45, 50, 57, 116, 204, 208.

6. *HC*, 57, 208–209; "On Humanity in Dark Times: Thoughts about Lessing," in H. Arendt, *Men in Dark Times* (London: Jonathan Cape, 1970), 13, 16, 30–31.

7. *HC*, 47.

8. *HC*, 116, 321; H. Arendt, *On Revolution* (London: Faber and Faber, 1963, referred to below as *OR*), 58. For a more extensive treatment of this topic, see M. Canovan, *Hannah Arendt: A Reinterpretation of Her Political Thought* (Cambridge: Cambridge University Press, 1992), 79–84.

9. N. O'Sullivan, *Conservatism* (London: Dent, 1976), 11.

10. Ibid., 9, 11.

11. Her criteria were in both cases concerned with the defense of a fragile human world against destructive processes let loose by human action. In *Totalitarianism*, in the course of her analysis of imperialism as a process of unstoppable expansion, she spoke of how "the French Revolution, with its conception of man as lawmaker and *citoyen*, had almost succeeded in preventing the bourgeoisie from fully developing its notion of history as a necessary process." In *OR*, by contrast, she presents the French Revolution as a tragedy in which the Jacobins were led by their pity for the poor to politicize "the social question" and thereby to unleash the torrential force of "the life process" against the fragile world of constitutional politics. See H. Arendt, *The Origins of Totalitarianism*, 3d ed. (London: George Allen and Unwin, 1967, referred to below as *OT*), 106, 144; *OR*, 55, 70, 86, 107–109.

12. See, e.g., N. O'Sullivan, "Politics, Totalitarianism and Freedom: The Political Thought of Hannah Arendt," *Political Studies* 21/2 (1973), 185; G. McKenna, "Bannisterless Politics: Hannah Arendt and Her Children," *History of Political Thought* 5/2 (1984), 339,

360. In both these cases, the condemnations were based on misunderstandings of Arendt's position.

13. E. Burke, *Reflections on the French Revolution* (London: Dent, 1910), 20, 33, 59, 85, 92, 123, 128, 164–165, 243.

14. "Hannah Arendt on Hannah Arendt," 334.

15. *HC*, 136.

16. *HC*, 98–100, 139; H. Arendt, "Franz Kafka: A Revaluation," *Partisan Review* 11/4 (fall 1944), 416.

17. *OT*, 478–479; *HC*, 178, 247.

18. H. Arendt, "The Crisis in Education," in *Between Past and Future: Eight Exercises in Political Thought* (New York: Viking Press, 1968), 192.

19. *OT*, 465; *HC*, 191.

20. *HC*, 148. "What I am pleading for ... is a new realization of the factually existing limitations of human beings" (H. Arendt, "The Archimedean Point," *Ingenor* (spring 1969), 25).

21. *OT*, 145; *HC*, 252.

22. *OT*, 465.

23. *OT*, 91, 124–147, 221, 461–467; *OR*, 156, 163; *HC*, 61–72, 251–252; H. Arendt, "Karl Marx and the Tradition of Western Political Thought," 2nd draft, 1953 (manuscript in the Library of Congress), section IV, 12–13. For a revealing attempt by Arendt to convince some radical members of the students' movement of the importance of legal guarantees (and of the U.S. Constitution in particular), see one of her contributions to the discussion recorded in A. Klein, *Dissent, Power, and Confrontation* (New York: McGraw-Hill, 1971), 16–17.

24. *OT*, 437.

25. *OT*, 459.

26. H. Arendt, *The Burden of Our Time* (London: Secker and Warburg, 1951), 434. (This was the first British edition of *OT*.)

27. *HC*, 2.

28. *HC*, 191.

29. H. Arendt, "Philosophy and Politics: What Is Political Philosophy?" (1969) (manuscript in the Library of Congress), 024437. Arendt was impressed by "Montesquieu's great insight that even virtue must have its limits" (*OR*, 86).

30. *OR*, 225.

31. *HC*, 244; *OR*, 92–93.

32. *OT*, 190, 192.

33. *OT*, 299–300; *OR*, 104, 174.

34. *OR*, 110; Klein, *Dissent, Power, and Confrontation*, 132.

35. 35. H. Arendt, "Reflections on Little Rock," *Dissent* 6/1 (winter 1959), 45–56.

36. See, e.g., H. Arendt, "On Humanity in Dark Times," 16; *Eichmann in Jerusalem: A Report on the Banality of Evil* (London: Faber and Faber, 1963), 132; "Collective Responsibility" (a contribution to a symposium in 1968), in J. W. Bernauer, SJ (ed.), *Amor Mundi: Explorations in the Faith and Thought of Hannah Arendt* (Dordrecht: Martinus Nijhoff, 1987), 47.

37. See, e.g., H. Arendt, "Peace or Armistice in the Near East?" *Review of Politics* 12/1 (1950), 63, 70; *Crises of the Republic* (New York: Harcourt Brace Jovanovich, 1972), 20, 31, 37, 42, 196, 227–228.

38. See, e.g., H. Arendt, "Personal Responsibility under Dictatorship," *The Listener* (6 August 1964), 186–187; *OT*, 468–477; "What is Authority?" in *Between Past and Future*, 107–117; "Hannah Arendt on Hannah Arendt," 310.

39. R. Grant, *Oakeshott* (London: The Claridge Press, 1990), 10.

40. Is there a family resemblance between the titles of Arendt's *The Human Condition* (1958) and Oakeshott's *On Human Conduct* (1975)?

41. M. Oakeshott, *Experience and Its Modes* (Cambridge: Cambridge University Press, 1933), 321. Note, however, that whereas for Oakeshott action must take place in "the mental fog of practical experience," which philosophy dispels, in Arendt's case the image is reversed, and it is the practical men, not the philosophers, who can see their way ahead. See H. Arendt, *The Life of the Mind* (London: Secker and Warburg, 1978), I, 82.

42. M. Oakeshott, *Rationalism in Politics and Other Essays* (London: Methuen, 1962, referred to below as *RP*), 22–23.

43. *HC*, 7–8, 188; "Truth and Politics," in *Between Past and Future*, 235–241.

44. Burke, *Reflections*, 84.

45. P. Franco, *The Political Philosophy of Michael Oakeshott* (New Haven: Yale University Press, 1990), 213.

46. *HC*, 40–46.

47. M. Oakeshott, *On Human Conduct* (Oxford: Oxford University Press, 1975, referred to below as *OHC*), 203.

48. *OHC*, 276.

49. *OHC*, 310.

50. *OT*, 311–317, 474–478; *OR*, 135.

51. *OHC*, 233.

52. Arendt, "Truth and Politics," *passim*; "On Humanity in Dark Times," 30–31; *HC*, 52; *OT*, 468–478.

53. *OHC*, 40–41.

54. *OHC*, 105.

55. Arendt, *The Burden of Our Time*, 439.

56. *RP*, 112.

57. *RP*, 122–126.

58. In a respectful review of Arendt's *Between Past and Future* in 1962, Oakeshott observed that in speaking of "the crisis of our time" as a break in historical continuity, Arendt was "guilty of some exaggeration" (*Political Science Quarterly* 77/1 (1962), 89.

59. *RP*, 170.

60. Robert Grant's charitable gloss on this sort of thing is that "it is a tribute to his humane, civilized outlook to say that in his writings the darker side of politics ... barely gets a look in" (Grant, *Oakeshott*, 89).

61. H. Arendt, "Tradition and the Modern Age," in *Between Past and Future*, 26.

62. H. Arendt, "Understanding and Politics," *Partisan Review* 20/4 (1953).

63. *RP*, 126.

64. For a similar criticism, see Grant, *Oakeshott*, 61.

65. *OR*, 182–215.

66. R. Beiner, "Hannah Arendt and Leo Strauss: The Uncommenced Dialogue," *Political Theory* 18/2 (1990), 251.

67. J. Gray, *Beyond the New Right: Markets, Government and the Common Environment* (London: Routledge, 1993), xi.

68. Ibid., viii, xi.

69. Ibid., 128.

70. *OR*, 285.

2

Hannah Arendt on Judgment: The Unwritten Doctrine of Reason

Albrecht Wellmer

I

The faculty of judgment played a preeminent role in Hannah Arendt's political and moral thought; however, despite the tenor of some of her earlier works, she certainly was no neo-Aristotelian philosopher of praxis. To be sure, we do not have her last word on the faculty of judgment. Nevertheless, from what we have it can safely be said that her theory of judgment was not meant as a reappropriation of an Aristotelian conception of phronesis, with phronesis understood as a virtue connecting sound deliberation with prudent action. Arendt's later thought was moving in the opposite direction, tending to dissociate judgment from action as well as from argumentation. The first dissociation is puzzling, because it was in the context of reflections about political action that the problem of judgment made its first appearance in Arendt's work; the second, because reflective judgment—and this is what Arendt really meant when she talked about judgment—is meant to lead to intersubjectively valid judgments, that is, judgments that everybody could agree on. Both of these curious aspects of Arendt's later account of judgment, however, fit into her attempt to assimilate political and moral judgment, structurally speaking, to aesthetic judgment in the Kantian sense. Aesthetic judgment is the judgment of a spectator—thus the dissociation of judgment from action. And the fact that consent to aesthetic judgment cannot be compelled by arguments accounts for its dissociation from argumentation. To be sure, Arendt at the same time wanted to preserve the internal relationship between judgment and discursive reason, that is, to preserve judgment as a *rational* faculty. She managed to do that by relating thinking and judging in a highly peculiar way: thinking for Arendt is primarily a destructive rather than a constructive activity that clears the ground and removes the obstacles for the exercise of the faculty of judgment. Those obstacles are the false generalities like rules, concepts, or values that tend to determine our judgments as the deceptive safeguards of an unreflective life. Dissolving the false generalities of unreflective social life, the "wind of thought" liberates the faculty of judgment as the faculty to ascend, without the guidance of rules, from the particular to the universal; and most particularly as the faculty "to tell right from wrong, beautiful from ugly."[1]

The most perplexing thing about Arendt's conception of judgment is the way in which she moves from almost Aristotelian premises to rather anti-Aristotelian conclusions. This movement of thought can be discerned in the relationship of her earlier reflections on action to her later reflections on thought and judgment. Judgment for Arendt is intrinsically related to the essential plurality of human beings, to our living in a common world which, *as* a common world, is opened up by speech. Matters of praxis, which belong to this common world, are not susceptible to scientific proof; they are not matters of knowledge but of *opinion.* At this point a theory of phronesis could have been expected to emerge, which would have analyzed the peculiar rationality related to the field of human praxis and explained the difference between good and bad judgment in terms of this peculiar rationality. At this point neo-Aristotelians usually rediscover Hegel's conception of "ethical life" ("*Sittlichkeit*") and/or move toward a theory of institutions. Arendt, in contrast, seems to move in the opposite direction. She proves to be a decidedly modern thinker in that she denies the existence of anything like an *ethical community* that could provide the basis for the exercise of phronesis. The common world of human beings, to which the faculty of judgment appeals, turns out not to be an existing ethical totality but a regulative idea, namely, the *sensus communis* that proves its reality above all in those rare moments when autonomous judgment breaks through the crust of established opinions and established generalities. The *existing* common sense, in contrast, is for Arendt rather like the sphere of Heidegger's "Man," the sphere of inauthentic being; correspondingly the paradigmatic cases of an exercise of the faculty of judgment are for her exceptional cases of independence from prefabricated opinions or of resistance against the indifference of the many.

That Arendt increasingly came to consider the faculty of judgment as an autonomous faculty, therefore, does not merely reflect her indebtedness to Kant's philosophy, whose architectonics she was to rely on in her last work. It also reflects the fact that her theory of autonomous judgment was, at the same time, a theory of the corruption of judgment in our time, and was thus implicitly related to a pessimistic theory of modernity. The autonomy of judgment manifests itself in those who, in a world without gods, metaphysical certainties, and ultimate values, resist the temptation to stop thinking and to succumb to the false consolations of ideology on the one hand, or to escape into sheer conformism on the other. It was in particular Arendt's experience of Nazi Germany that provided the negative background for her theory of judgment. It is not *The Human Condition* but her book on totalitarianism and *Eichmann in Jerusalem* that constitute the preparatory stages for her theory of judgment. This is true in a twofold sense: *First,* in both cases Arendt analyzes the condition of an utter corruption of judgment where people, either being in the grip of ideologies, or exchanging a discredited value system for a corrupt one, or out of sheer stupidity, become unable to perceive or to recognize what is going on. Arendt formulates the problem of personal responsibility under conditions of a collectively corrupted judgment—that is, the problem of how the justice of the Nuremberg and the Eichmann trials was to be understood—in terms of the demand

> that human beings be capable of telling right from wrong even when all they have to guide them is their own judgement, which, moreover, happens to be completely at odds with what they must regard as the unanimous opinion of all those around them.... Those few who were still able to tell right from wrong went really on their own judgements, and they did so freely; there were no rules to be abided by, under which the particular cases with which they were confronted could be subsumed. They had to decide each instance as it arose, because no rules existed for the unprecedented.[2]

The autonomy of judgment becomes manifest in those who, without the support of socially accepted rules and values—nay, *against* them—are still able to tell right from wrong. *Second,* however, Arendt's two books, besides providing the negative background for her theory of judgment, offer two powerful *positive* examples for the exercise of political judgment. Both books are paradigm cases of a nonconformist political interpretation of our time and both are written from the standpoint of a reflecting spectator. Therefore one could say that Arendt's theory of judgment is the attempt to give a philosophical account of the basic content of her two books as well as of her own way of coming to grips with the problems discussed in them.

To be sure, both works are highly discursive. They try to argue for certain interpretations and only in this sense can they be called examples of political judgment from a spectator's point of view. Otherwise, they could not have become the topic of extended and sometimes heated public or scientific debate. Moreover, both books certainly do have implications as far as practical orientations are concerned. Although they do not provide premises for a practical syllogism, one could not accept what they say as true and yet act as a neo-Nazi or a Stalinist. Therefore both books belong to a continuum of political discourse which occurs on many different levels. This discourse is not only concerned with the evaluation of past events, but affects future action as well. In the case of moral judgments it is even more obvious that there exists an unavoidable internal relationship to action, and not only past ones, as Arendt's own examples show. That every actor is a potential spectator, as Arendt admits, therefore not only means that he may become a judge *after* he acted; for certainly he may have been a *moral* judge *before* he acted. That judgment is possible only after the event, that the owl of Minerva begins to fly only after dusk, is therefore true only in the sense that the whole story can be told only after it is over. But is it ever over? It seems to me that Arendt's own critique of a teleological conception of history implies that the spectator's judgment is never final, rather it is always woven back into the unfolding web of human action and is waiting for those who will judge this judgment. But if this is indeed the case, would not an internal link between judgment, action, and argumentation have been restored as a necessary consequence of Arendt's attempt to rehabilitate the rational faculty of judgment? Although this might not be quite the recovery of an Aristotelian conception of phronesis, it might well be a modern, post-Kantian equivalent of it.

I think there are several possible reasons why Arendt's thought did not move in this direction. One reason, as Ronald Beiner has pointed out in his excellent interpretation of Arendt's theory of judgment, could have been that Arendt did not see any prospects for genuine action and for freedom in our world. Second could have been that Arendt's own theory of action, as she developed it in *The Human Condition*, did not—contrary to appearances—allow for such a move. Arendt was never able to explain what the content of genuine political action could be, because for her everything related to the material reproduction of society—to the societal sphere of labor and to material interests—had to be conceived of as lying outside the sphere of political action proper. Since, however, even under conditions of a democratic polity, political action and political debate can get their content, their theme, their "about" only from the ongoing life process of society, it appears that no form of political praxis could ever correspond to Arendt's model of action. Or rather, what Arendt called action could only be exemplified *either* by the revolutionary action of those who *found* a democratic polity *or* by the quasi actions of those disinterested spectators who try to form and publicly express an impartial judgment about what has happened in the sphere of action in the ordinary sense of the word. Paradoxically, it is a consequence of Arendt's own theory of action that the judging activity of the disinterested spectator may in the end become the only genuine form of political action. There would therefore be no place for an internal relationship between political judgment, political discourse, and political action in her theory of action. A *third* reason for Arendt's reluctance to move in the direction I have indicated could be that the Kantian framework of concepts from which she borrowed the term judgment, and in terms of which she tried to articulate her own theory of judgment, did not provide her with the conceptual "space" to weave together the different threads of her theory. This has been suggested by several of her critics including Bernstein, Habermas, and Beiner. To be sure, I do not really believe that Arendt's Kantianism gives us the explanation for the impasses of her theory; rather, I think it could as well be argued that she chose Kant—and it was, as everybody knows, a free extrapolation from Kant—because it was in Kant that she found what she needed for *her* theory of judgment. Nevertheless, I believe that it might be Arendt's Kantianism—her latent orthodox Kantianism, as it were—that defines the limits of her theory. I want to explore this possibility in what follows.

I will attempt to show that Arendt, in trying to overcome certain limitations of Kant's practical philosophy, remained fixated on basic presuppositions underlying these limitations, presuppositions that concern a *scientistic conception of truth* and a *formalistic notion of rationality*. This is why Arendt, in her attempt to uncover Kant's unwritten political philosophy, could not operate from within his practical philosophy, which she dismissed altogether. Instead she could only refer to the critique of aesthetic judgment as the place in the Kantian system that allows for judgments that are neither arbitrary nor compelling for every rational being, and where the idea of the validity of judgments is explicitly tied to the idea of an intersubjective agreement among a plurality of sensuous and worldly beings. Given the contextual presuppositions of Kant's notion of aesthetic judgment, however, there remains a gulf between "logical" and aesthetic judgements: the former, the intersubjective validity of which springs from concepts, are susceptible to rational argument; the latter, which are not based on definite concepts, are not open to argument but only to "contention." Now it is this very distinction between conceptual or objective and nonconceptual or subjective general validity, and the corresponding distinction between judgments that are open to argument or dispute (which, according to Kant, allow for a "decision by means of proof") and judgments that are only open to "contention," that might be questioned. Because Arendt, however, did not herself question these distinctions, her attempt to remove the problematic of political and moral judgment from the context of Kant's practical philosophy and assimilate it to the problematic of aesthetic judgment was bound to result in what I would call a *mythology* of judgment—a mythology of judgment because the faculty of judgment now begins to emerge as the somewhat mysterious faculty to hit upon the truth when there is no context of possible arguments by which truth claims could be redeemed. Of course, Arendt would not speak of "truth" here. The word does not matter, however, as long as it is clear that what is at stake is a claim to intersubjective validity, and *this* certainly belongs to the very notion of reflective judgment.

Because of presuppositions Arendt shared with Kant, there was no place in her thought for a broader conception of rationality that would have allowed her to tie reflective judgment to rational argument. Such a conception of rationality would have to be located, as it were, in between the formal rationality of logical demonstration and the speculative rationality of what she called "thinking"—in between, that is, the rationality of intellect and the rationality of reason. For Arendt, what is in between these two rationalities, or one might even say, what mediates between them, is the rationality of judgment. This means, however, that the faculty of judgment reveals itself as a kind of "place-holder" for a conception of rationality which would have exploded the formalistic constraints imposed on the idea of rationality in the empiricist-rationalist tradition of modern philosophy. If I say a "place-holder," this could be understood in a double sense: First, of course, in a theoretical sense, for we are trying to get clear about Arendt's theory of judgment. But second, it could also be understood in a more practical sense. Arendt, as a philosopher in dark times, certainly had good reasons to doubt the *reality* of such a broader conception of rationality. As a result, the faculty of judgment, exercised only by the few, became for her a place-holder for practical reason, which seemed to have finally disintegrated as an existing idea. Arendt's idea of this faculty of judgment, which for her was not least the faculty to perceive differences and to perceive the particular in its own right, has a deep affinity with Adorno's idea of nonidentifying thought, that is, a form of thought in which the concept, as Adorno says, would "transcend the concept, i.e. the manipulative and exclusionary character of the concept, and thereby reach the non-conceptual."[3] In both cases, however, I think the paradoxical character of those ideas—the faculty of judgment, nonidentifying thought—can only in part be explained by the fact that both thinkers must have felt a desperate disproportion between their attempt to defend reason on the one hand and the reality of a dehumanized world on the other. I believe that in both cases an undissolved residue of the philosophical tradition which they criticized was operative in their thinking and *forced* them into paradoxical constructions.

Let me, then, try to clarify some of those Kantian presuppositions that I believe prevented Arendt from pursuing the internal relations between judgment and rational argument. Moreover, I wish to indicate how this relationship may be understood once those presuppositions are questioned.

II

Kant, as Arendt has pointed out, uses the term "reflective judgment" in a rather broad sense. It can only somewhat deceptively be rendered by the usual definition, according to which reflective judgment allows us to find a universal or a universal rule under which a given particular can be subsumed. This definition has the advantage, however, in that it points to the role of imagination in reflective judgment. It therefore indicates the creative dimension of language use, which is always involved when we have to find appropriate descriptions, words, problem formulations, explanations, or rules to fit a given situation which do not lie ready at hand when we start to reflect on such situations. It seems, however, that Kant did not really pursue this line of thinking (which is suggested by his definition of reflective judgment), very far. And it might well be the case that to pursue it seriously would undermine the conceptual framework of a philosophy of consciousness. In the decisive passages of *The Critique of Judgement*, reflective judgment in its broader sense is related to what Kant calls an "enlarged mind;" the "maxim" of judgment is "to think from the standpoint of everyone else," or as he also puts it, to "reflect upon one's own judgement from a universal standpoint." Both quotations are from section 40 of *The Critique of Judgement* on "Taste as a kind of sensus communis," which became central to Arendt's reflections on political judgment. I want to quote one of the crucial passages at length.

> However, by the name *sensus communis* is to be understood the idea of a *public* sense, i.e., a critical faculty which in its reflective act takes account (*a priori*) of the mode of representation of everyone else, in order, *as it were*, to weigh its judgement with the collective reason of mankind, and thereby avoid the illusion arising from subjective and personal conditions which would readily be taken for objective, an illusion that would exert a prejudicial influence upon its judgement. This is accomplished by weighing the judgement, not so much with actual, as rather with the merely possible, judgements of others, and by putting ourselves in the position of everyone else, as the result of a mere abstraction from the limitations which contingently affect our own estimate.[4]

That Kant does not only refer to aesthetic judgment here becomes clear from other remarks in the same paragraph, as well as from remarks he made in letters to Markus Herz, from which Arendt has quoted in her lectures on Kant's political philosophy. I want to give one of these quotations in which Kant even hints at something like a dialectical progress in argumentation:

> You know that I do not approach reasonable objections with the intention merely of refuting them, but that in thinking them over I always weave them into

my judegments, and afford them the opportunity of overturning all my most cherished beliefs. I entertain the hope that by thus viewing my judgements impartially from the standpoint of others some third view that will improve upon my previous insight may be obtainable.[5]

Here we have the germ of a notion of reflective judgment that would be intimately related to a conception of rational argumentation, potentially covering the whole field of possible intersubjective validity claims. But Arendt did not draw this conclusion, and in this, as we shall see, she was faithful to Kant, even against his own explicit intentions. But let us first come back to Arendt. The autonomy of judgment as she conceives it is articulated in terms of a sharp opposition between thinking and judging on the one hand and cognition and truth on the other. "Truth," Arendt writes, "is what we are compelled to admit by the nature either of our senses or of our brain."[6] This statement is amazingly in accord with modern mainstream epistemology, even if in naturalistic disguise. The "brain" stands for logical deduction and demonstration, the "senses" for empirical evidence or sensual intuition. This is the monological conception of cognition and rationality that runs through modern philosophy from early empiricism via Kant to Husserl, to the early Wittgenstein and twentieth-century empiricism. As everything of importance for her lies outside this sphere of cognition and truth, Arendt does not even care about sticking to a transcendental formulation of this position. What Arendt accepts above all from the epistemological tradition of modern philosophy is the model of a singular cognitive subject (or organism) confronting an external world that leaves its imprint on the internal representations of this subject, the corresponding primacy of cognition over language, and the idea of rational compulsion or logical proof. The problem with this set of premises is that they are philosophically mistaken because, to put it in a nutshell, they ignore the fact that even our senses and our brain are symbolically structured and thus part of an intersubjective world opened up by speech. Therefore not even cognition in Arendt's sense—that is, scientific cognition—can be understood in terms of the compelling force of uninterpreted intuitions or the compelling force of a worldless, that is, speechless logic. This much has certainly become clear in the often puzzling debate about paradigm shifts in science. Because Arendt accepts a questionable epistemological model of cognition from the philosophical tradition, she must locate the human world, that is, the common world of men opened up by speech, the world of politics and poetry, of thinking and judging, *beyond* or *above* the sphere of cognition. But this is again something like a world of action *beyond* or *above* a sphere of labor and work. More important, because the strategically crucial concepts of truth and rational compulsion have been handed over, as it were, to the extraworldly subjects of cognition, those rational activities which for Arendt are the truly humane ones—thinking and judging—can only be characterized by a series of negations: Thinking has no definite results (as cognition has), it is destructive (rather than constructive); judgment is not compelling (as truth is) and is not arrived at by moving within a rule-governed calculus (as logical conclusions are). What Arendt fails to see, however, is that these negative characterizations of thinking and judging do not merely draw a legitimate boundary line with respect to scientific and instrumental rationality, but cede the whole field of conceptions which we need to articulate an idea of discursive reason to science and technology, which in fact had occupied this whole field of conceptions in modern times. The opposition of "meaning" versus "truth," on which Arendt relies to reclaim the idea of reason for the field of thinking and for the field of human affairs, is not sufficient to mark a distinction between poetry and discursive reason, between good and bad judgment, or between the merely eccentric and the intersubjectively valid.

Arendt accused Kant of using the notion of truth in the field of speculative reason, thereby assimilating thinking to truth. Something similar could have been said by the early Wittgenstein and, obviously, by Heidegger or Jaspers. And certainly Arendt was right in pointing to an inconsistency in Kant's thought: given his conception of knowledge, his idea of a future system of metaphysics appears as a scientistic aberration. Criticizing Kant, Arendt remains faithful to his concept of cognition and to his formal conception of rationality. These Kantian conceptions of cognition and of rationality, however, also affect his—and Arendt's—conception of judgment. Because Kant conceives the subject of cognition as well as the subject of moral reasoning in a monological way, there is no real place for the exercise of judgment—except for a marginal or a transcendental one—*within* the spheres of cognition and morality in his philosophy. Judging as a cognitive or a moral subject for Kant is *equivalent* to "thinking from the standpoint of everybody else."

When we apply the categories of pure understanding to sensuous phenomena or judge our maxims in the light of the Categorical Imperative, we eo ipso think from a "universal standpoint"—the universal standpoint being defined by the universal forms of cognition or the "form of lawfulness" of our maxims. Kant continues the passage concerning the "sensus communis" which I have quoted above: "This [i.e., the weighing of our judgements with the possible judgements of others, A. W.] ... is effected by so far as possible letting go the element of matter, i.e. of sensation, in our general state of representative activity, and confining attention to the formal peculiarities of our representation or general state of representative activity."[7] Although Kant already speaks here of aesthetic judgment, the sentence indicates that thinking from a universal standpoint is intimately connected for him with the distinction between *matter* and *form.* The formal element represents what is not merely subjective and what therefore belongs to a universal standpoint; in the case of empirical cognition and of moral judgment, however, the conformity to the universal form of thinking—to the form of lawfulness—is brought about essentially by the categories of pure understanding and the Categorical Imperative respectively. In both cases, therefore, the faculty of judgment could only play a subordinate role.

Arendt accepted the first part of Kant's solution but not the second. As far as moral judgment is concerned, she was too clearly aware that Kant's formal-monological conception of moral judgment cannot work as it stands; and I think she had good reasons to read Kant's conception of reflective judgment back, as it were, into his moral philosophy. However, she then stuck to Kant's *monological* concept of cognition and his *formal* conception of rationality, that is, to the conceptual presuppositions in terms of which Kant's notion of reflective judgment is articulated. Therefore Arendt could not use the notion of reflective judgment to uncover a suppressed dialogical dimension of Kant's conception of practical reason, but only to assimilate moral—and political—judgment to aesthetic judgment. Arendt remains entrapped within an epistemological framework, from the perspective of which physical science must appear as the paradigm of knowledge, physical facts as the paradigm of factuality, and logical demonstration as the paradigm of rational argument; correlatively, the activities of thinking and judging must appear as lying outside the sphere of cognition, truth and rational argument proper. If truth is "what we are compelled to admit by the nature either of our senses or of our brain," then truth is speechless, beyond or below speech, while thinking and judging, the truly humane faculties, because they depend on speech, that is, on a plurality of human beings, are beyond truth.

Now Arendt, as is well known, always liked to start with sharp analytical distinctions, and her distinction between a sphere of cognition and truth on the one hand and the sphere of thinking and judging on the other might be considered as just being one of those analytical distinctions. Arendt herself warns us against hypostatizing this analytical distinction when she points out that the sphere of cognition itself is shot through with elements of thinking and therefore, as one might conclude, cannot really correspond to the monological concept of cognition which she takes over from the epistemological tradition. On the other hand, one might argue that there *does* exist an internal relationship between the logic of modern natural science on the one hand and a monological concept of cognition on the other. The point therefore would not be to dismiss Arendt's distinctions altogether, but only to look at them from a different perspective which no longer forces us to oppose the domains of thinking and judging—that is, the domain of human affairs and of critical thought—to the sphere of rational argument proper through a series of negations. We could take the debate about paradigm shifts in science as a starting point for indicating such a new perspective. What this debate has shown is not that relativism is true even for science, but that even physical science does not correspond to that epistemological paradigm linking truth and cognition with calculative rationality which Arendt accepts—following a long tradition. However, if no formal account can be given of rational argument even with respect to physical science, we may well turn the tables and try to understand the peculiar rationality of science from the vantage point of a broader conception of rationality. Such a conception of rationality would allow us to recognize the internal relationship between different kinds of intersubjective validity claims—for example, moral, aesthetic, or scientific—and corresponding forms of argumentation, and the internal relationships, by which the different spheres of validity are also connected with each other. Rational argumentation—what we *call* argumentation—rarely corresponds in actuality to the model of deductive or inductive reasoning (where ultimate premises are either given by intuition, empirical evidence, construction, or mere fiat) which has been so widely accepted as a model of rationality in modern philosophy. Arguments always operate in contexts that are organized not in a linear, but in a holistic way. The compelling force of arguments is therefore always dependent on contextual presuppositions which themselves may be questioned as the argument goes on. This does not only mean that rational discourse cannot rest on ultimate premises that in principle could not be questioned, but also, and more specifically, that there are no universal and a priori criteria of what would count as a good argument in specific contexts. Moreover, arguments often have their own context of explication through which they attain their specific meaning and their specific force, if they have any. This means, however, that an intersubjective system of fixed meanings, that is, a common language, which for the formalist tradition always was an unquestioned presupposition and a condition of the possibility of rational argument, may be as much the *result* of rational discourse as it is its—always partially realized—starting point. What the debate about paradigm shifts in science has shown is that the deductive or calculative model of reasoning collapses whenever the presupposition of a stable and transparent intersubjective meaning system is put into question. But this is precisely one of the points where argument becomes *necessary*. Rational discourse understood in this way—and I think it is the way in which we do understand it when we begin to argue—would not least be an attempt to restore an intersubjective agreement which in the calculative model is always taken for granted (or taken as something to be brought about *before* we can begin to argue). Kuhn's original distinction between the rationality of "normal science" and the somehow irrational, rhetorical, or merely persuasive character of interparadigm debates still presupposes this calculative model of rationality. The interesting parallel to Arendt is that again only negative characterizations—as far as rationality is concerned—are available for the description of a nonformalizable type of discourse.

III

Once the presuppositions of the modern epistemological—empiricist-rationalist—tradition have been put into question, we can begin to redefine the role of the faculty of judgment, because now a broader conception of rationality will provide us with the missing link between the notion of judgment and the idea of intersubjective agreement. A philosophical strategy like this also underlies Habermas's theory of discursive rationality. If the validity of judgments could be explained in the Habermasian sense as the possibility of a consensus brought about by arguments, then the faculty of judgment would just be the faculty to hit upon what also could be agreed on in a rational consensus; and this faculty would certainly be inexplicable without some internal relationship to an ability to argue and deliberate well. So the Aristotelian connection between phronesis and deliberation would have been restored in a post-Kantian philosophical framework. I shall not, however, follow Habermas directly. For I think it can be shown that a procedural conception of rationality like that of Habermas, linked to a consensus theory of truth, ultimately requires the reintroduction of an autonomous faculty of judgment to become intelligible: a consensus brought about under conditions of an ideal speech-situation can be a criterion of truth only if a sufficiently developed faculty of judgment of all participants is presupposed. Of course, it might be suspected then that it is the very attempt to set up a formal standard of intersubjective validity that gives rise to the postulate of an autonomous faculty of judgment—as it did already for Kant. If we want to prevent the whole problem from reemerging, as it were, behind our back, we would therefore have to give up the attempt to ground the idea of rationality in some sort of formal-universal standard of intersubjective validity.

The same point could also be put in a positive way: we could now understand the faculty of judgment as a place-holder for a conception of *rationality* and of *intersubjective validity* respectively, for which no overall formal criterion and no overall formal explanation can be given. It seems to me that this would in fact be the only viable conception of rationality indistinguishable from that of discursive reason. This, to be sure, is an idea of discursive reason that can only be understood and practiced from *within*, from wherever we happen to be, with the standards, criteria, and arguments that are available to *us*, while we know these standards, criteria, and arguments may be questioned—although we may have no reason to question them—as time goes on. The only criteria of validity we have are those we happen to have inherited from an existing culture of reason. The next day may well show us that the only rational thing is to abandon or modify some of them; however, there can be no *outside* criterion of truth and we do not need any. Needless to say, this has nothing to do with relativism, given that the idea of intersubjective validity is still tied to that of rational agreement. This idea of rational agreement, however, no longer refers to a point outside history or at the end of history. Discursive reason only exists as "situated" reason, to use Benhabib's expression, and this pertains to its uniting and reconciling as well as to its disruptive and subversive force. If, however, we conceive reason or rationality in the broad sense I have suggested and yet allow it to be "situated," then the faculty of judgment loses its independent status as well as some of its mysterious character. It would simply be a faculty to hit upon the truth in situations where it is not easy to do so, or where—depending on the situation—experience, character, imagination, or courage is required. The *goodness* of judgment, however, could only prove itself by a judgment's being confirmed through either experience, or arguments, or—connected with these two—the independent judgment of others.

Disregarding for a moment Kant's distinction between reflective and determinant judgment—the latter being, I would claim, basically a matter of know-how in about the same sense that rule following is for Wittgenstein—the decisive point could be put as follows: If we say that someone has good judgment—about the character of persons, in political matters, in matters of art, with regard to moral or practical problems, or as a legal or medical expert—we are implying that his or her judgment has proven to be right either in a particular instance or in many cases. *We* say this, judging someone's judgment, after having convinced ourselves in quite ordinary ways that he or she has often been right, has often analyzed complex situations in the right way, has often seen at once what nobody else could see, or has often come up with the right argument at the right time. This certainly *is* a faculty, the value of which cannot be overestimated, a faculty moreover that Arendt herself seems to have had in an extraordinary degree with respect to political and moral matters. But we can call it an *autonomous* faculty in Arendt's sense only if we dissociate it from its natural context of rational argumentation. Good judgments must have the internal capacity of revealing themselves as good and of convincing "everybody else."

This brings me back to my initial reflections on the status of the faculty of judgment in Arendt's theory. How do we explain the functioning of judgment when a context of rational argumentation no longer exists? Or, to put it in more general terms, how do we account for the fact that the practical power of rational argument can sometimes be very limited indeed, so that valid judgments may not convince anybody? Here I think the response must be the following: Why do *we* call these judgments valid? Is it not because they convinced *us*? I think there is nothing mysterious in somebody's hitting upon the truth or doing the right thing while others are unable to see that *this* is the truth or that *this* is the right thing—either because they lack courage, imagination, or experience, or because their whole form of life has been corrupted. Stupidity, cowardice, self-deception, and irrationality are as much elements of human life as the faculty of reason; we do not need to postulate an autonomous faculty of judgment to account for the fact that the former do not always win over. What we do need, and here I agree with Beiner—as well as with Arendt and Kant—are institutional conditions under which everybody has a chance to develop his political, moral, or aesthetic judgment; for these are the only conditions under which a political, moral, or aesthetic culture can exist, and therefore the only soil, as it were, from which good judgment may still spring in those moments when the world is in shambles.

IV

As a conclusion, I want to illustrate my main argument by saying something about moral judgment and moral discourse. I want to show how from a Kantian starting point in moral philosophy one could give an account of moral judgment that might be considered as—if I may use this term—a "rational reconstruction" of Arendt's attempt to read a conception of "moral taste" into Kant's idea of the functioning of practical reason. Kant's moral philosophy may be summed up by the following statement: "We must be *able to will* that a maxim of our action should become a universal law—this is the canon for all moral judgement of action."[8] Now I think that Kant's principle of moral judgment makes sense only if we understand it in a "negative" way: We ought *not* to act in a certain way if we can*not* will the maxim of our action to become a universal law.[9] Thus we ought not to tell a lie to get out of a difficult situation, because the corresponding maxim cannot be universalized (i.e., I cannot will it to become a universal law). This is a very simple idea indeed that Kant thought, with good reason, every ordinary human being could grasp. Because of his tendency to give his moral philosophy a formalistic twist, however, Kant did not pay much attention to the fact that the right application of his *formal principle* of morality in more complex situations cannot be a matter of course. That is, Kant dismissed the problem of the possible intersubjective validity of our moral judgments because here, as always, he took the *formal criterion* at the same time to be a criterion of intersubjective validity: Applying the Categorical Imperative, I am judging—as a noumenal Ego—from a universal standpoint. What may be called the rigid formalism of Kantian ethics, which comes to the fore, for example, in his discussion of an "alleged right to lie for philanthropic reasons"[10], is the direct expression of this presupposition.

Now if we take the "negativistic" interpretation of the Categorical Imperative, which I have suggested, for granted, the problem of moral judgment as it has been left open by Kant could be stated in the following way: In complex situations, or in situations in which our moral judgment is not unambiguously supported by an existing moral culture, it may not be obvious which maxims—or which ways-of-acting-in-this-situation—are *not* universalizable in an *intersubjective* sense of the word. That a maxim is not universalizable in an intersubjective sense of the word means that *we* cannot will it to become a universal law. Which ways of acting *I* cannot will to become a universal law depend on how I describe a specific situation and the alternatives of action open to me. For example, it makes a tremendous difference whether I describe a specific action as handing over a fugitive person to the legal authorities who are searching for him, or whether I describe it as abandoning a helpless and innocent person to a band of terrorists called police. Both descriptions can be the right ones depending on the situation. But in a specific situation at most *one* of them can be the right one. Depending on the description I choose, the particular way of acting which is at stake will be or will not be universalizable *for me*. This shows, however, that the problem of moral judgment is not so much a problem of universalization as such, but rather a problem of getting the relevant facts of the situation right; that is, of interpreting the situation as well as the available alternatives of action in the right way. The right way would be the way in which "everybody else" who tries to form an impartial judgment would interpret this situation. I mention only in passing that an interpretation of a situation of action can obviously be the right one only if it takes into account the different perspectives of the concrete actors involved. Posing the problem of the intersubjective validity of moral judgment therefore also makes the suppressed dialogical dimension of Kantian ethics visible.

What I want to point to mainly is: (1) that if we see a situation of action in the right way, we usually have no choice morally speaking; (2) that we can and do argue about whether the interpretation of specific situations is the right one; and (3) that moral discourse takes place to a large extent as discourse about the "facts" in the widest possible sense. Again we need not be worried that there are no ultimate criteria of what the right description of a situation of action would be; as long as we are *in* situations (and not philosophizing), we usually know quite well how to go about arguing for or against certain interpretations, although there are also cases where things are so complicated that we may be unable to make up our mind. Practically speaking, there are of course limits of rational argument; but as Beiner has pointed out, we cannot consider these practical limits of rational argument as limits in principle as long as we distinguish between true and false and think that *we* do have arguments. I want to point to one specific limit of rational argument, however, which I believe might have induced Arendt to postulate an autonomous faculty of judgment. I think that all of us, or at least most of us, sometimes close our eyes to the facts of a situation, project *our* idiosyncratic conditions on others, are unable—for lack of imagination or good will—to take the perspective of others into account, or are unaware of our own motivations. What can prevent this from happening on a large scale or even collectively is a moral culture that certainly also requires good institutions. Now in many of the cases I have mentioned rational argument does not work because we do not *want* to recognize the truth. This not wanting to recognize the truth, however, goes together well with what I would call moral self-interest, that is, the interest of having a good moral opinion of ourselves. The false generalities and social clichés that Arendt was criticizing may often act as a mediating link between this moral self-interest and interested self-deception. But where this happens, we will consider ways of acting as universalizable which we could not consider as such if we dared to acknowledge or if we seriously tried to find out the facts—the facts about others, about ourselves, about the context of our action, and so on. Rational argument may not work in such situations because it *always* can only work under certain preconditions: experience and knowledge in the case of the physicist or physician, aesthetic education and experience in the case of art, and moral character or sincerity in the case of moral discourse. And needless to say, these are preconditions that certainly cannot be brought about by rational argument alone: they are rather the practical results of a scientific, aesthetic, or moral culture. Such a culture might be called a "culture of reason"[11] inasmuch as discursive rationality becomes the element in which it moves and develops. Now as far as moral character is concerned, it may often remain more or less invisible under normal conditions of social integration. It becomes visible only under extreme conditions. I think this is what Arendt really refers to when she claims that the faculty of judgment emerges as an autonomous faculty "when the stakes are on the table."[12] What really may become visible in such situations, then, is not a faculty of judgment as an autonomous mental faculty, but what kind of person somebody really is; for it shows itself only when good judgment has its price.

This then is the way in which a formal principle of morality may coexist with an account of morality in terms of "moral taste," that is, in terms of reflective judgment: The formal principle—a principle of generalization—defines the moral point of view from which we look at situations of action. But whether the "I can will . . . " is also a "we can will. . . ," that is, whether my moral judgments can claim intersubjective validity, depends on whether my interpretations of situations of action are the right ones. Only if they are the right ones, if they could be shared by "everybody else," can they lead to valid moral judgments. A well-developed faculty of judgment is certainly of immense importance in moral as well as political matters. But it is not an addition to, but rather an expression of what we might call the "faculty" of discursive reason.

Notes

1. H. Arendt, *The Life of Mind*, vol. 1: *Thinking*. New York and London: Harcourt Brace Jovanovich, 1978, p. 193.

2. H. Arendt, *Eichmann in Jerusalem: A Report on the Banality of Evil.* New York: Viking Press, 1965, pp. 294–295.

3. T. W. Adorno, *Negative Dialectics.* New York: Seabury Press, 1973, p. 9 (translation changed). German edition: *Negative Dialektik. Gesammelte Schriften*, vol. 6 (ed. R. Tiedemann), Frankfurt am Main: Suhrkamp, 1973, p. 21 ("[daß] der Begriff den Begriff, das Zurüstende und Abschneidende übersteigen und dadurch ans Begriffslose heranreichen [könne]").

4. I. Kant, *The Critique of Judgement* (trans. J. C. Meredith), Oxford: Clarendon Press, 1952, p. 151. German edition: *Kritik der Urteilskraft, Werke*, vol. 5 (ed. W. Weischedel), Darmstadt; Wissenschaftliche Buchgesellschaft, 1959, p. 389 ("Unter dem sensus *communis* aber muß man die Idee eines *gemeinschaftlichen* Sinnes, d.i. eines Beurteilungsvermögens verstehen, welches in seiner Reflexion auf die Vorstellungsart jedes andern in Gedanken (a priori) Rücksicht nimmt, um *gleichsam* an die gesamte Menschenvernunft sein Urteil zu halten, und dadurch der Illusion zu entgehen, die aus subjektiven Privatbedingungen, welche leicht für objektiv gehalten werden könnten, auf das Urteil nachteiligen Einfluß haben würde. Dieses geschieht nun dadurch, daß man sein Urteil an anderer, nicht sowohl wirkliche, als vielmehr bloß mögliche Urteile hält, und sich in die Stelle jedes andern versetzt, indem man bloß von den Beschränkungen, die unserer eigenen Beurteilung zufälliger Weise anhängen, abstrahiert.")

5. Quoted from H. Arendt, *Lectures on Kant's Political Philosophy*, ed. R. Beiner. Chicago: University of Chicago Press, 1982, p. 42. (Cf. *Kant's Briefwechsel*, vol. 1, *Kant's Gesammelte Schriften*, vol. 10 (ed. Königlich Preußische Akademie der Wissenschaften), Berlin/Leipzig: de Gruyter, 1922, p. 116 f.: "Daß vernünftige Einwürfe von mir nicht blos von der Seite angesehen werden wie sie zu wiederlegen seyn könten sondern daß ich sie iederzeit beym Nachdenken unter meine Urtheile webe und ihnen das Recht lasse alle vorgefaßte Meinungen die ich sonst beliebt hatte über den Haufen zu werfen, das wissen sie. Ich hoffe immer dadurch daß ich meine Urtheile aus dem Standpunkte anderer unpartheyisch ansehe etwas drittes herauszubekommen was besser ist als mein vorigtes.")

6. Arendt, *Thinking*, p. 61.

7. Kant, *The Critique of Judgement*, p. 151; German: *Kritik der Urteilskraft*, pp. 389ff. ("Welches [d.h., daß man sein Urteil an anderer mögliche Urteile hält, A. W.] ... dadurch bewirkt wird, daß man das, was in dem Vorstellungszustande Materie, d.i. Empfindung ist, so viel möglich wegläßt, und lediglich auf die formalen Eigentümlichkeiten seiner Vorstellung, oder seines Vorstellungszustandes, Acht hat.")

8. I. Kant, *Groundwork of the Metaphysics of Morals* (trans. H. J. Paton), New York: Harper and Row, 1964, p. 91. German edition: *Grundlegung zur Metaphysik der Sitten, Werke*, vol. 4, p. 54 ("Man muß *wollen können*, daß eine Maxime unserer Handlung ein allgemeines Gesetz werde: dies ist der Kanon der moralischen Beurteilung derselben überhaupt.")

9. See Albrecht Wellmer, "Ethics and Dialogue," in *The Persistence of Modernity*, Cambridge/Mass.: The MIT Press, pp. 123ff.

10. I. Kant, "Über ein vermeintliches Recht, aus Menschenliebe zu lügen", in *Werke*, vol. 4, pp. 637–643.

11. See F. Kambartel, "Vernunft: Kriterium oder Kultur?", in: F. Kambartel, *Philosophie der humanen Welt*, Frankfurt am Main: Suhrkamp, 1989.

12. Arendt, *Thinking*, p. 193.

3

The Moral Costs of Political Pluralism: The Dilemmas of Difference and Equality in Arendt's "Reflections on Little Rock"

James Bohman

Hannah Arendt was often embroiled in controversy, and in her most controversial writings she employed a unique style of philosophical journalism. Two of her more contentious philosophical interpretations of contemporary events produced the greatest furor: her analysis of the "banality of evil" in *Eichmann in Jerusalem* and her political essay in *Dissent* arguing against the "forced integration" of public education in the South, "Reflections on Little Rock."[1] However disparate they are in theme, both writings have an underlying philosophical point in common: Arendt's strict distinction between politics and morality, as well as her willingness to challenge the moralism of prevalent political views, especially when she thought that it created the conditions for the emergence of powerful institutions and the use of their accumulated means to violence beyond the proper limits of politics.

Both strands of her political philosophy are certainly to be found in her unpopular arguments against school desegregation in Little Rock. Many sympathetic commentators have given various reasons for this "unwise" essay, including how her European perspective on race problems in the United States were filtered through her experiences as a Jew in prewar Germany, as well as how her penchant for the abstract classification of historical events according to her own philosophical categories distorted her perceptions of the issues. Indeed, her notorious distinction of "the social" and "the political" led her astray on more than one occasion.[2] I shall argue that none of these explanations, and even the implied criticisms of Arendt's political thought that they contain, are adequate in understanding the philosophical motivations behind Arendt's stance on Little Rock. As deeply mistaken as she was about the particular circumstances and as much as she severely misinterpreted what was at stake in some of the issues involved, her arguments are deeper and far more troubling for pluralistic politics than they first appear to be. I shall argue that her real underlying concern is with defending pluralism among equal citizens, and thus with urging us to accept clear-mindedly the real moral costs of holding both diversity and consent as necessary political values.

Because Arendt seems to be so clearly wrong about many of the circumstances and effects of segregation, it was very easy for her contemporaries to dismiss her arguments. But in this period Arendt was very much concerned about the future of the American republic itself, which she saw as deeply threatened by measures such as the "enforced desegregation," measures that only lead us further into the modern trap of using politics to achieve the nonpolitical ends of social equality. Federal enforcement and intervention, she argues, should be restricted "to those few instances in which the law of the land and the principle of the Republic are at stake" (48). By the latter, Arendt meant to restrict federal intervention to threats to the very idea of citizen self-rule. Public education is simply the wrong target, according to Arendt, and its desegregation has nothing to do with the protection of the most basic human rights. Indeed, Arendt goes so far as to predict that equal opportunity in education will only make racism worse by heightening social competition and the awareness of differences. Arendt is arguing that such attempts to eliminate social inequalities create "the dilemma of difference," to use Martha Minow's phrase.[3] They may only heighten such differences, and in the end serve only to reinforce the very categories of difference, race, or social class that they sought to eliminate. Arendt's awareness of these dilemmas makes it more difficult for us some thirty-five years later to dismiss her arguments with the ease of most her contemporaries.

At the same time, Arendt argues social differences should not be dissolved into sameness and homogeneity. As can be readily seen in many of her other writings, in particular *Crises of the Republic*, Arendt otherwise had obvious sympathies with the civil rights movement and its demands for equal rights. It was a sign not only of the vitality of the American republic, but also of the superiority of political power over mere violence. But her endorsement was contingent upon the movement remaining within the boundaries of the rule of law and insisting only on demands of equal rights and political equality. Rather than aim at public education as do totalitarian regimes with their false utopias of equality, Arendt suggests that the movement is better served if it uses the power of legal coercion against antimiscegenation laws (which restricted the private right to marry) and against restrictive voting practices (which limited rights of political participation). The rule of law is thus better used against "enforced segregation," rather than against social discrimination and exclusiveness, which somehow for Arendt is all that is wrong with both public education and fair housing practices. "Segregation is discrimination enforced by law, and desegregation can do no more than abolishing laws enforcing discrimination;" it cannot, however, abolish discrimination itself (50). Apparently, Arendt interprets this requirement quite narrowly, given that she equates desegregating schools with forcing whites to accept social equality, even as they stood backed by police weapons to keep African American students out.

The decades and struggles that have come to pass since the publication of "Reflections on Little Rock" make it possible for us to read it in a new light. As I shall show, it is not that her contemporaries were wrong about what is so problematic in the essay. Rather, the many critiques of liberal equality from the point of view of both communitarianism and multiculturalism make it possible for us to see more readily the difficulties that Arendt was concerned about in her analysis. Moreover, many in the civil rights movement itself have come to question some of the wisdom of corrective measures adopted as legal remedies, from Lani Guinier's recent criticisms of "race-conscious redistricting"[4] to the growing number of African American critics of federally mandated school desegregation policies (including the first African American mayor elected in Saint Louis, Missouri) as undermining community schooling and neighborhood integrity. At the very least, we might now be able to see some of the complexities of Arendt's arguments, especially in recognizing the sometimes high costs of a commitment to the political value of pluralism in our fragile communities.

Reactions to "Reflections on Little Rock": Arendt's Defenders and Critics

From the beginning Arendt's "Reflections on Little Rock" was virulently attacked from many quarters. The critical reactions may be classified into three groups, and even Arendt's apologists fit into one of these categories: the first traces her analysis to a cultural misunderstanding of the situation by an uncomprehending European intellectual. Such a treatment of the "mistakes" of the essay range from the sharp criticisms of Arendt's contemporaries, including the American philosopher Sidney Hook and the political scientist David Spitz; a more moderate, but thorough moral rejection by the novelist Ralph Ellison; and, finally, sympathetic reconstructions by her biographer Elisabeth Young-Bruehl and her interpreter Margaret Canovan. Young-Bruehl argues that Arendt treats the situation as analogous to the situation of European Jews, especially to the extent that she was struck by the pictures of a young girl walking through the screaming racist mobs. As shown again in the powerful documentary film *Eyes on the Prize*, this historical moment, with the faces of that crowd contorted by hate, forms a shocking and unforgettable image. This African American child, Arendt claims, is being used as a means for social advancement, put in a situation of humiliation and assimilation, much like the class parvenu striving for social recognition. The second sort of treatment of this sort sees Arendt as a victim of her own philosophical categories and distinctions, which led her to misinterpret the situation and give it a philosophical significance it does not have. This sort of criticism is in fact the dominant one of Arendt's friends and critics alike.

In the same issue of *Dissent* in which the essay originally appeared, the title of David Spitz's sharp and insightful critical response captures the rejection of Arendt's strict and ontologizing use of philosophical categories: "Politics and the Realms of Being."[5] Seyla Benhabib sees the "difficult and risky art of making distinctions" behind Arendt's theoretical treatment of the issue. In particular, it is the "essentialism" of her notorious distinction between the social and political that is the problem. According to Benhabib, the Little Rock essay demonstrates that "the distinction between the 'social' and the 'political' makes no sense in the modern world," but not for the reasons that Arendt gave in *The Human Condition*. On the contrary, "the struggle to make something public is a struggle for justice."[6] The other predominant interpretation of this sort, forcefully articulated by Margaret Canovan, takes the opposite tack. She argues that Arendt's essay is no aberration, but follows from her entire political philosophy. Canovan argues that Arendt is defending an old-style liberal notion of political equality, one that shows the limits of legal coercion and preserves the autonomy of both the private and the public realm.[7] In my view, all of these interpretations are partially right, but in many respects they are also wrong. They are wrong because they misidentify one of the core issues: the problem of the moral and political costs of a justice that includes *both* equality and plurality.

Both of these interpretations seem to be verified by Arendt's own seeming repudiation of the essay after some very telling public criticisms by the African American novelist, Ralph Ellison. In particular, Ellison responded to Arendt's criticism of African American parents in the essay and made clear that the heroism of civil rights movement was based in the constant and daily struggles of "a people who must live in society without recognition."[8] By not understanding this fact, as well as by missing the constant undercurrent of violence and explicit terror in a segregated society, Arendt misinterprets why African American parents would send their children into angry mobs: through such events the child confronts "the terrors of social life," the life that the child will have to face in segregated society. Arendt wrote to Ellison that she now understood this ideal of sacrifice in the movement because she now "grasped the element of stark violence and elementary, bodily fear in the situation." Her criticism in this case is all the more ironic, given that Arendt generally applauded the civic courage manifested in social movements such as the antiwar and civil rights movements, seeing it as necessary to sustain the public world.[9] But does this admission change anything in her interpretation of political and social equality, or of the limits of the rule of law? Arendt grants only that she may not have understood the situation culturally, but all that she explicitly changes is her understanding of the role of children in the front lines of desegregation and nothing else in her analysis.

How do Arendt's admissions to Ellison affect her position on school desegregation? Very little indeed, precisely because it seems to me that one of the real core ideas of the essay has not yet been discussed by friends and foes alike. The operating contrast is not merely between the social and the political, but also between equality and difference. In many different contexts, Arendt insists that the problem with social equality is that it implies sameness, rather than the difference of political equality. Indeed, political equality is the very opposite of social homogeneity for

Arendt, and it is the latter that Arendt fears is being manifested in some of the demands for integration. When she concedes to Ellison that she did not understand the "terror" of segregation, she criticizes such terror too because it undermines the conditions of plurality that make citizenship possible; it makes a common world of the plurality of citizens impossible. With regard to eliminating violence, a genuine political goal is at stake: it promotes greater plurality. But for this reason she is suspicious of the hidden Rousseauian agenda behind the Little Rock demands: that education be used as a coercive instrument by those who seek to create a common will rather than a common world.[10]

It is my contention that Arendt's response to Ellison is hardly a "graceful retraction," as Benhabib puts it. Rather her admissions are unrepentant and still consistent with the thrust of her essay: with her peculiar understanding of the relation of power, equality, and diversity. On my interpretation, the main point of "Reflections on Little Rock" is a warning about the use of political power: no matter how noble its moral end, force should not be used at the cost of the plurality that is the condition of political life. The central claim of the essay is contained in the following lines, which at the time sounded quite conservative. Now, they sound very much like the critique of liberalism quite common among both contemporary communitarians and defenders of multiculturalism. Arendt writes: "Liberals fail to understand that the nature of power is such that the power potential of the Union as a whole will suffer if the regional foundations on which this power rests are undermined.... And states' rights in this country are among the most authentic sources of power not only for the promotion of regional interests and diversity but for the Republic as a whole" (54). This source of power is free association of people acting in concert, and the use of state power in this case undermines the formation of such power and consent and threatens to separate such communicative power from citizens' relation to state institutions. Such a state cannot maintain the twin necessary conditions of a republic and its public space: consent *and* plurality.

There is a further, nonpolitical aspect of Arendt's thinking about diversity in this essay that I shall not treat here: her basically conservative and elitist criticism of mass society, the result of modern homogeneity. One reason not to abolish social discrimination, Arendt argues, is that it is an important factor in preserving group formation in large-scale societies. In mass society all group distinctions and interests have disappeared, and thus group distinction is an important mechanism for preserving plurality, even when it inevitably entails social discrimination. Such discrimination is permissible and even desirable for Arendt, so long as it does not expand into areas of political equality. Arendt believed that many forms of segregation amounted only to such group distinction. Rather than the denial of difference, they are the means for preserving it. The question remains whether exclusion, rather than mutual recognition, is the more effective mechanism for maintaining diversity, and here Arendt provides no substantive argument for her position. Nonetheless, it points to the very high moral price that Arendt is willing to pay for plurality, given that it is a barrier to the forced inclusion of groups and individuals typical of totalitarian regimes.

In the rest of the essay, I want to look at the core arguments about diversity and equality as they are expressed in "Reflections on Little Rock." In the first, more brief section that follows I want to argue against Arendt's general claim that social equality undermines plurality. In particular, I want to defend a modified version of the basic Rousseauian claim against Arendt that there is a direct relation between social equality and political equality. This point is well known: there cannot be large social inequalities without there being political inequalities as well. In order for the argument to work against Arendt, I will have to show that social inequalities above a certain threshold reduce the potential plurality of the political, public sphere. While I reject Arendt's arguments about political equality and diversity, I shall then defend her general point about power and diversity on somewhat different grounds.

Taken together, my two arguments lead us to accept some of Arendt's strong philosophical medicine concerning the relation of equality and plurality. Arendt rejects the standard liberal solution that gives primacy to equality over plurality. If we give up this way of ordering the main values of liberalism, Arendt is arguing, then we must accept some rather uncomfortable conclusions. Although we may often have to pay a moral price for diversity, I shall argue that there is more to be said when this price has to be paid, and here a richer notion of equality is needed in order to have some criterion by which to decide. Moreover, Arendt herself gives us just such richer criterion that she should have used in the Little Rock case but does not: the price of diversity should not be so high as to risk the loss of common citizenship, the only mechanism for preserving plurality through a shared pubic sphere. Arendt does not pay sufficient attention to the requirements of plurality that her own account of civil rights entails when she is thinking about the difficult dialectic of reconciling political inclusion and exclusion in the Little Rock case. Political equality requires a minimum threshold: that all must have access to the public world.

Social Equality and Political Plurality: The Problem of Political Poverty

I have already noted that Arendt's main fear about social equality is that it produces *sameness*. For this reason, demands for equality lead to the loss of plurality that is typical of the modern public world. In this respect, she saw social exclusion not only as an inevitable result of spontaneous, free association, but also as a positive mechanism for preserving diversity in large-scale, mass society. But more than in terms of the positive and intrinsic value of diversity, Arendt argues that sameness undermines the condition of genuine plurality that is manifested most completely in politics. Arendt opposed all political theories and philosophical ideals that she thought undermined such a politics of plurality, and here she included not only the tradition's emphasis on "rulership," but more important, the theories of Marx and Rousseau who dangerously advocated norms of unanimity and equality and replaced politics with the social concerns of household management in the form of bureaucratic institutions.

For this same political reason, Arendt opposed all historical trends that produced homogeneity rather than plurality, including demands for "natural communities" of race and ethnicity, as well as the communities of religion and other authorities that demanded credal unanimity and a united will. According to her vision of politics, "citizens are held together not by a common will but by a common *world*, by sharing a set of worldly institutions."[11] Citizenship is not a matter of people having enough similar beliefs and desires, or even some minimal "overlapping consensus," but of the plurality of different persons inhabiting a common public space together. Perhaps the best analogy here is to see the extent to which Arendt models all politics and political institutions on international law, in which there is the most extreme diversity, no quasi-natural basis of community, and no more agreement than members can produce among themselves by respecting all their differences. On this analogy, participants could not conceive of forcing some other nation to desegregate its religious schools or to adopt some particular population policy, without undermining the plurality of "the union of social unions" that makes up any international institution. Such a public space can be maintained only if it remains open to many different perspectives and points of view.

Because politics does not aim either at uniting people in some common will or at producing some convergent interest of all as the tradition had thought, Arendt proposes an alternative notion of consent and agreement appropriate to her radical pluralism. Although arguing against both natural rights and the unity of the political will typical of social contract theory, she in no way rejects consent as the fundamental criterion of legitimacy. However, it has an entirely different role for Arendt. It is the basis of power in Arendt's special sense, of people acting in concert. People can act in concert only by maintaining their plurality in their common action. The political mechanism here is the free and plural consent of all citizens who both generate, share, and limit power by acting together.[12]

The main differences between plural and singular consent can be illustrated in light of Arendt's interpretation of Kant's theory of judgment. According to Kant, the public use of reason is manifested as an "enlarged capacity for thought" that permits a critical and impartial process of deliberating and judging "from the standpoint of everyone else." It is precisely by appealing to public reason that a plurality of persons can resolve what Kant calls "the perplexities of opposing claims" in ways acceptable to all. According to this version of Kantian impartiality, citizens are then unreasonable to the extent that they do not exercise their common public reason and put forth reasons that do not have public scope. Public reasons in a pluralist society will not presuppose some particular conception of the good, or Rawlsian comprehensive moral doctrine, because it is reasonable for everyone to assume that such reasons will not have public scope. This interpretation of mutual consent requires that citizens be impartial only to the extent that they all abstract from their own point of view, and adopt the standpoint of impartial reason. Arendt explicitly rejects the demand that public reason produce singular agreement or impartial consent in this sense. The assumption that there is such a unified standpoint is not pluralist enough: we cannot assume that there is *one* public standpoint in political life and not *many* different ones. Ideals of public reason usually imply some convergence of opinions or interests as the aim of deliberation.

Arendt's insistence on the rule of law should also be understood in light of her pluralism. The formal and procedural character of these constraints in the rule of law is not enough for singularity, nor does the issuing of laws as the basic form of political decision making require that all citizens adopt the same normative standpoint in deliberation. Even if individuals or groups each construe their public standpoint as appropriately abstracting from their concerns or interests, a variety of standards of impartiality or "individualized impartial concerns"[13] are inevitable in pluralist societies. The questioning of this assumption of singularity is in fact the core of many feminist criticisms of notions such as impartiality and the overly unitary forms of universality that they generate.[14] Whatever abstraction from one's own point of view impartiality requires, it cannot be at the price of the plurality of potential preferences, norms, and values. Arendt expresses her pluralism even in her interpretation of Kantian "common sense." Kant's "enlarged capacity for thought" means that the common social world and public opinion within it is "many sided." Impartiality consists of the capacity to make judgments that reflect this multidimensionality, not to come to a single rational opinion, but to use a many-sided common sense.[15] Such a common sense will emerge only in the interaction among diverse citizens in the public sphere.

It is only in light of the requirement of plurality in the public sphere that we can make sense of Arendt's particular interpretation of political equality. Equality only guarantees the same set of basic rights for all that in turn can only be exercised in the public world. The right to happiness enshrined in the American Revolution is not the right to the fulfillment of individual interests, or the right to egoism as Marx describes it in *On the Jewish Question.* According to Arendt's interpretation of the documents of the American Revolution, public freedom and happiness "consisted in the citizens' rights of access to the public realm, in his share in public power."[16] Other passages in Arendt suggest an equally broad notion of political equality as such access to the public sphere. But they also reveal an unresolved tension in her thought, a tension that led her astray in her analysis of desegregation. Such passages stand in marked contrast to the narrow interpretation of political equality in other works, including most notably for my purposes, "Reflections on Little Rock."

On her narrow reading, political equality is limited to the rule of law. Law is quite limited in its function: it guarantees the equal freedom of all citizens and nothing else. It is not a means to promote greater justice or to compensate for economic disadvantages, such as those of class. In passages in which Arendt wants to point out the limits of the rule of law, she typically refers to everyday politics, to the politics of managing the affairs of everyday life, such as the school systems of a complex nation-state. A much broader reading of political equality comes up in extraordinary contexts, such as her account of the American Revolution. It is also to be found in other analyses of extreme phenomena, not only of acts of founding but of political terror in which the most basic requirements of equality and plurality are challenged. In these contexts, Arendt speaks of equal rights of access to the public world, her "right to have rights."[17] Without being able to participate in the common world and to have equal footing or standing within it, the abstract "rights of man" have no reality. Without this right to have rights, we are deprived of "a place in the world that makes opinions significant and actions effective."[18] It is the right to have rights, I want to argue, that was at stake in Little Rock, not the sameness of social equality.

In these contexts, Arendt develops her "unofficial view." They give a clear indication of just what "access" to the public world entails. It means not only that our opinions have significance and that our actions are effective, but an even stronger condition. Human beings are free as citizens not by mere access, but only to the extent that they can *initiate* human action in concert with others. In the public world the human capacity for spontaneity (or natality) becomes a reality in which the ability to initiate becomes exercising the "freedom to call something into being which did not exist before."[19] This sort of freedom exists only in the artificial world of politics and makes possible a space for open, historical possibilities. Thus, on the broad view of political equality, citizens are free and equal only to the extent that they can initiate such creative actions, as for example when they initiate acts of deliberation about matters of common concern. Without the ability to initiate human action, citizens do not have genuine access to the public world, their actions are ineffective, and their opinions insignificant. But such in effectiveness and insignificance exactly describes the forms of exclusion that permeate the political world of segregation. If Arendt feared equal unfreedom, she also had to fear unequal freedom, as measured by the ability to initiate political action. Such inequality we may call "political poverty," to signify the blind spot of Arendt's thinking about the ill effects of the problem of economic poverty in modern political life.[20]

Extreme social inequalities produce a form of "political poverty" in the public world, a form of poverty that is manifested in the inability of groups of citizens to avoid being excluded from effective participation. They cannot avoid exclusion because they cannot successfully initiate politically significant joint activities of various sorts, such as public deliberation. These inequalities may persist even with the availability of genuine, procedural opportunities for participation. Conversely, such groups cannot avoid being included either, in the very deliberative outcomes and agreements over which they have no real control or public input. Because they cannot initiate deliberation, their silence is turned into tacit consent by the more powerful deliberators who are able to ignore them. In these cases, powerful groups can make presumptive claims about the "we" that has deliberated publicly or come to an agreement, a "we" that does not pass the tests of plurality and publicity contained in conceptions of political equality. A public world does not come about. The problem is that it takes a considerable degree of communicative power and capacity to contest such an inclusion in a nonpublic we. Asymmetrical inclusion succeeds by constantly shifting considerable political burdens on the challengers.

To be effective in deliberation, deliberators must be able to initiate discussion and dialogue, in which their reasons may receive deliberative uptake and thus acquire public significance. But unlike economic poverty, such capacity failure in the public sphere is often caused by the narrow interpretation of who can participate imposed by better situated deliberators. Just as economic agents must have the capacity to avoid acute hunger and severe malnourishment, so too public actors must have the ability to avoid being excluded from public life or having their concerns consistently ignored. Of course, being poor or wealthy in this political sense admits of degrees. The importance of avoiding such persistent disadvantage establishes the case for a threshold requirement of political equality in public deliberation.

There are two main advantages of such a capability-based analysis of equality as an operational measure of exclusion and inclusion that are particularly relevant to Arendt's legal status account. First, it shows that political equality admits of degrees and is not an all or nothing concept. Second, it shows that, by virtue of their nonpublic exclusion and inclusion, impoverished citizens may only choose to comply with political decisions. But because they cannot cooperate in deliberation or make politically significant contributions, their compliance in no way implies consent. African Americans in the South before *Brown v. Board of Education* and the events in Little Rock did not have equal standing in the public world. Arendt is correct to worry about the use of force in rectifying such inequalities and also in preferring alternative forms of power generated by communication and solidarity in the public sphere. But the problem is a genuinely political one: not to repeat any form of coercive inclusion and exclusion through the corrective measures themselves. Given the violence of segregation, this is a political risk worth taking for freedom and equality.

With the model of totalitarianism in mind, Arendt merely assumes that it is primarily through political means that the conditions of plurality can be violated. But groups can act in concert to exclude others, while other groups may simply be ignored; the actions of members of such groups are ineffective and their opinions insignificant precisely because their reasons are never taken up in public deliberation. Thus, Arendt seems forced to admit that promoting a threshold of political equality in the form of access to the public world and the development of requisite public capacities will not decrease plurality and difference but will make the public world more many-sided and multidimensional. If this argument is correct, the inclusion of more citizens in deliberation ought to be a primary goal of any democracy that is concerned not to lose the legitimacy of its institutions. Such inclusion not only maintains their public character, but in the case of public education it also prepares children to be citizens in a pluralistic society.

How is it that diversity can be promoted by citizens in the public spheres of pluralistic societies? It is here that we must consider Arendt's analysis of the positive role of institutions in creating the conditions of plurality as an alternative to mechanisms of social discrimination for preserving differences and diversity. The question here is not what best promotes plurality as such, which does not have intrinsic political value per se; rather, it a question of promoting the best kind of diversity, that is, of pluralism consistent with common citizenship. With equal access to the public world and equal capacity to initiate action within it, it will be a political world that is more diverse than imagined under liberal constraints, but one that must still be a common world as well if people are to act together and generate power. Against Arendt's narrow view, I shall argue that we can judge corrective measures, such as school desegregation, not on the narrow criterion of equality before the law, but on whether they succeed in promoting both social plurality and common citizenship at the same time. Such an argument is consistent with what I have been calling Arendt's own broader interpretation of political equality.

Plurality and Citizenship: The Problem of Moral Compromise and the Costs of Diversity

According to Arendt, discrimination is legitimate so long as it is "confined to the social sphere." Discrimination in this very odd sense (as in the common use of the French term *distinction*) is concerned with the process of group formation, and Arendt thinks that any kind of discrimination on the social level is consistent with the rights of access of all groups to the public sphere. Besides being a bulwark against Arendt's fear of a mass society of conformism, social discrimination is an unavoidable social fact of plurality, an outcome of having groups with distinct identities. In the modern world, once we leave the private realm "and cross over into the threshold of the public world, we enter first, not the political realm of equality, but the social sphere" (51). It is the sphere of an innumerable variety of groups and associations, including profession, income, ethnic origin in the United States, and class, education, or manners in Europe. Individual differences or personal distinctions are not as important as "the differences by which people belong to certain groups whose very identifiability demands that they discriminate against other groups in the same domain" (51). Such group identifiability follows simply from the "rights of free association," which includes also the rights of people to raise their children to acquire this same group identity, including its social discrimination against other groups.

For this reason, the social pluralism in Arendt can rightly be called "agonistic." These antagonisms emerge in the United States precisely because of its diversity, as well as controversies about the "right of people" to enter into various "social spaces" (such as hotels or vacation spots in Arendt's own examples), a right that Arendt wants to deny even while demanding a right of free access to the public sphere and to a share of political power. The right to free association protects these social spaces, which are not regulated by the plurality of the common world. It is in the public space in which we enter as equals under the rule of law that the space is created for politics and a form of power based on plurality rather than sameness, on common citizenship rather than particular identity.

But the public sphere is not a mere container for differences, even in Arendt's extreme pluralism. It is also a space in which "plural agreements," are worked out. Given the criticism of unanimity models of consent, Arendt seems to have a model of compromise among plural citizens in mind. Such compromise has as it theme the continuing basis for consent itself, which is the basis for cooperation, for acting in concert. In the American Revolution, the exemplar of a revolution of plural consent, such action was based on principles of "mutual compromise and common deliberation."[21] What Arendt is advocating is therefore a form of pluralistic civic republicanism which, rather than being Rousseauian in its emphasis on common culture, has Mill and Tocqueville's emphasis on difference and plurality of free association. Within the public sphere, citizens will act and deliberate together as more than just an association of associations; they inhabit a common world in which they are free, equal, and diverse. As Margaret Canovan puts it: "What unites the citizens of a republic is that they inhabit the same public space, share its common concerns, acknowledge its rules and are committed to its continuance and to achieving a working compromise when they differ."[22] Above all, they need not be committed to any particular policy or law that they may publicly disobey and remain citizens, but to the

Constitution, to the rules and institutions that make public freedom possible as well as the limits on political power that allow for plurality. Such a commitment has been described by Habermas as the minimum of unity, a common "constitutional patriotism."[23]

Once again, such a commitment to the principles of the Constitution can be interpreted either broadly or narrowly. If it is interpreted narrowly as a shared set of beliefs, then there is no reason to think that consent always has to be pluralistic. In fact, Rawls regards constitutional essentials in this way, to the extent that they provide a public basis for justification; in light of such shared political values, "there is but one public reason."[24] Contrary to Rawls, Arendt is committed to public reason being as many-sided and multidimensional as the political world and free associations out of which it emerges. It cannot be her view that there is then some core agreement of shared values or even of general principles.

However, Arendt faces a different, but related difficulty, even on the broad interpretation of political equality and consent. If there are a plurality of interpretations of the principles of the Constitution, how is it that there is any unity at all, even the unity that is only sufficient to permit the shared space of difference that is the public sphere? It seems that Arendt is ensnared on the horns of a dilemma: either too much unity and thus no plurality, or too much plurality and not enough unity even for common deliberation. In the first case citizens already agree sufficiently for unanimity and a common will; in the second case, we disagree so much that conflicting groups may only deliberate along side of, rather than with each other, in a world shared just enough for unceasing public contestation. Call this problem of unity and plurality the "republican dilemma of difference." In "Reflections on Little Rock," Arendt clearly wants to err on the side of plurality; but in other contexts when speaking of the political virtues required for the commitment to a Constitution she clearly falls on the side of unity.

There is a way out of this dilemma that accords well with Arendt's view of equality and difference: to view the ideal of common citizenship as the deciding criterion in cases of conflicts between the plurality and unity in the public sphere. The problem with basing plural consent on a commitment to a constitution, whether it be its political values or abstract principles, is that it is too substantive for pluralism. It leads to a politics of virtue, by which individuals and groups transcend their particular interests and goals and participate in the intrinsic goods of the public sphere. Given the crucial role of freedom of association and expression in the public sphere, it is better to fall of the plurality side of the dilemma and work out an account of how common deliberation is still possible, without requiring that citizens share some underlying orientation to the common good. Arendt is correct in those writings where she argues that this solution to conflicts of plurality and equality will require a politics of compromise, rather than of virtue. She also provides clear criteria with which to judge such compromises: they must be consistent with the broad interpretation of political equality outlined in the last section and with the ideal of common citizenship. In particular, specifically moral compromises exhibit the structure of pluralistic consent, the willingness to cooperate and act together with those who are not the same as us either in beliefs or ascribed characteristics. But such compromises can be reached only if we give up the priority of morality over politics.

Arendt and the Politics of Compromise

The willingness to compromise in public is not the same as tolerance, another of the main political virtues for pluralist republicans like Arendt. Tolerance may well be required by some particular compromise, as in cases when citizens leave an issue such as abortion up to the free conscience and private choice of each individual. More typically, compromise is the successful resolution of a conflict that threatens the breakdown of cooperation among plural citizens, in which citizens modify the deliberative framework by which they live together and make decisions. Given that the more diverse a society is the more likely it is to produce deep and enduring conflicts, making such compromises is the basic and constant task of the pluralist citizens. Such compromises must be guided by the goal of maintaining common citizenship, despite deep disagreements among groups and individuals that threaten such continued cooperation. In "Reflections on Little Rock," Arendt is arguing that forced integration not only decreases the diversity of American society, but that the use of force needed to carry out this policy undermines the basis for cooperation and compromise in the framework of the common Republic.

To the extent that desegregation is forced upon citizens, Arendt believes that it is not a diversity-promoting public compromise at all. Indeed, the use of force itself will provoke only resistance to the goals of the policy. Arendt is certainly historically correct, to the extent that this resistance continues today in almost all American cities with a virtual and de facto boycott of public schools by whites. The policy has not achieved the public goals that it set for itself, and these goals could have been reached only by mutual cooperation and the search for common ground.

But the moralist in us all is as outraged as Arendt's liberal commentators and rejects just this implication of radical pluralism. The demand for some sort of compromise and consensual solution in this case is difficult to accept on moral grounds: it is giving in to unreason and to a great moral evil, and certainly to the social discrimination of racism. Reaching a compromise demands some ability to separate moral and religious commitments on the one hand from political and legal concerns on the other. Just as in the principled commitment to freedom of expression advocated by groups such as the American Civil Liberties Union, such a normative politics will not always be on the side of the angels. The compromises that promote diversity, however, need not always protect the worst and most exclusionary groups in a society, nor force reasonable citizens to deal with the most intransigent holdouts. In order to make a clear distinction between successful and unsuccessful compromises, more must be required than the mere continuation of the Republic.

The ideal of common citizenship also helps to distinguish good from bad compromises. In order to make Arendt's view more defensible, we need to make this distinction more clearly, as well as make the process of compromise formation in deliberation more public and dynamic. It is not simply a matter of refusing to use force against those who resist a particular political decision, although obviously there must be limits on public power as well as on the coercive power of institutions. Citizenship must also be a positive criterion, one that supplements Arendt's typical interpretation of the rule of law. As I have argued, this interpretation is particularly narrow in "Reflections on Little Rock."

The best way to judge whether Arendt's discussion of desegregation represents a good or bad proposed compromise is to look first at several instances of compromises that are consistent with common citizenship. I propose two such examples: first, the special rights granted to Native Americans in the reservation systems of Canada and the United States; and second, recent changes in voting practices away from winner-takes-all, one-person-one vote to so-called cumulative voting systems. In both case, I shall argue, political compromises modify the framework of rules and procedures through which we cooperate, in such a way as to protect diversity, overcome problems of unequal and persistent minorities, and yet be consistent with the ideal of common citizenship and participation in the public sphere. In order to establish initial plausibility, it is enough to say that this is the way the federalists and antifederalists together constructed the "dual democracy" of checks and balances in the Constitutional Assembly, a primary forum for moral compromise and for the public construction of new frameworks for deliberation and discussion.

Let me begin with an example of how cultural diversity may produce "deep conflicts" that go to the core of the framework for ongoing cooperation. These conflicts can perhaps best be illustrated by the many problems concerning the unique legal status of Native Americans as citizens in both the United States and Canada. As Will Kymlicka points out in *Liberalism, Community and Culture*, interpretations of their rights based on the idea of political inclusion do not work for the simple reason that these interpretations are disputed by the tribal groups themselves. After the *Brown v. Board of Education* decision and the calls for the integration of all racial and ethnic groups into the political community with full and equal rights for all, the federal governments of both the United States and Canada began to dismantle the reservation system and the differential legal treatment of Native Americans.[25] Although the reservation system produced desperate and systemic poverty, groups like the American Indian Movement saw that it could be used for purposes of preserving cultural identity in the face of an overwhelming and invasive majority European culture. The capacity of specifically Native American political communities to protect their culture and identity depends on their ability to make use of the extraordinary rights and powers already present in the reservation system itself for this end. Kymlicka describes the solution this way: "The reservations form special political jurisdictions over which Indian communities have guaranteed powers, and within which non-Indian Americans have restricted mobility, property and voting rights."[26] Without these restrictions on universal rights and special powers not guaranteed in the Constitution, permanent minority cultures might otherwise disappear. Do such special powers and rights constitute a reasonable and legitimate compromise, or are they violations of the constitutional guarantees and rights to equal protection? On Arendt's view, they clearly violate both the rule of all and narrow political equality.

I take the solutions of restrictions on property and mobility rights of non–Native Americans described by Kymlicka to be an example of a fair compromise of this sort. Similar restrictions of rights of free expression and speech, however, would not be acceptable moral compromises, because they make impossible the very use of public reason needed for political compromise within these communities. Only certain circumstances of inequality and minority status make such compromises reasonable modifications of basic constitutional principles; rights of cultural membership do not reasonably override the political rights necessary for common citizenship, and certainly not rights of free speech. Indeed, the restrictions on rights of mobility proposed in the reservation policies discussed above are fair only because this compromise is for the sake of a disadvantaged minority within a larger and pluralistic political community. The same policies would be unfair under different circumstances (depending, for example, on the extent of social inequalities, who is in the majority, who is in the minority in the larger community; or if the tribal community were itself a nation state). They also cannot be used to assure the survival of the current set of communities or groups through legal means, if that goal is to be achieved by denying members of minority cultures access to the public sphere. Such restrictions for the sake of some vision of cultural identity are not permissible compromises, because they promote neither diversity within the culture, nor common citizenship in the pluralistic polity and larger public sphere.

This emphasis on common citizenship is particularly significant for how fair compromises are made in situations of unequal minorities, such as in the Native American example. The compromise about political jurisdiction on reservations has to do with not only the cultural values involved but also with the specific circumstances of inequality. Persistent social inequalities and extreme poverty, coupled with deep conflicts with the majority culture that can overwhelm them economically, produce a situation of public deliberation in which the concerns of Native Americans and their minority culture count for little in larger political institutions. These inequalities in deliberation make it such that a group becomes a permanent minority, consistently disadvantaged in civic deliberation. Its concerns do not receive reasonable consideration from other citizens and thus cannot reasonably be expected to affect outcomes. This extreme poverty, the large cultural distance from European collective goals and assumptions, and other deliberative disadvantages in the Native American case makes the restrictions on property, mobility, and voting rights appropriate and fair. The latter restriction is, however, the most problematic.

In the absence of persistent inequalities of this sort, as in the case of the Afrikaner minority in South Africa or even the Quebecois majority in the province of Quebec, similar calls for distinct jurisdictions and the restriction of rights are hardly illegitimate. Southern claims to their dominant "way of life" as based on the value of plurality have a similar status. Other measures are more important in cases of less extreme social and cultural inequalities: the universal application of separate jurisdiction would not promote public deliberation, nor the continued cooperation of minority groups in the larger public sphere. But sometimes separate jurisdictions can serve a public function, to the extent that they provide the public space needed for groups like Native Americans to have a more coherent and effective voice in the larger, civic public sphere. Representational voting is one way to insure that unequal minorities can reasonably expect to effect the outcome of deliberation.[27] The problem with such proportional schemes is that they do not promote public deliberation. The opposite is often the case: numerical formulas for representation may even bring about a further separation of the disadvantaged group from the larger public sphere. Given the quite predictable outcomes of such schemes, dominant groups need not take seriously the larger claims of smaller groups, except for strategic purposes. Such solutions leave the basis for continued conflict intact, as do ones suggested by theories that simply stop with the plurality of the civil society alone. These criticisms suggest two criteria for adequate moral compromise. They are fair if they meet the two main criteria: that they correct for persistent inequalities and that they make possible continued participation in a common framework of pluralist citizenship.

More appropriate than proportional representation schemes are forms of corrective voting that are still consistent within the framework of the political equality and common citizenship implied by both majority rule and "one-person, one vote." These standards need not be interpreted so narrowly in a fair moral compromise. Here proposals of "cumulative voting systems" are better than "group representation systems" as ways to overcome persistent inequality and permanent minority status. Put simply, cumulative voting gives each voter multiple votes, say seven votes for a seven-seat city council; in contrast, group representation apportions the council seats proportionately among the cultural groups, granting special status and voice to cultural minorities or other groups in need of protection.[28] Both representation and cumulative voting compensate for the disadvantages of underrepresentation in deliberative institutions. But cumulative voting does so in a way that incorporates principles of one person-one vote and majority rule even while compensating for the particular circumstances of many inequalities. More importantly, it encourages continued active cooperation and participation in a common public sphere, fostering cooperation and coalitions among diverse groups in ways that proportional representation schemes do not.

In this way, cumulative voting manifests the two main criteria for successful moral compromises: it takes into account persistent inequalities and promotes the ideals of common citizenship. By overcoming disadvantages, it helps make the reasons of disadvantaged groups count for more and thus establishes the reasonable expectation that they will be able to affect the outcome of civic deliberation. Contrary to schemes of group representation, this forms of voting promotes open, pluralistic, and dynamic group formation in the public sphere. Mere plurality is not enough: diverse groups in civil society promote equality only to the extent that groups and associations can then form and re-form themselves, changing the character of the public sphere as they do.

Do Arendt's claims that cultural diversity is at stake in Little Rock pass such tests? Democratic decision making places high demands on self-reflective and public uses of reason, particularly under the conditions of plurality. Liberals have long pointed out that democratic institutions cannot be based on the assumption of shared, substantive moral agreement. Good democratic arrangements and constraints promote such solutions by assuring deliberative liberties and the conditions of mutuality in dialogue. The former are related to achieving equality of citizens who possess political and human rights, now understood in terms of the equal conditions under which citizens publicly reason and deliberate. This may include compromises in which these rights are distributed differentially or in which voting procedures broaden majority rule to take into account the position of unequal minorities. The latter expand the framework of common citizenship to incorporate differences. Arendt certainly believes that common citizenship is at stake in Little Rock, but not because she is defending any positive proposal. She is arguing against the use of Supreme Court powers and federal troops to settle an issue about which no compromise had been reached. In the concluding section, I shall discuss Arendt's discussion as a proposal about what to do in situations of failed compromise. Even if the price of diversity is that there cannot be a public world without moral loss, diversity can hardly be maintained at the costs of the very conditions that maintain it: public equality and common citizenship. Arendt is caught in this paradox in her defense of diversity here, and this is a crucial failing of her argument.

Conclusion: The Costs of Diversity

The arguments of Arendt's "Reflections on Little Rock" are significantly more complex than both her few defenders and many detractors make them out to be. She raises a deep and enduring problem of democratic politics, one that has only recently been put with similar clarity in debates about multiculturalism and the dilemmas of difference. Arendt squarely faces the hidden question of these debates: at what cost diversity? Defending diversity is sometimes a dirty job, and it does not mean that one is always on the side of the victims and the downtrodden. She also raises another similar question for other contexts: at what price equality? Arendt's answer is that equality and diversity must mutually limit each other in the proper political arrangement: diversity, in the form of free association, limits equality to political equality; equality, in the form of equal access to the public world and the right to have rights, limits diversity through common citizenship and restrictions on the scope of political power. As political values, plurality and equality therefore have equal worth. When applied to Little Rock, this argument outraged Arendt's liberal friends and readers.

The application of this balancing of values of equality and plurality to the particular situation in Little Rock proved more difficult to do than Arendt had herself imagined. She admitted that she ignored the violence of segregation, which violates the most basic rights of access to the public world. Arendt's narrow version of political equality ignored the fact that segregation also produced a situation in which African Americans could not initiate political action and deliberation, except in the form of civil disobedience. For this reason, her arguments in favor of maintaining social discrimination as a bulwark against mass society ring false in a racist society, because there is no common sphere of citizenship and plurality that needed to be preserved and protected from the inroads of social equality. On the criterion of common citizenship, leaving in place discrimination in public education cannot be acceptable, especially given the historical conception of the civic role of public education in the United States.

Further historical facts complicate Arendt's position as well. The legal doctrine of "separate but equal" was already in place and was precisely the sort of compromise between equality and diversity that Arendt seems to be proposing. This compromise could no longer elicit plural consent, neither from African Americans themselves nor from their liberal allies. A satisfactory solution to this conflict and breakdown of cooperation could not be achieved by perfecting this doctrine into "socially separate but politically equal," which in effect Arendt is asking African Americans to do. Only a few nationalists may have been willing to take up such suggestions. A narrow version of Arendt's view on political equality and citizenship might require this sort of reformulation. I have given arguments why Arendt has to reject these narrow interpretations in order to save her view of active citizenship in a many-sided public world.

As wrong as Arendt is on so many of the particulars of the situation in Little Rock and about how her views might apply to it, she is correct about just how prevalent and disturbing the dilemmas of difference are in modern politics. Her views stand as a warning to a too facile version of pluralism and multiculturalism. Democratic pluralism is difficult to achieve and even harder to maintain; it means coming to terms with, and more important, even compromising with people not only with whom we "reasonably disagree," but also with the very groups we may even morally abhor. If the public world is truly many-sided, and if our democracy is truly governed by pluralistic consent, we will not find much moral comfort there. As in Isaiah Berlin's many clear formulations of unpleasant political truths, Arendt saw this moral discomfort clearly and used her political-philosophical journalism to articulate it, all the while she does not simply retreat to a defeated liberalism. As citizens in democratic and pluralistic polities with vibrant public spheres, we need not, indeed should not, surrender our moral abhorrence. As members of plural groups with different points of view, we will also engage in a shared political life of common citizenship. Even when governed by this ideal, this common life will inevitably require public compromises between equality and difference.

Note

1. Hannah Arendt, "Reflections on Little Rock," *Dissent* 6 (1959), 45–56. Page references in parentheses throughout the body of my essay refer to this article. It is the main focus of my analysis because it illustrates well the complexities of Arendt's view of the relationship between equality and difference.

2. Just to mention a few of the judgments that this categorical distinction led her to endorse: her generally negative evaluation of the political effects of the workers' movement in Europe on politics in *The Human Condition*; her one-sided view of the welfare state, as well as her rejection of political demands for economic equality; her assertion in *On Revolution* that the greatness of the Hungarian Revolution of 1956 lies in the fact that it had nothing to do with issues of "bread and poverty" and that the French Revolution lost its political significance by being coopted by the "impoverished masses." These negative judgments reflect the degree to which the distinction of the social and the political is tied to Arendt's own version of the conservative critique of "mass society," a vision of the pathologies of modernity that runs throughout her writings. On the other hand, it must also be said that her specifically republican view of politics did not lead her to reject all social movements, as her affirmative analyses of the civil rights and antiwar movements in the United States show. In this essay, I shall try to show that Arendt's prescient awareness of the deep problems of plurality in democracies contains valuable lessons for many current debates, such as those concerning the political implications of multiculturalism. These lessons can ultimately be separated both from the distinction of the social and the political and from Arendt's sometimes quite idiosyncratic political judgments.

3. Martha Minow, *Making All the Difference: Inclusion, Exclusion and American Law* (Ithaca: Cornell University Press, 1990), pp. 19–23

4. See Lani Guinier, *The Tyranny of the Majority* (New York: Free Press, 1994).

5. See David Spitz, "Politics and the Realms of Being," *Dissent* 6 (1959), 56–65; the other critical essay in this issue of *Dissent* is so polemical and ad hominem that it is hard to categorize; the next critic in the same issue, Melvin Tumin, calls the essay (at best) "a horrible joke." See Melvin Tumin, "Pie in the Sky," *Dissent* 6 (1959), 65–71. Arendt's response which follows, "A Reply to Critics" in the same volume, calmly emphasizes that the "real

issues" of the essay are the rule of law and the role of education in achieving integration and that her critics have misread her intentions.

6. Seyla Benhabib, *Situating the Self* (London: Routledge, 1992), p. 94.

7. Margaret Canovan, *Hannah Arendt: A Reinterpretation of Her Political Thought* (Cambridge: Cambridge University Press, 1992), p. 149. Chapter 6 is a masterful treatment of the essential role of plurality in Arendt's republicanism, and I base much of my treatment of plurality in Arendt on Canovan's suggestive analysis.

8. Elisabeth Young-Bruehl, *Hannah Arendt: For the Love of the World* (New Haven: Yale University Press, 1982), p. 316.

9. See Hannah Arendt, "Civil Disobedience," in *Crises of the Republic* (New York: Harvest Books, 1969), pp. 49–102. See also Canovan, *Hannah Arendt*, pp. 225ff.

10. This feature of the essay can be seen in the fact that Arendt considered her essay, "Crisis in Education" to be the sequel to her "Reflections on Little Rock." In the second essay, she claims that "education must be conservative" to preserve what is "new and revolutionary in each child." Ever dialectical, even her conservativism has a radical republican twist, always with the historical experience of totalitarianism in the background. See Hannah Arendt, "Crisis in Education," in *Between Past and Future* (New York: Viking Press, 1968), pp. 192–193. On the relationship between the essays, see Young-Bruehl, *Hannah Arendt*, p. 317.

11. Canovan, *Hannah Arendt*, p. 226.

12. See James Bohman, "Cultural Pluralism and Public Reason," *Political Theory* 23:2 (1995) 253–279; although I favor the use of the term "plural agreement," Canovan uses the term "pluralistic consent" to describe how freedom, plurality, and stable institutions are maintained all at once. See Canovan, *Hannah Arendt*, p. 217. But therein lies the difficulty of Arendt's view; when held together, these values produce political dilemmas and moral conflicts, as manifested in her problematic treatment of school desegregation. I shall argue that Arendt accepts that these conflicts are often irresolvable.

13. Thomas Nagel, *Equality and Partiality* (Oxford: Oxford University Press, 1991), p. 65.

14. See feminist critics of Habermas, such as Seyla Benhabib and Iris Marion Young: they criticize notions of the generalized other and impartiality, respectively. See Young, "Impartiality and the Civic Public," and Benhabib, "The Generalized and the Concrete Other," both in *Feminism as Critique*, ed. Seyla Benhabib and Drucilla Cornell (Minneapolis: University of Minnesota Press, 1987). Both of their arguments go beyond the less interesting claims that publicity or justice is simply one value among others, or that it is merely a value for a particular group. It is not clear how these criticisms can then avoid a radical form of the liberal dilemma, as smaller and smaller groups tend to construct more and more narrow and fragmented identities. So long as people form their reasons publicly and make decisions in common, they will have to adopt some public standpoint from which the reasons and interpretations given by others are mutually intelligible. For a defense of the idea of a plurality of publics and the implications of conflicts in the interpretation of needs, see Nancy Fraser, "Rethinking the Public Sphere," in *Habermas and the Public Sphere*, ed. Craig Calhoun (Cambridge: MIT Press, 1992), pp. 109–42. The plurality of publics is, however, insufficient for producing what I am calling "plural agreement" or "pluralistic consent," especially if each of them is dominated by its own single public point of view. In

democracies, as Fraser admits, there must be some institutions in which these diverse publics finally deliberate together. Only in such a diverse "civic" public sphere is deliberation exercised pluralistically, in the multifaceted meaning that Arendt gave to Kant's idea of a "common sense."

15. See Hannah Arendt, *Lectures on Kant's Political Philosophy*, ed. Ronald Beiner (Chicago: University of Chicago Press); see also her *Life of the Mind: Willing*, Vol. 2 (New York: Harcourt Brace and Jovanovich, 1978), pp. 242–243 and pp. 255–272; see also Richard Bernstein, "Judging: The Actor and the Spectator," *Philosophical Profiles* (Cambridge: Polity Press, 1986), pp. 228–230.

16. Hannah Arendt, *On Revolution* (London: Penguin Books, 1973), p. 127.

17. Hannah Arendt, *The Origins of Totalitarianism* (New York: Harvest Books, 1973), p. 298.

18. *Ibid.*, p. 296.

19. Hannah Arendt, "What is Freedom?" in *Between Past and Future* (New York: Viking, 1968), p. 151.

20. For a fuller development of this conception of political poverty, especially as it is applied to public deliberation in democratic institutions, see James Bohman, *Public Deliberation: Pluralism, Complexity and Democracy* (Cambridge: MIT Press, 1996), especially chapter 3, "Deliberative Inequalities."

21. Arendt, *On Revolution*, p. 214.

22. Canovan, *Hannah Arendt*, p. 227.

23. See Jürgen Habermas, "Citizenship and National Identity," *Praxis International* 12:1 (1992), 1–19. It is not clear what separates Habermas's view from Rawls's argument for a shared commitment to certain "political values," or "overlapping consensus." See John Rawls, *Political Liberalism* (New York: Columbia University Press, 1993), pp. 133ff.

24. Rawls, *Political Liberalism*, p. 220.

25. For a discussion of the role of liberal constitutional principles in these debates generally and the specific role of the *Brown* decision for the liberal Canadian "Just Society" policy of the late 1960s to dismantle the reservation system, see Will Kymlicka, *Liberalism, Community and Culture* (Oxford: Oxford University Press, 1989), pp. 140–150. This policy "recommended the end of special constitutional status of Indians" (p. 142) and integrating them into Canadian society. Integration is indeed often publicly desirable for citizenship, but not on the dominant group's cultural terms.

26. Kymlicka, *Liberalism, Community and Culture*, p. 136.

27. Iris M. Young, "Polity and Group Difference," in *Feminism and Political Theory*, ed. Cass Sunstein (Chicago: University of Chicago Press, 1990), 117–141; also her *Justice and the Politics of Difference* (Princeton: Princeton University Press, 1990), especially pp.184–186.

28. Cumulative voting procedures that grant each person multiple votes make it more likely that minorities and other disadvantaged groups will successfully elect at least one candidate and thus have a greater influence on the results of deliberation. In *The Tyranny of*

the Majority, Guinier gives the example of Chilton County, Alabama, where not a single African American had ever been elected by majority-rule, one-person, one-vote rules. For a discussion of this case and other voting schemes that are supposed to fulfill the Supreme Court's mandate for "the right to full and effective participation," see Lani Guinier, "Groups, Representation, and Race-Conscious Districting," *University of Texas Law Review* 71:7 (1993), 1539–1640, especially pp. 1639–1640. I agree with Guinier that gerrymandering does not ensure that this right of full effective participation can be achieved by persistent minorities. She is also correct in that it is only on the basis of being able to influence results and outcomes that disadvantaged groups will see decisions as legitimate and be willing to continue to cooperate, not on any intrinsic features of the decisions or the decision procedures themselves.

II

Ethics and the Nature of Evil

4

Socialization and Institutional Evil

Larry May

The nature of every bureaucracy is to make functionaries and mere cogs in the administrative machinery out of men, and thus to dehumanize them.
—*Hannah Arendt,* Eichmann in Jerusalem, *p. 289*

One of the paradoxes of democracy is that face-to-face interactions encourage participation but also often lead individuals to become intolerant of one another's differences. As a result, democracies tend to foster institutions whose goal is to preserve the sense of connectedness that makes people want to participate with one another, while leaving spaces between diverse individuals in which they can maintain their diversity.[1] Unfortunately, the institutions created in a modern community also have a tendency to become increasingly hierarchical and bureaucratic as a way of isolating people from the personal pressures and prejudices of others. Such bureaucratic institutions tend to dehumanize their members, making them less rather than more fit to act sympathetically toward their fellow humans in a participatory democracy.

In a series of writings, Hannah Arendt argued that certain institutions were able to instill in their members a willingness to do virtually anything, even to participate in great evil. The key component was the ability of bureaucratic institutions to instill in their members the idea that each member was completely replaceable, and hence completely vulnerable to the whims of the institution. If, in addition, the individual has the idea that one should support family above all else, then the individual is in the unenviable position of feeling pressured to do virtually anything that the employing institution requests. Indeed, certain institutions are able to "socialize" their members to be more loyal to the institution than to city, nation, or humanity.

In this essay, I want to look closely at the process of institutional socialization. In the first section I will reassess Arendt's claims about the role of bureaucratic institutions in the perpetration of the kind of dehumanization that sets the stage for great evil. In the second section, I will provide an account of institutional socialization, especially bureaucratic socialization, that draws on Arendt's work as well as work in anthropology and social theory. In the third section, I will confront recent models of institutional socialization in critical social theory, where such socialization is almost always seen as a positive contributor to the solidarity of communities. I conclude with a cautionary note to critical theorists, advancing the thesis that some hierarchical or bureaucratic institutions may in fact do more harm than good in terms of socialization of its members.

I Dehumanization in Bureaucracies

In her provocative book *Eichmann in Jerusalem*, Hannah Arendt sets out, among other things, to explain how relatively "normal" people could come to participate in one of the world's greatest evils, the Nazi extermination of millions of Jews in the late 1930s and early 1940s.[2] Adolph Eichmann, Hitler's director of the Final Solution, was as "everybody could see ... not a monster."[3] Yet he was able to send thousands to their deaths and to administer a program that he boasted had been ultimately responsible for the deaths of millions of Jews. Arendt portrayed her inquiry as one that explored Eichmann's conscience: how could a seemingly normal person come to believe that the right thing to do was to exterminate millions of innocent people? The answer to this inquiry was to be found in the institutional factors that socialized Eichmann, as well as so many other petty bureaucrats, into believing that their highest moral duty was to follow their superiors' orders. Moreover, the socialization was such that Eichmann and others felt driven to go beyond the call of duty to persevere with "painstaking thoroughness in the execution of the Final Solution."[4]

In this section, I will attempt to reconstruct Arendt's analysis of the role of bureaucratic socialization in the perpetration of the Holocaust. As I will describe it, this process of socialization, from which she attempts to generalize, involved four overlapping components. First, due either to societal or to institutional factors, individuals came to feel increasingly vulnerable economically, especially with regard to the continuance of their jobs. Second, these individuals experienced a loss of autonomy, or at least a loss of control over their lives within the institution. Third, loyalty to the institution was instilled as the chief moral value for these individuals. Fourth, the meaning of conscientiousness was transformed, to a point where following orders scrupulously and then going beyond the call of institutional duty was the most virtuous behavior a person could engage in. I will examine each of these components in turn.

For Arendt, it is important that the bureaucracies in Nazi Germany were peopled by solid, respectable men who had shown their ability to develop strong habits, rather than by unreliable "Bohemians," fanatics, adventurers, sex maniacs, or sadists. Bureaucratic institutions need to be able to secure reliable people, but also they need to secure those who are not self-sufficient. In Nazi Germany, bureaucrats were recruited from the ranks of "job holders and good family-men," focusing on the "devoted *paterfamilias*" who is determined "to make life easy for his wife and children." The first stage in the institutional socialization Arendt identified is the use of economic insecurity to redirect these individuals' single-minded devotion to family into a drive to do whatever seemed necessary to keep one's job.[5] The "devoted *paterfamilias* worried about nothing so much as his security" and that of his family. As a result, he was transformed into a very docile member of any organization or institution that would employ him.[6]

The economic climate itself put pressure on these men. "It became clear that for the sake of his pension, his life insurance, the security of his wife and children, such a man was ready to sacrifice his beliefs, his honor, and his human dignity."[7] On this analysis it is important that the bureaucratic man identify loyalty to his family with loyalty to his employer, and that he transfer his strong respectable habits of always doing his duty to doing whatever the institution put forth as his professional duties. "When his occupation forces him to murder people, he does not regard himself as a murderer because he has not done it out of inclination but in his professional capacity."[8]

The second component in the dehumanization of the bureaucrat comes in the loss of autonomy. Each individual bureaucrat's action becomes merely a "tiny cog" in a machine that is so large that the bureaucrat cannot see what the eventual effects will be of the actions of the overall machine. As Arendt points out, "the political form known as bureaucracy" is best described as "the Rule of nobody."[9] Most bureaucrats do not have control over the process by which decisions are made, nor even over the way that those decisions are to be carried out. And because the bureaucrats do not see themselves as in charge, their consciences are relieved of concern for the outcome of their actions.

In bureaucracies, there is a diffusion of responsibility due to the collective nature of the enterprise. Nazi bureaucrats therefore saw themselves as "fully exempted from responsibility" for their acts.[10] In fact, most individual Nazi bureaucrats could not easily tell what their role was in the collective activity of the whole machine. The point of "bureaucracies" is that a certain kind of division of labor occurs in which work is compartmentalized to such an extent that individual human action is transformed into mere "behavior," that is, the activity of people who are, nearly unreflectively, responding to conditioning.[11] The members of a bureaucracy come to see themselves as not in control, indeed they come to see that no one person is in control, and thus to see the bureaucratic institution as somehow outside the human realm in which they would normally have felt responsible for what occurred.

The third component in the dehumanization of bureaucracies is the rise of loyalty as the chief virtue. "The member of the Nazi hierarchy most gifted at solving problems of conscience was Himmler. He coined slogans like the famous watchword of the S.S., taken from a Hitler speech before the S.S. in 1931, 'My Honor is my Loyalty.' "[12] Once the individual Nazi bureaucrat had lost a sense of personal responsibility for his actions within the institution, normal moral scruples were thrown into chaos. To regain a sense of honor and virtuousness, the bureaucrat seized on the one moral concept left over from his previous set of norms: achieving honor and virtue through loyalty. Eichmann was ultimately impressed that "not just the S.S. or the Party, but the elite of the good old Civil Service were vying and fighting with each other for the *honor* of taking the lead in these 'bloody matters.'"[13]

This loyalty is cemented in the understanding that the goals and norms of the institution are ultimately much more important than any individual goals or norms because "of being involved in something grandiose, unique ('a great task that occurs once in two thousand years'), which must therefore be difficult to bear."[14] The importance of the institutional goals creates the feeling "Who am I to judge that the institution is pursuing these goals in the wrong way, let alone that these goals are themselves somehow wrongheaded?"[15] And for those individuals who still might raise such questions, loyalty to family, which calls for doing all that one can to keep one's job, comes into play.

The fourth component in bureaucratic dehumanization involves a thorough transformation of conscience. Here is how Arendt describes one of the most important elements of the socialization of Nazi bureaucrats:

> The problem was how to overcome not so much their conscience as the animal pity by which all normal men are affected in the presence of physical suffering. The trick used by Himmler ... was very simple and probably very effective; it consisted in turning these instincts around, as it were, in directing them toward the self. So that instead of saying: What horrible things I did to people! the murderers would be able to say: What horrible things I had to watch in the pursuance of my duties, how heavily the task weighed upon my shoulders![16]

Once loyalty is regarded as the chief virtue, then a Nietzschean "transvaluation of values" occurs whereby what was previously thought to be morally wrong is now thought of as merely something difficult to bear. The more one could bear to do these previously immoral things, now seen as one's institutional duty, the more loyalty, and hence the more virtue, one displayed.

From here it is only a short jump to the idea that the most virtuous bureaucrat is the one who not only follows orders but tries to do even more than that. Here "to be law-abiding means not merely to obey the laws but to act as though one were the legislator of the laws that one obeys. Hence the conviction is that nothing less than going beyond the call of duty will do."[17] For Arendt, this transformation helps to explain why the Nazi bureaucrats like Eichmann did more than merely follow what they were ordered to do, acting with "horribly painstaking thoroughness in the execution of the Final Solution."[18] In this way, these bureaucrats were able to seize back a slight bit of the autonomy they had been forced to relinquish, and hence also to see their honor and virtue as again somewhat under their control.

We have now come full circle in understanding how one bureaucracy was able to transform normal people with regular consciences into people whose consciences urged them to outdistance one another in becoming efficient murderers. It was not Arendt's intention, nor is it mine, to argue that *all* bureaucracies, let alone all institutions, are analogous to the Nazi bureaucracy. Yet, although it is clear that Arendt's view of bureaucracy is greatly influenced by her examination of an admittedly extreme case, there are important general lessons to be learned from her understanding of this case. I want to highlight two lessons that Arendt draws from the examination of the Nazi bureaucrats.

For Arendt, bureaucracies are all manifestations of "the Rule of nobody."[19] In *The Origins of Totalitarianism*, she argues that the rise of bureaucracies in Western European countries brings about a replacement of the rule of law by bureaucratic rule and an ensuing "disregard for law and legal institutions" as well as a diminished sense of participation in politics by many members of the populace.[20] Bureaucratic institutions, in her view, impede people's sense of participation because the rule by decree characteristic of bureaucratic order causes them to feel cut off from the decision-making structures that affect their lives. Put in other terms, bureaucratic institutions socialize people to see themselves not as actors but as acted upon. The ensuing feelings of powerlessness can give rise to an acceptance of, and even participation in, harms that one would never have found acceptable outside of the bureaucratic institution.

Arendt also draws the general conclusion that people can be socialized by bureaucratic institutions to do acts that they would otherwise see as evil. In her essay "Thinking and Moral Considerations," she succinctly articulates the thesis about the "banality of evil" that she had first propounded in *Eichmann in Jerusalem*. Arendt says that the "banality of evil" refers to "something quite factual, the phenomenon of evil deeds, committed on a gigantic scale, which could not be traced to any particularity of wickedness, pathology, or ideological conviction in the doer, whose only personal distinction was a perhaps extraordinary shallowness."[21] The reason that ordinary men and women can come to participate in great evil is that bureaucratic institutions socialize their members to be thoughtless, at least concerning what is right or wrong within the institution.

On Arendt's account, most people have a "need to think," but this can be erased by "more urgent needs of living."[22] Bureaucratic institutions are especially good at instilling people with a sense of this urgency and pressing it in such a way that otherwise conscience-driven individuals are able to accept even a total reversal of their previous value scheme. Socialization in institutions can have this negative effect, in Arendt's view, and it is one of the most important things to be countered if evil is to be diminished in the world. But in doing this it remains important to remember that it is not intentional acts of evil but acts that are socialized by institutions that are to be combatted.[23]

On my interpretation of Arendt, institutional socialization in bureaucracies transforms individuals into cogs; that is, individuals come to think of themselves as anonymous. As such, they escape the face-to-face confrontations with one another, and with the consequences of their actions, that are necessary in developing a sense of responsibility. Lacking this personal dimension in their institutional lives, they are likely to lose their sense of personal responsibility as well. And on this construal of Arendt's position, it is the anonymity, not necessarily the top-down structure, that is the key to the socialization that gives rise to the banality of evil.

As we shall see, anonymity is often a hallmark of many types of institutions. In this respect, then, Arendt's analysis of the negative side of bureaucracies can be extended to many forms of institution.

II Reconceiving Institutional Socialization

In this section I will focus on the loss of autonomy and sense of anonymity that are often felt by people involved with institutions. But before beginning that enterprise, I want to survey some interesting recent accounts of how socialization operates to organize conventions in institutions, with special attention to the work of Richard Titmuss and to Mary Douglas's *How Institutions Think.*[24]

Socialization is a form of learning, specifically a development of attitudes, beliefs, and habits concerning one's role in a social group. A society is a social group that is bound together by certain common beliefs and organizational structures. For a society or institution to operate smoothly, the members of these social groups need to know, or to learn, how to coordinate their actions with the actions of others to achieve certain collective goals. It is useful, I believe, to think of socialization as merely one of many possible forms of learning that occurs during the course of the human maturation process. Almost everyone is socialized into the ways of life of some institution or other. In the earliest years this occurs in the institutions of "family" (in a broad and flexible sense) and "school" as well as in the wider society into which each of us is born.

Institutions are mechanisms for organizing individuals by reference to various customs that assign roles to those who perform various tasks. Institutions may operate at a small-scale level, such as the institutions of handshaking[25] or gift giving; or they may operate at a large-scale level, such as the institutions of the army or General Motors. The organization of institutions can be hierarchical, such as those of a regiment or a bureaucracy; or it can be egalitarian, such as the handshake institution. Important for our purposes, institutions have effects on their members: most significantly, the customs that govern the corresponding roles create expectations for individuals to conform their behaviors in various ways.

It is important to distinguish institutions that instill anonymity from those that instill other forms of impersonal behavior. Many institutions are designed to protect individuals from harms that are made more likely by closeness of association. The institution of marriage is supposed to protect both partners by providing relatively clear roles as well as corresponding duties and rights, and yet the introduction of formal notions of duties and rights into a very personal relationship introduces an element of impersonality into marriage. In a similar way, the institution of "blind" refereeing of academic articles is supposed to protect both reviewers and those whose work is reviewed, by completely eliminating one of the most important markers of the personal, one's name. Such a practice often results in a reviewing process that is anonymous.[26]

In all cases of impersonality, some peculiarities of the individual person are eliminated, diminished, or hidden. Anonymity is an extreme form of impersonality. Some less extreme forms restrict a certain range of otherwise common emotional responses so that there is a greater likelihood that people will be able to respect each other as equals. The institution of free speech socializes people to be more tolerant of those whose speech they dislike, and the reciprocal nature of this institution's enforced impersonality is often said to breed a certain kind of distanced respect for those who are very different from oneself. Thus some forms of impersonality in institutions can serve a positive moral purpose.

The forms of socialization that occur within institutions (hereafter often "institutional socialization") can have both positive and negative effects. Anonymity can sometimes serve a positive moral purpose, as in blind refereeing, but it can serve negative moral purposes as well, as we saw in Arendt's account of the Nazi bureaucrats. In the previous section I surveyed some of the negative consequences of bureaucratic institutional socialization. I want to discuss some of the positive effects of certain forms of small-scale institutional socialization before turning back to large-scale (especially bureaucratic) institutional socialization. Throughout I will be guided by examples drawn from the rich literature in sociology and anthropology on these topics.

One of the best examples of small-scale socialization involves the institution of gift exchange: gift giving, gift receiving, and gift repaying. Ethnographic studies suggest that most societies have an institution of gift exchange into which the members of the society are socialized from an early age. The socialization to give gifts and especially to accept and repay gifts is so strong that the members of many societies come to feel that they are under a set of strict obligations that are triggered whenever a gift is given to them.[27] Gift exchange is clearly an institution in the sense that there are customs governing this set of practices, and the practices often organize a significant segment of social life.

The organization occurs in the realm of face-to-face interactions between members of a society. In some ancient societies, the gift relationship was the basis of a rudimentary economy and was extremely important in governmental affairs as well. Richard Titmuss claims that quite a bit was lost "by the substitution of large-scale economic systems for systems in which exchange of goods was not an impersonal but a moral transaction, bringing about and maintaining personal relationships between individuals and groups."[28] A similar kind of point can be made about the substitution of large-scale, impersonal bureaucratic institutions for small-scale, face-to-face ones.

Institutions that accentuate the personal rather than the impersonal can enhance humanistic impulses. This is well illustrated by Titmuss's argument that the institution of voluntary blood donation enhances altruism. Titmuss also claims, more controversially, that large-scale commercial institutions, such as those that buy and sell blood, diminish altruism.[29] A number of recent theorists, such as Jürgen Habermas, have claimed that institutions can play a positive mediating role in enhancing the impulse to display solidarity with one's fellow citizens, or even with the members of the human race. Such claims appear to be consistent with the studies of gift giving. But, as I will argue, it is only personal, face-to-face institutions, such as the gift relationship, that clearly function in this way. The ethnographic evidence examined by Marcel Mauss and Richard Titmuss does not show that bureaucratic and other impersonal institutions enhance humanistic impulses. Indeed, their research appears to support the opposite result.

One work that is often cited to show the positive effects of large-scale institutions is Mary Douglas's *How Institutions Think*, which argues that smallness of scale is not terribly important in ascertaining which institutions are likely to attain stability. Rather, the major factor is whether or not the institution can attain solidarity. Douglas follows Emile Durkheim in thinking that even very large-scale institutions can occasionally attain stability and enhance the moral sentiments of its members.[30] I agree with her that size of group alone is not the most important factor in determining whether an institution will be likely to attain stability and encourage altruistic impulses. She is right to think that collective belief formation and solidarity are the keys; but collective belief formation and solidarity are more difficult to achieve and sustain the larger the group gets.

Douglas rightly points out that there is a strong "political rhetoric" that romanticizes the small community based on mutual trust. Contrary to this rhetoric, however, many small communities turn out to be highly polarized. What distinguishes both successful small and large institutions, according to Douglas, is their members' "commitment to the given social order."[31] This is the factor that Durkheim identified as solidarity and that, on Douglas's interpretation, chiefly involves a sharing of beliefs. This is at least feasible for large-scale institutions. So far, Douglas's position seems unexceptional to me. But we need to ask further whether the impersonality of large institutions, especially bureaucratic ones, is likely to enhance or diminish the human impulses and attitudes that would support solidarity.[32]

Douglas is quite unsure about the likelihood of solidarity emerging in large-scale groups that are hierarchically structured. Coercion can also only go so far; it must be supplemented by what Douglas calls "extrarational principles" that produce and sustain a community.[33] These extrarational principles, such as habits and conventions, are both founded in analogy with and reinforced by institutional socialization.[34] And although Douglas thinks that these principles can be extended to institutions of any size whatsoever, it is not clear from her work whether large, impersonal institutions will be likely to generate the sense of commonality needed for strong social bonds. Indeed, she criticizes Durkheim's own attempt to link strength of social bond with loss of individuality and autonomy.

It is important to distinguish strong social bonds that contribute to evil from the kind of solidarity that can lead to the advancement of the common good. Loyalty to institution is not the same as solidarity in a community. The chief difference is that in some institutions, socialization will produce insensitivity to the needs of others, as the goals of the institution come to blot out the normal moral sentiments of individual members. Conversely, in communities where solidarity exists, an enhancement of normal moral sentiments occurs. What seems to make the difference is whether the members of a community or institution feel supported in or alienated from their personal values. If the institution is alienating, then the strength of social bonds within the institution can intensify the alienation. If the community is supportive, then the strength of social bonds can intensify fellow feeling. Of course group size alone will not determine whether the members of the group feel alienated or supported by the group. But there does seem to be a correlation with size, given that face-to-face interaction stresses the uniqueness of each member. In some cases, however, it is possible for large groups to convey support for the uniqueness of each of their members, and for the strength of bond felt by these members to result in moral good rather than evil.[35]

Following Hannah Arendt, I would argue that the strength of social bonding can contribute to the process of dehumanization, especially in bureaucratic institutions. Strong social bonds plus a diminished sense of personal autonomy are what create the "cogs in a machine" mentality of bureaucrats. Strong social bonds, especially in hierarchical institutions, often lead to a loss of autonomy and feelings of anonymity.[36] Certain institutions socialize most of their members to feel that decisions should be made by other, more knowledgeable and experienced members, the "experts." This is a theme that many, including Habermas, have discussed at length. But there have also been many recent writings, including some by Habermas, that have extolled the role of impersonal institutions in extending the realm of moral deliberation and discourse. I wish to turn to some of these writings with the hope of showing that we should remain deeply suspicious of bureaucratic and other impersonal institutions, especially when we focus on the effects of the forms of socialization most often employed by these institutions.

III Anonymity, Institutions, and Critical Theory

In some of his early writings, Habermas expressed worries similar to those expressed by Hannah Arendt about institutional socialization in bureaucracies. In *Legitimation Crisis* in particular Habermas spoke of "the political anonymization of class rule." Such rule is characterized by "traditionalistic ties, fatalistic willingness to follow, lack of perspective and naked repression."[37] In this work, Habermas defines socialization as "the adapting of inner nature to society." Habermas here worries about the negative effects of the kind of socialization that is necessary for individuals to become individuated.[38]

In his later works, Habermas seems so interested in pursuing the positive connections between socialization and individual maturation that he forgets the negative features of socialization he had once described. This shift parallels Habermas's move from strong support for participatory democracy to support for representative forms of government, with nonparticipatory political institutions now seen as having mainly positive effects.

These changes manifest themselves quite clearly in the second volume of Habermas's *Theory of Communicative Action.* Here Habermas links socialization with learning role competencies and with understanding authority in terms of the "generalized other."[39] Social control in institutions is understood, as it was for George Herbert Mead, intersubjectively. Individuals mature to the extent that they can "assume the attitudes of others who are involved with them in common endeavor." Institutions are then nothing but bases for "normative consensus among group members." Importantly, "institutions claim a validity that rests on intersubjective recognition, on the consent of those affected by it."[40] But such consent is merely hypothetical, because it encompasses what individuals would agree to if they were to assume the standpoint of the generalized other, not what individuals have actually agreed to.

The strong emphasis on how consent is implicit in all institutions, and especially in institutional socialization, has brought Habermas to the point where he is an outspoken supporter of the role of institutions in mediating between the individual and collective will. In his most recent book, Habermas continues to place increasing emphasis on the role of institutions in his political philosophy, with little corresponding attention to their possibly negative effects.[41] Indeed, Habermas has come lately to glorify the anonymous, faceless member of a political institution as the embodiment of the perspective of universality and rights within a democracy.

Habermas has come to be critical of participatory democracy because of his worries about the tyranny of the majority in popular political institutions that are unmediated by hierarchical institutions.[42] For example, he worries that the voices of ethnic minorities have not been heard in unmediated participatory democracies. But this is not comforting to those like myself who continue to follow Arendt in worrying about the dehumanization that occurs when hierarchical or bureaucratic institutions mediate between individuals. In the remainder of this section I will argue that Habermas has moved too far away from his earlier (Arendtian) skepticism about bureaucratic and hierarchical institutions.

Habermas clearly recognizes the differences between his own view and that of Arendt. After identifying Arendt with the republican tradition, especially with its emphasis on "decentralized self-governance" that takes over and controls "the bureaucratically independent state power," Habermas says that his own view does not go this far.[43] He offers strong support for governmental bureaucracies that render individuals anonymous rather than forcing them to confront each other as unique selves. Indeed, echoing Arendt's own language in describing the negative effects of bureaucracies in the *Origins of Totalitarianism*, Habermas extols the virtues of "subjectless forms of communication" and "anonymous" "popular sovereignty."[44]

For Habermas, anonymity makes it more likely that people will form judgments based on universalizable reasons rather than on considerations of sentiment, emotion, or prejudice. So Habermas would agree that anonymity depersonalizes, but he would disagree that anonymity dehumanizes, because he follows Kant in seeing the appeal to universal reasons as, in principle, the most human of appeals.[45] Habermas also has a pragmatic response to my criticisms. The justification given to admittedly problematic notions such as "anonymity" and "subjectless communication" ultimately rests on Habermas's increasing frustration with unmediated forms of popular sovereignty.

Although I am sympathetic to the practical difficulties of maintaining unmediated popular sovereignty at the national level, I cannot follow Habermas's rush to support anonymous and impersonal institutions, such as various administrative agencies or parliamentary bodies, that mediate between and transform the face-to-face interactions and deliberations among citizens. My main reason is that a person's intuitions, upon which judgments are made, are much more problematic when they are based on impersonal and general considerations than when they are based on personal and particular ones. As Arendt herself shows so well in her later works (especially *Thinking*), good judgment is based on the kind of intuitiveness or thoughtfulness that is vivid and intensely felt by being thoroughly immersed in the particularities of one's life. When those particularities are absent, people often lack a sense of personal responsibility, another important ingredient in good moral judgment. Institutions, especially ones that render their members anonymous, are likely to dehumanize their members in the sense that these members have less to base their autonomous moral judgments on.[46]

Arendt distinguishes between those legal institutions that protect individual action and judgment and those that do not. As Margaret Canovan has noted, Arendt supports the idea of "laws as fences [that] limit and protect the spontaneous movements of individual[s]."[47] But legal institutions can become problematic when they reduce individuals to some common denominator and thereby eliminate any basis for uniqueness and spontaneity. What is lost in anonymity is the sense of personal responsibility that will counteract the possible willingness to contribute to harm or evil in the world. This point is as true in economically and socially oriented institutions as it is in politically oriented ones.

Let us consider the business corporation. This is an organized institution with its own rules, customs, and ethos. Businesses may be organized hierarchically or nonhierarchically; but it is commonly believed that only hierarchically organized businesses can achieve significant profitability. Business corporations are able to socialize their members to be highly motivated and loyal in the pursuit of corporate objectives and goals. The hierarchical structure mediates between individuals and makes the personal interactions of these individuals much less important than they would be in a nonhierarchically organized enterprise. Indeed, the hierarchical structure imposes an impersonality on the business corporation in that the individual members are concerned to satisfy the requirements of a particular role, first and foremost, rather than to act autonomously as they would in a business that gave more independent authority to each of its members.

Institutional conventions could be established that encourage independent decision making, even in hierarchical institutions. This could occur, for example, if a supervisor designates a segment of the business in which an employee is to be "in charge," or if a supervisor regularly consults with supervisees, recognizing them as equals (as seems to happen in some of the businesses set up on the "Japanese model"). Such practices could form a basis for large-scale, nonhierarchical institutions that could be more supportive of autonomy than of anonymity. If nonhierarchical large-scale businesses can operate efficiently, then perhaps the same can be true at the political level. So, it is not largeness of institutions that is the problem, but rather the hierarchical nature of institutions that creates the increased likelihood of dehumanization.

Autonomy and institutional socialization are not necessarily opposed to each other, but it often turns out that bureaucratic and hierarchical institutions socialize their members in such a way so that autonomy (at least in terms of the choice of institutional ends) is diminished.[48] Autonomy involves the condition of being the ultimate source of authority in a certain realm of decision making. Hierarchical structures deny to some members of a group much if not all autonomy of judgment. But even within such institutions autonomy is rarely extinguished completely. Some may rightly claim that autonomy is encouraged in those nonhierarchical components of hierarchical institutions.

Autonomy is also not necessarily incompatible with anonymity. Anonymity makes one less concerned about what others might say about one's conduct. In some situations this produces an *increase* in autonomy. People who live in large cities are often less concerned about the opinions of their neighbors and more likely to act on their own principles. But in other situations, anonymity diminishes autonomy when one identifies too much with the role one plays (Arendt's conception of being a "cog") rather than with one's unique characteristics, and as a result sees oneself not as an agent but as a passive subject. Within most governmental and business institutions, socialization tends to work to the detriment of autonomy and in favor of "following orders."

The loss of autonomy and the increase in feelings of anonymity work to create the "dehumanization" that Arendt described. In my view, the feelings of shame or guilt at having contributed to a harm are chiefly what are diminished in this socialization process. In the remainder of this essay I will address these features of humanistic sentiments that are jeopardized by increasing institutional mediation and ensuing feelings of anonymity in economic, social, and political sectors of contemporary society.

IV Shame, Guilt, and Institutional Evil

One of Hannah Arendt's enduring legacies is the concept of the banality of evil. Arendt focused primarily on the way in which evil was often perpetrated because of thoughtlessness rather than intent. I wish to take her point one step further by explaining how thoughtlessness leads to a diminution of feelings of shame and guilt and hence to a greater likelihood that people will participate in acts of great evil. Along the way I will also try to explain why Habermas has gone wrong in not recognizing the implications of his support for institutional mediation, especially in the domain of morality. Here I will employ his important concept of the "colonization of the lifeworld."

Shame is best understood as the response that people feel when they believe that others (an anticipated audience) would judge them to have a particular failing or character defect. Shame has its origins in the feeling of wanting to hide from someone whose gaze betrays some sort of disapproval of one's person. Guilt is best understood as the response that people feel when they believe that they have engaged in a transgression. Guilt has its origins in the feeling that one has broken the law and hence that one stands in a position to be punished. Both shame and guilt turn on various cognitive factors, as well as the conative factors I have just mentioned. In the case of shame, one thinks that others would judge one to have a defect; in the case of guilt, one thinks that there is a law or rule that one's conduct has violated.[49]

Institutional socialization can affect the cognitive dimensions of shame and guilt in certain cases. Most importantly, the institutional audience may counteract one's normal anticipated audience, thus blocking shame from occurring. If none of one's associates give the slightest indication that one's behavior is defective and hence worthy of shame, then the normal internalized sense of shame will begin to change over time, perhaps resulting in the elimination of feelings of shame for certain kinds of institutionally approved acts. Indeed, there may be a reversal of the categories of behavior that trigger the feelings of shame such that a refusal to participate in harmful behavior may be seen as shameful. Guilt also may be blocked if institutional socialization causes one not to think that certain acts are indeed violative of legitimate laws or rules of conduct.

Institutional bureaucracies are especially well adapted to provide alternative bases of shame and guilt to those normally provided by family, church, or school. Two features are especially worthy of comment. First, institutional bureaucracies mimic institutions of family, church, and school in being top-down structures that rely on a group of easily known sources of authority to convey information about what is and is not acceptable conduct. Second, institutional bureaucracies connect self-interested motivations with normative motivations in significant ways, just as is true in family, church, and school. Few other institutions that adults encounter (with the exception of legal institutions) provide such strong impetus to conform to the institutional norms as do bureaucratic institutions.

In her essay "Thinking and Moral Considerations," Arendt focuses on the internal dialogue between me and myself that can be extinguished if one does not think about what one is doing. This analysis is in line with my own, but it lacks a developed, positive explanation of how moral thinking works. I will try to provide a plausible account, consistent with Arendt's conception of the banality of evil, of how the thoughtlessness instilled by bureaucratic institutions blocks moral thinking. Habermas's notion of colonization is helpful in this regard. According to this notion, ideas or categories from an institution can invade an individual's conception of his or her life to such an extent that the person conceives of his or her life in terms of the dominant categories of the institution. James Bohman notes that colonization occurs, for instance, "when the imperatives of the insurance industry and the defense bureaucracy begin to dictate the character of medical practice and the goals of scientific research."[50] Bureaucratic institutions are one example that Habermas employs to explicate the phenomenon of how a person's identity may be changed by institutional socialization, but he seems to downplay its effect.[51]

Shame and guilt can be colonized by an institution when it attempts to impose its own conception of what is to be done onto the existing conceptions of shame and guilt held by its members. Previously, people felt shame when they acted in a way that indicated that they were deficient in certain respects: for instance, in not displaying sufficient sympathy toward others. Institutional socialization can transform this sense of shame by changing the anticipated audience before whom one would feel shame. The new audience, the people who are the authorities in an institutional hierarchy, imposes a new sense of deficiency, one drawn in terms of the specific normative goals of the institution. The moral sense of the individuals who belong to the institution is thus colonized by internal rules and roles of the institution. And the idea of what constitutes pride in oneself is also transformed, so that one takes pride in satisfying the new audience, and greater pride in going beyond what this audience expects.

With guilt a similar transformation occurs. The social rules, concerning what is a transgression and what is not, which constituted the moral bedrock of these individuals, are replaced by the rules of the institution. As a result, a member of an institution comes to feel guilty for violating the rules of the institution, even when those rules conflict with the rules of the society at large or of the member's family. This helps us fill out the story that Arendt had begun to tell about institutional socialization. Indeed, at one point she discusses Eichmann as a kind of rule chameleon:

> He functioned in the role of prominent war criminal as well as he had under the Nazi regime; he had not the slightest difficulty in accepting an entirely new set of

rules. He knew that what he had once considered his duty was now called a crime, and he accepted this new code of judgment as though it were nothing but another language rule.[52]

Eichmann differs from most of us only in that he is seemingly easier for different institutions to colonize in terms of guilt feelings.

One of the reasons Habermas seems to be blind to these results of his own conception of socialization is that he regards guilt and shame as mere "affective responses to violations" of rules or conventions. This affects what he calls the realm of ethical life, but not of morality proper. On his view,

"Mere" conventions bind, so to speak, in a groundless fashion by custom alone; we do not associate a moral claim with them. Duties, by contrast, derive their binding force from the validity of norms of interaction that claim to rest on good reasons.

To focus on shame is, according to Habermas, to focus merely on the responses to what lies much more deeply within the individual, namely the sense of duty; to focus on guilt is to focus on an illegitimate basis of morality, namely, the institutional rules of "mere" conventions.[54]

Habermas does not come to terms with the way colonization applies to the moral domain because he denies that the ethical lifeworld has much connection to the moral domain in the first place. This has allowed him to ignore the negative effects of socialization on moral sentiments. But this should not be true even on Habermas's own terms. Duty is a cognitive concept, and anything that affects our cognitive capacities, especially in the moral domain, should be of great interest to Habermas. Yet his deontological conception of morality has rendered him blind to the consequences of socialization on both moral sentiments and moral understanding. Our feelings of shame and guilt are often important sources of moral understanding.

I have argued throughout this essay that institutional socialization can have a negative impact on one's understanding of right and wrong. Especially in the case of bureaucracy, the anonymity that results from institutional socialization can change the way that shame and guilt operate within an individual. Evil is made more likely, although it is not intentional evil that is at stake.[55] Perhaps this is the problem. Habermas, unlike Arendt, has been so focused on the intentional acts of individuals that he has failed to see that it is *unintentional* acts that need to be fought. In this respect, the anonymity of institutions is something about which we should be very suspicious. For in anonymous interactions, the face of evil is not easy to identify.[56]

Notes

1. One of the best discussions of this point occurs in Margaret Canovan's book, *Hannah Arendt: A Reinterpretation of Her Political Thought*, Cambridge: Cambridge University Press, 1992, chapter 6.

2. Hannah Arendt, *Eichmann in Jerusalem*, New York: Viking Press, 1964, p. 26.

3. Ibid., p. 54.

4. Ibid., p. 137.

5. Marilyn Friedman has been critical of the recent turn in moral theory toward an acceptance of the legitimacy of partiality. See her book *What Are Friends For?* Ithaca, NY: Cornell University Press, 1993, especially chapter 2.

6. Hannah Arendt, "Organized Guilt and Universal Responsibility," *Jewish Frontier*, 1948, reprinted in *Collective Responsibility*, edited by Larry May and Stacey Hoffman, Savage, MD: Rowman and Littlefield, 1991, p. 279.

7. Ibid., pp. 279–280.

8. Ibid., p. 281.

9. Arendt, *Eichmann*, p. 289.

10. Arendt, "Organized Guilt," p. 280.

11. Hannah Arendt, *The Human Condition*, Chicago: University of Chicago Press, 1958, p. 45.

12. Arendt, *Eichmann*, p. 105.

13. Ibid., p. 114 (my italics).

14. Ibid., p. 105.

15. See ibid., p. 114 and elsewhere.

16. Ibid., p. 106.

17. Ibid., p. 137. Arendt notes the obvious parallels between the moral philosophy of Immanuel Kant and the views of duty taken by some Nazi bureaucrats. On this same point see A. Zvie Bar-on's essay "Measuring Responsibility," *Philosophical Forum* vol.16, nos. 1–2 (1985), reprinted in *Collective Responsibility*, edited by Larry May and Stacey Hoffman, Savage, MD: Rowman and Littlefield, 1991.

18. Arendt, *Eichmann*, p. 137.

19. A similar point is made by Iris Young in her book, *Justice and the Politics of Difference*, Princeton: Princeton University Press, 1990, chapter 3.

20. Hannah Arendt, *The Origins of Totalitarianism*, New York: Harcourt Brace, 1951, p. 243.

21. Hannah Arendt, "Thinking and Moral Considerations," *Social Research* vol. 38, no. 3, autumn 1971, p. 417.

22. Ibid., p. 421.

23. See the postscript to *Eichmann in Jerusalem* for a thorough discussion of this issue, especially concerning the failure of the current concepts in jurisprudence to comprehend this phenomenon.

24. Mary Douglas, *How Institutions Think*, Syracuse: Syracuse University Press, 1986.

25. It is perhaps more common to refer to handshaking as a convention rather than as an institution. But it seems to me, and to many sociologists, that there are roles and even a certain amount of social organization that occur here as well.

26. This is not always true, for in very small subfields it is difficult to eliminate completely the possibility of identifying the persons involved because, for instance, of idiosyncratic writing styles.

27. See Marcel Mauss's groundbreaking study of the ethnography of the gift relationship, *The Gift: Forms and Functions of Exchange in Archaic Societies*, translated by Ian Cunnison, London: Cohen and West, 1954.

28. Richard M. Titmuss, *The Gift Relationship: From Human Blood to Social Policy*, New York: Pantheon Books, 1971, p. 72.

29. Ibid., p. 245. See Kenneth Arrow's criticism of this result of Titmuss's study, "Gifts and Exchanges," *Philosophy and Public Affairs* vol. 1, no. 4 (summer 1972). For a philosophical defense of Titmuss against Arrow's criticisms see Peter Singer's essay "Altruism and Commerce," *Philosophy and Public Affairs* vol. 2, no. 3 (spring 1973).

30. Douglas, *How Institutions Think*, chapter 4.

31. Ibid., p. 28.

32. I discuss solidarity and its applicability to large-scale groups in detail in my book *The Socially Responsive Self*, Chicago: University of Chicago Press, 1996.

33. Douglas, *How Institutions Think*, p. 29.

34. Ibid., p. 45.

35. I am indebted to William Rehg and Ralph Lindgren for making me aware of the importance of this point, and for showing how it may undercut some of my doubts, expressed here and elsewhere, about the possibility of large-scale solidarity acting as a positive moral force in the world. I discuss this a bit more at the end of this essay.

36. Some of the most persuasive evidence for this view can be found in Ervin Staub's book, *The Roots of Evil: The Origins of Genocide and Other Group Violence*, New York: Cambridge University Press, 1989, espcially chapters 2 and 5.

37. Jürgen Habermas, *Legitimation Crisis*, translated by Thomas McCarthy, Boston: Beacon Press, 1975, p. 22.

38. Ibid., pp. 13–14.

39. Jürgen Habermas, *The Theory of Commnicative Action*, vol. 2: *Lifeworld and System: A Critique of Functionalist Reason*, translated by Thomas McCarthy, Boston: Beacon Press, 1987, pp. 37–40.

40. Ibid., vol. 2, p. 39.

41. Jürgen Habermas, *Between Facts and Norms: Contributions to a Discourse Theory of Law and Democracy*, translated by William Rehg, Cambridge: MIT Press, 1996, chapter 8, p. 31, where Habermas does mention some negative effects of bureaucracy. (I will refer to the pagination of the penultimate typescript draft of Rehg's translation.)

42. Ibid., ch. 7, p. 9.

43. Ibid., ch. 7, pp. 15–16.

44. These phrases are embedded in the following quotations: "Both within and outside the parliamentary complex and its bodies programmed for deliberation, these subjectless forms of communication comprise arenas in which a more or less rational opinion- and will-formation can take place in regard to the entire society and in need of regulation." "The 'self' of the self-organized legal community disappears in the subjectless forms of communication that regulate the flow of discursive opinion- and will-formation in such a way that their fallible results enjoy the presumption of rationality . . . Popular sovereignty, even if it becomes anonymous, retreats into democratic procedures . . . only in order to make itself felt as communicatively generated power." *Between Facts and Norms*, ch. 7, pp. 17, 20.

45. I am grateful to James Bohman for suggesting this formulation of Habermas's point to me.

46. Arendt differs from Habermas in that she sees good judgment as proceeding from, and remaining tied to particulars, "without any overall rules." Whereas Habermas continues to follow Kant in thinking that good judgment proceeds by applying a universal rule to a particular case. See Arendt's fascinating discussion of this point in *The Life of the Mind*, vol. 1: *Thinking*, New York: Harcourt Brace Jovanovich, 1977, pp. 69–70.

47. Canovan, *Hannah Arendt*, p. 88. Habermas does still somewhat recognize this point, as when he worries about the "suffocation of spontaneous public communication," in *Between Facts and Norms*, ch. 8, p. 54.

48. See Irving Thalberg's provocative essay "Socialization and Autonomous Behavior," *Tulane Studies* vol. 28 (1979), pp. 21–36.

49. See John Deigh's helpful discussion of the concepts of guilt and shame in his essay "Shame and Self-Esteem," *Ethics* vol. 93, no. 2, January 1983.

50. James Bohman, *New Philosophy of Social Science*, Cambridge: MIT Press, 1991, p. 176.

51. On p. 311 of volume 2 of *Theory of Communicative Action*, Habermas discusses the effects of bureaucracies but says that these create serious problems for a person's identity "only if there is an *irresistible* tendency to an ever *expanding* bureaucratization."

52. Arendt, "Thinking and Moral Considerations," p. 417.

53. Jürgen Habermas, *Justification and Application*, translated by Ciaran Cronin, Cambridge: MIT Press, 1993, p. 41. It should be pointed out that earlier in this paragraph Habermas says that "*affective responses* to violations ... constitute the *experiential basis* of obligations, though they do not exhaust their semantic meaning." But he also says, in the next paragraph, that "Sanctions (however much they are internalized) are not constitutive of normative validity; they are symptoms of an already felt and thus antecedent, violation of a normatively regulated context of life" pp. 41–42.

54. For a critique of this overall approach to the place of shame in morality, see Bernard Williams, *Shame and Necessity*, Berkeley: University of California Press, 1993.

55. For a good discussion of this point see John Kekes, *Facing Evil*, Princeton: Princeton University Press, 1990.

56. The research for this essay was supported by a grant from the National Science Foundation's program in Ethics and Value Studies.

5

The Commodification of Values

Elizabeth M. Meade

The rhetoric of "family values," which has dominated every political campaign on the local and national level since 1992, exemplifies a phenomenon that Hannah Arendt was well aware of as early as the 1950s: that values in the modern age have become commodities. In "Tradition and the Modern Age" she wrote: "Values are social commodities that have no significance of their own but, like other commodities, exist only in the ever-changing relativity of social linkages and commerce."[1] We talk nostalgically about values we once held as if they were objects that have been lost or misplaced. Different groups offer competing sets of values for replacement. In the 1992 presidential campaign, for example, each of the three candidates promised a return to "family values," but each offered a different set for consideration. The values each candidate offered reflected those of his youth: Perot offered the work ethic of the Depression, Bush offered the entrepreneurial determination of the post–World War II era, and Clinton offered the public service ideals of the Kennedy Camelot. It was up to the voters to determine which set they wanted to "buy." Even after the election, America continued to shop for values. Most local and national candidates still promise a return to these ill-defined family values. The advertising campaigns they have launched for these wares center around the assumption that if we can only find the right set of values, the ills of society (crime, drug use, poverty, AIDS) will vanish as surely as "ring around the collar." Arendt would surely have condemned as naive this attempt to find a facile moral solution to a complex set of political problems.

That a consumer society would treat values as commodities is not really surprising. But Arendt's analysis of the nature of values suggests that there is a problem with using the terminology of values (which, she argued, originated in the marketplace) to talk about matters of ethics and morals. This vocabulary effectively precludes us from perceiving intrinsic worth in specific values or virtues, because in the context of the market, value is relative, dependent on any number of factors. In this essay I explore the genesis and development of Arendt's critique of values, which is part of a larger critique of traditional moral concepts, including commandments, laws, and standards. The first section details Arendt's analysis of the failure of both everyday morality and what we might call professional or philosophical morality. Specifically, Arendt diagnoses as fatal the assumption of both everyday and philosophical morality that we can take for granted that people know what is right and what is wrong. This section draws heavily on the lectures from a course Arendt gave at the New School for Social Research in 1965. The second section exposes the problematic nature of the concept of value as an ethical term, due to its conceptual descent from exchange value: it expands on Arendt's well-known criticism of the encroachment of economic concerns and categories into formerly public domains and activities in modern society, as detailed in *The Human Condition*. And finally, the third section assesses the currency of traditional morality in general as static and unyielding and consequently often useless in those times of crisis that call for a moral response.

Arendt's critique of values can be traced throughout her entire body of work, beginning with her critique of bourgeois society and institutions in *The Origins of Totalitarianism*. The political and economic aspect of the critique continues in some of the essays contained in the volume *Between Past and Future*, as well as in *The Human Condition*. All of those works were written or published in the 1950s and their concerns are almost exclusively political. The critique of values expanded to include other ethical concerns in the early 1960s, when the trial of Nazi Adolf Eichmann raised questions of good and evil, and of the complicity of people with apparently ordinary moral sensibilities in atrocities. Although her later works do not directly address the concept of value, her critique of other moral concepts, such as standards and codes of conduct, relies heavily on the earlier critique of values.

Although Arendt's concern with the questions of values can be discerned in all of her major works and many of the lesser-known works as well, the subject has seldom been treated by scholars of Arendt's work. This has been the case for a number of reasons. First, she was primarily and by her own designation a political thinker; consequently, questions of ethics in her work have been dealt with exclusively in a political context. Although that has been appropriate, I believe the question of value deserves a fuller treatment than it has yet received. Second, there has been a tendency in the past for scholars to consider either Arendt's early, completely political works (*Origins of Totalitarianism, The Human Condition*) or her later, more philosophical works (*Eichmann in Jerusalem, The Life of the Mind*). As a result, perhaps, the full impact of the development of her thinking about values has been missed. Margaret Canovan's recent book, *Hannah Arendt: A Reinterpretation of her Political Thought*, demonstrates the advantage of considering the full range of development of Arendt's thought in any interpretation of her work. Just as Canovan found her reinterpretation of Arendt's political thought greatly enriched by reading many of Arendt's unpublished lectures and manuscripts on political theory, so I found my consideration of her ethical thought focused by my reading of her unpublished lectures on morality. Specifically, Arendt's 1965 lecture notes for a course given at the New School for Social Research directed much of my thinking and research. This essay does not give a complete treatment of the question of value in Arendt's work, but it does try to give an idea of the scope of the critique.

I The Failure of Morality

Arendt's meditations on ethics began, as did her political work, with the seminal event of her personal life and professional career, the Holocaust. The question that haunted the world after the discovery of the death camps by the Allies was "How could such a thing have happened?" How could ordinary people with ordinary moral sensibilities participate in such a moral cataclysm? The events of the Holocaust struck a potentially lethal blow to how we view ourselves as human beings and how we think about matters of good and evil. We had thought we knew what was good and what was evil, and that we could rely on people not to participate willingly in evil, but after the war that assumption was no longer possible. What happened?

As Arendt described it in a lecture at the New School for Social Research in 1965, what happened was "the total collapse of all established moral standards," which people of her generation witnessed in the 1930s and 1940s in Hitler's Germany and Stalin's Russia.[2] When politicians today speak of the collapse of moral standards, they often mean that the standards themselves would still be valid if we could only get people to adhere to them once more. What Arendt meant, I think, was that the standards themselves collapsed, that they could not bear the weight of the actions they were supposed to measure. The standards proved inadequate both in preventing and later in comprehending the enormity of the crimes. The moral challenge lie not with those who masterminded the Holocaust—history has known evil people before and will surely know them again—but with the ordinary, generally good people "who only 'coordinated' themselves and did not act out of conviction" (Some Questions, p. 024582). The moral standards, which had evolved over centuries of religious and philosophical thought and had been taught to generations of pious schoolchildren could not prevent whole nations of people from turning on their Jewish populations, from bearing false witness, from collaborating in murder. And later, after the war, when the presumed madness was over, the language of moral standards seemed curiously inadequate to describe what had gone on. It must have been tempting to conclude, as some indeed did, that there *are* no such things as ethics and morals, given that "no one had to be a convinced Nazi to conform, and to forget over night, as it were, not his social status, but the moral convictions which once went with it" (Some Questions, pp. 024582, 024581).

But rather than conclude that morality was dead, Arendt chose to examine our assumptions about things good and evil and the vocabulary with which we talk about such things. Perhaps by the phrase "the collapse of moral standards" we could also understand that the way people had been thinking and talking about morality for centuries had been wrong all along. In the same lecture mentioned above, Arendt addressed the inadequacy of the traditional understanding of evil to explain or comprehend the evil of people like Adolph Eichmann and of the Holocaust in general:

> If the tradition of moral philosophy, as distinguished from the tradition of religious thought, is agreed upon one point from Socrates to Kant, and, as we shall see, to the present, then [that point is] that it is impossible for man to do wicked things deliberately, to want evil for evil's sake. (Some Questions, p. 024564)

It is so difficult for us to believe that people could willingly and knowingly participate in evil, Arendt argued in the 1960s, that we have neglected the moral challenge presented by the Holocaust. The most we have been able to do, perhaps, is to acknowledge that it seemed "to transcend all moral categories" (Some Questions, p. 024581). We have not been willing to rethink those categories.

What almost all moral philosophers since Socrates have taken for granted is that in most situations people know the difference between right and wrong, and consequently know the correct course of action. For their lapses there has been much explanation in terms of ignorance (Socrates), temptation (Aquinas), and inclination (Kant), but the morally correct course of action has been presumed to be both knowable and known. Most people have also assumed that this knowledge can be condensed—into laws, commandments, codes of conduct, standards, or values—and committed to memory. In the course of her critique of values, Arendt mounts a radical challenge to these twin pillars of moral philosophy: that most people always know the moral course of action, and that this knowledge is represented in the standards and rules of conduct that govern society.

II The Critique of Value

Until the age of industrialism, one spoke about ethics in terms of virtues. From the time of Socrates, and particularly by Aristotle, virtues have been defined as states of character that are unconditionally good. The catalogue of virtues changed from the primarily political virtues of classical Greece and Rome to Christianity's cardinal virtues of prudence, justice, temperance, and fortitude, but in each case virtues had absolute worth.[3] But with the demise of the terminology of *virtues* in the rise of the market economy, it was no longer possible to say that something was simply good, in and of itself. The term "good" was no longer absolute and self-sufficient—it came to imply a subsequent "for"—*good for* obtaining something else or *good for* (in the sense of relative to) another person.

If virtues are internal standards, self-imposed in the quest for goodness or the good life and absolute, values, in contrast, are externally determined or imposed and relative. What makes an object or quality valuable (instead of virtuous) is the demand for it, how much people are willing to pay for it, relative to other objects or qualities. Thus, the transition from the terminology of virtues to that of values entailed the loss of the concept of intrinsic worth. Virtue is a transcendent standard; value arises from the marketplace. As Arendt explained:

> The much deplored devaluation of all things, that is, the loss of all intrinsic worth, begins with their transformation into values or commodities, for from this moment on they exist only in relation to some other thing which can be acquired in their stead.[4]

One of the earliest philosophers to use this terminology of market and values when speaking of what were formerly known as virtues was Thomas Hobbes. He defines virtue, referring to intellectual virtue, as "somewhat that is valued for eminence; and consisteth in comparison."[5] In saying that virtue "consisteth in comparison," Hobbes is stating that virtue is relative to something else. In chapter 10 of *Leviathan* Hobbes enumerates a list of powers that enable a person to obtain some future good for himself. Among these powers are items that might have been included in some form in Aristotle's list of virtues from the *Nicomachean Ethics*. These include "riches joined with liberality," "reputation of love of a man's country," and "what quality soever maketh a man beloved, or feared by many" (pp. 150–151). By subordinating the worth of these qualities to their ability to obtain power or some other good for the possessor, Hobbes effectively denies that anything could have absolute value or worth. Instead of advocating patriotism as an attribute worthy for its own sake, Hobbes recommends the *reputation* of patriotism in order to gain more power. And the kind of power Hobbes is referring to is not so much *political* power (which the ancients certainly valued as well) as *purchasing* power. In other words, these qualities are desirable only insofar as they enable one to purchase the support of other people.

The most ominous consequence of this switch from virtues to values was Hobbes's challenge to the very notion of the absolute worth and dignity of a human being, when he declared that "The *Value* or Worth of a man, is, as of all other things, his Price; that is to say, so much as would be given for the use of his Power: and therefore is not absolute; but a thing dependent on the need and judgement of another" (pp. 151–152). Hobbes's philosophy sets market value, the price someone would be willing to pay according to supply and demand, as the moral standard for both human beings and their actions. As Arendt remarked ironically, "There is hardly a single bourgeois moral standard which has not been anticipated by the unequaled magnificence of Hobbes' logic."[6]

Arendt's investigation into the origin of the concept of value begins in *The Human Condition.* The book's primary concerns are: (1) the rise of work and labor, at the expense of action, as the dominant modes of human activity, and (2) the collapse of the public and private realms into society: "the rise of housekeeping, its activities, problems, and organizational devices—from the shadowy interior of the household into the light of the public sphere" (*HC,* 38). When the distinction between public and private vanishes, truly public concerns are edged out by the urgency of private concerns. The private realm is where activities necessary to the maintenance of life take place. The public realm, on the other hand, is a space created by the interaction of people. Whereas necessity and force characterize the private sphere of existence, the public is characterized by freedom, persuasion, and the pursuit of excellence. By bringing economic concerns that were formerly private into the public realm, we become once again enslaved to necessity. Two of the activities that characterize the human condition are essentially private: labor and work. Labor is the human activity most closely associated with the processes of biological life. Like the life of a species, labor is a cyclical and hence never-ending process of production and consumption. What is produced by labor has a very short life span, as it is consumed again almost immediately. Work, on the other hand, is a linear process that comes to an end with the finished product. That product, unlike that which is produced by labor, lives on after the activity of work has ceased. It is the activity by which people create a world for themselves from the materials provided by the earth. Only action takes place in public, as it is the only activity that goes on directly between and among people, and thus it creates the public or political space. Arendt's analysis of the collapsed distinction between public and private, and with it the triumph of labor over action, reveals the emergence of value as the moral standard.

Arendt believed that action was most highly prized during the classical era of first Greek and then Roman political dominance, as a way in which people could attain immortality. With the ascendence of Christianity and the promise of everlasting life, action lost its specifically political connotation and "was now reckoned among the necessities of earthly life," denoting all kinds of active engagement in the things of the world" (*HC*, p. 14). Contemplation was considered the highest human endeavor throughout the Middle Ages. Consequently, action, labor, and work had roughly equal rank as those activities concerned with temporal existence. With the rise of industrialism, however, work began to emerge as the defining human activity, as can be seen in Marx and Engels's declaration that production, rather than reason, is what distinguishes humans from animals. In the *German Ideology* they write that human beings "begin to distinguish themselves from animals as soon as they begin to *produce* their means of subsistence" (*German Ideology*, p. 151). With the decline of the importance of action and the political life in favor of the productive life, the concept of value emerged as our moral standard.

Arendt attributed this elevation of the productive life to the great labor theorists Adam Smith and Karl Marx. And here a word must be said about Arendt's somewhat controversial use of Marx's thought. *The Human Condition* presents a fairly sharp, if deferential, criticism of aspects of Marx's thought, which many commentators have argued represents a misunderstanding of Marx's thought.[7] Specifically, she criticized him for his role in the elevation of labor as the defining activity of the human condition at the expense of action, on the one hand, and for collapsing the distinction between labor and work by attributing the productivity of work to the life process of labor, on the other. Indirectly, she saw the collapse of this distinction as responsible for some of the worst aspects of consumer society, and the decline in the importance of political action.

Critics of Arendt's use of Marx have argued that she misunderstood what Marx meant by "labor." Even Jennifer Ring's attempt to reconcile Arendt's and Marx's thought had to acknowledge that "Arendt seems offbase in arguing that he overlooks the distinction between labor and work," doubting, in fact, whether the two concepts (labor and work) "can possibly remain distinct for long."[8] Few of these writers, however, acknowledge the fact that Arendt's critique of Marx takes place in the context of formulating her own political theory, and that she had a lifelong habit of appropriating historical and philosophical material for her own original philosophy. Karl Jaspers himself wrote on his evaluation of her doctoral thesis on Augustine (recommending her for the equivalent of a *cum laude* grade) that her

> method does some violence to the text. The foreword and the execution of the whole make clear that no attention is given to the great transformations in Augustinian thought that came about in the course of his life. Neither historical nor philosophical interests are primary here. The impulse behind this work is something not explicitly stated: through philosophical work with ideas the author wants to justify her freedom from Christian possibilities, which also attract her.[9]

What is significant about Arendt's use of Marx is not its critical view of Marx, but rather the more positive contribution to the development of her own thought.

In essence, Arendt argued that Smith and Marx established a particular kind of productivity as the standard of value (although clearly they used the term "value" exclusively in the economic sense)—one usually associated with what she called work. This standard is partly manifested in their distinction between productive and unproductive labor. Productive labor was more highly valued by these theorists because it leaves something behind when the activity has ceased. Durability becomes the criterion of value.[10] In many ways, these categories of labor reflect Arendt's distinction between work and labor. Arendt also criticized Marx, however, for not understanding all the implications of the division and for collapsing the distinction between labor and work. She characterized the "unutopian ideal that guides Marx's theories" as envisioning that "the distinction between labor and work would have completely disappeared; all work would have become labor because all things would be understood, not in their worldly, objective quality, but as results of living labor power and functions of the life process" (*HC*, p. 89).

Although to date the triumphs of socialism are mixed, the distinction between labor and work has been further obliterated in our modern consumer society, and along with it the distinction between use objects (the durable products of work or productive labor) and consumer goods (the immediately consumed products of labor). All activities and all objects are seen in terms not of production, but of consumption. People at all levels of society, Arendt argued, no longer see themselves as workers producing goods, but as wage earners producing the means of their own subsistence, that is, as laborers instead of workers. It is a common and deserved criticism of modern society that all objects are treated as consumer goods—from a loaf of bread, to a piece of furniture, to the earth itself—objects to be used up, consumed, disposed of at will. Values, in the context of a laboring society, are a commodity, but also a consumer good. It is a terrible state of affairs that virtues have come to be seen as values, that is, as objects to be used, but it is far worse that those values are also seen as consumable items, that is, as objects to be used up.

In her inquiry into the *vita activa*, Arendt found that the very concept of value, whether or not it is used in terms of moral values, means exchange value, and thus has its source in the experience of production and in the marketplace. In a work-oriented society, it makes sense that objects are valued according to their use and usefulness. But, Arendt argued, borrowing terminology from Marx, upon entering the market, use value becomes exchange value. The distinction is between producing items for your own use—where you are still the arbiter of their value—and producing goods for sale. The use value of a commodity is derived from its utility. Marx argued that a "commodity, such as iron, corn or diamond, is therefore, so far as it is a material thing, a use-value, something useful."[11] Exchange value, on the other hand, "presents itself as a quantitative relation, as the proportion in which values in use of one sort are exchanged for those of another sort" (*Capital*, p. 304). Arendt argued:

> For it is only in the exchange market, where everything can be exchanged for something else, that all things, whether they are products of labor or work, consumer goods or use objects, necessary for the life of the body or the convenience of living or the life of the mind, become "values." (*HC*, pp. 163–164)

If values are seen as arising from work and as displayed for sale in the market, then they must themselves be produced goods or commodities. If we speak of moral qualities as values, then they too must be commodities. Marx theorized that when people enter the exchange market, they do so not as producers of the commodities, but as the owners. This subtle shift in the relationship between workers and the goods they produce results in an estrangement from the commodity on the part of the producer/owner. The commodities are in fact separated from the labor or work that produced them, and consequently from the worker as well. On the exchange market, Marx said, the commodities "were separated from their direct connection with the mouths of the retainers etc. and transformed from use values into exchange values, and thus fell into the domain and under the supremacy of money wealth."[12] Marx deplored the transformation of use values into exchange values because of their separation from labor, their source. When the idea of exchange values is introduced into the moral realm, it becomes apparent that to speak of morals in terms of values is to envision them as commodities, that is, as objects whose value are determined by demand and easy exchange.

Arendt found two main difficulties with the triumph of exchange value as the dominant metaphor for ethics. The first and most significant problem is the origin of values in the marketplace, a pseudopublic forum that does not allow for truly public activities or action. Virtues had been located in the public forum by the Greeks and thus maintained a link with political action. Meaningfulness, which for Arendt is the guarantor of reality and the ultimate standard of action, cannot exist except in public. Hence values, if understood primarily as exchange values, are essentially meaningless. Persons in the exchange market are workers, their agents, or exploiters. Regardless, the exchange market is not the place for the actions of a free person. If values are expressive of the marketplace, then they are, in Arendt's lexicon, expressive of the actions of a private person, not a citizen.

The second difficulty Arendt had with the notion of value as an ethical measure is its instability and relativity. Classical morality had no "values." The very word, as we have said, implies that worth is derived from human need and estimation. The cornerstone of classical and especially Aristotelian morality was the notion of virtue and excellence—*arete*. Courage, for example, was for the ancients a virtue on its own merits. It was valued absolutely and not in terms of its utility or the conditions of the market. If we think of courage as a value rather than as a virtue, we might perhaps find that it had a higher value in times of war than in times of peace.[13] Arendt opposed this transformation of virtues to values because values are indeterminate, relying on human beings for their standard and worth.

According to Marxist interpretation, applying the terminology of the marketplace to moral values would have several other alarming implications. And it is with regard to these issues that we see the positive results of Arendt's creative use of Marx's categories and terminology. The first such implication is the estrangement or alienation of the producers of the values from the values themselves. In other words, those who manufacture the values do not necessarily see themselves in those values—in fact, they feel a certain disconnection from them. For instance, since the Conservative Party of England's Prime Minister John Major called for a return to family values early in 1994, ranking members have been embroiled in scandals involving extramarital affairs, illegitimate children, suicide, and sexual deviance.

The commodification of values implies a second problem, stemming from their identification as exchange values. Arendt argued that if all values are ultimately exchange values, then one set of values may be easily exchanged for another. One need only commit to one's values for as long as they are either effective or fashionable. Buying values, so to speak, puts one in the same relationship to them as to any other commodity. While the producer of an object puts something of himself into the object, making a commitment of self to it, a purchaser feels no such personal connection. A purchaser feels free to do what he likes with the object—keep it, use it, not use it, or discard it. This is especially true with items that can be easily replaced. Arendt saw confirmation of this easy exchangeability in the success of the Nazis in securing the collaboration of whole nations in their murderous agenda. Particularly with regard to their own citizens, the Nazi regime substituted the traditional values of the populace with what Arendt has called "a new set of German values."[14] Hitler needed only to show that his values would be more effective. Arendt found that Nazism was morally "more extreme" than Stalinism, precisely because it did "announce a new set of values and introduced a legal system designed in accordance with them. It proved moreover that no one had to be a convinced Nazi to conform, and to forget overnight, as it were, not his social status, but the moral convictions that once went with it" (Some Questions, pp. 024582, 024581).

More alarming than the initial exchange of traditional values for Nazi values was what happened after Germany's defeat. When the war was over and the new set of values had been proven not to work, the German people easily exchanged sets of values again. Typically, Arendt was more troubled by this second exchange than by the first, and by the moral problem it posed:

> The problem it raises is not resolved if we admit, as we must, that the Nazi doctrine did not remain with the German people, that Hitler's criminal morality was changed back again at the moment "history" had given the notice of defeat. Hence we must say that we witnessed the total collapse of a "moral" order not once but twice, and this sudden return to "normality," contrary to what is often complacently assumed, can only reinforce our doubts. (Some Questions, p. 024581)

She was not so much disturbed that an exchange of values could occur in the first place. But to revert so easily and unashamedly back to the former set of values indicated to Arendt that there had been no real commitment to either set.

Arendt's realization that value as a concept is derived from the process of work also revealed its dependence on the utilitarian relationship of means and ends. Arendt's investigation in *The Human Condition* revealed that work is generally seen as a means to an end—the product. Value, then, as a concept is also derived from this relationship of means and ends, having ultimately to do with how the work process achieves its end, or alternatively, how much demand there is for the product. So, for example, an object that has much work put into it is more valuable than a mass-produced item. Similarly, an object that was inexpensive to manufacture but is in high demand will be more valuable than one for which demand is low. The means/end relationship excludes the possibility of anything having intrinsic merit (worth) because the value of the object is derived solely from its relationship either to another object or to a buyer. In utilitarian terms, nothing can exist as an end in itself. And every end serves in turn as a means to another end. For Arendt, the consequence of seeing values as a function of the means/end relationship, or even as an end to be achieved, is again that values are divested of all meaning:

> The perplexity of utilitarianism is that it gets caught in the unending chain of means and ends without ever arriving at some principle which could justify the category of means and ends, that is, of utility itself. The "in order to" has become the content of the "for the sake of"; in other words, utility established as meaning generates meaninglessness. (*HC*, p. 154)

The principle difficulty of utilitarian ethics is that effectiveness is its criterion, rather than goodness. Moral action, judged by the standard of utility, is meaningless, because success is its ultimate standard. Speaking of Adolph Eichmann's opinion of Hitler even in 1961, Arendt remarked that

> What he fervently believed in up to the end was success, the chief standard of "good society" as he knew it. Typical was his last word on the subject of Hitler—whom he and his comrade Sassen had agreed to "shirr out" of their story; Hitler, he said, "may have been wrong all down the line, but one thing is beyond dispute: the man was able to work his way up from lance corporal in the German Army to Führer of a people of almost eighty million.... His success alone proved to me that I should subordinate myself to this man." (*EJ*, p. 126)

Eichmann's view—which is not so different from that of many people—is that the value of an action is entirely subordinated to the successful achievement of its end.

III The Critique of Traditional Moral Concepts

Arendt's critique of moral value is contained within her larger analysis of the loss of action in the modern age through the ascendence of work as the defining activity of the human condition. Moreover, elements of this critique can be found in most of her political writings—*The Origins of Totalitarianism*, *Between Past and Future*, and of course, *The Human Condition*. In these works, her concern was primarily political, and consequently, so was her interest in the commodification of value. But in her last, unfinished work, *The Life of the Mind*, Arendt began to take a more philosophical look at the problem of these traditional moral concepts.

Extending her analysis of the commodification of value, Arendt was able to discover other ways moral concepts are reified and thus rendered useless. But instead of approaching this analysis from the point of view of the most political of all activities, action, she approached it in this work from the most silent and isolating of activities: thinking. Although she addressed the issue of value directly in the above-mentioned political works, her discussion of other moral concepts such as codes of conduct and moral standards is a product of her investigation into the activity of thinking. That is, the inadequacy of these concepts is revealed not in a political reality (such as the events of the Holocaust), but in the course of her examination of the three activities that comprise the life of the mind: thinking, willing, and judging.

She began the first volume of The *Life of the Mind, Thinking*, by wondering if

> the activity of thinking as such, the habit of examining whatever happens to come to pass or to attract attention, regardless of results and specific content, could ... be among the conditions that make men abstain from evil-doing or even actually "condition" them against it?[15]

The question was raised for her by the trial of Adolph Eichmann in 1963, about which she wrote for the *New Yorker* and in *Eichmann in Jerusalem: A Report on the Banality of Evil*. She found that despite the crimes to which he openly and even proudly admitted (although not as crimes), he was not the traditional picture of an evil, depraved monster. He was an apparently normal person who saw his actions during the war as the actions of a law-abiding citizen. Eichmann's overwhelming character trait, in Arendt's view, was his complete thoughtlessness—not in the sense of carelessness, but in the literal sense of absence of thought. She wondered if it was in fact this lack of thought that enabled him to be a nice, "normal" man, yet one who was responsible for transporting millions of people to their death without any disturbance of conscience.[16] By not thinking about what he was doing, he could literally not know what he was doing.

Arendt does not pursue this question to any great depth in this volume: instead what emerges is her highly specialized definition of thinking. Arendt excludes the majority of cognitive activity that we would consider part of the activity of thinking. Rather, she characterizes the activity of thinking strictly as an internal dialogue with oneself, which she referred to as the "two-in-one." Thinking's strength as a possible means of preventing complicity in evil lie in Arendt's assumption that in thinking one splits into two and that one would not willingly do anything to jeopardize the harmony of that relationship with oneself. For a thinking person to go against what he or she knows to be right is to be condemned to live forever with a person for whom he or she has contempt.

For Arendt, one of the most significant indicators of Eichmann's thoughtlessness was his inability to formulate an original sentence. During his testimony, and in the text of his police examination, she noticed that he either used clichés and idiomatic expressions or, when forced to speak with some originality, he repeated his own phrasing over and over until it too acquired the status of cliché. Arendt believed that "the longer one listened to him, the more obvious it became that his inability to speak was closely connected with an inability to *think*, namely to think from the standpoint of somebody else" (*EJ*, p. 49).

Eichmann's use of clichés and other similar types of expressions struck Arendt as the result of Eichmann's inability to think. Moreover, such expressions (clichés, euphemisms, etc.) in general may also relieve the speaker of the responsibility of thinking. The phrases are automatic and familiar: in using them, one does not need to think about what one is saying. Arendt argued with great force that

> Clichés, stock phrases, adherence to conventional, standardized codes of expression and conduct have the socially recognized function of protecting us against reality, that is, against the claim on our thinking attention that all events and facts make by virtue of their existence (*LOM*, p. 4).

The problem with the sort of systematized concepts (values, standards, codes, theorems, etc.) that we use in speaking about moral issues is that they are all a kind of shorthand for a perceived moral truth. They have the advantage of being easily communicated and easily remembered. Whereas Socrates concluded after much discussion and thought that it is better to suffer wrong than to do wrong, Christians were taught a rule that was perhaps derived from that thought process: "Do unto others as you would have them do unto you." Many people in a situation that might call for that response simply need to recall its secularized version, the phrase "the Golden Rule," which acts as a mnemonic for that principle. But each moral precept represents a further step away from the thought process that led Socrates to conclude that he *personally* should suffer wrong rather than to do it. As Arendt understood Socrates' ethical action, the *thought process* rather than the precept compelled the moral action. But people can feel a certain disconnection from a memorized rule. They probably know that they are supposed to act in accordance with such rules, and maybe they often do, but the Golden Rule is not a part of them in the way that Socrates' thoughts were a part of him.

The mistake we make is in thinking that having standards means that we will act according to them, or even that simple possession (rather than implementation) of standards is sufficient to an ethical life. The implicit assumption is that it does not even really matter which standards or rules we have, as long as we have some. When ethical action is predicated solely on such things as rules and standards, Arendt argued,

> what people get used to is less the content of the rules ... than the *possession* of rules under which to subsume particulars. If someone appears who, for whatever purposes, wishes to abolish the old "values" or virtues, he will find that easy enough, provided he offers a new code, and he will need relatively little force and no persuasion—i.e., proof that the new values are better than the old—to impose it. The more firmly men hold to the old code, the more eager will they be to assimilate themselves to the new one, which in practice means the readiest to obey will be those who were the most respectable pillars of society. (*LOM*, p. 177)

Arendt speculated that the activity of thinking might be a precondition (although not a guarantee) of ethical action precisely because of its tendency to destroy, at least for the moment, whatever it examines closely. Arendt used Socrates as her model for the thinking activity, as well as her model of an ethical individual. She was, I think, particularly struck by the fact that Socrates' thinking always had negative results. Every dialogue between Socrates and another person who was sure he knew what a certain virtue was ended in aporia; that is, the person who had hoped to teach Socrates what that virtue was now found himself less sure than he had ever been about the virtue. Arendt interpreted Socrates' use of aporia as a purgative, to "purge people of their 'opinions,' that is, of those unexamined pre-judgements that would prevent them from thinking—helping them, as Plato said, to get rid of the bad in them, their opinions, yet without making them good, giving them truth" (LOM 173). For Arendt, this aporetic moment had a great deal of significance for her revaluation of morals. The concepts proposed for discussion in the Socratic dialogues—concepts like justice, piety, love, and friendship—are akin to moral concepts or values. As concepts they represent a consolidation of several complex ideas put together by some ancestor and handed down as a kind of necessary shorthand: using these concepts allows us to go about our everyday business without having to stop and examine everything that crosses our path, by subsuming the particulars automatically under these general concepts. But Arendt's analysis of the commodification of value demonstrated to her that matters of ethics and morals cannot be founded on anything of another person's making—either concepts in general or specific concepts, such as value. As Socrates found that to use a prefabricated definition of something obstructed a person's ability to examine and come to understand that thing, so Arendt found that maintaining a system of values obstructs a person's ability to value anything. Arendt warned of the danger of substituting one system of values for another for much the same reasons that Socrates could not provide his students with definitions or other supposed truths.

Thinking enables us to examine each situation we encounter. It carries with it the dangerous yet essential side effect of destroying the opinions we hold about it. Arendt cautioned that "thinking inevitably has a destructive, undermining effect on all established criteria, values, measurements of good and evil, in short, on those customs and trials of conduct we treat of in morals and ethics" (*LOM*, p. 175). Thinking destroys the kind of shorthand we use for ethics, of which I spoke earlier; it destroys the prefabricated values and standards that we arm ourselves with. This process is difficult and threatening. It was undoubtedly due at least in part to this phenomenon that Socrates was charged with undermining the morals of the youth of Athens. To be sure, Socrates' objective in his discussions was not purely negative. Although talking about justice or piety will not yield knowledge of justice or piety, Socrates fully expected that such an examination would help a person *become* just or pious. Arendt's proposition that thinking could be a precondition to acting ethically implies that true ethical action requires the willful destruction of what we have been raised to believe constitutes ethics. She even speculated that "if every man could be made to think and judge by himself, then indeed it might be possible to do without fixed standards and rules" (Some Questions, p. 024601).

IV Conclusions

Ethical action is therefore not a matter of the application of reified concepts like rules, values, and standards to the crisis situations that Arendt believed called for an ethical response, no matter how much thought or consideration is put into that application. When she hypothesized that thinking could be a precondition to acting ethically, she did not mean the kind of thinking used in applying rules and theorems. She meant the destructive force that prevents us from relying on those rules and standards. Whenever Arendt characterized true ethical action, she noted that the agent never consciously calculated the possible personal risks or consequences (like eternal damnation) and never consciously applied standards like the Golden Rule. An act of real virtue and real courage for Arendt was an authentic expression of self. Typically, such a person might say that he or she had no choice but to do it, that it would have been impossible not to.

The most tragic consequence of the commodification of value, or more precisely, the commodification of morality, is to subtract the self from consideration. Once that has been done, authentic action, action for which one is wholly and consciously responsible, is impossible. When morals and ethics are distilled into rules, theorems, definitions, standards, and values, they present a roadblock to authentic moral action.

Notes

1. Hannah Arendt, *Between Past and Future: Eight Exercises in Political Thought*, enlarged edition, (New York: Penguin Books, 1977), p. 32.

2. Hannah Arendt. Papers. Library of Congress, Washington, DC "Some Questions of Moral Philosophy," lecture series given at the New School for Social Research in 1965. Box 46, p. 024582. All other references will appear in the text.

3. And in any event, there would have been little dispute about what constituted a virtue. Aristotle would certainly not have disagreed that prudence, justice, temperance, and fortitude were virtues. He might have only disagreed about the relative ranking of the virtues.

4. Hannah Arendt, *The Human Condition* (Chicago: University of Chicago Press, 1958), pp. 165–166, hereinafter *HC*. All other references are to this edition and will appear in the text.

5. Thomas Hobbes, *Leviathan*, edited with an introduction by C. B. MacPherson (New York: Penguin Classics, 1986), p. 134. All other references are to this edition and will appear in the text.

6. Hannah Arendt, *The Origins of Totalitarianism*, new edition with added prefaces (New York: Harcourt Brace Jovanovich, 1979), p. 139. All other references will be to this edition and will appear in the text.

7. See especially Bikhu Parekh, "Hannah Arendt's Critique of Marx," in *Hannah Arendt: The Recovery of the Public World*, M. A. Hill, ed. (New York: St. Martin's Press, 1979). Parekh

argues that Arendt's "amazing misinterpretations" stem from her misunderstanding the rational aspect of Marx's concept of labor. His point that Arendt seems to assume that Marx used the term "labor" the way she, nearly a century later, would define it, is well taken. A similar point is made in W. A. Suchting's "Marx and Hannah Arendt's *The Human Condition*," *Ethics* 73 (October 1962), pp. 47–55.

8. Jennifer Ring, "On Needing Both Marx and Arendt: Alienation and the Flight from Inwardness." *Political Theory* 17:432–448 (August 1989), p. 439.

9. Hannah Arendt, Karl Jaspers, *Correspondence: 1926–1969*, edited and with an introduction by Lotte Kohler and Hans Saner. Translated by Robert and Rita Kimber (New York: Harcourt Brace Jovanovich, 1992), letter 2, n. 1, p. 690.

10. Arendt felt that establishing durability as the criterion of value was central to the theories of economics and property. In *The Human Condition* Arendt speaks of the use objects produced by work, which provided "the durability Locke needed for the establishment of property, the 'value' Adam Smith needed for the exchange market, and [which] bear testimony to productivity, which Marx believed to be the test of human nature" (*HC*, p. 136).

11. Karl Marx, *Capital*, in *The Marx-Engels Reader*, second edition, edited by Robert C. Tucker (New York: W. W. Norton, 1978), p. 303. All other references are to this edition and will appear in the text.

12. Karl Marx, *The Grundrisse (Foundations of the Critique of Political Economy)*, in *The Marx-Engels Reader*, second edition, edited by Robert C. Tucker (New York: W. W. Norton, 1978), p. 271. All other references will be to this edition and will appear in the text.

13. In the *Republic*, Plato ridicules this idea that some virtues might only be useful in a specific context, when he asks Polemarchus incredulously, if we should say that "for those who are not at war the just man is useless?" (332e).

14. Hannah Arendt, *Eichmann in Jerusalem: A Report on the Banality of Evil* Revised and enlarged edition (New York: Penguin Books, 1977). First published in the United States by Viking Press, 1963), p. 103, hereinafter *EJ*. All other references are to this edition and will appear in the text.

15. Hannah Arendt, *The Life of the Mind* (New York: Harcourt, Brace, Jovanovich Publishers, 1977), p. 5. Hereinafter referred to as LOM.

16. Arendt reported that "half a dozen psychiatrists had certified him as 'normal'—'More normal, at any rate, than I am after having examined him,' one of them was said to have exclaimed, while another had found that his whole psychological outlook, his attitude toward his wife and children, mother and father, brothers, sisters and friends, was 'not only normal but most desirable'—and finally the minister who had paid regular visits to him in prison after the Supreme Court finished hearing his appeal reassured everybody by declaring Eichmann to be 'a man with very positive ideas" (*EJ* pp. 25–26).

6

Did Hannah Arendt Change Her Mind? From Radical Evil to the Banality of Evil

Richard J. Bernstein

In 1945 Hannah Arendt declared: "The problem of evil will be the fundamental question of post-war intellectual life in Europe."[1] Arendt was wrong. Most postwar intellectuals avoided any direct confrontation with the problem of evil. But it did become fundamental for Arendt. She returned to it over and over again. Like a luminous red thread against a dark background, the concern with the *meaning* of evil—especially after the revelations of the horrors of twentieth-century totalitarianism—runs through all her thinking. She was still struggling with it at the time of her untimely death. In the "Introduction" to the posthumously published *The Life of the Mind*, she tells us that one of the origins of her preoccupation with mental activities was her attending the Eichmann trial where she had been struck by "the banality of evil." "After having been struck by a fact that, willy-nilly, 'put me in possession of a concept' (the banality of evil), I could not help raising the *questio juris* and asking myself 'by what right I possessed and used it.' "[2]

In this essay I want to think with—and sometimes against—Arendt in her own dialogue with herself (and others) about the meaning of evil, especially as it is manifested in the concentration and death camps—"the most consequential institution of totalitarian rule (*OT*, p. 441).[3] Exploring some of the main pathways that she pursues in her attempt to try to think what she claimed was "thought-defying" will enable us to gain a more profound understanding of her independent thinking. We will also see that Arendt raises some of the most difficult and treacherous questions that must be confronted by anyone seeking to grapple with the problem of evil at the close of the twentieth century—a century that future generations may label "The Age of Genocides."

Although it is well known that Arendt used the phrase "the banality of evil" and presumably abandoned her earlier understanding of "radical evil," there has been enormous confusion about the meaning of these expressions. The story of her struggle with the meaning of evil is far more complex and nuanced than it initially seems. Following its twists and turns is like following a detective story where there are all sorts of misleading clues (even misleading clues given by Arendt herself). It is not, however, one of those detective stories where all the loose ends are finally tied up. The loose ends of genuine independent thinking are never "finally" tied up. In this essay I want to focus on what Arendt meant by radical evil.

So let me begin by plunging in, and citing what appears to be conclusive evidence that Arendt emphatically changed her mind about the meaning of evil—her own direct testimony. Shortly after the publication of *Eichmann in Jerusalem*, a now famous exchange of letters between Gershom Scholem and Hannah Arendt was published.[4] Scholem concludes his letter with a damning critique of Arendt's "thesis" concerning "the banality of evil." I want to cite Scholem's critique and Arendt's response at some length because these texts are vital for everything that follows. Scholem, barely restraining his disgust and disdain, sarcastically writes:

> After reading your book I remain unconvinced by your thesis concerning the "banality of evil"—a thesis which, if your sub-title is to be believed, underlies your entire argument. This new thesis strikes me as a catchword: it does not impress me, certainly, as the product of profound analysis—an analysis such as you give us so convincingly, in the service of a quite different, indeed contradictory thesis, in your book on totalitarianism. At that time you had not yet made your discovery, apparently, that evil is banal. Of that "radical evil," to which your then analysis bore such eloquent and erudite witness, nothing remains but this slogan—to be more than that it would have to be investigated, at a serious level, as a relevant concept in moral philosophy of political ethics. I am sorry—and I say this, I think, in candor and in no spirit of enmity—that I am unable to take the thesis of your book more seriously. I had expected, with your earlier book in mind, something different. (p. 245)

Scholem here sums up what many of Arendt's critics at the time were saying in a much more hysterical fashion. For the very phrase "the banality of evil" was offensive. It seemed to trivialize not only what Eichmann had done, but the full horror of the Shoah.

Speaking directly to the issues raised above, Arendt in her reply writes:

> In conclusion, let me come to the only matter where you have not misunderstood me, and where indeed I am glad that you have raised the point. You are quite right: I changed my mind and do no longer speak of "radical evil." It is a long time since we last met, or we would perhaps have spoken about the subject before. (Incidentally, I don't see why you call my term "banality of evil" a catchword or slogan. As far as I know no one has used the term before me; but that is unimportant.) It is indeed my opinion now that evil is never "radical," that it is only extreme, and that it possesses neither depth nor any demonic dimension. It can overgrow and lay waste the whole world precisely because it spreads like a fungus on the surface. It is "thought-defying," as I said, because thought tries to reach some depth, to go to the roots, and the moment it concerns itself with evil, it is frustrated because there is nothing. That is its "banality." Only the good has depth and can be radical. But this is not the place to go into these matters seriously: I intend to elaborate them further in a different context. Eichmann may very well remain the concrete model of what I have to say. (pp. 250–251)

What could be clearer and more explicit? Arendt affirms that she has changed her mind. She now (1964) believes "evil is never 'radical'." Even Elisabeth Young-Bruehl in her perceptive biography reaffirms what Arendt says here. Young-Bruehl comments "Arendt rejected the concept she had used in *The Origins of Totalitarianism* to point at the incomprehensible nature of the Nazis—'radical evil.' As she did this, she freed herself of a long nightmare; she no longer had to live with the idea that monsters and demons had engineered the murder of millions."[5] So it would seem! But if we step back and reflect on the exchange between Scholem and Arendt, it is striking how *little* is said about the meaning of "radical evil." Only the barest hint is given. If we are to answer the question: "Did Hannah Arendt change her mind?" we must first find out what precisely did *she* mean by "radical evil." It is here that our detective work must begin in order to gather the relevant evidence.

In 1948 Arendt published a remarkable essay in the *Partisan Review* which was starkly entitled "The Concentration Camps."[6] It is among her most powerful and trenchant essays. It still stands as one of the most penetrating analyses of the horrors of the concentration camps and the role they play in totalitarian regimes. I also think that if one reads this essay carefully there is a discernible subtext—one in which we discover the "essentials" of her understanding of action, plurality, and politics, which she fully developed only in *The Human Condition* (published ten years after this essay). Arendt does not use the phrase "radical evil" in this article, but she does speak about "absolute evil." She writes:

Murder in the camps is as impersonal as the squashing of a gnat, a mere technique of management, as when a camp is overcrowded and is liquidated—or an accidental by-product, as when a prisoner succumbs to torture. Systematic torture and systematic starvation create an atmosphere of permanent dying, in which death as well as life is effectively abstracted.

The fear of the absolute evil which permits of no escape knows that this is the end of dialectical evolutions and developments. It knows that modern politics revolves around a question which, strictly speaking, should never enter into politics, the question of all or nothing: of all, that is a human society rich with infinite possibilities; or exactly nothing, that is, the end of mankind.[7]

One reason why this 1948 essay is so important is because Arendt reworked it and included it in the final section, "Total Domination," of the penultimate chapter of *The Origins of Totalitarianism* (the chapter that precedes her inconclusive "Concluding Remarks"). Arendt was dissatisfied with her "Concluding Remarks" and deleted it from subsequent editions of her book. She did, however, incorporate some of her comments from these remarks in the main body of her text. In the original "Concluding Remarks" this is what she has to say about absolute evil:

Until now the totalitarian belief that everything is possible seems to have proved only that everything can be destroyed. Yet, in their effort to prove that everything is possible, totalitarian regimes have discovered without knowing it that there are crimes which man can neither punish nor forgive. When the impossible was made possible it became the unpunishable, unforgivable absolute evil which could no longer be understood and explained by the evil motives of self-interest, greed, covetousness, resentment, lust for power and cowardice; and which therefore anger could not revenge, love could not endure, friendship could not forgive. Just as the victims in the death factories or the holes of oblivion are no longer "human" in the eyes of their executioners, so this newest species of criminals is beyond the pale even of the solidarity in human sinfulness.

Difficult as it is to conceive of an absolute evil even in the face of its factual existence, it seems to be closely connected with the invention of a system in which all men are equally superfluous. The manipulators of this system believe in their own superfluousness as much as in that of all others, and the totalitarian murderers are all the more dangerous because they do not care if they themselves are alive or dead, if they ever lived or never were born. The danger of the corpse factories and the holes of oblivion is that today, with populations and homelessness everywhere on the increase, masses of people are continuously rendered superfluous if we continue to think of our world in utilitarian terms. (*OT* I, p. 433, emphasis added)

When Arendt dropped her "Concluding Remarks" from the revised second (1958) and subsequent editions of *The Origins of Totalitarianism* she incorporated most of the above passage into her discussion of "Total Domination." But she also made a very significant *addition.* Immediately after the first paragraph cited above, she added the following sentences:

It is inherent in our entire philosophical tradition that we cannot conceive of a "radical evil," and this is true both for Christian theology, which conceded even to the Devil himself a celestial origin, as well as for Kant, the only philosopher who, in the word he coined for it, at least must have suspected the existence of this evil even though he immediately rationalized it in the concept of a "perverted ill will" that could be explained by comprehensible motives. Therefore, we actually have nothing to fall back on in order to understand a phenomenon that nevertheless confronts us with its overpowering reality and breaks down all standards we know. There is only one thing that seems to be discernible: we may say *that radical evil has emerged in connection with a system in which all men have become equally superfluous.* (*OT*, p. 459, emphasis added)

Before attempting to make sense of these several texts, I want to cite one further piece of evidence in order to clarify what Arendt meant by "absolute evil" or "radical evil."[8] In early 1951, before *The Origins of Totalitarianism* appeared in bookstores, Arendt sent a copy to Karl Jaspers so that he would receive it before his birthday. Delighted that his former gifted student had used a quotation from his writings as the epigraph of the book, he immediately acknowledged receiving it. After a first reading of the preface and concluding remarks of the book, Jaspers added a note with the following cryptic question: "Hasn't Jahwe faded too far out of sight?" In her next letter to him, Arendt wrote that his question "has been on my mind for weeks now without my being able to come up with an answer to it." But Jaspers's question did provoke the following reflections on radical evil.

Evil has proved to be more radical than expected. In objective terms, modern crimes are not provided for in the Ten Commandments. Or: The Western Tradition is suffering from the preconception that the most evil things human beings can do arise from the vice of selfishness. Yet we know that the greatest evils or radical evil has nothing to do anymore with such humanly understandable, sinful motives. *What radical evil really is I don't know but it seems to me it somehow has to do with the following phenomenon: making human beings as human beings superfluous (not using them as means to an end, which leaves their essence as humans untouched and impinges only on their human dignity; rather, making them superfluous as human beings). This happens as soon as all unpredictability—which, in human beings, is the equivalent of spontaneity—is eliminated.* And all this in turn arises from—or, better, goes along with—the delusion of the omnipotence (not simply with the lust for power) of an individual man. If an individual man qua man were omnipotent, then there is in fact no reason why men should exist at all—just as in monotheism it is only God's omnipotence that makes him ONE. So, in this same way, the omnipotence of an individual man would make men superfluous. (emphasis added)[9]

What are we to make of these claims about absolute or radical evil? Initially, what is most striking is what Arendt does *not* say. There is *no* suggestion in any of these passages that radical evil is to be understood as the "idea that monsters and demons had engineered the murders of millions."[10] I want to be even more emphatic. There is no evidence that Arendt ever held anything like this belief. On the contrary, she categorically rejected such a claim—long before she witnessed the Eichmann trial. Already in her 1948 article, "The Concentration Camps," Arendt sharply distinguishes between what happened when the camps were run by the S.A. and when they were taken over by the S.S. The S.A. represented a "criminal and abnormal mentality." They might well be thought of as sadistic monsters.

Behind the blind bestiality of the S.A., there often lay a deep hatred and resentment against all those who were socially, intellectually, or physically better off than themselves, and who now, as if in fulfillment of their wildest dreams, were in their power. This resentment, which never died out entirely in the camps, strikes us a last remnant of humanly understandable feeling.[11]

But although such behavior was perverse and sadistic, it was still "humanly" understandable. This was not yet the real horror—the transformation that took place when the "desk murderers" took control. In a passage that sounds very much like, and seems to anticipate Foucault, Arendt writes:

The real horror began, however, when the S.S. took over the administration of the camps. The old spontaneous bestiality gave way to an absolutely cold and systematic destruction of human bodies, calculated to destroy human dignity;

death was avoided or postponed indefinitely. The camps were no longer amusement parks for beasts in human form, that is, for men who really belonged in mental institutions and prisons. The reverse became true: they were turned into "drill grounds" ... on which perfectly normal men were trained to be full-fledged members of the S.S.[12]

Arendt not only categorically rejects the all too popular image of the Nazis as "insane" monsters, she makes a much stronger and provocative claim—that "radical evil" cannot be accounted for by "evil motives." This is compatible with one of the main points that she stresses much later in *Eichmann in Jerusalem* when she emphatically states: "one cannot extract any diabolical or demonic profundity from Eichmann."[13]

Now it may be thought that Arendt's reference to Kant is helpful for grasping what she means by "radical evil." After all, she tells us that Kant coined the expression "radical evil." It is, of course, true that Kant speaks of radical evil in his *Religion within the Limits of Reason.* There are commentators who have argued that this is an essential concept for understanding Kant's moral philosophy, and in particular, his analysis of human freedom. So it seems sensible to try to grasp what Arendt means by radical evil by first probing Kant's meaning—and then focusing attention on what Arendt appropriates from Kant.[14] This, however, is another misleading clue that can divert our attention. Even if we set aside the complex scholarly question of precisely what Kant meant by "radical evil" and how it does (or does not) fit with the rest of his moral philosophy, Arendt herself indicates that her understanding of radical evil is quite different from Kant's. Consider once again what she says in her all too brief reference to Kant. "Kant, the only philosopher who, in the word he coined for it, at least must have suspected the existence of this evil *even though he immediately rationalized it in the concept of a 'perverted ill will' that could be explained by comprehensible motives*" (*OT*, p. 459 emphasis added). Whether Arendt is being fair to Kant is a debatable issue. But it is clear that Arendt does *not* think that Kant grasped what *she* intends by "radical evil." This is why she goes on to say "we actually have nothing to fall back on in order to understand a phenomenon that nevertheless confronts us with its overpowering reality" (*OT*, p. 459).

The question that must be asked is: What does Arendt mean by radical evil? She provides an essential clue in her letter to Jaspers: "it seems to me it somehow has to do with the following phenomenon: making human beings as human beings superfluous (not using them as means to an end, which leaves their essence as human untouched and impinges only on their human dignity; rather, making them superfluous as human beings)." This is also the point she makes when she introduces the expression "radical evil" in *The Origins of Totalitarianism.* So the question now becomes: What does Arendt mean when she says "radical evil has emerged in connection with a system in which all men have become equally superfluous" (*OT*, p. 459)?

Superfluousness is one of the most persistent and most pervasive themes in *The Origins of Totalitarianism.* This theme is crucial for her analysis of the decline of the nation-state and the end of the Rights of Man—her analysis of statelessness and what happens when human beings are stripped of the right to have rights. For example, she tells us:

> The calamity of the rightless is not that they are deprived of life, liberty, and the pursuit of happiness, or of equality before the law and freedom of opinion—formulas which were designed to solve problems *within* given communities—but that they no longer belong to any community whatsoever. Their plight is not that they are not equal before the law, but that no law exists for them; not that they are oppressed, only in the last stage of a rather lengthy process is their right to live threatened; *only if they remain perfectly "superfluous," if nobody can be found to "claim" them, may their lives be in danger.* Even the Nazis started their extermination of Jews by first depriving them of all legal status (the status of second-class citizenship) and cutting them off from the world of the living by herding them into ghettos and concentration camps; and before they set the gas chambers in motion they had carefully tested the ground and found out to their satisfaction that no country would claim these people. The point is that a condition of complete rightlessness was created before the right to live was challenged. (*OT*, p. 295 emphasis added)

It is, however, in her analysis of the concentration camps in the section "Total Domination" that she is most explicit about the phenomenon of superfluousness. It is here that she speaks directly of radical evil. Arendt poignantly analyzes the three successive steps of total domination. "The first essential step on the road to total domination is to kill the juridical person in men" (*OT*, p. 447). "The next decisive step in the preparation of living corpses is the murder of the moral person in man. This is done in the main by making martyrdom for the first time in history, impossible . . . " (*OT*, p. 451). Finally, there is the systematic destruction of individuality.

After the murder of the moral person and annihilation of the juridical person, the destruction of the individuality is almost always successful. . . . For to destroy individuality is to destroy spontaneity, man's power to begin something new out of his own resources, something which cannot be explained on the basis of reactions to environment and events. Nothing then remains but ghastly marionettes with human faces, which all behave like the dog in Pavlov's experiments, which all react with perfect reliability even when going to their own death, and which do nothing but react. This is the real triumph of the system. . . . (*OT*, p. 455)

To make human beings superfluous is to eradicate the very conditions that make humanity possible—to destroy human plurality, spontaneity, natality, and individuality. Arendt sums this up in the paragraph that immediately precedes her brief discussion of absolute or radical evil.

What totalitarian ideologies therefore aim at is not the transformation of society, but the transformation of human nature itself. The concentration camps are the laboratories where changes in human nature are tested, and their shamefulness therefore is not just the business of their inmates and those who run them according to strictly "scientific" standards; it is the concern of all men. Suffering, of which there has been always too much on earth, is not the issue, nor is the number of victims. Human nature is at stake, and even though it seems that these experiments succeed not in changing man but only in destroying him, by creating a society in which the nihilistic banality of *homo homini lupus* is consistently realized, one should bear in mind the necessary limitations to an experiment which requires global control in order to show conclusive results. (*OT*, pp. 458–59)

Earlier I suggested that the kernel of Arendt's understanding of the human condition, especially her emphasis on plurality as the condition for human action, is contained in this culminating chapter of *The Origins of Totalitarianism.*[15] It is as if by "dwelling on the horrors" of the concentration camps that she came to the shocking realization that the not-so-hidden aim of totalitarianism was to make human beings qua human superfluous, that is, to transform "human nature" so that what is essential to live a *human* life—plurality, spontaneity, natality, and individuality—are themselves destroyed. This is what Arendt meant by radical evil—a new and unprecedented phenomenon that "confronts us with its overpowering reality and breaks down all standards we know." Mass murder, genocide, unbearable large-scale suffering by innocent people, systematic torture and terror had happened before in history. But the aim of totalitarianism was not oppression, not even "total domination"—if this is still understood as the total domination of *human beings.*

Totalitarianism, as Arendt understood it, strives to obliterate one's humanity and the very conditions required to lead a human life. This is why one of the main reasons why Arendt insisted that Nazi crimes (if we can even speak of them as "crimes") are "crimes against *humanity*." She tells us in *Eichmann in Jerusalem* that: "There was not the slightest doubt that Jews had been killed *qua* Jews, irrespective of their nationalities at the time," but nevertheless this unprecedented crime "was a crime against humanity, perpetuated upon the body of the Jewish people."[16] Radical evil differs from the main traditional Western understandings of evil because it has nothing to do with "evil motives"—indeed it has nothing to do with *human* motives. And this is precisely what Arendt says about Eichmann when she speaks of the "banality of evil"! "Except for an extraordinary diligence in looking out for his personal advancement, he had no motives at all.... He merely, to put the matter colloquially, *never realized what he was doing*."[17] Radical evil, as Arendt so straightforwardly and devastatingly phrases it, is making human beings "superfluous as human beings." This is why I agree with Margaret Conovan when she writes Arendt "never had thought in terms of 'monsters and demons,' and 'banality' was really a more accurate way of describing the self-abandonment to inhuman forces and the diminution of human beings to an animal species of totalitarianism."[18]

Nevertheless, it looks like there is a crucial gap at this stage in Arendt's thinking, even if one accepts the claim that totalitarianism aims at "the transformation of human nature itself" and that "the concentration camps are the laboratories where changes in human nature are tested." We may ask, why call this radical or absolute evil? Arendt, it would seem, is presupposing a normative concept of human nature that is itself in need of justification. I think this way of putting the issue is misleading, for it misses the poignancy of her shocking insight. It is of course true that in *The Origins of Totalitarianism* Arendt does not hesitate to speak about "human nature" and the "transformation of human nature." In *The Human Condition*, however, she is much more cautious.

> To avoid misunderstanding: the human condition is not the same as human nature, and the sum total of human activities and capabilities which correspond to the human condition does not constitute anything like human nature....
>
> The problem of human nature, the Augustinian *quaestio mihi factus sum* ("a question have I become for myself"), seems unanswerable in both its individual psy-

chological sense and its general philosophical sense. It is highly unlikely that we, who can know, determine, and define the natural essences of all things surrounding us, which we are not, should ever be able to do the same for ourselves—this would be like jumping over our shadows. Moreover, nothing entitles us to assume that man has a nature or essence in the same sense as other things. In other words, if we have a nature or essence, then surely only a god could know and define it, and the first prerequisite would be that he be able to speak about a "who" as though it were a "what."[19]

Arendt expresses a philosophic motif that she finds in Augustine, and which had been reinforced by her philosophic mentors, Heidegger and Jaspers. But there is another important aspect concerning her questioning of the concept of a fixed human nature.

Arendt, who insisted that her thinking was rooted in her experience, claimed that with the event of totalitarianism, one could no longer believe in the fixity of human nature, or that there is something deep down in human beings that will resist the totalitarian impulse to prove that "everything is possible"—even the most radical transformation of "human beings" into a species that is not quite human. When Eric Voegelin sharply criticized her for claiming that "human nature as such is at stake," she replied that:

The success of totalitarianism is identical with a much more radical liquidation of freedom as a political and as a human reality than anything we have ever witnessed before. Under these conditions, it will hardly be consoling to cling to an unchangeable nature of man and conclude that either man himself is being destroyed or that human freedom does not belong to man's essential capabilities. Historically, we know of man's nature only insofar as it has existence, and no realm of eternal essences will ever console us if man loses his essential capabilities.[20]

In many places Arendt affirms how profoundly she was affected by the realization that what she had been brought up to believe was impossible turned out not only to be possible but all too real. She began her 1965 New School lecture course, "Some Questions of Moral Philosophy," by citing a passage she admired from Winston Churchill: "Scarcely anything material or established, which I was brought up to believe was permanent and vital, has lasted. Everything I was sure or taught to be sure was impossible happened." This was the bitter "lesson" of totalitarianism. It was not only the evil of totalitarianism that so deeply affected Arendt. Even more significant for questioning the meaning of evil was the almost universal collapse of moral standards in the face of totalitarianism. She declared "We ... have witnessed the total collapse of all established moral standards in public and private life during the thirties and forties ... without much notice all this collapsed almost overnight and then it was as though morality suddenly stood revealed ... as a set of mores, customs and habits, which could be exchanged for another set with hardly more trouble than it would take to change table manners with an individual or a people."[21] Arendt makes a similar point in the introduction to *The Life of the Mind*:

> The fact that we usually treat matters of good and evil in courses in "morals" or "ethics" may indicate how little we know about them, for morals comes from *mores* and ethics from *ethos*, the Latin and Greek words for customs and habit, the Latin word being associated with rules of behavior, whereas the Greek word is derived from habitat, like our "habits."[22]

Consequently, I do not think it is accurate to say that Arendt is uncritically presupposing a normative conception of human nature which is the basis for her conception of radical or absolute evil. Rather I think it is more perspicacious to say that Arendt's own thinking was deeply affected by the traumatic experience of witnessing what seemed to be *impossible*—that an unprecedented totalitarian movement could arise whose ideology was based on the "principle" that "everything is possible" including the transformation of the "human" species into something less than human—where spontaneity, individuality, freedom, and even natality could be eradicated from "human" life. The specter that haunted Arendt—the specter of totalitarianism—is one where human beings would become superfluous, and even the concept of humanity itself would be obliterated.

Against Scholem who states that radical evil and the banality of evil are *contradictory*—I want to support further the *compatibility* of these conceptions of evil. I want to pursue a clue that initially does not even appear to be a clue. Let us return to Arendt's reply to Scholem. She casually remarks: "(Incidentally, I don't see why you call my term 'banality of evil' a catchword or a slogan. As far as I know no one has used the term before me; but that is unimportant.)" Arendt is wrong again! The "banality of evil" had been used before—in a very significant context which Arendt seems to have forgotten. In 1946, some fifteen years prior to *Eichmann in Jerusalem*, Arendt discussed the question of Nazi war crimes in her correspondence with Jaspers. Let us review what was said in their exchange of letters.

In 1946, a year after Arendt and Jaspers resumed their correspondence which had been interrupted by the war, Jaspers sent Arendt his monograph *Die Schuldfrage* which dealt with the question of Nazi war crimes and German guilt. Commenting on the book, this is what she writes about Nazi "crimes" (17 August 1946):

> Your definition of Nazi policy as a crime ("criminal guilt") strikes me as questionable. The Nazi crimes, it seems to me, explode the limits of the law; and that is precisely what constitutes their monstrousness. For these crimes, no punishment is severe enough.... That is, this guilt, in contrast to all the criminal guilt, oversteps and shatters any and all legal systems.

Responding to this criticism, Jaspers writes:

> You say that what the Nazis did cannot be comprehended as "crime"—I'm not altogether comfortable with your view, because a guilt that goes beyond all criminal guilt inevitably takes on a streak of "greatness"—of satanic greatness—which is for me, as inappropriate for the Nazis as all the talk about the "demonic" element in Hitler and so forth. It seems to me that we have to see those things in their total banality, in their prosaic triviality, because that's what truly characterizes them. Bacteria can cause epidemics that wipe out nations, but they remain merely bacteria. I regard any hint of myth and legend with horror. (19 October 1946)[23]

These are the words of Jaspers in 1946, but they could very well be the words used by Arendt in her reply to Scholem. There is even an uncanny echo of Jaspers's comparison with bacteria and Arendt's comparison of the spread of evil to a fungus: "Evil possesses neither depth nor any demonic dimension. It can overgrow and lay waste the whole world precisely because it spreads lie a fungus on the surface."[24]

Returning to our original question, "Did Arendt change her mind?" we may ask, however, how did Arendt understand the evil of Nazi "criminality" in 1946 when she discussed the issue with Jaspers—before she publicly wrote about radical evil and long before she wrote about the banality of evil. We do not have to speculate. In her 17 December 1946 letter to Jaspers this is what she says:

> I found what you say about my thoughts on "beyond crime and innocence" in what the Nazis did half convincing; that is, I realize completely that in the way

I've expressed this up to now I come dangerously close to that "satanic greatness" that I, like you, totally reject. But still, there is a difference between a man who sets out to murder his old aunt and people who without considering the economic usefulness of their actions at all (the deportations were very damaging to the war effort) built factories to produce corpses. One thing is certain: we have to combat all impulses to mythologize the horrible, and to the extent that I can't avoid such formulations, I haven't understood what actually went on. Perhaps what is behind it all is only that individual human beings did not kill other individual human beings for human reasons, but that an *organized attempt was made to eradicate the concept of the human being.* (emphasis added)[25]

It is difficult to imagine a more forceful rejection that "satanic greatness" is an appropriate concept for describing Nazi crimes—this is what Arendt "totally rejects." Like Jaspers she strongly affirms the need to combat all impulses to mythologize the horrible. She is even self-critical about her own formulation insofar as it might suggest this dangerous sort of mythologizing of radical evil. Radical evil has nothing to do with "satanic greatness." Radical evil, strictly speaking, is neither punishable nor forgivable, because punishment and forgiveness presuppose what radical evil seeks to eradicate, that is, *human* action.[26] What the Nazis attempted to do in the concentration camps was to "eradicate the concept of the human being." This is what had seemed to be impossible. This is what is so "thought defying." For it is even "beyond" the horror of the extermination of millions of human beings.

The exchange that took place between Jaspers and Arendt in 1946 (which is only three years after Arendt herself first learned what was happening at Auschwitz) helps to clear up another confusion—one to which Arendt herself contributes. At one point in responding to Arendt's criticism of his book *Die Schuldfrage*, Jaspers writes:

The way you do express it, you've almost taken the path of poetry. And a Shakespeare would never be able to give adequate form to this material—his instinctive aesthetic sense would lead to falsification of it—and that's why he couldn't attempt it.[27]

Jaspers's reference to Shakespeare is especially illuminating because Shakespeare is the poet who created some of the greatest and most compelling characters who exemplify "satanic greatness." Arendt herself frequently refers to Shakespeare when speaking about evil, especially when she attempts to distinguish the banality of evil from traditional conceptions of evil. Because her rhetorical constructions sometimes suggest that *the* alternative to the banality of evil is evil, which is theologically or aesthetically categorized as "satanic greatness," one can easily be misled into thinking that she identifies radical evil with satanic greatness. Thus in one of her first attempts to explain and clarify what she means by the banality of evil, she writes:

> Eichmann was not Iago and not Macbeth, and nothing would have been farther from his mind than to determine with Richard III "to prove a villain. . . ." [Eichmann] was not stupid. It was sheer thoughtlessness—something by no means identical with stupidity—that predisposed him to become one of the greatest criminals of that period. . . . That such remoteness from reality and such thoughtlessness can wreak more havoc than all the evil instincts taken together which, perhaps, are inherent in man—that was, in fact, the lesson one could learn in Jerusalem.[28]

We find a similar rhetorical contrast more fully elaborated in the introduction to *The Life of the Mind.*

> Factually, my preoccupation with mental activities has two rather different origins. The immediate impulse came from my attending the Eichmann trial in Jerusalem. In my report of it I spoke of "the banality of evil." Behind that phrase, I held no thesis or doctrine, although I was dimly aware of the fact that it went counter to our tradition of thought—literary, theological, or philosophic—about the phenomenon of evil. Evil, we have learned, is something demonic. Its incarnation is Satan, a "lightning fell from heaven" (Luke 10:18) or Lucifer, the fallen angel ("The devil is an angel too"—Unamuno) whose sin is pride ("proud as Lucifer"), namely, that *superbia* of which only the best are capable: they don't want to serve God but to be like Him. Evil men, we are told, act out of envy. This may be resentment at not having turned out well through no fault of their own (Richard III) or the envy of Cain, who slew Abel because "The Lord had regard for Abel and his offering, but for Cain and his offering he had no regard." Or they may be prompted by weakness (Macbeth). Or, on the contrary, by the powerful hatred wickedness feels for sheer goodness (Iago's "I hate the Moor: my cause is hearted"; Claggart's hatred for Billy Budd's "barbarian" innocence, a hatred considered by Melville a "depravity according to nature"), or by covetousness "the root of all evil" (*Radix omnium malorum cupiditas*). However, what I was confronted with was utterly different and still undeniably factual. I was struck by a manifest shallowness in the doer that made it impossible to trace the incontestable evil of his deeds to any deeper level of roots or motives. The deeds were monstrous, but the doer—at least the very effective one now on trial—was quite ordinary, commonplace, and neither demonic nor monstrous. There was no sign in him of firm ideological convictions or of specific evil motives, and the

only notable characteristic one could detect in his past behavior as well as in his behavior during the trial and throughout the pre-trial police examination was something entirely negative: it was not stupidity but *thoughtlessness*.[29]

This passage is important because it shows how radically Arendt departs from those traditional entrenched understandings of evil where evil is understood to be an expression of "evil motives." This departure from the tradition is what is so disturbing in her analysis of the banality of evil. But, *in this respect*, she already made the same point about radical evil; it is not a matter of "evil motives," but rather seeking "to eradicate the concept of the human being," making *human* beings superfluous qua *human beings*. And Arendt also indicates here what she takes to be the essential clue for understanding Eichmann's "monstrous deeds"—his thoughtlessness, his inability to think and judge.

Let me return to the original question: "Did Arendt change her mind?" Phrased in this unqualified manner, the question is too vague and ambiguous; it invites misleading answers. But we can break down this vague question into more specific and determinate questions that can be answered. Does the concept of radical evil that Arendt analyzes in *The Origins of Totalitarianism* "contradict" (as Scholem claims) Arendt's notion of the banality of evil? No! I have argued that what Arendt means by radical evil is making human beings superfluous—eradicating the very conditions required for living a human life. This is compatible with what she says about the banality of evil. Eichmann lacked the thoughtfulness to even grasp that this was the consequence of his "monstrous deeds." Did Arendt ever believe that Nazi crimes could be adequately explained as the "deeds of monsters and demons"? No! She explicitly and consistently "totally rejects" such an understanding of Nazi criminality. Did Arendt ever think that anything like "satanic greatness" was a relevant concept for understanding the evil of totalitarian domination? No! Already in 1946 she makes it perfectly clear that she rejects such a notion—and even criticizes those formulations that she uses that suggest such an understanding of Nazi evil.

To answer these questions emphatically in the negative is not to deny that there was a shift of focus when she spoke of "the banality of evil." There was a major shift. The key concept in her earlier analysis of radical evil is *superfluousness*. After she witnessed the Eichmann trial she turned her attention to *thoughtlessness*. It is as if Arendt initially felt the need to understand what was unprecedented in the evil that erupted with twentieth-century totalitarianism. Her answer was that never before had there been such a thorough and systematic attempt to change human nature—to make human beings in their plurality, spontaneity, and individuality superfluous. But after the Eichmann trial she became obsessed with a new and different question. How could one account for the "monstrous deeds" committed by persons who in other circumstances seemed so "normal" and "ordinary?"

After witnessing the Eichmann trial, Arendt revised her understanding of the role of Nazi ideological indoctrination. As she says in the passage cited above, "there was no sign in [Eichmann] of firm ideological convictions." What Arendt took to be the indisputable *phenomenon* of the banality of evil opened up a whole new line of questioning for her. For she became obsessed with asking "by what right I possessed and used it." What precisely she meant by the banality of evil and how it is related to thinking, willing, and judging became the themes with which she struggled in the unfinished *The Life of the Mind*. And the full story of her struggle with the meaning and consequences of the banality of evil is itself as complex and nuanced as her struggle with the meaning of radical evil. (In a sequel to this essay I plan to examine in detail her independent thinking about the banality of evil.)

In her recent book on Arendt, Margaret Conovan uses the metaphor of "thought trains" in describing what is so characteristic of Arendt as a thinker. Arendt always insisted that her thinking was set off by, and grounded in, events and experiences. What is so exciting about Arendt as a thinker (and sometimes so frustrating for her readers) is the ways in which her mind sets off in a variety of different ways—pursuing different "thought trains"—some of which we have not fully followed here; for example, how her understanding of evil is related to her understanding of goodness; how little evil has to do with our traditional notions of morality and ethics. We have seen, however what Arendt means by "thinking without banisters;" how she struggled to comprehend what appears so "thought defying"—the unprecedented evil manifested in twentieth-century totalitarianism. Her own ongoing struggle with various aspects of "the problem of evil" provides fresh insight into many other dimensions of her thinking. Her "dwelling on the horrors"—in particular totalitarian concentration camps—shaped the contours of her understanding of what is so distinctive and vital for *human* life—freedom, spontaneity, plurality, and natality. It is by unflinchingly looking into the abyss that she "discovered" what is quintessential to living a human life.

The terrible fact that one has to live with—the specter of totalitarianism—is that there is no ontological guarantee that these fragile human conditions will always exist; there is the real possibility that the concept of humanity itself can be eradicated. This is what totalitarianism sought to achieve with its ideological conviction that "everything is possible." This is an all too real and present danger. Parodying Heidegger, we might say this is the supreme danger—the danger of radical evil where human beings in their distinctness, uniqueness, and plurality become superfluous. And this is the danger that Arendt—in all her thinking—sought to combat.

Notes

1. Hannah Arendt, "Nightmare and Flight," reprinted in Arendt, *Essays in Understanding, 1930–1954*, ed. J. Kohn (New York: Harcourt Brace, 1994), p. 134.

2. Hannah Arendt, *The Life of the Mind* vol. 1, *Thinking* (New York: Harcourt Brace Jovanovich, 1981), p. 5.

3. Several editions of *The Origins of Totalitarianism* have been published. The most easily available is the third edition (1973) published by Harcourt Brace Jovanovich. This is the edition (*OT*) to which I normally refer. However, important changes were made in successive editions. *OT* I is the abbreviation that I use for the original 1951 edition published by Harcourt Brace; and *OT* II is the abbreviation I use for the 1958 second enlarged edition published by World Publishing: Meridian Books.

4. "Eichmann in Jerusalem: An Exchange of Letters between Gershom Scholem and Hannah Arendt" was originally published in *Encounter*, January 1964, pp. 51–56. The exchange is reprinted in Hannah Arendt: *The Jew as Pariah*, ed. R. H. Feldman (New York: Grove Press, 1978), pp. 240–251.

5. Elisabeth Young-Bruehl, *Hannah Arendt: For Love of the World* (New Haven: Yale University Press, 1982), p. 367.

6. Hannah Arendt, "The Concentration Camps," *Partisan Review* 15/7 (July 1948), pp. 743–63.

7. Ibid.

8. Arendt, it seems, uses "absolute" and "radical evil" as synonyms, although she favors "radical evil."

9. See Jaspers's letter, 15 February 1951, and Arendt's reply, 4 March 1952, in *Hannah Arendt–Karl Jaspers Correspondence 1926–1969*, ed. L. Kohler and H. Saner (New York: Harcourt Brace Jovanovich, 1992), p. 166.

10. See note 5.

11. Arendt, "The Concentration Camps," p. 758.

12. Ibid.

13. Hannah Arendt, *Eichmann in Jerusalem: A Report on the Banality of Evil*, revised and enlarged edition (New York: Viking, 1965), p. 288.

14. Concerning the interpretation of radical evil in Kant, see John Silber, "The Ethical Significance of Kant's *Religion*," introductory essay to *Religion within the Limits of Reason Alone*, trans. T. M. Greene and H. H. Hudson (New York: Harper and Row, 1960); Henry E. Allison, *Kant's Theory of Freedom* (New York: Cambridge University Press, 1990), especially chapter 8; and Sharon Anderson-Gold, "Kant's Rejection of Devilishness: The Limits of Human Volition," *Idealistic Studies*. Anderson-Gold claims "There is a certain parallel between Kant's concept of radical evil and Arendt's concept of banal evil in *Eichmann in Jerusalem*" (p. 48, n. 30).

15. Consider the following passage, which Arendt added to the 1958 (and subsequent editions) of *The Origins of Totalitarianism*.

> Total domination, which strives to organize the infinite plurality and differentiation of human beings as if all humanity were just one individual, is possible only if each and every person can be reduced to a never-changing identity of reactions, so that each of these bundles of reactions can be exchanged at random for any other. Totalitarian domination attempts to achieve this goal both through ideological indoctrination of the elite formations and through absolute terror in the camps; and the atrocities for which the elite formations are ruthlessly used become, as it were, the practical application of the ideological indoctrination—the testing ground in which the latter must prove itself—while the appalling spectacle of the camps themselves is supposed to furnish the "theoretical" verification of the ideology.
>
> The camps are meant not only to exterminate people and degrade human beings, but also serve the ghastly experiment of eliminating, under scientifically controlled conditions, spontaneity itself as an expression of human behavior and of transforming the human personality into a mere thing, into something that even animals are not; for Pavlov's dog, which, as we know, was trained to eat not when it was hungry but when a bell rang, was a perverted animal. (*OT*, p. 438)

16. Arendt, *Eichmann in Jerusalem*, p. 267.

17. Ibid., p. 287.

18. Margaret Canovan, *Hannah Arendt: A Reinterpretation of Her Political Thought* (Cambridge: Cambridge University Press, 1992), p. 24, n. 30. Canovan has written one of the most perceptive recent books on Arendt in which she makes extensive use of Arendt's unpublished manuscripts. She shows in detail how central *The Origins of Totalitarianism* is for all of Arendt's subsequent thinking. In her interpretation of the theory of totalitarianism Canovan brings out another central aspect of Arendt's theme of superfluousness—how dangerous totalitarian murderers are because they believe in their *own* superfluousness as

much as in that of all others; they abandon themselves to "superhuman laws of Nature and History."

19. Hannah Arendt, *The Human Condition* (Chicago: University of Chicago Press, 1958), pp. 9–10.

20. Hannah Arendt, "A Reply to Eric Voegelin's review of *The Origins of Totalitarianism*," *Review of Politics* 15 (January 1953), pp. 83–84.

21. Hannah Arendt, "Some Questions of Moral Philosophy," Arendt Archives in the Library of Congress, p. 024585.

22. Arendt, *The Life of the Mind*, p. 5.

23. *Arendt–Jaspers Correspondence*, pp. 54, 62.

24. "Eichmann in Jerusalem: An Exchange," p. 251.

25. *Arendt-Jaspers Correspondence*, p. 69.

26. In *The Human Condition*, when Arendt analyzes human action she explains that the "true hallmark" of those offenses we call "radical evil" is that they are unpunishable and unforgivable.

> The alternative to forgiveness, but by no means its opposite, is punishment, and both have in common that they attempt to put an end to something that without interference could go on endlessly. It is therefore quite significant, a structural element in the realm of human affairs, that men are unable to forgive what they cannot punish and they are unable to punish what has turned out to be unforgivable. This is the true hallmark of those offenses which, since Kant, we call "radical evil" and about whose nature so little is known, even to us who have been exposed to one of their rare outbursts on the public scene. All we know is that we can neither punish nor forgive such offenses and that they therefore transcend the realm of human affairs and the potentialities of human power, both of which they radically destroy wherever they make their appearance. (p. 241)

27. *Arendt-Jaspers Correspondence*, p. 62.

28. Arendt, *Eichmann in Jerusalem*, p. 287.

29. Arendt, *The Life of the Mind*, pp. 3–4.

7

Evil and Plurality: Hannah Arendt's Way to *The Life of the Mind*, I[1]

Jerome Kohn

"When all the world dissolves . . .
All places shall be hell"

Hannah Arendt was interested in what people do and the ways their doings affect the world, for better and worse. The focus here is not the natural earth but the human world, an artifice arising between men and women,[2] continuously affected by what they do to flourish and endure, and also by the ways they think in order to become reconciled to their existence. Mortal beings do not ask or come prepared to live in this world. It is rather as if they emerge from nowhere, first appearing as strangers, then communicating and interacting until, more or less gradually, they disappear. These notions of appearing and disappearing are relative not to the earth but to a *common* world, and they are not exactly the same as living and dying. Human lives are passed on the face of the earth, but are related, distinguished, and remembered congruent with the conditions and the limitations of an *enduring* world. Unlike the natural earth, the human artifice cannot be understood as if it were, in any sense, necessary or its course determined. That is why Arendt lays such stress on the stories of what men and women do as the only way of experiencing the meaning, of grasping the changes, the newness, and the play of the world. The great story of those stories, woven together, becomes human history, which also cannot be comprehended causally,[3] nor simply as a concatenation of events.[4] In the modern age, the history of the world has been variously and profoundly told as a tale of overall enhancement and progress. It is conceivable that one day an unremittingly hostile or offended nature may erupt or otherwise overwhelm all civilization and destroy its memory. Then any "posthistoric" survivors will be like "prehistoric" peoples, living without "a human world," without "human reality."[5] But apart from natural vicissitude, there are different and perhaps more conclusive ways that the world may be ruined and lost as the effect of what men do.

I

The Human Condition, published in 1958 and probably Arendt's most scrutinized book, deals analytically with three kinds of doing that together constitute the active life of human beings: labor, work, and action. "To think what we are doing" is, she tells us, the book's "central theme."[6] Except for the reversals time and circumstance have wrought in our understanding of active life—in particular the emergence during the last three centuries of a social realm in which the ancient separation of public from private life has become less distinct—her treatment of the activities themselves is positive. They rise from labor's capacity "to sustain life," proceed through work's ability "to build a durable world," and culminate in action, the realm in which "the relationships between men who live on the earth and inhabit the world" are established and maintained.[7]

But she had been led to her considerations of the modalities and possibilities of active life only after years of deliberating on a new form of political domination that tended, distinct from previous tyrannies, toward world destruction. She called it totalitarianism, and recognized concentration camps as its essential phenomena. In these places the institutions that for centuries had been carefully wrought to provide the human artifice with stability and durability were systematically eliminated. It was there that human beings were concentrated, massed together, neither distinct nor related, in preparation for extinction. Arendt saw this phenomenon as the appearance of hell on earth (*OT*, 445–47).[8] Wrested from its traditional location in an afterlife, where since Plato it had been used by temporal powers to keep the "multitudes" in check, hell had now been *realized* in the midst of life. This was what men had done, men of her own country and generation had established, filled and kept full places of torment on the earth's surface without (and this in sharp contrast to the traditional conception of hell) any humanly comprehensible pretension of justice. Thus what had been done was, for her, unprecedentedly evil. It was an evil that, unchecked, might ravage and perhaps obliterate the world before ultimately destroying itself. As such it defied human understanding, for it "exploded our categories of thought and our standards of judgment."[9]

The Origins of Totalitarianism was first published in 1951. Arendt, who wrote fast but thought long, labored over that passionate and intensely personal work for at least five years. Its form took shape gradually as she told of emerging "subterranean streams" and "crystallizing elements" that finally fully appeared in totalitarian regimes, breaking the thread of a long tradition and fundamentally altering human history. She changed the book in subsequent editions, adding to and deleting from it until its structure could no longer accommodate her thought. *The Origins of Totalitarianism* is, on the one hand, a work of erudition and reflection, presenting a startling interpretation of modern European intellectual currents and political events. But it is also a work of the imagination whose originality still disturbs readers and eludes analysis. Arendt's indignation and outrage at the evil men had done in bringing forth an "entirely new form of government," one that is now "an ever-present danger," are far from easily aligned with the "promise" of the "new beginning" with which she ultimately chose to end her book (*OT*, 478).[10]

In that respect it would be ironic to read *The Origins of Totalitarianism* solely or primarily as a study of a kind of political domination that once threatened the world, which the world rose up against and overcame, and which (to be sure) still demands the vigilance of peoples who enjoy some measure of freedom directed across their borders toward those who do not. That the book is more than an "introduction" or "background" to Arendt's subsequent thought is clear if one takes seriously her own "unavoidable conclusion," namely that what she had been concerned with was "no mere threat from the *outside.*" On the contrary, she believed that "the crisis of our century" not only did not disappear with the defeat of the Nazis or the death of Stalin, but that "the true predicaments of our time will assume their authentic form" only when both those forms of totalitarianism have "become a thing of the past" (*OT*, 460, emphasis added). The "true predicaments" of understanding and judging the unprecedented evil that became manifest under totalitarian domination are critically important for the human capacity to think as she conceived it. According to an ancient tradition, the solitary activity of the thinker had been considered a turning away from the realm of "becoming" in order to behold its "truth,"[11] thereby gaining access to a nonappearing and unchanging realm underlying or transcending the merely apparent one. But for Arendt, living in the midst of the twentieth century, the meaning (not the "truth") of "what man may do and the world may become" had become both urgent and also peculiarly difficult to experience, requiring a willingness and an ability, not typical of philosophers, to confront the transience and phenomenality of the "realm of human affairs ... *directly*," in "wonder" or "horror" ("Concern With Politics," *EU*, 445, emphasis added).

Later, in the early 1960s, Arendt's concerns were once again, and similarly, divided. On the one hand, *On Revolution*, published in 1963, is her most sustained and focused work of political analysis. In it she develops her conception of political action, which in *The Human Condition* had been classically evoked as the highest activity of active life, by tracing it in the revolutions of modern times. These were complex and perhaps never entirely successful attempts to establish new, or anew, the foundations of political freedom. On the other hand, her attendance at the trial of the Nazi bureaucrat Adolf Eichmann prompted her most controversial book, *Eichmann in Jerusalem: A Report on the Banality of Evil*, also published in 1963. *Eichmann in Jerusalem* clearly recalls, in many obvious ways, the last sections of *The Origins of Totalitarianism*, but in at least one important respect it differs. What in the earlier work, as well as in *The Human Condition*, she had called "radical" evil—what could be more radical than the reality of hell without justice?—is now, at least in the case of one Nazi functionary, termed *banal*. But the problem of the comprehension of evil is by no means thereby resolved, for in *Eichmann in Jerusalem* the "banality of evil" is emphatically stated as "word-and-thought-defying."[12]

When she spoke of "radical" evil Arendt was clearly influenced by Kant. When Kant deconstructed the unity of thought and being by demonstrating the "antinomies" of pure reason, the way was opened for him to conceive a specific "root" of evil (as distinct from "original sin") in man as he exists, a rational and sensuous being. There is no indication that Arendt agreed with Kant about the nature of such a root: for her it was rather that evil in itself, "absolute" evil, had become manifest in the world. But when she changed her terminology and spoke of the banality of evil and of its thought-defyingness, did she, as might be reasonably supposed, revert to a pre-Kantian conception of evil as "privation" or "deficiency" of being? Augustine, for example (always an important example for Arendt), in *De libero arbitrio voluntatis* had originally interpreted evil in terms of human freedom, the free choice of the will. And ultimately for him, evil in itself (*natura mala*) is "nothing": it "consumes" itself, it "cannot exist at all without the good," it "has no mode of existence except as an aspect [a "corruption"] of what is good."[13]

But it is in his *Confessions*, written after *De libero arbitrio voluntatis* and some twenty years before the *Enchiridion*, that Augustine, recounting the story of his conversion to faith in the God of Christ as the savior of the world, most vividly and personally wrestles with the problem of evil. He admits that he can "not see clearly" that "the will's free choice" is the "cause of evildoing."[14] The strength of Augustine's faith stems from the fact that he is fully and intimately aware of human weakness, of his own yearnings and failures, and especially of his ability to sin (there is no *imitatio Christi* in Augustine). Sin is, of course, pride, but there is also a sort of ignorance in man's turning from reliance on God, as the source of his being, to his own power to achieve the objects of his desires, expressed as concupiscence and lust.[15] In a great flash of poetic insight, Augustine imagines the whole of creation, all that is material and visible, but also all that is invisible, "all the angels and all spiritual things," arranged in "one vast mass," a "sort of sponge, huge but finite on every side." "Encircling, penetrating, and filling" this sponge "in all its parts" is God, imaged as an "infinite and immeasurable sea everywhere through measureless space." Augustine asks, "Where, then, is evil, and whence does it come and how has it crept in?" He asks, specifically, "*What is its root and what its seed*?" According to Augustine's image, as well as God's plan and ordering of the world as the scene of human salvation, man is "all good," even if a "lesser" good than God himself. "Whence, then, is evil?" Did God make man out of "evil matter," and was he powerless to convert "the whole lump" to good, or to destroy it and start afresh? Why, then, would he "*make anything at all* out of such stuff," why does anything or anyone exist? (*Conf* 7, 5, emphasis added).

Augustine answers this altogether new question, a question he later locates within the workings of his own mind (*quaestio mihi factus sum* [*Conf* 10, 33]), by saying that even if men are "corrupt" they are nevertheless good, for although "they could not be corrupted if they were supremely good, unless they were good they could not be corrupted." For "corruption harms, but unless it could diminish goodness it could not harm." This is the heart of Augustine's encounter with evil, and it is tied to his faith in the perfection of God. God is immutable and as such superior to his creation, which qua his creation is also good but its goodness is subject to alteration in time,[16] either increase or decrease. What is "corrupted" is "deprived of good," but if it were deprived of good altogether it would no longer be corruptible. It would have become incorruptible, and *as such its goodness would be augmented.* "What can be more monstrous," Augustine asks, than to suppose that what has lost "all good" has "become better?" Augustine's long search for the origin of evil therefore led to the conclusion that evil "has no substance at all." "Whatever is, is good," for otherwise it would "cease to exist" (*Conf* 7, 12).

In other words, it is not possible to do evil for the sake of evil. All sin and evildoing, no matter how wicked, are false pursuits of goods, of kinds of pleasure, or power, or whatever. For "there is no such thing as evil," nor is there anything from "beyond" God's creation "that can burst in and destroy the order which thou hast appointed for it." Only of nothing can it be said that it "should not be" (*Conf* 7, 13). In the later "handbook," Augustine writes that good and evil are not logical "contraries," for while "good can exist without evil ... evil cannot exist at all without good." When he says that there is "good in what is evil," he is not thinking only in terms of the whole order of creation, but also of evildoing and evildoers themselves. "For a man or an angel could exist and yet not be wicked, whereas there cannot be wickedness except in a man or an angel." It is "evil to be wicked," but "good to be a man, good to be an angel."[17]

It is not necessary, fortunately, to speculate whether or not Arendt shared anything like Augustine's faith to assess her debt, or to put it more precisely, her gratitude to him. Although Augustine is nowhere mentioned by name in *Eichmann in Jerusalem*, it is evident that he was present in her thought, as was Kant,[18] and that she was thinking with them both as she followed the train of her own thought, and its object, Eichmann. In the first place, the banality of the evil Arendt saw in Eichmann is not less but more real than the growth from any possible "root" of evil. Banal evil is able to spread over the face of the earth precisely because, like a "fungus," it has neither a "root" or a "seed." But because it is not a "substance" (in Augustinian terms), evil cannot be done for its own sake, just as, for virtually opposite reasons, it cannot be done for its own sake if it *is* radical and has a "root" that can be thought. For then (as Kant might have said) no rational being can be "determined to prove a villain" in the requisite sense.[19] Insofar as it has no "root," banal evil is not "demonic" (Arendt is no more Manichean than Augustine), yet nevertheless thought is "frustrated" by it, for what "*ought not to have happened*" is not "nothing."[20]

Furthermore, the case of Eichmann (in a sense a limiting case[21]) revealed to her that at least one evildoer was not "corruptible": by resisting any inclination he might have had to halt or hinder the evil he perpetrated, Eichmann believed he was doing his duty.[22] Whatever "banality" may mean to others, for Arendt it denotes a kind of behavior, unknown and unimagined by either Augustine or Kant. Conforming to the rules derived from the ideology with which the Nazi movement responded to the world in which it arose, a man had become conditioned to commit murder, albeit murder at a distance,without emotion,[23] without motive, and very much as Pavlov's dog was conditioned to salivate without feeling hunger. Eichmann was not a dog but a man, but no more than a conditioned animal did he exercise free choice. Arendt is intent to show throughout her "report" that Eichmann did not act spontaneously or take initiative, that he avoided responsibility and did not judge.[24] He did as he was bid.

As perhaps no one else, Arendt was struck by the absence of thought in Eichmann, a fact that became apparent to her in the sheer meaninglessness of the cliché-ridden accounts he gave of his doings and of himself, whether or not they had any moral relevance. One outstanding example was his speech from the gallows: while "in complete command of himself," in a situation that almost always calls forth some measure of thought—or remorse, shame, or defiance—Eichmann on the contrary managed to become "elated" and "forget" that it was he himself who was about to die (*EJ*, 252). Yet Eichmann's thoughtlessness is not, as has sometimes been suggested (and Arendt herself in her published work does not give the reader much direct help in this regard), either the completion or the solution of the problem of comprehending the banality of evil. It is indeed a first step: the thoughtlessness of conditioned behavior may permit, in the sense that it does not prevent, evildoing on a vast scale. But neither Eichmann nor anyone else was ever hanged for being thoughtless. Such a notion is ludicrous. Criminals are indicted for what they do and murderers are punished for the sake of the world, not for what goes on, or does not go on, in their inner lives (cf. *EJ*, 278; *LM* I, 182).

As a Nazi bureaucrat Eichmann had arranged for countless thousands of people, innocent of any crime and for the most part harmless nonbelligerents, to be "transported" to their deaths. It was probably because he was not particularly stupid, nor morally insane (in his own "muddled" way he distinguished between right and wrong), nor criminally motivated, nor an ideological anti-Semite, nor in any obvious psychological sense even "abnormal," that Arendt was able to discern in his *untroubled conscience* a connection between his thoughtlessness and the evil he perpetrated. "Only 'good people' are capable of having a bad conscience" (*LM* I, 5), yet it seems that Eichmann's conscience *would* have troubled him if, like many S.S. officers toward the end of the war (including Himmler himself), he *had* been corruptible (*EJ*, 116). That is at least part of the complexity of what Arendt means by the "banality of evil." What is certain is that after publishing her "report" on the proceedings in the Jerusalem courtroom, and in the wake of the bitter controversy that immediately ensued, she was impelled to reconsider and rethink the concept of the banality of evil in order to justify her use of it (*LM* I, 5).

The relation of philosophical thinking to the world was an old concern of Arendt's, but it never before had been so sharply focused. A new vista was opened on the traditional distinction between contemplative and active life. What might be the real relation of thinking—thinking as a pure, simple, and free activity—to evildoing? Can thinking itself be a kind of "conditioning" *against* it? (*LM* I, 3–5) What, conversely, is its relation to doing good, to "morality"? Moreover, early in her life Arendt had learned as a student of Augustine that there was more to mental life than thinking, that the mind itself was "trinitarian," and now she was led to question the "events and experiences" that were connected with the discovery of *different* mental activities, their interpretation throughout history, and what had become of them in "the modern age." "And behind all these seemingly academic problems," she wrote, "looms the question: How can we approach the problem of evil in an entirely secular setting?" (HA-KT). In this letter Arendt was asking for relief from her academic job, for time to think about the meaning of evil in a world in which traditional religious, moral, and even legal sanctions had become not only irrelevant but inverted. It was the failure of sociallv accepted rules, of the norms (or "yardsticks," as she preferred t[illegible] them) that were thought to govern (or "measure") human conduct, which fully determined Arendt's conception of the task of moral and political thought.

II

In the latter half of the 1960s and early 1970s, Arendt embarked on a variety of studies for her final, tremendously ambitious, yet strange work, *The Life of the Mind.* The existing two volumes comprise more than 400 pages, thus making it the longest, after *The Origins of Totalitarianism,* of any of her books, and it would have been the longest of them all had it been completed. Still, although there has been speculation about its final, unwritten part, the extant text has received relatively little attention and less analysis in the considerable body of scholarship devoted to Arendt. The tension between philosophy and politics, or thinking and acting, has been noted, but that is an old story in Arendt. From the fact that the tension is not resolved in the first volume on *Thinking,* it does not follow necessarily that Arendt intended to resolve it there. The opposition of free will and free action is likewise an old story, but neither in this case, by turning her attention to the faculty of the will in the second volume on *Willing,* does it follow that she intended to overcome it. The fact that many great philosophers throughout history have not exercised sound political judgment is a *very* old story in Arendt, and should make us at least think twice about what she might have meant in speaking of judging as the realization of "thinking, making it manifest in the world" (*LM* I, 193).

Does *The Life of the Mind* represent a change in Arendt's orientation from politics to philosophy? From the first she was an avid student of philosophy, and virtually all her work is shot through with philosophical reflection, more often than not polemical in nature. The last work may be more apparently philosophical than political, but to specify her own concerns from the first two volumes is by no means easy. The question of orientation seems crucial, and it is why I have been trying to trace a way—that there are other ways I have no doubt—which Arendt followed to *The Life of the Mind.* Before continuing to do so, a few general remarks about her last work may prove helpful. It was planned as a set of critical inquiries into three activities comprising mental life: thinking, willing, and judging, the last of which was not written at the time of her sudden death in December 1975. Fortunately we have her 1970 lecture course on Kant's political philosophy that in part deals with the faculty of judgment and as such is an important source for speculation as to what the final inquiry might have become. But it would have been odd, to say the least, if *The Life of the Mind* had culminated, as those lectures do, with a critical account of Kant's political philosophy.[25] Surely—there is so much evidence—the final part on the faculty of judgment was intended to be the completion of her own thought.

The tripartite structure of *The Life of the Mind* recalls the threefold division of labor, work, and action in *The Human Condition*, in the sense that Arendt was asking what we are *doing* when we are engaged in mental activities. But any attempt to coordinate the activities of active and mental life is stymied by the lack of symmetry between them. On the other hand, the relation of the tripartite structure to Kant's three Critiques is more suggestive and quite symmetrical, but with certain stipulations: Arendt is primarily concerned with the limitations of knowledge as set forth in the *Critique of Pure Reason*; Kant's understanding of the will in the *Critique of Practical Reason* differs markedly from Arendt's in *Willing*; and the *Critique of Judgment* is a work of aesthetic philosophy, which the unwritten *Judging* surely would not have been in anything like the same sense.

Arendt's last work also may be considered the *completion* of her earlier project on the activities of active life, for the traditional opposition of the *vita contemplativa* to the *vita activa* no longer holds. Mental activity, although reflective, is not contemplative in the usual sense.[26] For Arendt thinking does not attain, much less come to rest in "truth." Years earlier she had written to a friend that "Truth, on the contrary, is always the beginning of thought ... Thinking starts after an experience of truth has struck home, so to speak." She said then that the belief "that truth is a result which comes at the end of a thought process" is "probably ... the oldest fallacy of Western philosophy." For Arendt, as expressed here and elsewhere, truth is rather the a priori condition of the possibility of thought, as well as its "beginning."[27]

Put differently, but still in Arendt's idiom, when the mind has suffered the passion of wonder (or horror) at *what is*, at existence as such, thinking initiates a quest for meaning that is inseparable from its activity. She thus takes "meaning" as a gerund, or verbal noun, indicating thereby an active experience rather than the conclusion of one. In this sense (developed throughout much of *LM*, I) cognitive truth *is* the result not of thinking, but of sequential logical reasoning.[28] In Arendt all roads lead to activity, and mental activity in general is more sheerly active—less impeded—than either labor, work, or even action. Yet all mental activities, in one way or another, and to a greater or lesser extent, are in operation *withdrawn* from the world. In that sense they are "private" activities, but not, for her, *deprived* of the world. It is in Arendt's late and original inquiry (an inquiry with both Augustinian and Kantian roots to be sure) into the ways that nonappearing mental activities *affect* the world that her divergent concerns of the 1950s and early 1960s may be seen to coalesce. In the present context I am suggesting that in *The Life of the Mind*, among much else, Arendt sought to compose her long deliberations over evil, both evildoing and evildoers, at a deeper, inner level, and that encountering her on that level requires turning one's attention to a different word.

At the conclusion of her exemplary reinterpretation of Hannah Arendt's political thought, Margaret Canovan cites Arendt's belief "that each of the key political thinkers of the past 'has thrown one word into our world, has augmented it by this one word, because he responded rightly and thoughtfully to certain decisively new experiences of his time'."[29] Canovan goes on to say that "Arendt also 'augmented' the world by one word: the word 'plurality'." Canovan is clearly right: "the word 'plurality'" appears throughout Arendt's work and, in one way or another, informs virtually all the *topoi* (or occasions) of her thought.

In its reverberations and richness of contextual meanings, plurality is difficult to define. It connotes more than the many members of the human species and more than a collection of subjects or subjectivities. The reality of the whole realm of appearances, all that is various, beautiful, and new depends on the viewpoints of a plurality of spectators. Political reality, contingency as the price of freedom—given that we cannot know the ends of our actions we can only misconceive them as means to ends—makes no sense apart from a plurality of actors. Moreover, the evil Arendt at first called radical (and it may be one reason she did so) was its attempt to *eradicate* plurality from the face of the earth: to dehumanize human beings, to make them interchangeable, and above all to make them *superfluous*. While singularity is one opposite of plurality, the superfluity of masses of human creatures is likewise the opposite of a "plurality of unique beings" (*HC*, 176).[30]

Fifty years ago, with extraordinary effort, a totalitarian power was defeated by greater powers allied against it. The war against the Nazis is generally considered a "just" and necessary war and its outcome, despite doubts over strategic decisions such as the bombing of Dresden, as the victory of right over wrong. That is one thing. But the problem of understanding the unprecedented evil of totalitarianism is an entirely different matter, and judging that evil requires a way of thinking somehow reflecting the experience of superfluousness. For her that experience was forced by terror upon the victims of totalitarian domination, but it was also the *mass* experience from which the unreal or inverted "world" of totalitarianism was fabricated. Although seeing superfluity both in and out of the concentration and death camps has been the real source of vast misunderstanding regarding Arendt,[31] it also is the core of her concern with totalitarian evil and the complex of predicaments associated with it. Although Arendt never diminished, in terms of human suffering, the difference between the murdered and their murderers, from the very beginning her focus shifted from one to the other. In 1946, immediately after describing the hideous "primal equality" of those who were "dragged to their deaths ... like things that had neither body nor soul," she noted that "those whom an accident of birth condemned to death obeyed and functioned to the last moment as frictionlessly as those whom an accident of birth condemned to life" ("The Image of Hell," *EU*, 198). Long before encountering Eichmann she realized that the aim of totalitarianism was "to establish the superfluity of man," of man as such, of *all* men and women (*OT*, 457).

It is tenable to suggest that even Arendt's renowned description of the threefold process by which human beings in the camps were dispossessed of their humanity applies, mutatis mutandis, to their dispossessors. First there was the destruction of juridical or political man by placing him outside the law; second, the destruction of the moral person by rendering his conscience impotent; and third, by eliminating his uniqueness and spontaneity, the human individual was destroyed, as if the meaning of his life was not to have been a beginning but to have become a corpse (cf. *OT*, 447–454). The S.S. officers in charge of the camps were also in a position beyond the laws of any land (the Nazis never formally revoked the constitution of the Weimar Republic but scorned its laws when they conflicted with the Führer's will); "ideally" they had to rid themselves of any promptings of "conscience" or even feelings of "animal pity," and become "superhumanly inhuman" in order to carry out "a great task that occurs but once in 2000 years" (Himmler) (*EJ*, 105–106); and even Eichmann, in his own defense, spoke of "the obedience of corpses, (*Kadavergehorsam*)" (*EJ*, 135).

In a sense the first two parts of *The Origins of Totalitarianism* are the stories of how a people, the Jews, came to be regarded as superfluous and of how superfluous masses were brought about as a byproduct of the industrial revolution and, in particular, the policies of imperialism. They are long and complex stories, both pointing the way to alienation from a common world, a situation exacerbated after World War I by the presence of large numbers of stateless refugees and the economic burdens of unemployment, among other factors. But Arendt also has different thoughts about the meaning of superfluousness. Chief among them, perhaps, is the loss of *common sense*. When individuals are, for whatever reason, rejected from the plurality of men, no longer sharing common interests but thrown back upon themselves, then the common world begins to break down. That is just another way of naming the loss of common sense. Arendt's profound animosity against the "social" stems from this loss, for what she essentially means by it is the increasing *functionalization* or *socialization* of man that takes the place of common sense, the sense that orients us in the world.

Closely related, also, is what Arendt calls *loneliness*, which she distinguishes from the dialogic solitude of the thinker. It is always a possible human experience. As she puts it, "we have only to remind ourselves that one day we shall have to leave this common world which will go on as before and for whose continuity we are superfluous in order to realize loneliness" (*OT*, 476). Loneliness, however, when it is no longer a marginal experience for those who have lost their common sense and become functions of society is "so contradictory to the human condition of plurality that it is simply unbearable for any length of time [without] the company of God" (*HC*, 76). For Arendt loneliness is a condition of the "desert," and the human desert is where totalitarianism is likely to occur by appearing as an *answer* to the predicaments of those who live there.

It answers their predicaments by replacing lost common sense and a lost common world with "logical reasoning" (*OT*, 477), the self-evident logic of an idea, or ideology, thereby catching men up in a process that fabricates a literally senseless "world" in which "everything is possible." As Arendt sees it, the "totalitarian world and its ideologies ... reflect the radical aspect of the functionalization of men," offering them "salvation" from an atomized and meaningless existence by transforming them into "functions of some higher historical or natural forces" ("Religion and Politics," *EU*, 379). It destroys human *psyches*, whether those of "concentration camp inmates" or "S.S. men," making them both "inanimate" (*OT*, 441). And ultimately, that is the reason she can speak of thinking as "an ever-present faculty in everybody" and, in the same sentence, of *losing* that faculty as "an ever-present possibility for everybody" (*LM* I, 191). Arendt found a remarkable sentence in the preface to Montesquieu's *Spirit of the Laws*, which seems to presage this state of affairs:

> L'homme, cet être flexible, se pliant dans la société aux pensées et aux impressions des autres, est également capable de connaître sa propre nature lorsqu'on la lui montre, et d'en perdre jusqu'au sentiment lorsqu'on la lui dérobe. [Man, this flexible being, who submits himself in society to the thoughts and impressions of his fellow-men, is equally capable of knowing his own nature when it is shown to him and of losing it to the point where he has no realization that he is robbed of it.] ("A Reply to Eric Voegelin," *EU* 408, Arendt's translation)

Elsewhere she translates the last part of the sentence with a slightly different nuance: "losing the very sense of it (*d'en perdre jusqu'au sentiment*) when he is being robbed of it." She goes on to say: "What is envisaged here is ... the loss of the quest of meaning" ("Understanding and Politics," *EU*, 318). When the plurality of human beings is no longer *represented* in the dialogue of thought, that dialogue ceases.

Because for Arendt plurality was a pilot in uncharted seas, locating and conceptualizing a diversity of predicaments, the word itself may have functioned for her less as a concept than, in a somewhat Kantian sense, a schema. A schema is not an image of anything objective, of anything that can be made present again in the usual sense of an image, but nevertheless it is "something *like* an image ... beyond or between thought and sensibility." It is not "given to sensibility;" it "exists in thought" but is not, like a concept, "a product of thought." According to Kant, it is "an image for a concept," produced by "pure *a priori* imagination ... an art concealed in the depths of the human soul, whose real modes of activity nature is hardly likely ever to allow us to discover and to have open to our gaze." Without a priori imagination, which is not derived from but rather the source of experience, "there would be neither the objectivity of the world ... nor any possibility of communication" (*LK*, 81–84).[32]

Arendt was somewhat impatient with the notion of "an art concealed in the depths of the human soul," and her own analyses of mental processes in *The Life of the Mind* may be viewed as an attempt to reveal the experiential ground of plurality. Such an attempt is fraught with difficulty because there is nobody, no *one* to observe the thinking, willing, or judging ego. Not only because that ego does not appear to anyone else, but more important because it itself is divided and plural, mental activities can only be experienced. Thus a major task for Arendt is to find signs in the world that indicate their reality, their presence or absence. Her fidelity to the world at this level accounts for the specific quality, the "strangeness" of *The Life of the Mind* as a work of "philosophy," just as it also, at a different level, accounts for the passion that pervades her political writings.

III

Karl Jaspers once wrote that "there are two kinds of Kantians: those who settle forever in the framework of his categories, and those who, after reflecting, continue on the way with Kant."[33] There are many senses in which Arendt was "on the way with Kant," including her conviction that, regardless of what she sought to understand, understanding itself is always tied to the faculty of imagination.[34] For example, the break in tradition is an important *fact* for Arendt, not "part of the 'history of ideas' but of our political history, the history of our world" (*LM* I, 212). Understood as a "fact" that as such does not appear, the break in tradition is an insight of imagination. She does not take it from Kant, who, on the contrary, she finds firmly rooted "in a tradition that regards philosophy as essentially identical with contemplation, a tradition that Kant himself, half unknowingly, helped to destroy" ("What Is Existential Philosophy?" *EU*, 172). The philosophic consequences of what Kant did are fundamental for her own insight both at this relatively early period (1946) and thereafter. By placing severe limits to the scope of human knowledge, Kant had, for Arendt, liberated thinking from what at times she calls the "tyranny" of truth. For her the importance of such liberated thinking cannot be overstressed, especially in times of transition, when traditional moral standards have lost their validity and the human world is no longer stable, even though, as we have seen, it bears no "results." What matters most in the present context is that "we cannot expect any moral propositions or commandments, no final code of conduct from the thinking activity, least of all a new and now allegedly final definition of what is good and what is evil."[35]

When Arendt reflected on the meaning of the break in tradition she was very much "on the way" with Kant. "Kant robbed man of the ancient security in being by revealing the antinomy inherent in the structure of reason; and by his analysis of synthetic propositions, he proved that in any proposition that makes a statement about reality, we reach beyond the concept (the *essentia*) of any given thing" (*EU*, 168). More depends, for her, on Kant's shattering "of the ancient unity of thought and being than we generally realize in the history of secularization." By depriving man of access to a "realm of ideas and universal values" which previously had gone unchallenged, including certainty of the existence of God and of divine laws, Kant had "called into question the reality not only of the individual but also of everything." With the loss of philosophy's "faith in concepts" Arendt finds that "philosophers have never quite been able to shake ... the guilty conscience they feel for indulging in philosophy at all" (*EU*, 169–170).[36]

Of course Arendt is aware that Kant, by these same means, was intent on establishing an entirely new sense of human autonomy: "He is the first philosopher to attempt to understand man entirely within the context of laws inherent in man and to separate him out from the universal context of being." But moral autonomy in Kant's sense is a paradox for Arendt, and a tragic one. Withdrawn from the world, the solitary thinker is indeed free to do what is morally right, yet forfeits that freedom as soon as he acts into a "world alien to him." Thus Arendt states Kant's "paradoxical legacy . . . : just as man comes of age and is declared autonomous, he is also utterly debased." It is this conjunction of autonomy and debasement that becomes, in her long journey toward *The Life of the Mind*, a crucial consequence of "the antinomical structure of human being *as it is situated in the world*" (*EU*, 169–171, emphasis added).[37]

For the world, understood by Kant as subject to natural causality, has become not only "alien" to the solitary thinker but hostile to the plurality of men and women who inhabit it. Because thinking no longer guarantees reality we are homeless in the world in a twofold sense: spiritually homeless in the bereavement of God, and "physically" homeless in the sense that our conduct, what we deem right and wrong to do, can no longer reliably be guided by "universal" thoughts transcending the phenomenal world. Arendt says explicitly that the modern world's background of nihilism "came about through Kant." Of course Kant did not cause the broken bond between thought and reality, and if he was the first to articulate it he was also the first to reject and, as it were, refute in anticipation the consequences that Arendt almost two centuries later descried. It is not in Kant but in the "history of secularization" that man's loneliness, his loss of common sense, and his functionalization become apparent. In terms of totalitarian evil we have already seen how this history developed, but it is interesting that Arendt, when she thought with Kant, regarded it not in universalist terms of any sort, but in terms of individual human experience. And it is also interesting that, in view of these phenomena, she asked in purely secular terms the Augustinian question: "Why is there anybody rather than nobody?" For Arendt that is an anti-nihilistic question.[38]

After the publication of *The Origins of Totalitarianism* Arendt searched in Jaspers, Heidegger, and French existential and Catholic thinkers,[39] finding clues to be sure, but never precisely what she was looking for in order to understand human plurality. And she continued to read Kant, where by 1957, she found fresh illumination. On 29 August of that year Arendt wrote to Jaspers:

I'm reading the [*Critique of Judgment*] with increasing fascination. There, and not in the[*Critique of Practical Reason*], is where Kant's real political philosophy is hidden. His praise for "common sense," which is so often scorned; the phenomenon of taste taken seriously as the basic phenomenon of judgment . . . ; the "expanded mode of thought" that is part and parcel of judgment, so that one can think from someone else's point of view. The demand for communicativeness.

On 8 September Jaspers wrote back that he "would like to give a seminar on the [*Critique of Judgment*] with you right away." And, on 16 September, Arendt replied that

it would be fun to do a seminar, one on the beautiful, as Kant understood it, *as the quintessence of the worldliness* [*Weltlichkeit*] *of the world. For every single human being.* And on his so closely related concept of humanity, which only becomes possible through the ability to "fight" over the things about which one cannot "debate," because hope is "finding agreement among ourselves," even when one cannot finally convince the other.[40]

Arendt and Jaspers never taught that seminar, but one can be fairly sure they talked about the *Critique of Judgment* in the ongoing conversations they both cherished. Enthusiasm for the seminar may have waned when Jaspers discovered the highly unusual significance of Kant's text for Arendt, their profound "agreement" with one another *not* being a matter of her ability to "convince" him of it.[41] Arendt says rather bluntly in the first of her *Lectures on Kant's Political Philosophy* that "Kant became aware of the political *as distinguished from the social*, rather late in life," that is, in the period of "decrease of his mental faculties." Her point is not that he did not have time or energy to write a '"fourth Critique"' (of Political Reason) but that *The Critique of Judgment* "should have become the book that is otherwise missing in Kant's great work." Her ensuing lectures seek to "justify" this highly controversial claim (*LK*, 9).

For Arendt what Kant in the *Critique of Judgment* discerned as "aesthetical reflective judgments" or "judgments of taste" (relegating them to the realm of the beautiful) in fact constitutes a major philosophical discovery, that of the autonomous faculty of judgment. But insofar as it is autonomous it is also a major philosophical problem. The point is that the *criteria* of such judgments are always "empirical, and consequently can never serve as determinate *a priori* laws by which our judgment of taste must be directed. On the contrary, our judgment is the proper test of the correctness of the rules."[42] For Kant this meant that in judging some particular object to be beautiful the *judgment itself* will validate or invalidate any given rules or standards of beauty, will determine or, so to speak, "sit in judgment" on what is general. When I judge that the Madonna del Parto is beautiful and ought to be admired, I am not saying that it is beautiful because it is a painting (or a painting by Piero), any more than I am saying that it simply pleases me to look at it. Rather *this particular painting* has become the rule or standard of beauty in my judgment. In every case of aesthetic judgment it is a particular object that is judged. And this appears to be logically impossible. In *thinking* the particular when the particular alone is given and "the general standard has to be found"—as Kant defines reflective judgment[43]—there is nowhere even to look for a "general standard." There is nothing to rely on but other particulars, be they works of art or nature for which, also, a "general standard has to be found" ad infinitum: how can what is particular ever, rationally, become general?

If we read Kant through Arendt's eyes, concerned as she was to understand and judge events for which traditional categories and standards are inadequate, but which have nothing whatever to do with "aesthetics," we become aware of an altogether different dimension of this problem. If I judge that Auschwitz was wrong and ought never to have happened, and Auschwitz was unprecedented, what standard am I employing? If Auschwitz cannot become "general," what *meaning* has it apart from its "truth," the brute fact of its horror? How can that horror be understood so that it will not be forgotten—or denied, distorted, or in any number of ways mythologized—but be borne and made past? Even before writing *The Origins of Totalitarianism* Arendt had said that the "story of the Nazi-constructed hell is desperately needed for the future," for "[o]nly from this foundation, on which a new knowledge of man will rest, can our new insights, our new memories, our new deeds, take their point of departure" ("The Image of Hell," *EU*, 200).

But there is more than that to the philosophical problem. Kant calls judgment of the beautiful "reflective," and understands it in contrast to "determinate" judgment in which the particular *is* subsumed under a rule or standard. Determinate judgments figure in the first two Critiques, that is, in matters of knowledge and morality, but even in those cases the faculty of judgment is problematic. In the first Critique it is the schemata, previously mentioned, that make judgments relating general rules to particular phenomena *possible*, and examples that are their "go-carts." But there are no rules for the application of rules, and if there were there would have to be rules for the application of those rules ad infinitum: in every case the rule, "for the very reason that it is a rule, again demands guidance from judgment." Similarly, judgment is required to find the right example if the "go-cart" is not to go astray. In that context Kant calls judgment a "natural gift," and adds that there is "no remedy" for its lack, and more or less leaves it at that.[44]

But in the second Critique even the possibility of "judgment under laws of pure practical reason seems to be subject to special difficulties." For there simply is no correspondence between the "morally good," which is "supersensuous," and anything that "can be found in sensuous intuition." No schemata, as they are employed in theoretical reason, are therefore possible. What is now in question is the "law" of moral freedom, the law inherent in human reason, that alone determines the good will. It is only the nonappearing will, the intention of the agent "and not the action with reference to its consequences" that matters, and thus what is needed is a "schema (*if this word is suitable here*) of the law itself." For Kant, therefore, it cannot be imagination but rather cognition (*Verstand, intellectus* [cf. *LM* I, 13–14]) that determines the will in particular cases, and today it is at least questionable if Kant's recourse to a "typic" of pure practical reason, conforming to "the sensuous world as the type of an intelligible nature," a regulative idea, is convincing in regard to such determination.[45]

For Arendt it clearly is not.[46] And at least in part that is what turned her to investigate the autonomous faculty of judgment, how it operates and why it is, as she says, of "some relevance to a whole set of problems by which modern thought is haunted, especially to the problem of theory and practice and to all attempts to arrive at a halfway plausible theory of ethics" (*LM* I, 216). Arendt is not generally considered a moral but a political thinker, and for her (as for Aristotle) politics is the more inclusive category. If ultimately the two are inseparable, she is nevertheless an original moral thinker and, as usual, a controversial one. In any case, moral factors in matters of policy are always problematic, and never more so than today. And is not the difficulty of understanding why we as individuals, as well as peoples, ought *not* to behave immorally peculiarly prominent among "the true predicaments of our time"? In the very last pages of *Eichmann in Jerusalem* Arendt puts great emphasis on "individual moral responsibility" that, in regard to criminal acts, she distinguishes clearly from political responsibility. And it is surely no accident that her first published study for *The Life of the Mind* is entitled "Thinking and Moral Considerations" (see note 35 above).[47] In conclusion, I propose to turn briefly to two series of lectures that Arendt delivered in 1965 and 1966, entitled "Some Questions of Moral Philosophy" and "Basic Moral Propositions."[48]

IV

These lectures are, as far as I know, the first place that Arendt's interest in thinking, willing, and judging as a triad of mental activities appears. Unlike *The Life of the Mind*, they are not formal inquiries into the activities as such, but rather thinking, willing, and judging lead from one to the other in her ongoing discussion of moral issues. Thus there is rather strong evidence that this was at least one of the ways that Arendt followed to her final work. On the other hand, these lectures do not constitute anything like a conventional course in moral philosophy. Her impetus is, once again, totalitarian evil, and one of her main emphases is the inability of traditional moral and religious thought to deal with "evil for evil's sake" (QMP, 761).

But she is not concerned here with convinced Nazis, or any sort of criminal, but with all individuals. In part she is also concerned with the phenomenon of "conscience" that, in one way or another, generally has been thought to speak clearly and tell every "normal" person the difference between right and wrong, whether or not it is listened to and obeyed. In distinction to her political writings, it is not the world that is the immediate focus of her reflection, but the "self." I say "immediate" because eventually the two are brought together. In Arendt's outline of the topics of her lectures she indicates that she will address four questions: "Why is it better to suffer than to do wrong?"; "How can I tell right from wrong?"; "What does it mean to render good for evil?"; and "Who am I to judge?" The last question is meant to *connect* "moral and political activity." For present purposes this is important insofar as it suggests a way of *experiencing* the world as a "plurality of unique beings."

The first of the four questions is associated with Socrates, the second and fourth primarily with Kant, and the third with Jesus, Paul, and Augustine.[49] Nietzsche is cited throughout the lectures, not only as someone who saw "how shabby and meaningless morality had become" (QMP, 742), but more important as having discerned the "egoistic" or "self-related" nature of moral activity as such. His insights, particularly in *The Will to Power*, are stressed by Arendt, and although she considers them exemplary she places them in perspectives quite unlike Nietzsche's own. For instance, in her own day Arendt saw a supposedly sound and secure moral structure collapse and show itself in "the original meaning of the word, as a set of "*mores*, customs" that could be exchanged for another, diametrically opposite set, and then later re-exchanged (QMP, 744–745). Morality as *mores* may owe something to Nietzsche.[50] But then she is genuinely astonished that in "two thousand five hundred years of thought" no other "word" has been found for telling right from wrong (QMP, 740–741). Closely connected to this lack of a new word is her own experience, stemming from her "report" on Eichmann, for which she was widely criticized for having dared to *judge* not a system, or a function, or a cog in "administrative machinery," but an individual whose circumstances she had not shared (QMP, 747–749). Be that as it may, Arendt proceeds to her questions in relation to every human individual, for it certainly does concern us all "if, for want of a better term, there is something we call morality."

Why Is It Better to Suffer than to Do Wrong?

Socrates says (*Gorgias*, 482 b–c) "it would be better for me that my lyre or a chorus I direct were out of tune and loud with discord, and that most men should not agree with me and contradict me, rather than that I, *being* one, should be out of tune with myself and contradict myself." This *being* one was not a question of simple identity but meant for Socrates that he was related to a self and that this self was not an "illusion." He can leave the company of others with whom he is in disagreement, but he can never leave himself. It is better to suffer than do wrong because in the latter case he can never be quit of the wrongdoer. It is a question of living with oneself rather than of a transcendent standard of what is right. For Arendt this is the description of moral personalities in a philosophic sense, of those who, confronted with wrong, simply say "I cannot." To these persons, living with themselves, moral propositions are self-evident, "evident to themselves." But this "I cannot" is entirely negative and, as far as wrongdoing in the world is concerned, those who say it mainly refrain from acting at all. One of the most striking points Arendt makes in these lectures is that moral propositions reflect the self to the self, hence that they are anything but "selfless." Thus Aristotle speaks of the self-love (*philautos*) of the ethically good man (*Nic. Eth.* 1168b28–1169a5) and the Bible commands us to "Love thy neighbor as thyself." Neither implies that we should love ourselves as we might love another, but that we are *dependent* on ourselves as on no other. There is an experience of inner plurality in such morality, but it is not the world of other human beings that is "between," or of primary interest to, one *being* one. For philosophers and philosophy in general, according to Arendt, this is a "marginal" or "borderline" experience, but in Socrates it attained exemplary validity. Socrates did suffer rather than commit wrong as he saw it: having staked his life on his belief in the goodness of the inner dialogue of thought, he elected to die for the sake of his conviction.[51]

How Can I Tell Right from Wrong?

Arendt found in Kant's Categorical Imperative the strongest of all explanations of the phenomenon of "conscience," itself an experience of inner *plurality*. Kant himself thought of it as a "compass" pointing out right from wrong and available to everybody, "moral knowledge" but not "moral conduct" following as "a matter of course" (QMP, 751–752). For our concerns what is most important is "the issue of inclination and temptation." Why did Kant equate them? Every inclination to do right as well as wrong is a temptation to be led "astray" from the self. As Arendt puts it in a striking metaphor, it is "through inclination, through leaning out of myself as I may lean out of the window to look into the street, that I establish contact with the world." What matters for Kant is that in self-reflection, being with myself, I am *free* of all objects of inclination. None can "affect" me. Anything I may "desire or for which I may feel a natural affinity" does not arise from myself, and insofar as I am determined by anything other than my "reason and my will," by anything or even any person "outside" myself, I lose my autonomy. If I obey the law I give myself in the Categorical Imperative, I *cannot* do wrong. This is why Arendt finds the notions of *law* of freedom, *freedom* of the will, and the *good* will in Kant ultimately incoherent (QMP, 759–760).[52] To Arendt Kant is the greatest modern moral *philosopher*, because no more than Socrates does he take recourse in transcendent standards. She even questions if after him there has been moral philosophy worthy of the name (QMP, 756). Yet because the ultimate standard in Kant is responsibility to oneself—to respond only to oneself—Arendt sees even here an "evasion" of the problem of wrongdoing insofar as it may not be a matter of inclination. She did not mean, of course, that Kant evaded a problem he did not know of, but that she herself found in his moral thought little help in understanding the evil she had witnessed.

Who Am I to Judge?

Arendt says that Kant responded to the old Latin saying *Fiat justitia, pereat mundis* (Let justice be done though the world perish) by saying, in effect, that without justice life would have no meaning or worth (QMP, 742). Arendt might have replied: But what about the world? Arendt was never concerned with a *theory* of justice, yet at the same time nothing mattered more to her than the *doing* of justice, which goes to the heart of her final concern with the autonomous faculty of judgment. "Justice ... is a matter of judgment." If one had to be present in order to judge then obviously "the administration of justice" would be impossible (*EJ*, 295–296). She might have continued her reply to Kant by saying: If judgment completely disappeared, the human world would have already vanished. Action had defeated the Nazis in 1945, but in her view judgment was required to release the world from the conditions of totalitarian evil, which, after all, had occurred here "in the midst of human society [and] not on the moon" ("A Reply to Eric Voegelin," *EU*, 404).

It is by way of the faculty of judgment that morality and politics almost effortlessly fit together. Kant discovered the faculty of judgment in his "outrage" that any claim to validity might be left to the sheer subjectivity of taste, to the *De gustibus non disputandum est*, and thereby be shut off from reason. It is crucial in seeking to understand Arendt that, after the break in tradition—the philosophical implications of which were the spiritual and physical homelessness that Kant himself had adumbrated—morality, the whole "field of human intercourse and conduct," had shown itself in the twentieth century to be equally as problematical as aesthetics in the eighteenth. There had been a shocking "collapse of moral and religious standards" on the one hand, and, on the other, persons who had not been "sucked into the whirlwind" were by no means those who formerly had taken the supposed "objective validity" of those standards for granted. To put it simply, some people do what is right, and others do not. Some follow the example of Socrates and refuse to do wrong, but there are no valid rules, transcendent or otherwise, for doing right. This is not only the case in "catastrophic" matters—although it is there also—and it is fair to say that Arendt was as equally outraged by this situation as Kant had been regarding the arbitrariness of taste. It is interesting that in these lectures she takes the arbitrator, in his "disinterestedness" and "impartiality," as her model of the judge. He is someone who cannot "be at odds with the whole world," who must "renounce himself for the sake of others," and "overcome" his "egoism."

As opposed to subjectivity, Kant saw *common sense* as the "very ground from which judgment springs." He did not mean that common sense (*sensus communis*) was *another* sense all men have in common but a sixth sense, a community or communicative sense through which human beings *relate* to one another, become part of a community by communicating what their five "private" senses have commonly perceived. That does not refer to everything that one or more of our five senses presents to us, but only that which our common sense, through its "imaginative" or "representational" capacity, *shares* with others. When I judge reflectively I have no object but other subjects, who are absent, present to my mind: I *think* "in the place" of others, so that when I say "this is pleasant" I do not mean that "chicken soup," for instance, pleases me whether or not it pleases others. Rather, I claim agreement because my act of judging *is* taking others' taste into account. That is what imagination, in one way or another, always does—*it makes present what is absent*—and it is why Kant says of his own concern with reflective judgment, "That is beautiful which pleases in the mere act of judging it."[53] It is this activity, and not any "objects," that Arendt refers to in the final sentence of the extant text of *The Life of the Mind* when she says that an "analysis" of "the faculty of Judgment . . . may tell us what is involved in our pleasures and displeasures" (*LM*, II, 217).

What Arendt described as happening in the example of the chicken soup is what Kant calls an "enlarged mentality."[54] It is a literally "considerate" mentality, taking "into consideration" the viewpoints of others. But it is not a question of empathy or "counting noses" (statistical empathy). Arendt gives an example of what she means:

> Suppose I look at a specific slum dwelling and I perceive in this particular building the general notion which it does not exhibit directly, the notion of poverty and misery. I arrive at this notion by representing to myself how I would feel if I had to live there, that is, I try to think in the place of the slum-dweller. The judgment I come up with will by no means be the same as that of the inhabitants whom time and hopelessness may have dulled to the outrage of their condition, but it will be an outstanding example for my further judging of such matters.

The validity of reflective judgments is "exemplary," and it is by taking the positions or viewpoints of others, not their feelings, into account when I judge that I claim agreement. The more positions I take into account, the *plurality* of them, the greater will be the scope of the community in which the examples guiding my judgment are likely to be shared. Thus also the likelihood of gaining agreement in that community is increased, the condition of political solidarity. Although such exemplary validity is never certain and can always be contested by members of the judging community, it "is not up to people who refuse to judge to dispute my judgment." Here the *being* one *appears* as one in the world, speaking "with the single voice of one unexchangeable person . . . one unchangeable individual whose identity can never be mistaken for that of any other," claiming the agreement of other equally unique individuals (*OT*, 476). Judgment is not a matter of knowledge. It is not "objective" and universal, but, although it is the act of a subject, it not "subjective" either: it is *intersubjective* in a literal sense. My own viewpoint becomes increasingly *formed* by considering more and other viewpoints than my own. That is the sense in which the *plurality* of viewpoints and their communication constitutes, for Arendt, human reality and the reality of the human world. For however much a private, nonappearing world might be "intimately and exclusively [my] own," it would be "without reality" (*HC*, 199).

For Kant the moral law is absolute: it holds not only for every human being but also for every rational being in the universe, regardless of its nature in any other respect. It would hold for God and his angels, if they exist. Moreover, whatever the consequences of an autonomous agent's acts may be for others or the world, they can never affect the unqualified goodness of the moral law itself. The dutiful agent, like God, is unimpeachable and alone.

But when Kant inquired into the realm of the beautiful he discovered both the autonomy of the faculty of judgment and that in its autonomy it is never alone. Judgment is actual only *between* people, so that in effect he discovered what Arendt calls the law of human plurality: *Not Man but men inhabit the earth.* It was her discovery that the world can turn into a desert when that law is broken. For Arendt's concern with evil this is crucial. She writes that our "choice of company, our choice of those with whom we wish to spend our lives" is itself a judgment, guided by particular "examples of persons dead or alive." We would do well simply to avoid anyone who, for instance, had chosen "Bluebeard as his example." But what is more likely and far more dangerous is "indifference." The loss of common sense, the "unwillingness or inability to choose examples and relate to others through judgment," makes possible crimes dictated by the logic of ideas, literally senseless crimes that "human powers cannot remove because they are not caused by human or humanly understandable motives," crimes committed without passion that in a disgusting and sometimes comical sense *resist* inclination.[55] It is his own essence, *plurality*, that the dutiful criminal offends, which is the reason that his crimes are unreconcilable obstacles that confound understanding.

But it is for exactly the same reason that they can be judged. It is the meaning of "thought-defyingness"—the activity of thinking having reached an impasse, of having come up against something it cannot endow with meaning—that releases Arendt's own judgment. Her judgment lets "thought-defyingness" *appear* in the world as the meaning of the offenses she likens to the *skandala*, the stumbling blocks mentioned (without elaboration) by Jesus. Of their perpetrator Arendt cites Jesus' words, "It were better for him that a millstone were hanged about his neck and he cast into the sea" (Luke 17:2). She repeats them with emphasis, "It were better *for him* had he not been born." Her own judgment is remarkably similar. The last sentence of Arendt's lectures reads: "Therein lies the horror and, at the same time, the banality of evil." What can that mean but that the evildoer, without choosing to do so, does "evil for its own sake"—that he crosses a line, losing or "extinguishing" himself without even being aware of it? It is not possible to be reconciled to Auschwitz. In judging it, however, making it exemplarily valid for what should never have happened, it is possible to be reconciled to the world in which it did happen. It might seem that thinking in its depth and evil in its rootlessness meet in that judgment to signal the end of an era of world loss (*Weltlosigkeit*) and a century of world destruction. Today as always we are at a threshold, but it may be idle, or perhaps even banal, to dream of a new beginning as long as that judgment is denied the agreement it claims.[56]

Notes

1. A second paper will complete this study of the way, or at least a way, that brought Arendt to her last work, *The Life of the Mind* (New York, Harcourt Brace Jovanovich, 1978), vol. 1: *Thinking*, vol. 2: *Willing* (hereafter cited as *LM* I and *LM* II). It will be concerned with freedom and the faculty of the will in relation to plurality. I want to acknowledge several long conversations with Elisabeth Young-Bruehl, in the course of which this project took shape.

2. Arendt typically just says "men" (and sometimes, for convenience, I will also) when she wants to emphasize not the differences between the sexes but their common humanity. (In German she says *Menschen*, without gender specificity, not *Männer*.)

3. "Causality ... is an altogether alien and falsifying category in the historical sciences." The historian who "honestly believes in causality actually denies [his own] subject matter." H. Arendt, "Understanding and Politics" in *Essays in Understanding*, ed. J. Kohn (New York: Harcourt Brace, 1994), 319 (hereafter cited as *EU*).

4. "... no fact that is a cause is for that very reason historical ... A historian who takes this as his point of departure stops telling the sequence of events like the beads of a rosary." W. Benjamin, "Theses on the Philosophy of History" in *Illuminations*, ed. H. Arendt (New York: Schocken Books, 1969), 263.

5. H. Arendt, *The Origins of Totalitarianism*, 2d ed. (New York: Meridian Books, 1958), 192 (hereafter cited as *OT*).

6. H. Arendt, *The Human Condition* (Chicago: University of Chicago Press, 1958), 5 (hereafter cited as *HC*).

7. The quotations are from Arendt's letter to Kenneth Thompson of the Rockefeller Foundation, dated 31 March 1969, in the Arendt collection in the manuscript division of the Library of Congress (hereafter cited as HA-KT).

8. Cf. "The Image of Hell" and "A Reply to Eric Voegelin," *EU*, 199–200, 404.

9. "Understanding and Politics" in *EU*, 310. Significantly, Arendt's original manuscript bears the title "The Difficulties of Understanding" (cf. *EU*, xx).

10. In the second edition of *OT* she added an "Epilogue: Reflections on the Hungarian Revolution" as if to instantiate the "promise." It was dropped from all subsequent editions.

11. Throughout her work Arendt refers to Plato's image of the cave (*Republic* VII, 518 C–D) as the clearest example of such a turning.

12. H. Arendt, *Eichmann in Jerusalem: A Report on the Banality of Evil* (New York: Viking Press, 1963) 252 (henceforth cited as *EJ*).

13. Augustine, *Enchiridion*, Chapters XII–XIV.

14. Augustine, *Confessions* book 7, chapter 3 (hereafter cited as *Conf*).

15. Arendt's early work, *Der Liebesbegriff bei Augustin* (Berlin, 1929), considers in detail the role and forms of concupiscence in Augustine's thought.

16. "... this mutable world stands in flux (*constat et non constat*)" for in the world "mutability itself is apparent, in which tracts of time ... are made from changes of things" (*Conf* 7, 8).

17. Augustine, *Enchiridion*, Chapter XIV.

18. Kant is mentioned in a single, albeit a crucial passage (*EJ*, 135–137).

19. Arendt was extremely fond of quoting Shakespeare's *Richard III*, I, i, 30, as a poetic example, developed throughout the play, of the contradiction of the "self" in all such "determinations."

20. Cf. Arendt's letter to Gershom Scholem, 24 July 1963, in H. Arendt, *The Jew as Pariah*, ed. R. Feldman (New York: Grove Press, 1978) 251; "'What Remains? The Language Remains'," *EU*, 14.

21. It is fair to say that she saw in Eichmann "the model 'citizen' of a totalitarian state," whereas previously she had thought that "such a citizen can be produced only imperfectly outside the camps" (*OT*, 456). Eichmann's humanity was not removed from him by force or violence of any kind.

22. See chapter 8, "Duties of a Law-Abiding Citizen," *EJ*, 135–150, in particular Eichmann's declaration "that he had lived his whole life ... according to a Kantian definition of duty."

23. Arendt wholeheartedly agreed with the judgment of the district court—"it was more than correct, it was the truth"—that "'*the degree of responsibility increases as we draw farther away from the man who uses the fatal instrument with his own hands.*'" Virtually everything that

seemed to her most judicious in the lower court's judgment was ignored or contradicted by the court of appeal (*EJ*, 246–49, her emphasis).

24. During the trial, and to the detriment of his defense, no one, including Eichmann, remembered the one time he had acted and judged (*EJ*, 94).

25. *Lectures on Kant's Political Philosophy*, ed. R. Beiner (Chicago: University of Chicago Press, 1982) hereafter cited as *LK*. These lectures, as Beiner rightly says, "give access to ideas ... that [Arendt] herself did not live to develop in the way she intended." But they are in no sense a "substitute for the work that was not written" (*LK*, vii–viii).

26. In HA-KT Arendt writes that in *The Human Condition* "[i]t had been one of my purposes to criticize the traditional dichotomy [of the *vita contemplativa* and the *vita activa*] and the conceptual framework on which it rested." But at that time she "was perplexed and did not know adequately how to deal with mental processes."

27. Arendt to Mary McCarthy, 20 August 1954, in *Between Friends: The Correspondence of Hannah Arendt and Mary McCarthy*, ed. C. Brightman (New York: Harcourt Brace, 1995), 24–25.

28. Arendt became frustrated and impatient when students asked her about "the meaning of meaning," since for her that question confused what she was intent on distinguishing, meaning and truth. The meaning of a poem, for instance, is in the particular work of art only insofar as that "work" is *done*, either by the poet or (to use Heidegger's term) the poem's "preserver." Analogous to Arendt's distinction between meaning and both senses of truth is the difference between doing such work and (1) being struck by the sheer beauty of the poem and (2) a logical argument leading, presumably, to a poetic theory.

29. M. Canovan, *Hannah Arendt: A Reinterpretation of Her Political Thought* (Cambridge: Cambridge University Press, 1992) 280–281. The interior quotation is from Arendt's 1955 "Lectures on the History of Political Theory," in the Library of Congress's collection of her papers.

30. Arendt's judgment of Eichmann was also that he was guilty, essentially, of a crime against human plurality: the fact that "you supported and carried out a policy of not wanting *to share the earth* with the Jewish people and the people of a number of other nations is the reason, and the only reason, you must hang" (*EJ*, 279, emphasis added).

31. It lies behind her harsh criticism of some Jewish leaders who in their wisdom selected members—relatively superfluous ones it would seem—of their own people to precede them to the death camps. Arendt asks: "'Why did you cooperate in the destruction of your own people and, eventually, in your own ruin?'" If this "darkest chapter of the whole dark story" had come out at Eichmann's trial "the prosecution's general picture of a clear-cut division between persecutors and victims would have suffered greatly" (*EJ*, 124, 117, 120).

32. The quotations are from a report entitled "Imagination," included in *LK* but not part of the lectures themselves. Arendt delivered the report at the second meeting of a seminar on the *Critique of Judgment*, conducted concurrently with the lecture course, as a model for student reports that were to follow. The quotations from Kant are from the *Critique of Pure Reason*, B 180–181.

33. K. Jaspers, *Kant*, from *The Great Philosophers*, vol. 1, ed. H. Arendt (New York: Harcourt, Brace and World, 1962), 152.

34. Cf. "A Reply to Eric Voegelin," *EU*, 404. Imagination here has nothing to do with "fictional ability."

35. H. Arendt, "Thinking and Moral Considerations," *Social Research* 38/3 (1971), 425.

36. This may at least apply to Arendt: cf. the strong statement she made in 1964: "I have said good-bye to philosophy once and for all" ("What Remains? The Language Remains," *EU*, 2), and her late rejection of any "claim" or "ambition" to be a philosopher (*LM* I, 3).

37. In the same context Arendt calls this paradox "unfree freedom," a notion to be developed in the second part of the current project in regard to the "potential immortality" of the political realm.

38. In this paragraph I have drawn on and quoted from two batches of Arendt's lecture notes in the Library of Congress, headed "The Spiritual Quest of Modern Man: The Answer of the Existentialists, New School, 1952," and "Totalitarianism: Lecture Oberlin College, 10/28/54."

39. Cf. "Concern with Politics in Recent European Philosophical Thought," *EU*, 428–447.

40. *Hannah Arendt-Karl Jaspers Correspondence 1926–1969*, eds. L. Kohler and H. Saner (New York: Harcourt Brace Jovanovich, 1992) 318–321, emphasis added. In the last letter Arendt quotes from Kant's *Critique of Judgment* § 56, "Representation of the Antinomy of Taste." The "antinomy" is that we cannot dispute or "debate" judgments of taste because we lack "definite concepts" by which they could "be *decided* by proofs." Yet, because we contest or "fight" such judgments, somehow they must be "based on concepts."

41. Cf. Arendt's remarks on their conversations in *Hannah Arendt: The Recovery of the Public World*, ed. M. Hill (New York: St. Martin's Press, 1979), 338–339, where Kant is not mentioned by name but the matter under discussion ("*ein gute Vers ist ein gute Vers*") is entirely apropos. Arendt esteemed Jaspers's lucid reading of Kant—"Jaspers, the only disciple Kant ever had"—not least for the attention it pays to Kant's political thought. But certainly there is no hint of what Arendt makes of reflective judgment in Jaspers's work on Kant (see note 33 above). Nor is there any hint of it in "the only [disciple] Jaspers' ever had" (*LK*, 7), Hans Saner, whose *Kants Weg vom Krieg zum Frieden: Widerstreit und Einheit* (1967)—translated as *Kant's Political Thought: Its Origins and Development* (1973)—purports to show that Kant's "method" of proceeding from opposition to unity is political throughout.

42. The quotation is from a footnote in the *Critique of Pure Reason*, B 35–36, where Kant is justifying his use of the word "aesthetic" "for that doctrine of sensibility which is true science," as *opposed* to its use in judgments of taste.

43. *Critique of Judgment*, Introduction, IV.

44. *Critique of Pure Reason*, B 172–174. The whole passage, which immediately precedes the discussion of the "Schematism," is of interest.

45. *Critique of Practical Reason*, trans. L. B. Beck (Indianapolis: Bobbs-Merrill, 1956), 71–72, emphasis added. Again, the entire passage entitled "Of the Type of Pure Practical Judgment" is of great interest.

46. "This rigid morality [of Kant's] disregards sympathy and inclination; moreover, it becomes a real source for wrongdoing in all cases where no universal law, not even the

imagined law of pure reason, can determine what is right in a particular case" ("On the Nature of Totalitarianism," *EU*, 334).

47. This essay was first delivered at a conference held at the New School in October 1970. I attended it and can attest that Arendt's talk was received, by both her respondant and her audience, with a degree of stupefaction. (The essay is incorporated, virtually verbatim, into different parts of *LM* I.)

48. The lectures will be published in a forthcoming volume of Arendt's unpublished and uncollected writings. The introductory lecture of "Some Questions of Moral Philosophy" appears under that name in *Social Research* 61/4 (1994), hereafter cited as QMP. I want to thank Elizabeth M. Meade for applying, tirelessly, her keen editorial skills in the preparation of that text. Unannotated quotations in what follows are from the unpublished lectures.

49. The third question deals with action and the will and will be considered only in the second part of this project.

50. Cf. *The Will To Power*, nos. 265, 283.

51. Cf. N. A. Greenberg's "Socrates' Choice in the *Crito*" (*Harvard Studies in Classical Philology*, vol. 70, no. 1, 1965) 45–82, especially 76–77. Arendt frequently recommended this brilliant essay to students.

52. This incoherence depends on Arendt's understanding of the activity of willing, which relies heavily on Augustine and is beyond the scope of the present paper.

53. *Critique of Judgment*, §45.

54. *Critique of Judgment* §40 (*eine erweiterte Denkungsart*).

55. "... if [Eichmann] had anything on his conscience, it was not murder, but, as it turned out, that he had once slapped the face of Dr. Löwenherz, head of the Vienna Jewish community" (*EJ*, 46–47). Arendt really was "of the opinion that Eichmann was a buffoon" ("What Remains? The Language Remains," *EU*, 16).

56. To avoid misunderstanding—and to repeat—such "agreement" by no means precludes contestation. Arendt's judgment asks not for passive consent or "acquiescence" but to be heard as a voice of reason in the "tacit agreement, a sort of *consensus universalis*" (Tocqueville) that underlies every principle and possibility of republicanism (cf. *Crises of the Republic*, New York: Harcourt Brace Jovanovich, 1972, 85, 88).

8

The Banality of Philosophy: Arendt on Heidegger and Eichmann

Dana R. Villa

Hannah Arendt was a uniquely controversial thinker. From *The Origins of Totalitarianism* to *The Life of the Mind*, her work has occasioned vehement, mystified, and often outraged response. And although controversy attends her entire oeuvre, it particularly surrounds two moments. First, there is her description of the amazing shallowness of Adolf Eichmann's personality, a shallowness that led her to formulate the idea of "the banality of evil."[1] Second, there is her characterization of Heidegger's political engagement with National Socialism as an "error" in her tribute essay "Martin Heidegger at Eighty."[2] If the portrait of the "thoughtless" bureaucrat Eichmann scandalized because it stripped his monstrous deeds of any particularly wicked motivation, the description of the "unworldly" philosopher Heidegger provoked because it reduced 1933 to an "error in judgment." Arendt apparently let Heidegger off the hook, in a way that disallowed deeper investigation into the links between his philosophy and his politics.

Controversial in themselves, the analyses of Eichmann and Heidegger provoke something akin to disbelief when they are juxtaposed to the reflections contained in "Thinking and Moral Considerations."[3] In this 1971 essay, Arendt returns to the phenomenon of Eichmann's sheer thoughtlessness, wondering whether the presence and efficacy of conscience ultimately rests on the capacity for thought. From a theoretical standpoint the case of Eichmann exercised a peculiar fascination:

> This total absence of thinking attracted my interest. Is evildoing, not just the sins of omission but the sins of commission, possible in the absence of not merely

> "base motives" (as the law calls it) but of any motives at all, any particular prompting of interest or volition? Is wickedness, however we may define it, this being "determined to prove a villain," *not* a necessary condition for evildoing? Is our ability to judge, to tell right from wrong, beautiful from ugly, dependent upon our faculty of thought? Do the inability to think and a disastrous failure of what we commonly call conscience coincide? The question that imposed itself was: Could the activity of thinking as such, the habit of examining and reflecting upon whatever comes to pass ... could this activity be of such a nature that it "conditions" men against evildoing?[4]

Arendt's answer to this question, by way of a meditation on the "resultless" nature of thinking in general and the "dissolvant" quality of Socrates' thinking in particular, is a qualified yes. By throwing out of gear our everyday deduction of actions and judgments from ready-to-hand principles, thinking interrupts all doing and initiates an internal dialogue between me and myself.[5] It is this dialogue that Socrates tried to incite, and that Arendt traces back to the internal plurality of consciousness itself. Only those who have cultivated their inner plurality through the activity of thinking can be said to have truly awakened the voice of conscience. Thus thinking, although not an immediately political force, is of the greatest importance in those rare moments when "Things fall apart; the centre cannot hold/Mere anarchy is loosed upon the world." In such moments, when "everybody is swept away unthinkingly by what everybody else does and believes in," thinking asserts the claims of conscience. *Inaction*, the refusal to join in, becomes a kind of action.[6] Subjecting accepted principles, values, and norms to its dissolvant, purging effect, thinking and its "byproduct" conscience offer one of the few real bars to complicity with evil performed by popular political regimes.

In "Thinking and Moral Considerations" Arendt relies on the "representative figure" of Socrates to make her case for the moral efficacy of thinking. This case appears to be animated by a very traditional association of philosophy with virtue. In "the rare moments when the chips are down," thought and reflection promote the faculty of judgment, "the ability to tell right from wrong, beautiful from ugly."[7] Against Eichmann, whose thoughtlessness indicated a complete absence of judgment, Arendt poses the thinker Socrates, whose "resultless enterprise" has the all-important ability to prevent catastrophes, "at least for myself."[8]

The trouble with this of course is that the capacity for thought, which Heidegger possessed in spades, did nothing to prevent him from engaging with National Socialism in 1933. Indeed it did not even stop him from referring to "the inner truth and greatness" of the movement after his break with the ideologues of the party.[9] To put it bluntly, Heidegger presents Arendt with a problem: either she must give up her tradition-inspired association of philosophy with virtue, thinking with judgment, or she must make an exception in the case of Heidegger. In "Martin Heidegger at Eighty" she evidently chose the latter course.

Robert Bernasconi has suggested that it was not only personal loyalty to Heidegger that led Arendt to characterize the engagement of 1933 as an "error" but, more deeply, a loyalty to one of the most cherished prejudices of the Western philosophical tradition: the Socratic idea that thinking/philosophy makes us moral.[10] Heidegger is "excused" by the notion of an unfortunate but brief "change in residence" (from the withdrawn "abode of thinking" to the realm of human affairs), one that blinded him, as in the *Republic*'s cave allegory, to the reality of what he encountered.[11] The difference between Socrates and Heidegger is not between the genuine item and an impostor, but between a "passionate thinking" *performed* in the marketplace and one enacted more purely in seclusion and withdrawal.[12]

Is Bernasconi right? Is "Martin Heidegger at Eighty" a torturous attempt not only to preserve Heidegger's "rightful place in the history of thought," but also the ideal of philosophy as somehow the home of virtue?

I do not think this is the case. And although I have enormous problems with the characterization of Heidegger's engagement as an "error," it is important to see that Arendt's "defense" of Heidegger is, in fact, an attack on philosophy and the activity of thinking in its pure unadulterated form. She wants not to excuse Heidegger or defend philosophy so much as to reveal what George Kateb has called the "strange alliance" between *thoughtlessness* and *philosophy*.[13] In this regard, the critique of Heidegger that she mounts in *The Life of the Mind* should be seen as driving home her fundamental critical point: the "unworldliness" of the philosopher *does not* excuse him, rather, it reveals an emphatic form of alienation from the world, one that is the enemy of "ordinary" (Socratic) thinking and oddly harmonious with everyday thoughtlessness or preoccupation (what *Being and Time* dubbed "fallenness," *Verfallenheit*). As the representatives, respectively, of sheer thoughtlessness and a pure thinking, Eichmann and Heidegger are strangely complementary, despite the vast difference in their persons and actions.[14]

Three years before she attended Eichmann's trial, Arendt wrote in the prologue to *The Human Condition* that "thoughtlessness—the heedless recklessness or hopeless confusion or complacent repetition of "truths" which have become trivial and empty—seems to me among the outstanding characteristics of our time."[15] Confronted with the reality of Eichmann, she was forced to take the full moral-political measure of such thoughtlessness. Eichmann's apparently disingenuous insistence that "with the killing of Jews I had nothing to do" makes sense when placed against the background of his depthless "normality."[16]

Eichmann was neither a bald-faced liar nor feebleminded. He could in all honesty claim to have never killed anybody, nor even to have harbored any feelings of ill will toward the Jewish people, because of his almost pathological normality. He was, as Arendt observed, the kind of individual who always respected laws and followed orders, and whose conscience would have been troubled "only if he had not done what he had been ordered to do—to ship millions of men, women and children to their death with great zeal and the most meticulous care."[17] The fact that he insisted on the distinction between his duty as transport organizer and the act of killing in the extermination camps flowed not from a legalistic cynicism, but rather from a moral sensibility utterly defined by his station, its duties, and his respect for the laws of a criminal regime. Of course, no one believed him for a moment. To do so, as Arendt writes, would have been too disorienting:

> The judges did not believe him, because they were too good, and perhaps also too conscious of the very foundations of their profession, to admit that an average, "normal" person, neither feeble-minded nor indoctrinated nor cynical, could be perfectly incapable of telling right from wrong. They preferred to conclude from occasional lies that he was a liar—and missed the greatest moral and even legal challenge of the whole case.[18]

What becomes of our traditional moral-legal categories once we recognize that "no wicked heart . . . is necessary to cause great evil"?[19] How do we judge an individual who, precisely because of his excessive normality, is incapable of telling right from wrong? Such questions bring us up short. In the case of Eichmann, Arendt hardly intended them to mitigate his responsibility for his actions—quite the contrary.[20] The fact of monstrous deeds committed by an unmonstrous doer, however, demands an investigation into the ways such normalcy diminishes the capacity for moral judgment.

What struck Arendt during the course of his trial was Eichmann's habitual reliance on "stock phrases and self-invented clichés."[21] Over and over again, Eichmann's account of his life and activities turned on the availability of a different "elating cliché" by which the actual event—joining the S.S., acknowledging his role in the Extermination, facing the gallows—could be rendered innocuous. Armed with his clichés, Eichmann's version of events proved impervious to reality. Thus he could, when confronted, readily acknowledge his role: if he had not transported the Jews, "they would not have been delivered to the butcher."[22] But in his mind, this acknowledgment did not constitute an admission of guilt, because in wartime there is "nothing to admit": everyone's activities could be linked to killing. Hence Eichmann's completely inappropriate wish to "find peace with [his] former enemies," a self-formulated stock phrase that neatly converted his victims and the Israelis trying him into wartime opponents with whom he might honorably make amends.[23]

Eichmann's reliance on clichés and stock phrases to insulate himself from the reality and significance of his deeds was hardly atypical. As Arendt points out:

> Eichmann needed only to recall the past in order to feel assured that he was not lying and that he was not deceiving himself, for he and the world he lived in had once been in perfect harmony. And that German society of eighty million people had been shielded against reality and factuality by exactly the same means, the same self-deception, lies, and stupidity that had now become ingrained in Eichmann's mentality.[24]

What made Eichmann exceptional was his chameleonlike capacity to adapt to a new set of language rules and the roles such rules prescribed, whether S.S. man or war criminal. Eichmann's retreat from reality into the clichés of ideological thinking or postwar reconciliation signaled not a peculiar mendacity, but a bizarre and unsettling form of honesty: the honesty of the other-directed conformist who literally "never realized what he was doing."[25] It was not so much stupidity as sheer thoughtlessness that "predisposed him to become one of the greatest criminals of the period."[26] Eichmann was capable of performing great evil, and not merely being complicit with it, because the purity of his thoughtlessness insured a terrible "remoteness from reality." In the postscript to *Eichmann in Jerusalem* Arendt writes: "That such remoteness ... and such thoughtlessness can wreak more havoc than all the evil instincts taken together which, perhaps, are inherent in man—that was, in fact, the lesson one could learn in Jerusalem."[27]

At a conference held on her work in Toronto, in 1972, Arendt vehemently repudiated the idea that her analysis of the "banality of evil" demonstrated that "Eichmann is in each one of us."[28] Her goal was not to suggest that, given the right circumstances, we are all potential Eichmanns (nothing, in her view, could be further from the truth). Rather the sense in which her description of Eichmann's personality had a wider relevance has to do with a general atrophy in our powers of judgment. As the distance from "participation in judgment and authority" (Aristotle) increases in mass society, there is a broad-based decline in our capacity to "think without rules," that is, to *judge* moral and political matters.[29] With this decline comes an increasing reliance on the various "bannisters" (ready-to-hand principles and value judgments) that enable us to navigate everyday life without having to stop and think.

The trouble is that these bannisters work to prevent us from recognizing novel—and potentially disastrous—configurations. Worse, they lull us into a kind of automatic judgment in which what matters is not the singularity of the event or situation, but the availability of such "yardsticks." Eichmann's constant appeal to clichés and stock phrases is the *reductio ad absurdum* of this trend. What Arendt fears is not the "Eichmann in us all," nor even a "loss of values," but the increasingly automatic quality of our judgments.[30] This worry comes out quite clearly in her response to Hans Jonas in Toronto:

> If you go through such a situation [as totalitarianism], the first thing you know is the following: you *never* know how somebody will act. You have the surprise of your life! This goes throughout all layers of society and it goes throughout various distinctions between men. And if you want to make a generalization then you could say that those who were still very firmly convinced of the so-called old

values were the first to be ready to change their old values for a new set of values, provided they were given one. And I am afraid of this, because I think that the moment you give anybody a new set of values—or this famous "bannister"—you can immediately exchange it. And the only thing the guy gets used to is having a "bannister" and a set of values, no matter.[31]

Supplied with such a bannister, the "good family man" can become a fascist in good conscience.[32]

It is precisely such everyday thoughtlessness that led Arendt, by way of Eichmann, to posit an "inner connection between the ability or inability to think and the problem of evil."[33] Thinking, the internal dialogue between me and myself, turns out to be a prerequisite for the exercise of an autonomous faculty of judgment, one able to operate independently of all "bannisters." However, if the faculty of judgment—the "ability to tell right from wrong"—turns out to be dependent on the ability to think, then "we must be able to demand its exercise in every sane person no matter how erudite or ignorant, how intelligent or stupid he may prove to be."[34] The extraordinary thoughtlessness of Eichmann, combined with the everyday thoughtlessness of countless Germans, seems to suggest that we need philosophy, the "exercise of reason as the faculty of thought," to prevent evil.[35]

The need to inject thinking into the realm of unreflective everydayness sends Arendt in search of a "model" thinker, one whose activity was philosophical without making him a philosopher, one who never stopped being "a citizen among citizens."[36] In "Thinking and Moral Considerations" she finds such a model in Socrates.

In Arendt's view, what Socrates does, is to "make *public*, in discourse, the thinking process—the dialogue that soundlessly goes on within me, between me and myself."[37] Performing the thought process in the marketplace, Socrates interrupts the activities of his conversational partners, forcing them to stop and think. Acting not as a teacher, but rather as a kind of "electric ray," he paralyzed them with his own perplexity, dissolving the solid ground of their unreflective opinions. Thinking has a paralyzing effect, one manifest in the uncertainty it induces:

[This paralysis] is inherent in the stop and think, the interruption of all other activities, and it may have a paralyzing effect when you come out of it, no longer sure of what had seemed to you beyond doubt while you were unthinkingly engaged in whatever you were doing. If your action consisted in applying general rules of conduct to particular cases as they arise in ordinary life, then you will find yourself paralyzed because no such rules can withstand the winds of thought.[38]

Thinking is intrinsically dangerous: it "inevitably has a destructive, undermining effect on all established criteria, values, measurements for good and evil, in short on those customs and rules of conduct we treat of in morals and ethics."[39] It is "equally dangerous to all creeds and, by itself, does not bring forth any new creed."[40] Yet it is precisely in this seemingly nihilistic character of thought that Socrates (and Arendt) locate its "saving power."[41] Throwing the automatic derivation of judgment and action out of gear, thinking awakens conscience and prompts a withdrawal from "what everybody else does and believes in." Generally no friend of withdrawal and inaction, Arendt stresses their importance in emergency situations where the majority makes itself available for the legitimation of evil. At such moments, "thinking ceases to be a marginal affair in political matters."[42] It possesses the power to prevent catastrophe—if not for the polity, as Socrates hoped, at least for oneself. The hope is that the thinker's abstention from supporting an immoral course of action will prompt others to "stop and think."

But if Socrates provides a model for the political import of thinking, he also provides a model for thinking as a resultless, unworldly enterprise. Put in the context of *The Life of the Mind*, much of the material Arendt employs in "Thinking and Moral Considerations" takes on a different cast. Considered in terms of a phenomenology of thinking itself, the moral efficacy of thought emerges as *essentially* a "side effect," a "marginal affair."[43] For while Socrates' strangely destructive "midwifery" is, according to Arendt, "political by implication," the process it enacts has, strictly speaking, no goal beyond itself.[44] Thinking may indeed "condition" men against evildoing, but it does not aim at doing so. What drives thinking—Kant's "need of reason"—is no moral imperative, but a relentless quest for meaning.[45]

It is the nature of this quest that it constantly unmakes its own results, subjecting them to the destructive "wind of thought." The purer the thinker—and Arendt, like Heidegger, views Socrates as the "purest thinker of the West"[46]—the less likely he will succumb to the temptation to set down the "results" of this quest as a philosophy or (worse yet) a metaphysical system. Strictly speaking, thinking has no results. The one thing that from the standpoint of the world saves it from utter uselessness is the curious fact that it actualizes our inner plurality (what Arendt calls the "two-in-one"), and thereby stimulates the development of conscience.[47] The notion of a secular conscience that Socrates gives birth to when, in the *Gorgias*, he declares that "It would be better for me that my lyre or a chorus I directed should be out of tune and that multitudes of men should disagree with me than that I, *being one*, should be out of harmony with myself and contradict me," is not pregiven, but a byproduct of the restless, erotic quality of thought itself.[48]

The consideration of Socrates in *The Life of the Mind* underlines Arendt's ambivalence toward thinking in its "pure" form. If "Thinking and Moral Considerations" often seems one step away from the cliché that "critical thinking is very important," the restoration of this material to its "systematic" context brings out the suspense implicit in Arendt's positive valuation. She endorses thinking despite its unworldly quality, despite the fact that a rigorously maintained withdrawal from the world is the sine qua non of thought.[49] This withdrawal from the realm of the senses and the city of men makes thinking, as Plato noted in the *Phaedo*, resemble death. It is, in Arendt's formulation, "*contrary to the human condition.*"[50] The quest for meaning turns out to be animated by something akin to Nietzsche's "spirit of revenge," by a resentment of the human condition and a profound alienation from the world. Viewed from the perspective offered by *The Life of the Mind*, Arendt's Socrates is closer to Nietzsche's than to Mill's.[51] What saves his thought for Arendt is his performance in the marketplace: if it were not for this "impurity" Socratic thinking would be bereft of "byproducts," a pure enemy of worldliness.

If Socrates points, albeit obliquely, to the possibility of an "ordinary" thinking, a form of reflection we can legitimately demand of everyone, then Heidegger stands for thinking in its resolutely pure, most extraordinary form. Indeed, the distinction between the few and the many, basic to Greek thought, is turned by Heidegger against philosophy itself. Thus in the "Letter on Humanism" (1947), we read "What is needed in the present world crisis is less philosophy, but more attentiveness in thinking."[52] Heidegger thematizes the requirement of pure thought which most philosophy fails to live up to, namely, its utterly unpractical character. *Contra* the metaphysical tradition begun by Plato and

Aristotle, Heidegger insists that thinking be released from the demand that it serve either acting or making, *praxis* or *poiesis*. Qua theory, thinking has always been inscribed in what Heidegger calls a "technical" horizon.[53] Against this bad faith of philosophy, which is always anxious to prove its utility, Heidegger insists that "thinking is a deed. But a deed that also surpasses all *praxis*. Thinking towers above action and production, not through the grandeur of its achievement and not as a consequence of its effect, but through the humbleness of its inconsequential accomplishment."[54]

What is the nature of this humble accomplishment? Putting it somewhat crudely, thinking for Heidegger is a kind of therapy, one that overcomes what the "Letter on Humanism" calls "the widely and rapidly spreading devastation of language."[55] In the public sphere, language functions primarily as a means of communication; it is codified in a way "which decides in advance what is intelligible and what must be rejected as unintelligible."[56] In its reified, public form, language is essentially a tool, a "mere container for sundry preoccupations": its world-disclosive character fades into oblivion.

It is precisely the world-disclosive character of language—its capacity to "clear" a space within which beings can disclose themselves—that leads Heidegger to call it the "house of Being."[57] Thinking devotes itself to the recovery of this dimension of language. It attempts to offset the denaturing effects of communicative speech by *listening* to language rather than manipulating it. The hope is that such a meditative, responsive attitude toward language will allow it to slip back into its more primordial element, Being. Learning to "exist in the nameless," the thinker allows language to open out, to provide spaces of silence around those words and practices that seem so unquestionable from our everyday standpoint, the standpoint of doing and acting.[58] Adopting an attitude of "releasement" (*Gelassenheit*), thinking allows language to resonate beyond the understanding of Being that gives our form of life both coherence and self-evidence. Thus in its saying, thinking does not grasp, manipulate, or facilitate anything; thinking merely "brings the unspoken word of Being to language."[59] This is the nature of its humble accomplishment.

Thinking begins then with a withdrawal from the public sphere and a suspension of the perspective of doing and acting. Heidegger's objection to previous philosophy is that it is not thoughtful enough: it has not succeeded in bracketing the demands of practice and everydayness. Hence the peculiarly "technical" interpretation of thinking that rules the Western tradition from Plato and Aristotle to the present. In the metaphysical tradition, thinking is theory, the securing of atemporal grounds or standards for action. Practical philosophy stands in a deductive relation to first philosophy, the "science of grounds."[60]

We need to be clear about the nature of Heidegger's complaint. He is not saying that the problem with philosophy/metaphysics is that it is too worldly. On the contrary, he, like Arendt, views the tradition as defined by its withdrawal from the world to a realm of essence beyond that of "mere" appearance. It is in this "true realm" of pure or constant presence that philosophers from Plato forward have made their abode. Implicit in this withdrawal is an ontological and ethical hierarchy: metaphysics' two-world theory makes the value and meaning of *this* world depend on the accessibility of the "true" world. Withdrawal from the world of appearances—"taking on the color of the dead"—ultimately provides access to "invisible yardsticks" for the realm of human affairs. Armed with the idea of the Good, philosophers since Plato have been able to return to the cave with the demand that this "shadow realm" conform to the measures discovered in the realm of essence or pure reason. For metaphysics, the withdrawal from the world of appearance/realm of human affairs is, in fact, a prelude to the subjugation of that realm. The idea of first principles expresses, in a nutshell, the intensity of philosophy's will to power.

As Arendt points out in "What is Authority?," this appeal to transcendent standards defines the concept of authority in the West.[61] However—and this is the theme of the remarkable introduction to *The Life of the Mind*—this appeal is no longer possible: God is dead. Glossing Nietzsche's aphorism from *The Gay Science* and the section of *Twilight of the Idols* entitled "How the true world became a fable," Arendt writes:

> What has come to an end is the basic distinction between the sensory and the suprasensory, together with the notion, at least as old as Parmenides, that whatever is not given to the senses—God or Being or the First Principles and Causes (*archai*) or the Ideas—is more real, more truthful, more meaningful than what appears, that it is not just *beyond* sense perception but *above* the world of the senses. What is "dead" is not only the localization of such "eternal truths" but also the distinction itself.[62]

With the collapse of the hierarchical relation posited between the suprasensory and the realm of human affairs, thinking finds itself confronted by two possibilities. It can return to the realm of appearances, now viewing that realm as the only locus of meaning (the tack taken by Arendt), or it can consummate its prior withdrawal, severing the last inauthentic link to the world of "sundry preoccupations." In other words, the collapse of the distinction between the "real" and "apparent" world implies the closure of the "technical" interpretation of thought. Liberated from the mission of securing atemporal "bannisters" for the realm of human affairs, thinking can become either the prolegomenon to judgment or it can at last fully realize its authentic, unworldly impulse: the pursuit of the invisible, of the *absent.*[63]

There is never any doubt as to which path Heidegger takes at "the end of philosophy." His pure or "passionate" thinking is carried out in a "place of stillness," a solitary realm far from the habituations of human affairs.[64] For Arendt, the tenacity and singlemindedness of this withdrawal is nothing less than heroic. However, the pure thinking enabled by the collapse of metaphysics (a collapse Heidegger makes no small contribution to[65]) carries its own specific dangers. The most extreme danger is the remoteness the activity of such pure thought demands:

> Seen from the perspective of thinking's abode, "withdrawal of Being" or "oblivion of Being" reigns in the ordinary world which surrounds the thinker's residence, the "familiar realms . . . of everyday life," i.e., the loss of that with which thinking—which by nature clings to the absent—is concerned. Annulment of this "withdrawal," on the other side, is always paid for by a withdrawal from the world of human affairs, and this remoteness is never more manifest than when thinking ponders exactly those affairs, training them into its own sequestered stillness.[66]

As her critique in *The Life of the Mind* makes clear, Arendt sees Heidegger as concerned from first to last with overcoming the "self-withdrawal" of Being through such sequestered stillness. Hence her interpretation of *Being and Time* as centering on an "entirely inner action" by which "man opens himself to the actuality of being thrown."[67] This inner action is, according to Arendt, nothing other than thought. Hence her interpretation of Heidegger's "reversal" (the *Kehre*) as a radical desubjectivization of thinking, one designed to allow the concealed history of Being (*Seinsgeschichte*) to come to pass in a thinking that obeys not the will, but the call of Being.[68] Hence, finally, her startling interpretation of the 1946 essay *Der Spruch des Anaximander*, in which she discovers Heidegger despairing of any trace of Being to be found in the realm of human history. Here thinking is no longer the only "genuine" acting, given that *all* acting is erring, going astray.[69] The only thing left for the thinker is to commune with Being in its enduring withdrawal, its perennial absence.

According to Arendt, the arc of Heidegger's thought is from the more or less traditional philosophical withdrawal of *Being and Time* (the polarity of *Eigentlichkeit/Uneigentlichkeit*), through the spectatorial distance of *Seinsgeschichte*, culminating in the truly radical remoteness of the "reversal" and the will to self-obliteration that is found in the Anaximander essay. Far more than Plato, Heidegger succeeds in taking on the color of the dead. He suspends not only the needs of the self, but even the thinking ego's instinct for self-preservation. This is world alienation with a vengeance.

The extreme quality of the late Heidegger's world alienation—extreme even by the standards of a philosophical tradition that cultivates it—is, Arendt suggests, a function of the moment he left the solitary abode of thought and got involved in the realm of human affairs.[70] The "shock of the collision" revealed to Heidegger the extent to which the will to power still animated his own thinking, and the need for a even more radical purging of its effects. Thus, the "will-not-to-will" is, according to Arendt, the force underlying the *Kehre* and his later thought. The engagement of 1933 revealed to Heidegger that his thought had not attained sufficient remoteness; 1945 revealed that the realm of human history did not bear even the trace of the meaning that thinking so relentlessly pursues.

If Heidegger's self-criticism questions the degree of his own remoteness from the realm of human affairs, Arendt's critique reveals the degree to which this remoteness characterizes the entirety of his thought (including even *Being and Time* with its existential themes of worldliness and historicity). Heidegger's "cure" for the "error" born of his remoteness in 1933 is, unsurprisingly, more of the same. And it is here that the "strange alliance" between philosophy and thoughtlessness reveals itself. For if the "bannisters" provided by metaphysical thought encouraged a kind of thoughtlessness, the closure of metaphysics leaves philosophical thought free to pursue its solitary vocation unburdened by any residual "care for the world." The irony is that while metaphysical thinking denied the reflective character of judgment in favor of a crudely deductive model, it at least retained a connection between thinking and judgment. In Heidegger, that is, in the purity of "extraordinary" post-metaphysical thought, this connection between thinking and judgment is severed once and for all. It is not only evasiveness that leads him in the *Spiegel* interview to refuse to offer philosophical guidance.[71]

In "Martin Heidegger at Eighty" Arendt repeats the famous story about how the philosopher Thales, his eyes fixed on the stars, fails to see where he is going and stumbles into a well. This provokes an outburst of laughter from a Thracian girl who witnesses the plunge, astonished that "someone who wants to know the sky should be so ignorant of what lies at his feet."[72] Taken at face value, the story presents Thales as a pre-Socratic absentminded professor. The implication seems to be that Heidegger was similarly absentminded and that 1933 was his stumble into the abyss.

There is, however, another way of reading Arendt's essay, one that does not reduce it to the level of lame apologetics. As I have tried to suggest, Arendt's persistent emphasis on the withdrawn quality of Heidegger's thought about Being does not simply reduce 1933 to an "error in judgment." Rather the point is that Heidegger pushes the philosophical devaluation of judgment qua independent faculty to new extremes, ultimately achieving an unprecedented autonomy for thought. The engagement of 1933 points not to an "error in judgment," but to the far more disturbing fact that *there was no judgment.*

That this was not a "mistake" to be rectified by sad experience is shown by Heidegger's postwar silence about the Holocaust. The same astonishing absence of judgment that led to 1933 appears again in Heidegger's inability to provide a thinking response to this cataclysmic event. The "strange alliance" between philosophy and thoughtlessness is manifest in the way their respective modes of alienation from the world (thinking withdrawal versus unthinking absorption in everydayness) issue in the same result: the death of judgment. The two extremes of Eichmann's extraordinary shallowness and Heidegger's extraordinary thinking meet at this zero point. The philosopher's lack of judgment, it is true, does not lead to any crime against humanity. But it does make him incapable of recognizing what "lies at his feet"—even after he has crawled out of the abyss.[73]

Notes

1. Hannah Arendt, *Eichmann in Jerusalem: A Report on the Banality of Evil* (New York: Viking Press, 1963), pp. 21–7, 49, and 252.

2. Hannah Arendt, "Martin Heidegger at Eighty," in Michael Murray, ed., *Heidegger and Modern Philosophy* (New Haven: Yale University Press, 1978), hereinafter cited as *MHE.*

3. Hannah Arendt, "Thinking and Moral Considerations," in *Social Research: Fiftieth Anniversary Issue*, 1984. Hereinafter cited as *TMC.*

4. Arendt, *TMC*, p. 8.

5. Ibid., pp. 13, 33.

6. Ibid., p. 36.

7. Ibid., p. 37.

8. Ibid.

9. See Martin Heidegger, "The Self-Assertion of the German University" in Gunther Neske and Emil Kettering, eds. *Martin Heidegger and National Socialism* (New York: Paragon House, 1990). The "inner truth and greatness" remark comes, of course, from *An Introduction to Metaphysics*, trans. Ralph Manheim (New Haven: Yale University Press, 1959), p. 199.

10. Robert Bernasconi, "Habermas, Arendt, and Levinas on the Philosopher's 'Error': Tracking the Diabolical in Heidegger," in *Heidegger in Question: The Art of Existence* (Atlantic Highlands, NJ: Humanities Press International, 1993), p. 70.

11. Arendt, *MHE*, pp. 300–302.

12. See Arendt's description of Socrates' activity in her *Lectures on Kant's Political Philosophy*, ed. Ronald Beiner (Chicago: University of Chicago Press, 1982), p. 37.

13. George Kateb, *Hannah Arendt: Politics, Conscience, Evil* (Totowa, NJ: Rowman and Allanheld, 1984), p. 195.

14. I do not want to be read as suggesting some sort of "moral equivalence" between Eichmann and Heidegger—an obviously absurd notion that even Heidegger's contemporary detractors would refuse.

15. Hannah Arendt, *The Human Condition* (Chicago: University of Chicago Press, 1958), p. 5. Bernasconi's essay reminded me of this passage.

16. Arendt, *Eichmann in Jerusalem*, p. 23.

17. Ibid., p. 25.

18. Ibid., p. 26.

19. Arendt, *TMC*, p. 13.

20. See, in this regard, *Eichmann in Jerusalem*, pp. 277–279; also 294–295.

21. Ibid., p. 49.

22. Ibid., p. 52.

23. Ibid., p. 53.

24. Ibid., p.52.

25. Ibid., p. 287.

26. Ibid., pp. 287–288.

27. Ibid., p. 288.

28. Hannah Arendt, "On Hannah Arendt," in Melvin Hill, ed. *Hannah Arendt: The Recovery of the Public World* (New York: St. Martin's, 1979), p. 308.

29. This worry makes its explicit appearance with John Stuart Mill's reflections in *On Representative Government.*

30. See Ronald Beiner's analysis in his "Interpretive Essay" in Arendt's *Lectures on Kant's Political Philosophy.*

31. Arendt, "On Hannah Arendt," p. 314. Cf. Arendt, *TMC*, pp. 26–27.

32. Hannah Arendt, *The Jew as Pariah*, ed. Ron H. Feldman (New York: Grove Press, 1978), pp. 231–232. Cf. Hannah Arendt, *The Life of the Mind*, vol. 1 (New York: Harcourt Brace Jovanovich, 1978), p. 177 (hereafter cited as *LM*).

33. Arendt, *TMC*, p. 15.

34. Ibid., p. 13.

35. Ibid.

36. Ibid., p. 17. Cf. Arendt's treatment of Socrates in "Philosophy and Politics," *Social Research* vol. 57, no. 1 (spring 1990).

37. Arendt, *Lectures on Kant's Political Philosophy*, p. 37.

38. Arendt, *TMC*, p. 25.

39. Ibid., p. 24.

40. Ibid., p. 26.

41. See the *Apology*, 30a, and Arendt, *TMC*, p. 26.

42. Ibid., p. 36.

43. Arendt, *LM*, vol. 1, p. 192.

44. Ibid., pp. 15, 174, 192.

45. Ibid., p. 15.

46. Ibid., p. 174. The phrase is from Heidegger's *What Is Called Thinking?*

47. Ibid., pp. 179–193.

48. Plato, *Gorgias*, 482c. Quoted in Arendt, *LM*, vol. 1, p. 181.

49. Arendt, *LM*, vol. 1, pp. 69–80.

50. Ibid., p. 78.

51. It is here that the analysis offered in *LM* connects with that offered in *The Human Condition*. Despite the strong distinction Arendt makes between the thinking activity and contemplation, it is clear that the two share an underlying continuity in their withdrawal from the world.

52. Martin Heidegger, "Letter on Humanism," in *Basic Writings*, ed. David Farrell Krell (New York: Harper and Row, 1977), p. 242.

53. Ibid., p. 194.

54. Ibid., p. 239.

55. Ibid., pp. 197–198.

56. Ibid., p. 199.

57. Ibid., p. 239.

58. See Richard Rorty, "Heidegger, Contingency and Pragmatism," in his *Essays on Heidegger and Others* (New York: Cambridge University Press, 1990), p. 31.

59. Heidegger, "Letter on Humanism," pp. 193, 239.

60. Heidegger, "The End of Philosophy and the Task of Thinking," in *Basic Writings*. See also Reiner Schurmann, *Heidegger on Being and Acting: From Principles to Anarchy* (Indianapolis: University of Indiana Press, 1987), pp. 1–8.

61. Hannah Arendt, "What Is Authority?," in her *Between Past and Future* (New York: Penguin Books, 1977), pp. 97–98, 104–115.

62. Arendt, *LM*, vol. 1, p. 10. Cf. Heidegger, "The Word of Nietzsche: 'God is Dead,'" in his *The Question Concerning Technology and Other Essays*, trans. William Lovitt (New York: Harper and Row, 1977), p. 64.

63. Ibid., pp. 75–76.

64. Arendt, *MHE*, p. 299. The "place of stillness" is from Heidegger, *Zur Sache des Denkens*.

65. Ibid., p. 296.

66. Ibid., p. 300.

67. Arendt, *LM*, vol. 2, p. 185.

68. Ibid., pp. 174–175.

69. Ibid., p. 194.

70. Arendt, *MHE*, pp. 300–301.

71. Martin Heidegger, "*Der Spiegel* Interview," in *Martin Heidegger and National Socialism*, ed. Gunther Neske and Emil Kettering, p. 60.

72. Arendt, *MHE*, p. 301.

73. See, in this regard, the analyses of Philippe Lacoue-Labarthe and Richard Bernstein in *Heidegger, Art and Politics* (Cambridge, MA: Basil Blackwell, 1990), and *The New Constellation: The Ethical-Political Horizons of Modernity/Postmodernity* (Cambridge: MIT Press, 1992), chapter 4.

III

Self and World

9

Thinking about the Self

Suzanne Duvall Jacobitti

Many contemporary political theorists have taken to thinking about the self. In America, this recent interest in the self may have been sparked by Michael Sandel's criticisms of John Rawls's *A Theory of Justice*. Rawls had offered a new approach to defend liberal principles, an approach that purported to avoid controversial normative and philosophical commitments. His principles of justice, he claimed, were simply those that would be chosen by any rational human self as long as the choice was made in ignorance of its particular characteristics, socioeconomic status, and preferences regarding the good life. Sandel attacked as untenable this concept of an abstract, disembodied self, "unencumbered" by ends or purposes or community attachments. Real selves, he argued, are always "thick" with particular characteristics stemming from genetic, family, and cultural influences; social and economic advantages or disadvantages; and concepts of the good life.[1]

Sandel's notion of a "situated" self found resonance with many critics of liberal proceduralism and individualism. Real, concrete, living selves have strong social attachments to family, friends, and community, as well as to shared moral and religious traditions. Real selves are not neutral among versions of the good life and do not want their political principles and institutions to be. Liberal neutrality seemed to many communitarians to be the cause of a decline of morality, patriotism, and community values that has plagued America since the 1960s.

Liberals have not let these charges go unanswered. Few liberals would deny that all real selves are "situated," in the sense that each concrete self begins in a particular genetic, cultural, and social situation. What is at issue is whether a self can or should be encouraged to transcend that situation. A self that cannot transcend its nature and nurture at all would seem incapable of critical reflection or free action. Such a self could not justly be held responsible for its actions, nor would it have the moral dignity to be worthy of having rights. Finally, a community of wholly situated selves, committed to their inherited traditions and unable to reflect critically on them, would surely be oppressive to minorities of all kinds. Defending liberal notions of rights, freedom, and responsibility, then, requires a stronger concept of the self than communitarians provide.[2]

Beyond the debate between communitarians and liberals, there are other reasons to think about the self. Feminists debate whether and to what extent the identity of women has been defined by traditional ideas and practices. Some argue that the autonomous, responsible self typical of liberal political thought is a social construction elevating the white male bourgeois self into the Self as such, in which form the idea has worked to oppress women and others whose experiences are "different." On the other hand, if women are to be capable of social criticism and of rising above the gender definitions and roles into which they have been socialized, a somewhat disencumbered, free self is required. Representatives of other groups that have been marginalized raise similar questions.[3] Indeed it is hard for any human self not to be fascinated by questions about its own nature, freedom, and limitations.

Thinking about the self is not easy of course; and any complete account must deal with the conflicting positions of the great thinkers since at least Augustine, including Descartes, Locke, and Hume, down to Nietzsche and Heidegger. What I attempt to do here is much more modest. Drawing mainly on the ideas of only one thinker, Hannah Arendt, I attempt to develop an account of a self that is neither disembodied and unsituated nor wholly a product of its situation, a self that is sufficiently autonomous to be a responsible, morally accountable agent of its actions, a self that has enough moral dignity to be the bearer of individual rights.

Arendt never wrote a sustained account of the self. Her discussions of the self are scattered throughout her works; and the pertinent passages include some of her most dense writing.[4] Some of what she said about the self appears contradictory. Perhaps no single account can remove all the puzzles contained in Arendt's many sayings on the self; and in any case such an argument would be beyond the scope and purpose of the present essay. What I have done here is to build on many of her ideas to construct my own account of the self, an account that I maintain is responsive to the issues raised in today's debates.

I A Preliminary Account of the Self

Fundamental to Arendt's political theory is the notion that each of us is a unique individual with the capacity of free action, of spontaneously initiating something new in the world. In *Origins of Totalitarianism*, Arendt used the word "individuality" to name that aspect of our personhood in which the capacity of freedom inheres. It is our "individuality," she said, that enables us "to begin something new out of [our] own resources" (*OT*, 455). Because of this individuality, she implied, we have the capacities traditionally associated with human beings—free action and reflective thinking—capacities that make us morally accountable for our actions and that entitle us to personal respect, legal recognition, the rights of citizenship in a body politic. Without this individuality, we are less than humans, mere bundles of reactions, determined by the functional requirements of physical survival (*OT*, 455, 438).[5]

Much of Arendt's writing was inspired by the fear that it was possible to destroy this individuality in human beings, a fear sparked by the "experiments" with human nature undertaken by Hitler and Stalin (*OT*, 437–441). She remained convinced that conditions in the twentieth century were such that what made totalitarian movements attractive once might well do so again, so that human individuality and the capacity of freedom continued to be at risk (*OT*, 458–459).[6]

Arendt's discussion of individuality in *Origins of Totalitarianism* includes several ideas that pertain to an account of the self. The phenomenon of individuality was, she suggested, revealed with unusual clarity in the stark situation of the concentration camps because the more familiar aspects of personal identity had been stripped away. First, most inhabitants of the camps had been denied identity as citizens of a particular country with a legal status and civil rights (*OT*, 450–451). Second, the inhabitants of the concentration camps were deprived of "moral personhood" by being made accomplices of the crimes of the regimes that had imprisoned them, as when inmates were made to choose which of their children should die or to share in managing the camps (*OT*, 451–452). What remained to these persons was sheer individuality. "In a sterile form," Arendt proposed, "individuality can be preserved through a persistent Stoicism;" and many took refuge in this "absolute isolation of a personality without rights or conscience" (*OT*, 453). When this too was destroyed, the inhabitants became mere animal specimens, bundles of reactions, no longer what we think of as human beings (*OT*, 438, 453–457).

What is this sheer individuality? "This part of the human person," Arendt argued, was the most difficult part to destroy "precisely because it depends so essentially on nature and on forces that cannot be controlled by the will" (*OT*, 453). This implies that there are parts of the human person that *do* and parts that *do not* depend on the "will." Indeed, Arendt said explicitly that one's "individuality" is "shaped in equal parts by nature, will, and destiny" (*OT*, 454).

How are we to understand this? Arendt was proposing, I suggest, that the part shaped by "nature" is the part we were born with, the part shaped by "destiny" is the socially constituted part of the self, and the part of the self shaped by the "will" is that part which, through deliberate choices, the self has shaped and for which it can be held responsible.[7] Let us take up these three aspects of how the person or self is formed:

First, what is that part of our person that we owe to "nature"? Each of us is endowed with a particular body with its own combination of physical traits and talents. We also are born with psychological dispositions to have certain feelings, desires, emotions, and motivations. Even though these dispositions are certainly shaped by experiences after birth, Arendt suggested they have a natural base. Although she did not specify, such a base might include such traits as a greater or lesser tendency to become angry, to be driven by physical desires, to be bold or shy, and so on.[8] Obviously, we are not responsible for our bodily traits and basic physical needs, nor on this account are we responsible for our basic psychological dispositions.

Our "nature" is not limited, however, to physical and psychological features. "Who" we are is always more than a list of general characteristics. There is, in the "nature" one was born with, a deeper uniqueness that, in a sense, governs a person's life. "The fundamental trait of a man's nature," Arendt said, "lies at a deeper level, as it were, than all gifts and talents, than all psychologically describable peculiarities and qualities [which] grow out of his nature" (*MDT*, 111–112).

Arendt tried to capture this deeper uniqueness in some of her biographical essays. For example, in Hermann Broch, this uniqueness was the demand that his life unify the different activities of art, science, and politics. Sometimes one can be a victim of one's unique nature, as Arendt argued Broch was (*MDT*, 114f). The continuous bad luck of Walter Benjamin seems to have been an attribute of his unique nature, in Arendt's view (*MDT*, 157ff).

In part, then, we owe our individuality, our unique personal identity, to "nature." The second source of our personal identity, our "destiny," comes from our society and culture. Each of us was born into and shaped by a particular cultural milieu, with a shared language and shared beliefs, stories and customs. Arendt's biographical essays always emphasize the cultural origins of her subjects. Thus, to understand Rosa Luxembourg, it was essential to know of the peculiar culture of the "Polish-Jewish 'peer group'" that was always her "home" (*MDT*, 40–41, 44–45). To understand Walter Benjamin, one had to understand the German-Jewish environment in which he was raised (*MDT*, 181ff); and one needed to know of Rahel Varnhagen that she was German, Jewish, and a woman.[9] In Arendt's own case, the facts that she was educated into German language and culture, that she was a woman and a Jew, were particularly salient to her own identity.[10] Arendt also did not minimize the importance of the social pressures each individual faces throughout life to conform to current traditions, beliefs, and fashions—to do what others do and think what they think (*HC*, 40).[11]

On Arendt's account, then, each of us is a concrete self, situated in a body, with a concrete set of psychological dispositions, and also situated in a particular cultural milieu, "encumbered" with inherited notions of the good life, morality, and religion. But each of us also has the capacity, within limits, to transcend this "thrownness." Each of us has the capacity to think critically and to initiate action. Because of these capacities, we are also capable, within limits, of shaping our own unique self. In *Origins of Totalitarianism*, Arendt attributed this third and final aspect of our "individuality" to the "will."

How are we to understand this aspect of the self that we *are* responsible for? Arendt's clearest discussion of this is in a passage in *The Life of the Mind,* where she compared how animals and humans "appear" in the world. Humans, like animals, simply appear in the world when they are born; they have no choice in the matter. In addition, both animals and humans engage in "self-display"—that is, they actively do things that are seen by, and attract the attention of, other sentient creatures. However, whereas animals do whatever they do without deliberation (apparently), humans "*up to a point* ... choose how to appear to others"; and this involves an "intervention of the mind," a "deliberate choice" (*LM* I, 34–35).

The difference between "self-display" by an animal and the "self-presentation" of a person is an "active and conscious choice of the image shown" (*LM* I, 36). When one shows anger, for example, unless one is simply swept away by rage and hence acts utterly without conscious choice, one's action reflects a decision about "what is fit for appearance." Arendt made it clear here that the *feeling* of anger is not a matter of choice; this feeling springs from our "soul." But the *show* of anger is deliberate (*LM* I, 31–32). Similarly, when a person displays courage, this does not indicate absence of the emotion of fear but a decision that "fear is not what he wants to show" (*LM* I, 36).[12]

Thus deliberate choice is involved in what, of the many things simmering in our souls, we wish others to see. In this context, Arendt spoke of "self-control": "we need a considerable training in self-control," she said, "to prevent the passions from showing" (*LM* I, 72). Although one cannot prevent the surge of internal emotion, one can conceal it or express it in deliberately chosen ways.

It is by choosing repeatedly and over time how we wish to appear, which of the "welter of happenings" in our soul we wish to show, that we shape our character. Thus one who repeatedly shows courage becomes a courageous person; courage has become "second nature or a habit" for that person (*LM* I, 36). Out of many such acts of self-presentation, Arendt said, "arises finally what we call character or personality, the conglomeration of a number of identifiable qualities gathered together into a comprehensible and reliably identifiable whole, and imprinted, as it were, on an unchangeable substratum of gifts and defects peculiar to our soul and body structure" (*LM* I, 37).[13]

In sum, then, we have here the outlines of a promising account of the self. This self is neither fully situated nor fully autonomous. It is an embodied self with a variety of particular, inherited and culturally acquired traits; but this self is also, because of the capacity of freedom, able partially to transcend its situation. This account of the self is compatible with a morality of virtues, in which an individual, through childhood learning and later free choice, acquires dispositions to act in desired ways. In this respect, this account is responsive to some of the communitarian critics who are troubled by the decline of virtue and character in moral education today.

On the other hand, a self that can consider how it wishes to appear also has the capacity to reflect on itself and on social norms. Hence it has a capacity of social criticism in the Socratic sense. Finally, because this self can, within limits, actually determine how it presents itself, it can be held accountable for what it does. It is not wholly transparent either to itself or to others because it has a depth in which much is concealed. Yet it is the agent of its actions and sufficiently free of forces beyond its control to be worthy of moral dignity and political rights.

II Problems of the Self

If an account such as this is plausible and coherent, it is very attractive, taking into account, as it seems to, much of what is desirable in both liberal and communitarian accounts of the self. It is not self-evident, however, that all of the above elements do cohere. Some readers may also object that the account is unfaithful to the spirit of Arendt's work. I wish here to take up some potential objections to this account, developing it further as I go.

The Fragmented versus the Unitary Self

It might be argued that this account ignores the powerful criticisms of the unitary self made by Nietzsche, criticisms Arendt herself took seriously, and by later deconstructionists. The account also suggests an interior dimension to the self that some may find at odds with Arendt's frequent claims that personal identity is manifested in action and better known to the others who witness it than to the actor.

Arendt did in fact argue, especially in *The Life of the Mind*, that many of our *experiences* of the self suggest a multiple, fragmented self. When we look into ourselves, we are aware of a variety of bodily and psychological needs, sensations, passions, feelings, and motives—all of which we "suffer" rather than control. What we encounter in our "soul," Arendt suggested, is "a more or less chaotic welter of happenings which we do not enact but suffer (*pathein*)" (*LM* I, 72).[14] Each of us is also aware, Arendt said, of various "mental" capacities: we can imagine, remember, reflect on the meaning of experience, will projects for the future, and make cognitive, moral, and aesthetic judgments. Our mental capacities also have "needs" that seem to compel us; for example, we experience a need to think and a need for the will to project into the future (*LM* I, 69, 129).

The experiences associated with this multiplicity of capacities and needs of body, soul, and mind are diverse and conflicting. Indeed each set of experiences generates its own perspective so that, for example, when bodily needs dominate our attention, we are led to see ourselves and the world in one way; but when experiences of thinking have primacy, we see things very differently. Thus a hungry person experiences things differently than one who is sated. A person who is always active in the world experiences things differently than one who spends most of her time in thought. To complicate things further, Arendt argued that the major mental faculties are themselves internally divided so that thinking seems to be an internal dialogue with oneself and willing is often experienced as a struggle of one will that tries to command an opposing will.[15]

The experiences one associates with one's self are, then, complex and multiple. This might lead to the conclusion that there is no self or perhaps that there are multiple selves, as Nietzsche at times suggested. But there is also, Arendt said, a direct experience of the self as a single phenomenon, which she calls "consciousness," that provides an internal testimony to personal identity. Consciousness, Arendt said, is an awareness of self that accompanies all our activities. This "awareness of the sameness of the I-am ... guarantees the identical continuity of a self throughout the manifold representations, experiences and memories of a lifetime" (*LM* I, 74–75). Now this formulation may sound like a regression to the early modern disembodied self of Locke and Kant; and indeed, Arendt cited Kant in this context: "I am conscious of myself, not as I appear to myself, nor as I am in myself, but only that I am." This consciousness, Kant said, "expresses the act of determining my existence" [Kant's words]. But Arendt corrected Kant for giving too idealist an account of this experience. "Consciousness ... not only accompanies 'all other *representations*' [Kant's words] but all my *activities*" (emphasis mine). Because it accompanies all my activities, "this sheer self-awareness ... is the guarantor of an altogether silent I-am-I" (*LM* I, 74–75). This "I" is not just a thinking self, but a self with a body and soul—a self that also expresses emotions and acts in the world.[16]

Here Arendt appears to have followed Heidegger's criticism of Kant for failing to appreciate that the unity of the self is prior to the theory/practice distinction and that "the whole of the being that in ourselves we are [involves] body, soul and mind" (*BPP*, 146). Heidegger said that Kant failed "to determine originally the unity of the theoretical and practical ego" (*BPP*, 146). Arendt's position also is in accord with Heidegger's view of the self as ontologically prior to particular experiences (including particular experiences of itself).

Of course, the fact that we are conscious of a sameness of the self—and that we cannot conceive of experience except on this assumption—does not demonstrate that there is a real referent for this awareness. There is no reason, however, to think Arendt doubted that there was such a "real" self. Where else could lie the natural uniqueness, mentioned above, that Arendt thought lies behind the various natural gifts and talents of each individual, and that is disclosed in speech and action (*HC*, 175–181)? Indeed, Arendt's very important argument that thinking may prevent evildoing depends on this unity of the thinking and acting self. She argued that a person who "stops to think"—rather than going along with what others are doing or with the clichés of the times—will not want to do something he cannot live with later when he is again alone in dialogue with himself. This argument makes no sense if there is not a real, unitary self.[17]

Character versus Spontaneity

A second possible objection to this account of the self is that a strong character, a "second nature," with stable dispositions and habits, may seem to be at odds with the capacity of freedom, the capacity spontaneously to initiate something new in the world.[18] If this objection were valid, I would be required to give up Arendt's account of action—a most unfortunate consequence, for this was surely one of her major contributions to political thought.

The capacity for action might be incompatible with strong character in the above sense if action were an everyday occurrence. In fact, it is not. Arendt was quite clear that most of what most of us do most of the time is not "action" at all, but more like "behavior," a term she used to describe activity that is habitual or determined by social conventions, dogma, or ideology (*HC*, 40f).[19] What we do for the most part in our everyday lives is a product of our habits, dispositions, socialization, needs, and so on. Such "doings" are free in the sense that we *could* have done otherwise than we in fact did. (If this were not so, we could not fairly be held responsible for such acts.) Such acts are free in a stronger sense to the extent that they result from habits we have freely chosen to develop.

The real question is whether having a strong, self-shaped character is compatible with free action in Arendt's special sense—the action that occurs in those rare cases when an individual breaks spontaneously with life's ordinary routine and initiates something new. An affirmative answer to this question is possible only if we can conceive of character constraining action without eliminating its spontaneous, unpredictable quality. A complete solution to this puzzle would require an account of action and freedom beyond the scope of this essay. My brief answer is to propose that character does constrain action somewhat, but that it does so only in a negative sense. That is, an actor of strong character may indeed set off something new, acting in a way no one could have predicted, but there are certain things a person of a given character will almost certainly *not* do.

I believe one could convincingly apply this suggestion to Arendt's exemplary cases of actors in history and literature—to the leaders of the American Revolution or to Pericles and Achilles. Surely none of these men lacked strong character. But here let us consider a nonheroic example: Let us say that I—being of a certain strong, self-shaped character—have a student with serious personal problems; perhaps he is deeply depressed, even suicidal. As a professor following normal routine, I may well ignore the situation. It is not my job after all to deal with the private lives of my students. Nor need I, to "live with myself" and the character I have helped to shape over the years, intervene in such a case. One cannot after all solve every problem in the world, not even those one sees firsthand. But suppose I do intervene.

It seems to me one can safely say several things. First, I may not know, until I actually take some step (confronting the student, speaking to an official counselor, etc.), whether I will act at all or what I will say or do. In this sense, my intervention would be quite spontaneous. Second, I can have no idea what the results of my intervention will be: the consequences of such an action are "boundless" and unpredictable. However, I can be very confident that there are some things I will *not* do, assuming my character is of a certain sort. I will not, for example, kill the student or initiate a love affair with him or promise him all A's. How, if my action is spontaneous, can I be confident that I will not do such things? For two good Arendtian reasons: First, because I know that I could not live with myself if I did such things; and I want to be able to live myself. And second, because I have chosen over the years to present myself *to others* as the sort of person who does not murder or seduce students and who does not compromise academic standards; and hence I have good reason to believe that I *am and will continue to be* that sort of person.

Indeed, if I could not be sure of such things, I would seriously doubt my sanity. Arendt herself may indeed have believed that possession of a strong character was a requisite of sanity—at least for those who were self-reflective and aware of free choices. In her discussion of how we shape our character, Arendt suggested that when we choose to present ourselves in a certain way, as in displaying a certain virtue, we imply making a commitment or promise to remain that way, to *be* the sort of person we presently, in this virtuous action, appear to be (*LM* I, 36–37). Such implied promises *to others* are, she suggested, essential to our own sense of self-identity. If we were isolated selves, capable only of self-reflection, we would become lost in the confusion of our inner experiences—of conflicting feelings, motives, capacities, thoughts, needs, and projects. Because of this ability to choose how we will appear to others and to make the same choice again and again, we can have stable identities. As she put it much earlier, in *The Human Condition*, "Without being bound to the fulfillment of promises, we would never be able to keep our identities; we would be condemned to wander helplessly and without direction in the darkness of each man's lonely heart, caught in its contradictions and equivocalities." The others before whom we appear confirm back to us "the identity between the one who promises and the one who fulfills" (*HC*, 237).[20]

Having a strong character and being able to make and keep commitments to others is a sine qua none of sanity, on this analysis—at least for the person who is not wholly a creature of socialization. This cannot, then, be incompatible with the capacity of action. Arendt's action in its purest form was a political phenomenon; so let us briefly consider some political examples.

We know a good deal about the character of former President Jimmy Carter, including that he prides himself on being a peacemaker. It was predictable—to Carter and to others—that should he intervene in international affairs, it would not be as a covert assassin nor would he attempt to insult a foreign leader. But such constraints imposed by his character certainly did not make it predictable that he would go to North Korea in the summer of 1994 as a private negotiator; and it certainly was not predictable what the outcome of the processes that action set in motion would be.

Voters' demands for strong and reliable but vaguely defined character traits in our presidents are also suggestive. Perhaps the most important trait in national leaders is the capacity to recognize dangerous or critical situations and to take forceful, creative initiatives. Because we cannot know what situations will arise or what actions will be required, we cannot know in advance what character traits are needed. What may have troubled voters most about George Bush (after the initial success of the Gulf War) and about Bill Clinton is the suspicion that they have *no* firm character at all, and hence there is *nothing* they can be counted on not to do.

If the above analysis is persuasive, it appears that having a strong, well-defined, self-shaped character is compatible with the human capacity of action. Hence Arendt's important insights into the nature of action need not be sacrificed if we adopt the account of self proposed here.

How Much Autonomy? How Much Self-Knowledge?

Each individual person is, then, in part shaped by her inherited characteristics, in part by socialization, and in part by her own deliberate choices. Not everyone of course takes advantage of the capacity to shape her character; perhaps indeed most people do not. Even for those who do, the choices are not unlimited; and how we in fact appear to others is not solely up to us for a number of reasons. A discussion of these reasons should also help address a further objection that might be made to the above account of the self—that it disregards Arendt's important and valid arguments that we do not control the meaning or consequences of our actions.

One of the most important reasons why we do not have this sort of control is that, as Arendt argued in *The Human Condition*, when we act, we act into a world inhabited by a plurality of other people, each distinct from the others. We cannot be sure what these others will do in response to our initiatives, nor what those who respond to their actions will do—and on and on. Thus each new action initiates a process which is, in a sense, "boundless" and the ultimate outcome of which is unpredictable.[21] This element of unpredictability is one reason why Arendt objects to images of mastery and sovereignty in connection with the self.[22]

It is also why forgiveness plays such an important role in Arendt's account of action. If the initiation of action sets off a process of reactions that is unpredictable and potentially endless, the burden of responsibility on the actor is terrifying. The horror of such responsibility is captured in the Greek tragedies where a single deed results in a curse on a whole family line, such as the House of Atreus. The same notion is captured in the ancient Hebrew saying that the sins of the fathers are visited on future generations of sons. Forgiveness, by contrast, is a free act that releases actors and their heirs from such unbearable responsibility (*HC*, 236–243).

There are other reasons why how we appear to others is not solely up to us. These are brought out in another dense passage in *Life of the Mind*, where Arendt says that our choices of how we wish to appear are

> determined by various factors; many of them are predetermined by the culture into which we are born—they are made because we wish to please others. But there are also choices not inspired by our environment; we may make them because we wish to please ourselves or because we wish to set an example, that is, to persuade others to be pleased with what pleases us. Whatever the motives may be, success and failure in the enterprise of self-presentation depend on the consistency and duration of the image thereby presented to the world." (*LM* I, 36).

This passage warrants careful attention.

First, it reflects awareness on Arendt's part that one's acts of self-presentation—one's actions, words, and gestures—will be described and interpreted by others in their own language and from their own individual and cultural perspectives. Hence, "what" one's action is and what sort of person one is judged to be are subject to different descriptions. When I choose how I wish to appear, I cannot disregard this. If, for example, in a typical American context, I call a person a "pig," I cannot claim this was not really an insult because I like pigs. In a certain context, calling someone a pig is simply an insult.[23]

Second, Arendt says, to the extent that "we wish to please others," what we choose to do will be greatly determined by what is culturally acceptable. To take an ordinary example, if a teenager wants to be "popular," current teen culture makes rather rigorous demands on how that teenager must present herself. Or if a woman in twentieth-century America wants to be liked or successful, she had best not be too aggressive or assertive in pressing her opinions or her career aims. The same limitations apply even if one wants to "displease" others. Thus, even romantic or bohemian "individualists," in their determination to be "unique personalities," have to choose outrageous or bizarre appearances, that is, what appears bizarre to their contemporaries.

If we want to please others in a more historical sense (that is, be remembered for our actions, be "immortalized"), we once again will be limited by cultural expectations. To take Arendt's classic example, if Achilles wanted to be a hero (that is, be remembered by others as courageous, as what a hero ought to be), Homeric culture offered him only one course of action—to die in battle. And this of course is what he chose.[24]

Even if we do not particularly care what others think of us, if we wish to have any influence in the world, if we wish to persuade others to our point of view or to act effectively, we must pay careful heed to how we appear. Michael Dukakis damaged his presidential prospects severely by forgetting that men are supposed to get angry, not engage in moral ruminations, when their wives are attacked. Similarly, a woman who wishes to free herself from dominant social definitions must still be careful that she not be judged insane; and if she wants perhaps to set an example for others, to be a role model for younger women, she must be cognizant of existing social definitions, so that she may communicate with those she wants to influence and still carefully and deliberately deviate from some of those definitions.

In choosing how we will appear and who we will be, we are, then, greatly limited—not just by our own individual nature and acculturation—but also by the fact that we continue to share with others a sociocultural world of preexisting roles and meanings. In this respect, there is always a tension between our individual self and the self we present to others. As Arendt once put it, "if we wish to take a part in the world's play at all," we must take on "masks or roles which the world assigns to us"; and yet through such masks, "something else manifests itself, something entirely idiosyncratic and indefinable and still unmistakably identifiable."[25]

And of course, in the end, the judgment of who we were will be made by others, because it is they who will determine whether we are remembered or forgotten and how our life story, if remembered, will be written. Here again, Arendt anticipated the postmodern notion of "narrativity."[26] Arendt insisted that using the form of a story is the only way to tell who someone was. A description will not do because of the fact that language, consisting of general words, is inherently unsuited to capturing individual uniqueness, which "confounds all efforts toward unequivocal verbal expression. The moment we want to say *who* somebody is, our very vocabulary leads us astray into saying *what* he is"—that is, we use general descriptive terms (tall, handsome, smart, clever, etc.), all of which refer to traits that this person shares with others. We end up describing a "type" and "his specific uniqueness escapes us" (*HC*, 181).[27] Such a story can best be written (and only definitively written) at the end of the person's life. "The unchangeable identity of the person, though disclosing itself intangibly in act and speech, becomes tangible only in the story of the actor's . . . life, but as such it can be known . . . only after it has come to its end" (*HC*, 193). Obviously, such a story is not written by the actor but by others.

In this sense, Arendt said, "nobody is the author or producer of his own life story." The stories that result from one's words and deeds "reveal an agent, but this agent is not an author or producer" (*HC*, 184). This should not be understood to mean, as some have argued, that Arendt shared Nietzsche's position that there is no doer behind the deed (*GM* I, xiii), so that the actor is entirely a creation of the storyteller, of the spectators who grant meaning.[28] Arendt meant only that the actor loses control of the meaning and consequences of the action the instant the action occurs, for all the reasons indicated above. Arendt was of course well aware that a storyteller is a creator and that it is possible to tell different stories about the same action or actor. But storytellers who write about historical figures are also, Arendt believed, "truthtellers" and have a responsibility to tell the story "straight."[29]

Arendt also suggested that part of who a person is remains forever elusive. This follows directly from our capacity of freedom, of initiating something new, a capacity that remains ours as long as we live. Of course, it ends when we die; but up until the moment of our death, there is always unrevealed potentiality. This is why Arendt said that we cannot be identified exclusively with what we make and do, that each individual is "essentially and forever more than anything he can produce and achieve," and that there is behind the works "a being that remains greater and more mysterious because the work points to a person behind it whose essence can be neither exhausted nor fully revealed by whatever he may have the power to do" (*MDT*, 257).[30]

It may be tempting to assume that this elusive aspect of the self can be captured by psychobiography, which claims to delve into the "inner self" in the sense of "real" underlying motives and desires. But Arendt correctly objected to this approach. The soul, as we have seen, is "dark"; what is there is unknown both to the self and to the spectator and nothing is gained by trying to pry into it (*OR*, 92).[31] It may be that psychologists have some insights into odd behaviors that result from frustration of functional needs of all humans. This would follow insofar as "inside we are all alike"—that is, that in the basic economy of psychological needs, humans do not differ. But this could shed no light on the elusive aspects of an individual's unique nature (*LM* I, 34–35).

There is simply no access, Arendt believed, to the particularities of the individual "soul." Motives and other psychological traits lie deeply buried; they *never* appear and hence remain unknown to actor and observers. Any attempt to force them into the open, she argued, is likely only to raise suspicions about the actor's integrity. The latter is true because of the very fact that, although we cannot control what is in our soul, we can choose what we wish to present (*OR*, 91f; *LM* I, 34–35). Hence it may seem that because we do not show our "true" selves, we are hypocritical, and that this hypocrisy needs to be exposed. But how, if Arendt is correct, does the observer know that the actor is not merely "making a show," that the action is not a disguise for some underlying motive?

In any particular case, Arendt said, we cannot know; and inquiring into motives will not shed any light. The only sense in which we can know a person's "true" character is by judging whether that person presents regularly, over time, a consistent appearance. "Only self-presentation [and not animal self-display] is open to hypocrisy and pretense ... and the only way to tell pretense and make-believe from reality and truth is the former's failure to endure." As we have said, Arendt argued that there is a sort of promise made each time one presents oneself that one will continue to present oneself the same way. The hypocrite is one who breaks that promise (*LM* I, 35–36).

We cannot, then, control either the events our actions set in motion or the way our life story will be seen, interpreted, and remembered by others. But we do, by our ability to present ourselves and to keep the "promises" implicit in our self-presentations, have the capacity to shape the character that determines our everyday activities and that constrains even our most spontaneous actions.

Conclusion

This account of the self is, I maintain, an attractive one. It acknowledges that all selves are firmly "situated" in particular bodies and sociocultural experiences. They are born with or learn identities involving gender, family relationships, language, cultural and social norms, and habits. But at the same time, individual selves have the capacity to think and act freely, to rise above their situations—never totally but to some degree—in both thought and action. They can, to a degree, shape their own character and remain true to that character. This account of the self allows for moral and legal responsibility, while offering a reminder that forgiveness has much to recommend it in the unpredictable world of human affairs. It does not appear to exclude any "others"—except those who might somehow be demonstrated incapable of freedom. Hence it could be the basis for a moral and political argument that all human beings deserve both respect as moral individuals and citizenship with equal rights in a body politic. It is, finally, an account of the self with which I find it plausible to identify my own self; and this, although not a sufficient criterion for a satisfactory account, certainly must be a necessary one for me.

This account has the key elements for any plausible account of the self: the element of depth and darkness, of unknowability; the element of complexity and contradiction in experiences of the inner aspects of the self; the element of "thrownness" in a given body and culture; the element of freedom, of the potential for unpredictable action; and finally, the element of unity—the fact that it is the same person who thinks, feels, wills, and acts. All of these elements must be included in any account of the self that remotely captures the "wonder-ful" phenomenon of the human self—the phenomenon that, from at least Socrates on, has prompted philosophers and poets to pause in admiring wonder.

Notes

Acknowledgment: I would like to thank Jerome Kohn, Larry May, Sandra Luft, Emily Gill, and Elaine Buker who read and made very helpful suggestions on earlier versions of this article.

1. John Rawls, *A Theory of Justice* (Cambridge: Harvard University Press, 1971), and Michael Sandel, *Liberalism and the Limits of Justice* (Cambridge: Cambridge University Press, 1982).

2. A useful survey of this debate is found in Stephen Mulhall and Adam Swift, *Liberals and Communitarians* (Oxford: Blackwell, 1992). See also Nancy Rosenblum, ed., *Liberalism and the Moral Life* (Cambridge: Harvard University Press, 1989), and the communitarian journal, *The Responsive Community*, edited by Amitai Etzioni. Some major related works focusing on the self are Charles Taylor, *Sources of the Self* (Cambridge: Harvard University Press, 1989), and Jack Crittendon, *Beyond Liberalism: Reconstructing the Liberal Self* (Oxford: Oxford University Press, 1992).

3. See, for example, Diana T. Meyers, *Self, Society, and Personal Choice* (New York: Columbia University Press, 1989); Seyla Benhabib, *Situating the Self* (New York: Routledge, 1992); and William Connally, *Identity/Difference: Democrat Negotiations of Political Paradox* (Ithaca: Cornell University Press, 1991).

4. This led me in an earlier work to argue that she lacked a coherent concept of the self; see Suzanne Jacobitti, "Hannah Arendt and the Will," in *Political Theory* 16 (February 1988, pp. 53–76). Bonnie Honig's "Arendt, Identity, and Difference" in *Political Theory* 16 (February 1988, pp. 77–98) stimulated me to reconsider this.

5. *The Origins of Totalitarianism*, 3d ed. (New York: Harcourt, Brace and World), 1966, pp. 455, 438. (Hereinafter cited in text as *OT*.) Indeed, we would be even less than animals, at least higher animals, Arendt suggested, because we would be like Pavlov's dogs—animals perverted by an unnatural conditioning. Cf. *The Human Condition* (Chicago: University of

Chicago Press, 1958) [hereafter cited *HC*], pp. 175–176, where she linked the fact that each human is "distinct" to the capacity of free speech and action, as the capacities that differentiate humans from animals.

6. As others have argued. See, for example, Margaret Canovan, *Hannah Arendt: A Reinterpretation of Her Political Thought* (Cambridge: Cambridge University Press, 1992), and Jeffrey C. Isaac, *Arendt, Camus, and Modern Rebellion* (New Haven: Yale University Press, 1992).

7. The term "destiny" here might relate to Heidegger's notion of our "destiny" or "fate" pertaining to our situatedness in a particular culture and tradition.

8. Arendt often wrote of our endowment of physical and psychological "gifts and talents" or "gifts and defects." See Hannah Arendt, *Men in Dark Times* (New York: Harcourt Brace Jovanovich, 1968 [hereafter cited as *MDT*]), pp. 111–112, and Hannah Arendt, *The Life of the Mind*, vol. 1 (New York: Harcourt Brace Jovanovich, 1978 [hereinafter cited as *LM*]), p. 37. Among our physical endowments is "brainpower," which Arendt described as "the most precious gift with which the body has endowed us" (*LM* II, p. 56, I, pp. 60–61). Arendt often referred to the psychological realm as a realm of "soul" or "heart."

9. *Rahel Varnhagen: The Life of a Jewish Woman*, rev. ed. (New York: Harcourt Brace Jovanovich, 1974).

10. See especially her 1975 speech in Copenhagen on receiving the Sonning Prize (with her papers in the Library of Congress). How Arendt chose to identify herself in particular situations was a different matter. Where Jews were being persecuted, she thought it essential to identify herself simply as a Jew (see *MDT*, p. 16). Dagmar Barnouw is interesting on Arendt and her German and Jewish inheritance; see *Visible Spaces: Hannah Arendt and the German-Jewish Experience* (Baltimore: Johns Hopkins University Press, 1990).

11. Each of us, to this extent, is what Heidegger called a "They-self." See also Arendt's discussion of "good society" in the eighteenth and nineteenth centuries: Hannah Arendt, *Between Past and Future*, enlarged ed. (New York: Viking, 1968), pp. 198–200; *OR*, pp. 100–101.

12. This is not an argument that reason rules the passions. Arendt rejected the traditional ideal of "self-mastery" that is rooted in Plato's notion that reason should rule the passions (*HC*, pp. 237–238, 244). For Arendt, the soul is entirely passive. Neither reason nor any other mental capacity can control psychological happenings, any more than they can control our need for food and air.

13. This account of how virtues are acquired is quite Aristotelian, as are her notions of courage and moderation as political virtues.

14. Cf. *HC*, p. 237, and *On Revolution* (New York: Viking, 1963 [hereinafter cited as *OR*]), pp. 92–94.

15. Arendt said parenthetically that this duality explains the "futility of the fashionable search for identity," adding that "our modern identity crisis could be resolved only by never being alone and never trying to think" (*LM* I, p. 187).

16. Arendt's quotes from Kant are from his *Critique of Pure Reason*, B 157–158. Cf. Martin Heidegger, *The Basic Problems of Phenomenology*, trans. A. Hofstadter, rev. ed. (Bloomington: Indiana University Press, 1988 [hereafter cited as BPP]), p. 158.

17. Arendt here quoted Socrates in the *Gorgias* (l., pp. 474b–484) saying it would be better for him that his lyre or his chorus be out of tune and all men at odds with him than that he, "*being one*, should be out of harmony with [himself] and contradict [himself]" (*LM* I, p. 181). Arendt emphasized the "being one."

18. See Honig, "Arendt, Identity, and Difference," pp. 89–90.

19. See Bhikhu Parekh, *Hannah Arendt and the Search for a New Political Philosophy* (Atlantic Highlands, NJ: Humanities Press International, 1981), p. 114.

20. Arendt argued that promising, understood in this way, is the only alternative to the traditional notion of self-mastery. Unlike the latter, it is compatible with freedom (*HC*, p. 244). In this context, Arendt noted that Nietzsche said the faculty of promising is what distinguished humans from animals (*HC*, p. 245).

21. Arendt used the image of acting into a "web" of other wills and actions (*HC*, pp. 182–184). This feature of Arendt's concept of action has been well explained by many interpreters.

22. The other reason is her objection to the Platonic notion that reason can rule the soul. The two objections are related. It is the plausibility of the notion of reason ruling the soul that gives legitimacy to the notion that the wise or "those who know" should rule others. In both cases, what is sacrificed is freedom (*HC*, pp. 222–225).

23. This point has been made in various ways by Wittgenstein, Heidegger, and others. It is part of what is often called "narrativity" (see Benhabib, *Situating the Self*, pp. 5, 214).

24. In a few cases such as this, where one chooses to die in "one supreme act," one can, Arendt suggested, be "indisputable master of his identity and possible greatness." Even Achilles, of course, depended on the storyteller for a final judgment (*HC*, pp. 193–194). Arendt may have had Achilles in mind when she said earlier that the disclosure of one's unique personal identity "can *almost* never be achieved as a willful purpose" (*HC*, pp. 179). Emphasis mine. Cf. Honig, "Arendt, Identity, and Difference," p. 83.

25. See Hannah Arendt, untitled speech on receiving the Sonning Prize, Copenhagen, Denmark, April 18, 1975, Arendt papers, Library of Congress.

26. See Taylor, *Sources of the Self*, pp. 44–48.

27. Public recognition has the same liability, Arendt suggested, in her acceptance of the Sonning Prize in 1975. Although she appreciated the prize, she also would be happy to return to her "naked 'thisness'—"; for recognition "can only recognize us *as* such and such, that is, as something which we fundamentally are *not*."

28. Honig, "Arendt, Identity, and Difference," pp. 88–89. Benhabib, *Situating the Self*, is truer to Arendt on this point, pp. 217–218.

29. In explaining the Greek notion of the poet, Arendt mentioned the incident from *The Odyssey*, where Odysseus hears a bard sing about the heroes at Troy, including himself. Here Odysseus hears what "actually happened" and can now "become fully aware of its meaning" (*LM* I, pp. 132). The poet does turn the real events into a story with a meaning—and may do this by "transformation and condensation" (*HC*, pp. 187). This does not, however, imply that the hero of the story was not a true agent with an inner dimension.

The task of the Greek bards—as of a biographer or historian today—was to capture as best they could the truth about this person whose story they told, even though, given the perspectival limits of our understanding, no one story can ever capture the whole. See also Arendt's discussion of the "telling of factual truth" in contemporary times in the essay "Truth and Politics" in *Between Past and Future* (New York: Penguin, 1977), pp. 227–264, quote on p. 261.

30. The comment is made about Waldemar Gurian. See also *HC*, p. 211 where Arendt criticized the perspective of *homo faber*, who sees the artist's work as greater than the artist.

31. On the darkness of the human heart or soul, Arendt is in the tradition of Augustine and Pascal.

10

Novus Ordo Seclorum: The Trial of (Post)Modernity or the Tale of Two Revolutions

David Ingram

History is the subject of a structure whose site is not homogeneous, empty time, but time filled by the presence of the now. Thus, to Robespierre ancient Rome was a past charged with the time of the now which he blasted out of the continuum of history.

—*Walter Benjamin,* Theses on the Philosophy of History

There is the question of this ungraspable revolutionary instant that belongs to no historical, temporal continuum but in which the foundation of a new law nevertheless plays, if we may say so, on something from an anterior law that it extends, radicalizes, deforms, metaphorizes, metonymizes, this figure here taking the name of war or general strike.

—*Jacques Derrida,* Force of Law: The "Mystical Foundation of Authority"

While ruminating on Abbé Sieyès's celebrated appeal to national sovereignty in legitimating the Constituent Assembly, Hannah Arendt mentions two problems that appear to render all revolutions necessarily illegitimate:

> the problem of the legitimacy of the new power, the *pouvoir constitué,* whose authority could not be guaranteed by the Constituent Assembly, the *pouvoir constituant,* because the power of the Assembly itself was not constitutional and could never be constitutional since it was prior to the constitution itself; and the problem of the legality of the new laws which needed a "source and supreme master, the higher law" from which to derive their validity.[1] (163)

Let us call the first problem the problem of *preconstitutional* legitimation. Formulated as a paradox, it says that all constitutional assemblies authorize their own historical authority; they constitute the people in whose name they act. The only way out of this circle, it seems, is to argue that assemblies do not constitute the people in whose name they act, but merely accede to it as a kind of preconstituted authority. Despite its considerable appeal, this commonsense resolution of the problem seems to imply the redundancy if not illusoriness of constitutional "foundings," and it raises an important question: Why should any historical appeal to "the preconstituted authority of the people" be binding on persons whose founding acts ostensibly aim to affirm their own radical autonomy? For persons such as these, only social conventions (or contracts) concluded by their own voluntary consent are legitimate and morally binding.

This response suggests another alternative to the circle mentioned above. If we assume that the people (or perhaps their representatives) *create* (constitute, or found) their moral tie through their own voluntary consent, then we are left with a notion of constitution that internalizes the circle in a seemingly more acceptable and less problematic—modern and enlightened—way. Rather than retrospectively "constituting" the historical tradition that ostensibly constitutes us, we the people simply constitute ourselves directly without mediation of the past; we exercise democratic *self*-determination.

Rousseau notwithstanding, this "solution" to the problem of the social contract will still strike many as viciously circular. To begin with, the social contract is not a civil contract in which two persons contract with one another over the exchange of goods and services; in order for persons to be obligated to one another in this *civil* sense, there must already be a *social* framework of mutually recognized rights and duties—a legal institution, if you will—that *constitutes* the legitimate scope and meaning of civil acts as such. The social contract that constitutes this framework cannot, therefore, be conceived as a civil contract without begging important questions. Because I must consent to the framework *prior* to engaging in civil or political acts with others, my initial "contract" is with myself, or rather that autonomous part of my self I call my conscience.

But can I ever be said to meaningfully contract with myself? It is precisely discomfiture over this circle, however internalized, that has led philosophers to postulate a foundation for constitutional rights that precedes (or transcends) any *contingent* consent, be it personal or political. This is where the second of the two problems mentioned by Arendt—let us call it the problem of *prepolitical* legitimation—kicks in. Equally paradoxical, this problem concerns not the historical title but the radical autonomy of equals who freely contract with one another to constitute a new political foundation: The free consent that morally binds the contractors can break from the constraints of conventional law only by deriving its authority from a higher, more universal law; but this law, in turn, apparently emanates from an *external*—naturally, rationally, or divinely preordained—force that imposes itself on the contractors independently of their free consent. And so we are back to the problem with which we began: Why should any metaphysical appeal to nature, reason, or divinity of the sort implicit in the notion of universal rights and duties be binding on persons whose founding acts ostensibly aim to affirm their own radical autonomy?

The paradoxes of legitimation recounted above have recently come under scrutiny by "postmodernists," who conclude that they render any constitutional act incoherent and, therefore, illegitimate. Interestingly, they argue this point by showing how these paradoxes are *necessarily* concealed by the *language* of legitimation itself. This concealment is effected by conflating the partisan language of politics, civil contract, and so on, with the impersonal language of metaphysical universality and necessity. Such a conflation not only substitutes a *single*, metaphysical "speaker" (e.g., humanity) for a *plurality* of historically situated speakers (e.g., the signers of the Declaration of Independence), but it also commits a kind of naturalistic fallacy; it involves inferring a prescriptive utterance (that certain rights *ought* to be freely accepted) from a descriptive one (that they *must* be accepted). These violations of logical inference and rhetorical address in turn conceal the inherent partiality and violence of any legal regime, thereby paving the way for systems of domination that masquerade as contracts between free and equal subjects.

Although I do not deny that attempts by revolutionaries to justify their acts on universal principle have often had the consequences described by postmodern critics, I doubt that these consequences are necessary. In particular, I will argue that they are not, so long as the principle appealed to is understood as a *procedural* rule for agreeing on rights rather than as a direct prescription of them. In a nutshell, *if* the "higher law" that binds the activity of consenting is a *procedural condition* for its possibility, and *if*, moreover, such a law is constituted in turn as a *meaningful and determinate prescription* (or set of rights) within this very same activity, then it need no longer confront the contractors as an *external* constraint on their autonomy.

Is *this* circularity—which in fact undermines the logical and ontological distinction between procedural rules and prescriptive rights—vicious? I will argue that it is not. If we assume that application of a general norm to a particular case involves a reciprocal determination of the one by the other that is as unavoidable—and thus as legitimate—as the reciprocal determination of part and whole that transpires in understanding a text, then why not assume the same regarding the reciprocal determination of procedure and outcome? This latter circle is analogous to the hermeneutic circle of application, in that the general idea regulating democratic discussion gets concretely defined (as a specific list of rights) only within that discussion. It is also analogous to the circle by which a constitutional tradition determines its own subsequent *re*interpretation.[2] Given that these circles (of application and appropriation) are equally present in all constitutional foundations, and that, moreover (as I shall argue), both are as legitimate as any hermeneutical circle, one must conclude that the problems of preconstitutional and prepolitical legitimation that ostensibly undermine such foundations do not in fact do so.

My defense of these claims will be framed in terms of a confrontation between the "postmodernist" camp, here represented by Jacques Derrida, and the "modernist" camp, represented by Hannah Arendt. I intend to show that Arendt acknowledges both the presence of the aforementioned circles in constitutional foundations and their legitimacy, whereas Derrida at most acknowledges their mere presence. Thus, although Arendt shares Derrida's opinion that the Declaration of Independence cannot avoid appealing to "absolute" foundations in its declaration of inalienable rights, she argues that these can refer to legitimate, nonmetaphysical principles of rational discourse as well as to illegitimate, metaphysical ones.[3] In her opinion, such principles not only adhere in the human condition—wherein they "enjoin" the pluralistic constitution of political identity through free communication among equals—but they augment it. They enhance political freedom only to the extent that they themselves are translated into *positive* law, specifically, in the form of a durable constitution providing for a separation of powers.

Here I think one must appeal to Arendt's own commonsense view of politics as *minimally* aim-oriented against her own antiutilitarian tendency to treat it as if it were a self-contained display of forensic virtuosity—speaking having no other aim than its own continuation.[4] For even its continuation would depend on the resolution of at least one aim—the implementation of a system of rights. This fact, I submit, is amply registered in Arendt's superior estimation of the American Revolution vis-à-vis its French counterpart. Despite the pathos of Arendt's assessment of the American Revolution—that it deprived later generations of the opportunity to freely constitute themselves, and privileged the pursuit of happiness (social welfare) at the expense of freedom—one also detects the glimmering of a less fateful and tragic outcome. The Founding, she speculates, might have provided an institutional basis for its own permanent and popular revolutionary emendation, had it incorporated provisions for the local establishment of direct participatory democracy modeled after Jefferson's "wards." Far from being vicious, the circularity implicit in *this* mediation of principle and practice, happiness and freedom, ends and means, would be legitimate in the hermeneutical sense mentioned above as well as faithful to Arendt's identification of freedom with political dialogue.

I The Postmodern Critique

Postmodernists like Derrida are skeptical about philosophical legitimations of any sort. It therefore comes as no surprise to find them deconstructing the revolutionary documents of the Enlightenment. Their intent is not to impugn revolutions or revolutionary actions, much less to impugn universal responsibilities with respect to fellow human beings. It is rather to expose the nonsense of conflating universal ethical obligation and partial law. In their opinion, the ethical command to respond to others openly is something akin to an existential presupposition. This universal idea ought not to be confused with any concrete declaration of political rights, because doing so is not only fallacious but ideological—endowing contingent and partial *legal* systems with the sanctified aura of a timeless justice. Given that every modern constitution commits this fallacy when it enjoins universal human rights, none, according to postmodernists, is truly legitimate. Hence revolutionary action is always legitimate for some persons simply because no legal system can be legitimate for all.

The fact that all constitutions are partial in their protection and advancement of political interests would seem to make them easy targets for revolutionaries bent on realizing justice for all. Yet, ironically, postmodernists discard a critical distinction—between morally just (legitimate) and unjust (illegitimate) political regimes—that revolutionaries routinely deploy in justifying their actions. Arguing that there is a rational distinction, or logical incommensurability, between descriptive (constative) and prescriptive (performative) speech acts, speculative and political language games, and so on, they submit that revolutionary initiatives, which are framed as prescriptions of political rights, cannot be justified on metaphysical grounds, which are framed as assertions of natural laws. However, the revolutionary documents of the Enlightenment apparently effect such a justification, they contend, because the language of legitimation itself inevitably renders the distinction between performance and constation indeterminate.

Poststructuralists criticize this language by deconstructing its rationality, or well-foundedness. The appearance of absolute legitimacy effected by such language, they shrewdly observe, depends on simultaneously invoking *and* erasing the rational distinction between free act and necessary law. Now, one of the most illuminating attempts to deconstructively expose this sleight of hand is contained in a public lecture that Derrida delivered at the University of Virginia in 1976, in which he argued that the "meaning and effect" of the Declaration of Independence depends on masking its own historical contingency and political partiality. It ostensibly accomplishes this by conflating two kinds of speech acts, constative and performative, and then conceals this fallacy behind an appeal to God as the highest authority—the "last instance" and "ultimate signature"—of the Declaration.[5]

Derrida initially raises the question of authorization in conjunction with the first problem of circularity mentioned above, the problem of preconstitutional legitimation. The signers of the Declaration claim authorization from the very people whose sovereignty their Declaration authorizes. The signers state that they are acting "in the name and by the authority of the good people of these colonies" when they declare that "these united colonies ... ought to be free." According to Derrida, by simultaneously asserting and enjoining the sovereignty of the American people, they do not *represent* so much as *create* this people. In the words of Derrida,

> This people does not exist. They do *not* exist as an entity, it does *not* exist, *before* this declaration, not *as such.* If it gives birth to itself, as free and independent subject, as possible signer, this can hold only in the act of the signature. The signature invents the signer.... In signing the people say—and do what they say they do, but in differing or deferring themselves through (*différant par*) the intervention of their representatives whose representativity is fully legitimated only by the signature, thus after the fact or the coup (*après coup*)—henceforth, I have a right to sign, in truth I will already have had it since I was able to give it to myself. I will have given myself a name and an "ability" or a "power," understood in the sense of a power- or ability-to-sign by declaration of signature. (*DoI,* p. 10)

In this passage Derrida alludes to the postmodern, future-anterior modality of the Declaration; that is, the unstated assumption that each representative *will have had* the right to sign the Declaration upon signing it. The signature supposedly creates the people that is presumed to authorize the signing.

Stated in such bald terms, this reading of the Declaration seems false. Surely the American people existed *before* the signing; indeed, as Arendt points out, the signing of the Declaration merely reenacted prior political compacts which the colonists believed had been violated by the Crown. And yet, there is a sense in which this new Declaration can be said to officially ratify and authorize the sovereignty of the American people for the first time, namely, in its appeal to a *universal* right to self-determination.

In fact, a closer reading of Derrida's deconstruction of the Declaration shows that he is aware of both possibilities: the American people already possessed the sovereign title to authorize the declaration of its independence *and* this title was first conferred on it by the signers. According to Derrida, the power of the Declaration actually depends on collapsing these two possibilities; on the one hand, the Declaration *does* something; it *makes* the American people free (i.e., it normatively constitutes the sovereign being of the United States). On the other hand, it *represents* a fact; it asserts the historical freedom of Americans. So construed, the viciousness of this circle consists in its commission of the "is-ought" fallacy first discussed by David Hume in the *Treatise*; it infers a prescriptive (or performative) utterance of the form, "There ought to be. . . ," from an assertoric (or constative) utterance of the form "There is. . . ."

Derrida's suggestion that the Declaration commits such a fallacy appears at the conclusion of a long commentary in which he seems to be saying that the problem of preconstitutional legitimation is not satisfactorily resolved by internalizing the circle of authorization in the guise of democratic self-determination. For one thing, this notion limits the binding scope of the Declaration to the signers, who contract with themselves, when its intended scope is the American people and, beyond them, humanity. For another, given that contracting with oneself seems absurd, we are forced to rethink our explanation of political obligation at a higher level, locating the source of obligation in some external agent or divine force.

Although he would probably not admit it—at least not in precisely these terms—I think that Derrida's own ethics of responsibility follows this same logic. It does so, however, by problematizing the traditional metaphysics of presence and cognate notions of democratic representation and self-determination. In Derrida's opinion, to exist humanly is to have one's freedom and identity questioned by an "other" (*l'autre*). Presumably, our ethical *obligation* to respond to something beyond us *follows from* the *necessity* to respond to this questioning. If so, it is incumbent on Derrida to explain how this relationship of "following from" does not commit a naturalistic fallacy of the sort he criticizes in the Declaration. His interpretation of the metaphysical "fact" of responsibility as a kind of "absence" or nonfact might be understood as a step in this direction. In Derrida's opinion, the kind of perpetual suspension, openness, and interruption of identity that signifies responsibility leads away from a metaphysics of presence toward a deontology of existence. Such a nihilistic "metaphysics" supposedly explains why even the most modest acts of political representation and self-determination are incoherent. One cannot represent oneself to oneself, or be obligated to oneself in the Rousseauean sense, because what is supposedly represented (one's own self) was never fully present in the first place, but is at best a promise, or idea, whose conditions of satisfaction—the closure of dialogue and the termination of responsibility—are forever deferred.[6] Thus, by being unconditionally obligated to the Other, one avoids the exclusionary violence of a *self*-contained and *self*-centered type of autonomy that relates to the Other as if (s)he were a dependent *thing*.

Now, it is just this violence that the signers of the Declaration perpetrate when they affirm the rights of "Man" while deliberately denying the full humanity of slaves, native Americans, and women. As we all know, what enabled them to entertain this hypocrisy was a metaphysics of racial and gender superiority. However, in Derrida's opinion, this rather trite observation conceals a more sinister rationale—one buried deep within the Western metaphysical tradition dating back to Plato. Ostensibly, the binary, foundational mode of truth-functional reasoning characteristic of Western *logos* directly implicates a dual hierarchy of being and value with God—the quintessential archetype of Eurocentric masculine self-possession—as supreme lord and master.

But God is not only the final command in a long chain of authority and domination; He is what makes possible the very transition from being to act (value) in the first place. That is why the Declaration must appeal to God—the "coup of force (that) makes right"—as the final judge authorizing man-made law (*DoI*, p. 11). This is explicit in the second paragraph of the Preamble of the Declaration, which begins with the famous words, "We hold these truths to be self-evident, that all men are created equal; that they are endowed by their Creator with certain inalienable rights ... " Although the signers of the Declaration presume to represent not just themselves, their constituencies, or humanity but the Creator Himself in asserting these rights, it is only the Creator who can effect the transition from what is essential and necessary in the natural order of things to what is right (permissible) in the domain of human affairs. Indeed the very logic of the deduction demands that it *should* be so. In claiming that "these united colonies are and of right ought to be free and independent states," the representatives violate what, in Derrida's opinion, is a logical distinction between "the to be and the ought to be, the constation and the prescription, the fact and the right" that only God—the "creator of nature and ... supreme judge of what is" (*DoI*, p. 13)—can bridge. In other words, it is only God—the foundation of reason and being—who can bridge the fact/value dualism posited by reason, for it is He alone, after all, who "founds natural laws and thus the whole game which tends to present performative utterances *as* constative utterance" (*DoI*, p. 11).

Since it is God who founds the laws of reason and nature that supposedly legitimate the racial and gender exclusions implicit in the Declaration's linking of European manhood with humanity, and the latter with moral agency and right, it is not surprising that Derrida should focus on the distinctly *metaphysical* violence effected by *this* transition from being to act. But he then misses what is perhaps of greater interest in the Declaration's assertion of inalienable rights, namely its foundation in a nonmetaphysical, nonhierarchical transition from being to act—or from social fact to moral obligation—of the sort implicit in the *performance* of a social contract, conceived as the outcome of a distinctly *dialogic* mode of reasoning and deliberation.

Derrida overlooks this alternative foundation because he conceives rationality too narrowly, as a *self-contained* mode of *monological* deduction premissed on a logical dualism between performative and constative utterances.[7] Is he right about this? J. L. Austin, who invented the distinction between performatives and constatives, thought that constatives might also be regarded as performative. Unlike factual propositions that play no role in actual conversation and interaction, such "speech acts" explicitly raise expectations for future justification.[8] John Searle—who is Austin's leading contemporary proponent and one of Derrida's harshest critics—elaborated further on the possibilities of this ambiguity. In a paper written some years ago Searle sought to show how a prescription, such as "Jones ought to pay Smith five dollars," might follow—either deductively *or* nondeductively—from a factual statement asserting that "Jones uttered the words 'I hereby promise to pay you, Smith, five dollars.'" Simply put, Searle used speech act theory to show how promising is both factually constituted and normatively regulated by certain sorts of *institutional rules*.

By parity of reasoning, one could argue that social contracts, as factual instances of mutual promising, imply normative obligations to the extent that the actual conditions underlying their performance approximate the *ideal* expectations of the contractors. In other words, one can conceive social contracts as the "conclusion" of a dialogue in which each contractor *responds* to the Other as both a fellow human being and as a unique individual possessing specific needs and interests that will have to be respected and attended to. By presenting *reasons* in support of certain legal principles, viz., by showing how these principles respect the reasonable needs and interests of all, the contractors actually *constitute* their own individual and collective identities in a manner that continually disrupts (puts at risk) the identity of the self-contained, self-sufficient ego.

Each contractor, we suppose, respects the Other's equal right to present arguments and counterarguments (which may or may not take the form of deductive inferences) free from internal and external constraints. The dialogic expectations of mutuality, equality, freedom, sincerity, inclusiveness, and good faith are purely ideal and regulative, so that the binding nature of the obligation, that is, its validity as a collective inference, can never be absolute. However, to the extent that these expectations are *reasonably approximated in reality*, its binding authority and rational validity will have to be conceded, at least conditionally, as a just agreement mutually concluded by all.

Without entering into a detailed discussion of this demonstration, we can see that, just as certain utterances containing words such as "promise" instantiate *both* prescriptions and descriptions, so certain dialogic agreements, constituted by uttering such words in appropriate circumstances, instantiate *both* facts and values. For in uttering performative words and in concluding agreements in the appropriate circumstances one has in fact promised and concluded; and having taken on the appropriate institutional obligations, one ought (all things being equal) to abide by them.[9] As we shall see, something like this point also underlies Arendt's take on the promissory act authorizing the Declaration.

If Derrida acknowledges the ambiguous, performative/descriptive status of speech acts such as contracting, he does so in order to *de*construct their monological logic, not *re*construct their dialogical rationale. Lacking recourse to a dialogic conception of rational authorization, he prematurely concludes that there are no satisfactory solutions to the problems of preconstitutional and prepolitical legitimation. As for the former problem, he submits that sovereignty—be it personal or national—is never present, but remains deferred in light of future acts of political questioning. Logocentric notions of representation and self-determination that imply the contrary—a *closed* and *self-contained* circle—are therefore vicious and violently exclusive of the absent Other. As for the problem of prepolitical legitimation, Derrida argues that the attempt to derive political rights from metaphysical absolutes commits a naturalistic fallacy. This in turn conceals the partiality of legal regimes no less than the ethical responsibility of agents engaged in voluntary political acts.

II The Modern Counter

Let us grant for the sake of argument that, from the standpoint of formal logic, the languages of philosophy and politics, constation and performance are radically incommensurable, so that you cannot infer a phrase belonging to one of them from a phrase belonging to another. Does it then follow that these different kinds of speech cannot supervene on one another without commission of a fallacy? Can we conceive the circle of legitimation in a nonvicious, *hermeneutical* way, so that appeal to an objective authority—be it historical tradition or "timeless" principle—does not collide with the free constitution of a future?

My reading of Arendt, whom I see as responding positively to this question, will doubtless strike many as too facile and optimistic given the favorable reception accorded her writings by Derrida and other postmodernists, who are more circumspect about the tragic consequences of modernity and more hesitant about affirming the legitimacy of any regime.[10] Yet, despite her denunciation of legitimating ideologies based on metaphysical absolutes, Arendt found nothing inherently illegitimate about at least *one* universal right—the right to have rights—and for that reason alone one can conclude that she regarded both the general idea of rights and its particular legal instantiations as legitimate. In her opinion, the grounds for making this positive judgment could only be secular. Neither nature, reason, nor tradition suffice to legitimate rights, but just those constitutive rules or procedures of common deliberation definitive of human political life, including the obligation—proclaimed by Derrida among others—to respond openly to one's interlocutor as a singular person. These procedural rights, she insisted, remain empty and impotent—rights that are not rights—so long as they remain unincorporated into a democratic constitution. In short, what secures their meaningfulness and efficacy—and with it, the actor's autonomy and responsibility—are just those political actions and legal judgments (or narratives) that they themselves regulate.

Arendt frames her discussion of these hermeneutical circles (of application and appropriation) in terms of a decisive contrast between premodern and modern revolutions. The *premodern*, astronomical sense of revolution as a recurrent cycle still survived in the "Glorious Revolution of 1688" that understood itself to be "a restoration of monarchical power to its former righteousness and glory" (p. 43). By contrast, the first *modern* revolutions—the American Revolution of 1776 and the French Revolution of 1789—not only restored ancient liberties, but also refounded them on a totally new, universal order. Between past and future, they revolved back to the republican models of Greek and Roman antiquity in order to revolve ahead to a final, lasting, constitution of freedom. Hence their need for some higher authorization beyond the transient realm of politics.

But how is such authorization possible? The inherent open-endedness of the hermeneutical circle speaks against it. Caught between the antipodes of modernity—universal finality and fleeting novelty—legitimation seems all but inconceivable. Hence the revolutionaries' tendency to collapse these poles into one timeless absolute.

Now, a superficial reading of her "deconstruction" of the Declaration suggests that Arendt is in basic agreement with postmodernists in criticizing the philosophical appeal to absolutes.

Jefferson's famous words, "We hold these truths to be self-evident," combine in a historically unique manner the basis of agreement between those who have embarked on revolution, an agreement necessarily relative because related to those who enter it, with an absolute, namely with a truth that needs no agreement since, because of its self-evidence, it compels without argumentative demonstration or political persuasion. (p. 192)

In this passage Arendt seems to agree with Derrida that political and philosophical modes of speech are incompatible. Indeed, she makes the case more strongly by suggesting that philosophical assertions about necessary and universal laws contradict human freedom: "By virtue of being self-evident, these truths are prerational—they inform reason but are not its product—and since their self-evidence puts them beyond disclosure and argument, they are in a sense no less compelling than 'despotic power' and no less absolute than the revealed truths of religions or the axiomatic verities of mathematics" (p. 192). The impression that philosophical language has no legitimate place in the Declaration is further reinforced by another curious remark. As if to get Jefferson off the hook, she adds that if he had solely intended to justify his claim that "all men are created equal" philosophically, he would have dispensed with the performative (or practical) speech act "We hold . . . " and simply asserted: "These truths are self-evident" (p. 193).

From this last remark it is apparent that Arendt agrees with Derrida that Jefferson's declaration illegitimately conflates performative political speech and constative philosophical speech, but disagrees with him about whether this particular conflation was necessary in order to procure the declaration's authority. For unlike him, she thinks that its rhetorical effect is entirely secured by the performative act alone. The constation of divinely preordained right was redundant, she submits, because what really legitimated the declaration was its own *reenactment* of the sorts of social contracts that had been made by the colonists dating back to the Mayflower Compact, and its *reassertion* of the kinds of rights that typically entered into such agreements.

But surely that cannot be the whole story, for Arendt herself insists that what was distinctly modern about the American Revolution was not its restoration of local and contingent rights, but its declaration of their universality. Indeed, recalling the passage cited above, it is possible to understand her objection against metaphysical truths ("they inform reason but are not its product") as an objection *not* against universal principles, but against any absolute that claims to be valid *independently of supplemental political acts of collective justification and interpretation.*

Now, Arendt expressly adverts to one such praxis-immanent absolute. In her opinion, "it is futile to search for an absolute to break the vicious circle in which all beginning is inevitably caught, because this 'absolute' lies in the very act of beginning itself" (p. 204). The "beginning" she had in mind is both philosophical—referring to a principle of free action—*and* historical—referring to contingent precedents. Let us start with the historical beginning, as Arendt's treatment of it illustrates the circular relationship of justification and interpretation that obtains between principles and practices as well as between past, present, and future.

For Arendt, "no revolution is even possible where the authority of the body politic is truly intact."[11] So, faced with the dilemma of either having to invoke an old authority in violation of their emancipatory ideal or having to relinquish any historical title to their newly acquired power, the revolutionaries compromised: they filled old bottles with new wine. They not only justified their acts as *restorations* of ancient liberties that had been illegitimately suppressed under absolutist government. They did so in an absolutist manner that mimicked the very power and authority they were rebelling against. For, "just as the old concept of liberty, because of the attempted restoration, came to exert a strong influence on the interpretation of the new experience of freedom, so the old understanding of power and authority, even if their former representatives were most violently denounced, almost automatically led the new experience of power to be channeled into concepts which had just been vacated" (p. 155).

According to Arendt, the revolutionaries could scarcely avoid appealing to absolutes given the fact that preceding generations of monarchs had solved the problem of authority "within the given frame of reference in which the legitimacy of rules . . . had always been justified by relating them to an absolute source" (p. 160). The revolutionaries' appeal, however, reconfigured that frame of reference. For they argued that the absolute power and authority presumed by the monarchs usurped the power and authority of God's messengers along with the power and authority of political agents engaged in radical acts of self-determination:

> The specific sanction which religion and religious authority had bestowed upon the secular realm could not simply be replaced by an absolute sovereignty, which, lacking a transcendent and transmundane source, could only degenerate into tyranny and despotism. The truth of the matter was that when the Prince "had stepped into the pontifical shoes of the Pope and Bishop," he did not, for that reason, *assume the function* and receive the sanctity of Bishop or Pope; in the language of political theory, he was not a successor but a usurper, despite all the new theories about sovereignty and the divine rights of princes. (pp. 159–169, my italics)

For the revolutionaries, then, the illegitimacy of absolute monarchy consisted in transferring a spiritual conception of power and authority to public life, with the result that the *proper functions* of both religion and politics—the former being the absolute relationship between private moral conscience and God, and the latter a contingent, social contract between political equals—were violated.

Clearly, if the legitimacy of modern revolutions depended on historically appropriating the absolutist framework of authority and power, it could only be the bare *form* or *function* of that framework, not its specific *substance*.[12] In fact, there was a profound substantive difference between the deistic God of the revolutionaries, who allows human beings to interact freely and equally in accordance with their own rational natures, and the paternalistic God of the monarchs, who assigns their governance to His divinely anointed trustees.

By attenuating divine intervention in human affairs, deism brought about a profound reversal. It transferred the final authority and absolute power that had formerly been vested in God to human beings acting in accordance with their own secular principles. That might explain why Arendt held that the inalienable rights proclaimed by Jefferson "were in principle independent of religious sanction" (p. 171). As she later notes,

> The absolute from which the beginning is to derive its own validity and which must save it, as it were, from its inherent arbitrariness is the principle which, together with it, makes its appearance in the world.... The principle that came to light during those fateful years (of the American Revolution) when the foundations were laid—not by the strength of one architect but by the combined power of the many—was the interconnected principle of mutual promise and common deliberation. (p. 214)

Contrary to Arendt's earlier discussion of Jefferson's famous proclamation, the above acknowledgment of absolute foundations rather reaffirms the lesson implicit in Searle's derivation of "ought" from "is," namely, that performative *acts* such as promising and deliberating depend on institutional *facts*. This alternative reading of Jefferson's proclamation is suggested by Arendt herself, when she says that the principle of open discussion (p. 268) regulating political argumentation and demonstration comprises "the very grammar of political action." (pp. 173, 192).[13] As she later remarks, the principles (*archai*) on which the architects act are also *origins* as well as *ends*; they are a "law of action ... that remains *apparent* as long as the action lasts" (p. 213). In other words, acts of promising and deliberating both enact—bring to finality—and constate (present) their a priori conditions of possibility. They constitute substantive rights in a manner that accords with, interprets, and realizes the universal idea of right—the very procedure that constitutes the constituting (the democratic act of promising and deliberating). In acts of promising and dialogic deliberation, revolutionary lawmakers *factually* assume the equality, autonomy, mutual openness and responsibility of their fellow interlocutors *and* they *normatively* enjoin and *constitute* it.

Significantly, the "entirely new concept of power and authority" (p. 166) revealed by the Declaration of Independence is *not* based on a "homogeneity of past and origin" (that is, on a *particular* language community bound by common traditions), but on practices of promising and deliberation that are virtually identifiable with the possibility of *any* human community. If we look to the past of particular cultures—say, the republican culture of ancient Greece and the absolutist culture of Catholic Christendom—for guidance in founding these practices, it is a past that, in the words of Arendt, exemplifies something universal—a relatively *constant* function. This *timeless* past can be invoked by revolutionaries to liberate the present from an oppressive and *parochial* past. But if these exemplary *archai* are more compelling than the contingent outcomes of dialogic deliberation, it is not because they are axioms from which we might *logically* derive such outcomes.[14] Rather, as general presuppositions *of* reasoning their own substantive meaning and institutional concretion unfolds *in* reasoning, namely, in discursive reflection and interpretation.

Arendt's argument that the American Revolution succeeded where the French Revelution failed also confirms this reading. As she points out, "the most obvious and the most decisive distinction between the American and French Revolutions was that the historical inheritance of the American Revolution was 'limited monarchy' and that of the French Revolution an absolutism which apparently reached far back into the first centuries of our era and the last centuries of the Roman Empire" (p. 155). The legacy of absolutism that burdened both revolutions was philosophical and theological. In the case of the French Revolution, however, the legacy in question equated freedom with a united will (Robespierre's "Il faut une volonté UNE"). That legacy proved useful to revolutionaries confronting the daunting task of saving Europe's starving masses, whose need for material security they ensconced as a *natural* right. But substituting the utilitarian satisfaction of a natural necessity for the active pursuit of freedom could not but prove disastrous for politics. This explains why, for Arendt, the French Revolution betrayed its emancipatory promise and degenerated into a caricature of the very absolutism it had overthrown. In what is perhaps an ironic gloss on the *instrumental failure* of that revolution, Arendt notes that the French leaders could not have allowed their revolution to succeed—that is, congeal into a permanent constitutional democracy—without consenting to the lawful disruption of their won dictatorship through regular election of new majorities. To have done otherwise would have frustrated the achievement of their own transcendent aims. Yet their Rousseauean equation of democratic polity with a sovereign general will that can never bind itself suggests that, for them, any *fixed* aim—even that of freedom—would have been too binding. That explains why the totalitarian descendants of the French Revolution in our present century manifested themselves as *movements* whose centers of power, Arendt incisively observed, resided in the anarchic forces of the secret police, not in the lawful powers of an enduring constitutional regime.

By contrast, nothing more clearly attests to the greater success of the Founding Fathers in breaking with the absolutist legacy than the durable authority of their accomplishments. Unburdened by the thought of starving masses, slaves, and general wills, their aim was to fashion a lasting constitution that would safeguard and *progressively augment* the freedom they already enjoyed.[15] Their belief—inherited from Montesquieu—that power is augmented through its constitutional division and opposition testifies to the inherent plurality of the human condition. More importantly, it mirrors the principle of the social contract—agreement based on a free and equal exchange of opinions—without which communication, responsibility, and identity would be impossible.

Contrary to Derrida, then, Arendt suggests that the rights and duties concordant with the idea of responsibility are *indirectly* grounded in the universal grammar of politics. This enables her to avoid the paradox of prepolitical legitimation as well as the naturalistic fallacy that ostensibly accompanies it; for the conditions that determine and constrain political acts partially derive their force from these very same acts. The laws that citizens voluntarily give themselves interpret *and* constitute the moral presuppositions underlying lawmaking as such. Without constitutional acts like these, the force of that moral imperative so extolled by postmodernists—the obligation to behave responsibly toward others—would be indeterminate and weak.

Yet this hermeneutical circle is not quite so unproblematic as it seems. If Derrida is correct about the open-ended historicity of interpretation, the Arendtian idea of politics as the making present (or the making appear) of some universal principle is absurd. The problem is not simply that the meaning and validity of a constitutional principle is always suspended, or open to further questioning and reinterpretation. It is that the *progressive realization* of the founding principle that is necessary for its *continuing* efficacy, validity, and meaning diminishes the meaning and legitimacy of its origin. Not only is the legitimation of a revolution a desideratum that can never be fulfilled, but *in retrospect* the revolution was never as free as the contemporary practice it founded, because those who have benefited from its *progressive realization* are by definition freer than those who founded it.

III The Progressive Deferral of Legitimation

In order to address these problems of preconstitutional legitimation we must take a closer look at the *temporal* space in which they emerge: suspended between past and future, the moment of legitimation never fully appears or presents itself. The reader will recall that, for Arendt, the legitimacy of a revolution descends from both a prior claim entitling (or *empowering*) it and a subsequent success *authorizing* it. These temporal dimensions recall her earliest "transcendental" reflections on the nature of freedom, which is not surprising, given that, in her judgment, revolutionaries not only act in the name of freedom, but also exemplify it.[16] In beginning something radically new and unpredictable, they reveal the extent of their own undetermined "natality." Conversely, in founding a democratic constitution providing for its own progressive emendation, they continue their revolution into the future, bringing about a greater freedom than they themselves had previously enjoyed.[17]

Herein lies a tension. Thanks to the constitution and its continuous progression, our political assent is in some measurable sense freer than that given by our forefathers, just as theirs was vis-à-vis their unenlightened predecessors. But we ourselves are in no better position to confer legitimacy, for our own sovereign rights are in the process of being constituted by the unfinished event.

The denial of natality and legitimacy that comes with the *progressive realization* of the constitution is but the mirror image of the same that comes with its *regressive diminution*, or devolution into mundane utilitarian politics. Our contemporary efforts at constitutional reform seem conventional and routine in comparison to the original founding act, just as that act seems conventional and routine in comparison to the archaic republican event that inspired it.

Recalling that the dilemma elaborated above plays on philosophical beginnings and ends no less than historical ones, we now detect at least *four* legitimation problems. On the one hand, there are problems of historical and philosophical entitlement, which concern the originary grounds that regressively empower revolutionary acts. On the other hand, there are historical and philosophical problems of retroactive validation, which concern the final purposes that progressively authorize their continuation.

Let us begin with the problem of entitlement. It raises the following question: In whose name and by what right was the act originally undertaken? Suppose we try to give a historical answer to this question. In that case we are caught in the following double bind. Either the new regime accepts as legitimate the basic concepts and institutions of the political tradition it opposes (in which case it can claim to be a legitimate heir—but not a revolution); or it does not (in which case it seems arbitrary and without apparent reason or cause). In both cases its legitimacy seems diminished in comparison to what preceded it. If we try to give a philosophical answer to this problem we encounter a different kind of legitimation problem, one revolving around the concept of freedom (natality). Either revolutionaries act in the name of some absolute principle that constrains the mutual assent of humanity—in which case they are not spontaneously self-determining agents. Or they do not, in which case, being unprincipled—driven by natural need and constrained by conventional sanction—they remain as unfree as before.

A similar dialectic applies to the problem of retroactive validation, which concerns the end rather than the origin of revolutionary acts. In inquiring into the authoritative attraction a revolution exerts on its proponents we ask: Why revolt? For what purpose? Suppose we give a historical answer to this question: We revolt for the sake of progress, to establish an enduring constitution in which people will be freer than they are *now*. If the revolution succeeds, it will have violated its own principle of self-determination. For how can it be progressive to deny subsequent generations the opportunity to exercise real—that is, revolutionary—self-determination? To reiterate Jefferson's concern, how can subsequent generations be legitimately bound by an act they could not have possibly authorized? The democratic self-determination that they enjoy is not of their own making; and its institutional framework may even frustrate constitutional emendation. Of course, if the revolution does not succeed all at once, there will indeed be plenty of opportunities for the people to reconstitute themselves freely through progressive efforts of reform. But that will have meant that at no point along the axis of reform will the people have succeeded in fully constituting their own freedom. The revolutionary moment in which self-determination and legitimacy coincide will have been deferred until the utopian moment of completion.

The double bind is somewhat different if we give a philosophical answer to the question. Suppose I want to revolt for the sake of realizing some transcendent, absolute ideal. If the end is truly final, then no constitution will be able to embody it. But short of actually doing so, no constitution will be legitimate, and our revolution will have been declared a failure. The alternative to this kind of utopian anarchism is a more qualified, immanent idealism that identifies the purposes to be achieved with what was resolved and realized, once and for all, by the concrete articles set forth in the constitution itself, or in some emendation of it. But in that case success is again purchased at the cost of legitimacy. Having no other purpose but to be itself, the revolution cannot progress, and indeed, seems pointless—a dead end that ought not to be continued for fear of extinguishing the very political life in whose name it was instituted.

Does Arendt's appreciation of the hermeneutical circle informing these paradoxes provide a better "resolution" of them than the postmodern alternative—one that enables us to say, for example, that despite their historical suspension between past and future, beginning and end, *some* declarations of rights *are* (presently) legitimate? The answer is yes. For a *proper* appreciation of the hermeneutical circle would seem to suggest that a free act of legitimation is no less realizable as a phenomenal *presence* than as an open-ended interpretation of meaning. Of course, Derrida would demur; the hermeneutical circle portends aporetic—if not tragic—consequences for even the most (seemingly) unproblematic shibboleths of common sense. For him, insisting that no law is truly legitimate seems as right as insisting that no text is truly meaningful; in both cases meaning and legitimacy get swallowed up in the abyssal non-presence of past and future. Despite these nihilistic implications, Derrida wants to affirm the "deconstructibility" of law as "a stroke of luck for all politics, for all historical *progress* [my stress]," and he wants to do it, no less, by linking deconstruction to the open-ended imperative to be just (*FoL*, p. 15).

In "The Force of Law" Derrida observes that this transcendent ethical imperative supervenes on law from the outside (*FoL*, p. 14–15). Presumably, it is the continual interruption of business as usual by ethical conscience that explains inventive deviations from standard legal practice. This inventiveness, in turn, supposedly makes "progress" possible.

But does it? Because, in Derrida's account, transcendent justice commands openness vis-à-vis the *wholly* Other, he can only conceive the interface between ethical principle and legal precedent as a *catastrophic* moment. In its deconstructive capacity interpretation is destructive; the judge decides as if he or she "invented the law in every case" (*FoL*, p. 23). But as Derrida points out, such inventiveness is no more legitimate than mechanical application:

> If the rule guarantees (the decision) in no uncertain terms, so that the judge is a calculating machine, which happens, and we will not say that he is just, free and responsible. But we also won't say it if he doesn't refer to any law, to any rule or if, because he doesn't take any rule for granted beyond his own interpretation, he suspends his decision, stops short before the undecidable or if he improvises and leaves aside all rules, all principles. It follows from this paradox that there is never a moment that we can say *in the present* that a decision *is* just (that is free and responsible), or that someone *is* a just man—even less, "I *am* just." (*FoL*, p. 23)

Here Derrida poses—without resolving—the four paradoxes of legitimacy mentioned above. First, he tells us that ethical responsibility requires acting in the name of justice, not the law. In elevating private moral conscience above legal precedent, however, jurists act irresponsibly, without the guidance of established criteria of reasonableness. Yet mechanically adhering to the strict letter of the law is equally irresponsible when the matter to be decided is unprecedented and recalcitrant to legal calculation (or subsumption). Second, Derrida insists that the ethical imperative remain open-ended and indeterminate. But then it will not be able to move judgment in any determinate direction. This movement will be effected by the force of law. Third, in Derrida's moral universe, the rebellious reinvention of the constitution in every legislative and adjudicative act ensures that the constitution does not ossify into an oppressive force constraining the freedom of future generations.

Its fleeting legitimacy, however, will be purchased at the expense of liberties that might otherwise have had the protection of standing law. Fourth, consonant with their lack of authority, Derrida quite rightly concludes that legal systems cannot possibly realize the utopian ends of justice. As he puts it, "in the founding of the law or in its institution, the same problem of justice will have been posed and violently resolved, that is to say buried, dissimulated, repressed" (*FoL*, p. 23).

Needless to say, the antipodes of permanent repetition and permanent revolution do not leave much room for that historical progress so sought after by Derrida. In this scheme, progression of the past (origin) toward a future (end) remains essentially enigmatic. However, once we see that ethics and politics, idea and reality, future and past mediate each other as necessarily as narrative part and whole do, the progressive nature of revolutionary action sheds its aporetic guise. As noted earlier, the impact of theocentric and political absolutism on the secular thinking of revolutionaries illustrates the powerful effects of tradition in shaping ideas. The revolutionaries could not have understood their own actions as reasonable responses to the provocations of a failed political tradition had they not done so in terms of the categories and expectations of that very same tradition. Second, however, this example shows how human understanding applies the tradition within which it moves in a way that invests it with new meaning and validity so that it always interprets *differently* the frame of reference it has inherited. In the case before us, the difference involved a radical reversal; the deistic interpretation of an absolute, divine legislator legitimated the humanistic idea of radical self-determination.

In summarizing the lessons provided by this example, one could say that revolutions inherit their legitimate title only on condition that they found a new lineage. Conversely, the radical overthrow of the old line of descent—in this case, the reversal of its authoritative meaning—does not completely break with it; at best, it interrupts it. To paraphrase Hegel, the revolutionary destruction of an oppressive political reality by an ethical idea (freedom)—or perhaps what amounts to the same thing, the repudiation of the present by a past pregnant with the future and a future pregnant with the past—has the character of a determinate negation, or *representation* that reapplies and reappropriates as much as it reverses (overturns).[18]

Of course the kind of progress that builds on the interpretative appropriation of authoritative precedents need not involve a revolutionary reversal of meaning. More typically, it involves eliminating anachronism and expanding meaning. The successful reinterpretation of a constitution generally preserves and augments its authority, that is, it demonstrates its "timeless" and "universal" validity as an exemplar of philosophical principle. In that case the authoritative meaning and legitimacy of a revolutionary act is never finally determinable.[19] Indeed, it is not inconceivable that a constitutional tradition might exhaust its meaning and validity for future generations faced with a new revolutionary crisis. But under more felicitous circumstances the provision for constitutional amendment or reinterpretation enables the original act of self-determination to be carried forward in ways that can be quite revolutionary in their own right (p. 202).

Here the history of American constitutional law provides a good benchmark for assessing the extent to which future generations can radically redefine the extent of their freedom.[20] Just as the Civil War amendments extended the protections afforded by the Bill of Rights to all persons (at least in principle) and redefined the limits of state intrusion, so too the New Deal "superstatutes" compensated for new restrictions on contractual and property rights by expanding the scope of personal privacy and political inclusion.[21] On the basis of this type of progress one might well conclude (*pace* Arendt) that the opportunity for *all* American citizens to exercise rational self-determination through "revolutionary" emendation of the Constitution has increased, rather than decreased, since the time of the Founding.

However relative it might be to changing circumstances, progress in the field of American law would have been all but inconceivable had the Constitution and the Declaration of Independence not been inspired by universal principles. The hermeneutical circle, in which human understanding moves, explains why the ideal demands of justice can never be absolutely transcendent and opposed to the legal traditions that give them concrete force and meaning, just as it explains why these same traditions tend to expand or generalize their meaning in the course of repeated application. Thus, although the Fourteenth Amendment to the constitution was originally interpreted as applying only to former slaves, it eventually took on the meaning of a philosophical principle enjoining equal protection for all persons.

In conclusion, I have argued that Arendt's explanation of the problems of political legitimation in the modern era can meet some or all of the objections raised by postmodernists, like Derrida, who question whether any state can be legitimated on any grounds. Her explanation also provides a better understanding of how revolutionary foundations are free, contingent undertakings, continuous with the past in only the most formal sense. Ultimately it provides a better interpretation of the Declaration of Independence than Derrida's, because it enables us to understand how revolutionaries could appeal to necessary and universal conditions (or absolutes) in a way that was consistent with their freedom and hence in a way that was legitimate. For the universals in question are not substantive rights that impose specific constraints, but abstract principles of procedural justice that, in a far less determinate way, regulate the free, democratic constitution of rights generally. Arendt's interpretation is also better because it accounts for the possibility of legal progress, which presupposes the mediation of transcendent ethical principle and contingent political action. Although Derrida himself adverts to the inseparability of these moments, he does so in order to cast aspersions on their rationality. But only someone so committed to conceiving rationality as a presuppositionless, foundational form of thinking would draw such skeptical conclusions about the hermeneutical circle. And only such a skeptic would be drawn to the politically paralyzing view that no revolutionary founding can be legitimate, because either politics corrupts the pristine transcendence of ethics with secular biases, or the pristine transcendence of ethics corrupts politics with metaphysical mystification, thereby concealing from us our own responsibility. Rulers since time immemorial have indeed cloaked their domination of the Other in ideologies that have served to rationalize the necessity of their violence. All that this shows is that the line separating legitimate from illegitimate foundations is often vague, and so requires ongoing clarification in the freest, fairest, and most in(con)clusive dialogue possible.

Notes

Acknowledgment: I am indebted to Larry May, Doug Litowitz, Liam Harte, and an anonymous reader for recommending revisions of earlier drafts of this essay.

1. Unless otherwise specified, all page references are from H. Arendt, *On Revolution* (London: Penguin, 1973).

2. Following Hans-Georg Gadamer's compelling demonstration in *Wahrheit und Methode* (1960), I take it that the part/whole, universal/particular, and past/present circles are all present and of a piece in every act of understanding.

3. As used in this essay, a metaphysical absolute is any necessary and universal presupposition (condition, principle, or ground) that remains essentially unqualified by contingent historical circumstances. A nonmetaphysical absolute, by contrast, is any condition that possesses universality and necessity in a historically qualified sense. Arendt's "grammar of politics," like the pragmatic rules (or ideals) regulating rational communication, are "absolutes" in this latter sense; having historically emerged in modern times, their concrete force and meaning varies with respect to the manifold ways in which historically situated political agents have interpreted them.

4. This distinction is grounded in her differentiation of the "human condition" into three distinct spheres of activity: political action (the realm of freedom), cultural fabrication (the realm of meaning), and labor (the realm of material reproduction). Roughly speaking, instrumental action aimed at the production of some use-value (happiness) functions within the economy of labor, whereas political action oriented toward freedom, functions within the space of spontaneous expression. Arendt's taxonomy of action spheres—which also survives in a more attenuated form in Habermas's own assignment of workplaces and public spaces to system and lifeworld, respectively—problematizes not only workplace democracy but any goal-oriented democratic politics (as Habermas himself acknowledges). Yet Habermas and Arendt are surely right to distinguish the praxis of collective deliberation definitive of public opinion formation from the economics of administrative decision and preference aggregation definitive of voting. Suffice it to say, the distinction does not rule out all utilitarian (instrumental) motives for political action, given that one of the purposes for entering into political debate will be to ensure its continuation through the successful establishment of constitutional guarantees. See note 10 below for further discussion of this issue; for Arendt's treatment of the distinction between political and purposive action, see *The Human Condition* (Chicago: University of Chicago Press, 1958); for my examination of Arendt's taxonomies of the *vita activa* and *vita contemplativa*, especially as these bear on Habermas's and Lyotard's political theories, see *Reason, History, and Politics: The Communitarian Grounds of Legitimation in the Modern Age* (Albany: State University of New York Press, 1995), pp. 286–288, 293–298.

5. J. Derrida, "Declarations of Independence," trans. Tom Keenan and Tom Pepper, *New Political Science* 15:7 (1986), p. 12, hereafter *DoI.*

6. Arendt reaches a similar conclusion by a somewhat different train of reasoning. She thinks the problem of political representation permits no solution, because either representatives are messengers—bound to convey their constituents' interests and hence replaceable by plebiscites—or they are independent judges of the common good—rulers rather than representatives. Because plebiscites require the administrative aggregation of interests, both instances amount to "elective despotism" (p. 237). Given this paradox, Arendt could only endorse representative government with the gravest of reservations. Although she conceded that representation enabled poor people and others "exclusively given to their personal interest" to control their rulers without having to directly participate in political debate (p. 133), she firmly denied that it enabled them to *present* themselves in a free, publicly recognizable way.

7. Besides entailing the illegitimacy of inferring performatives from constatives, the logical incommensurability between "is" and "ought" renders an important class of ethical utterances illegitimate as well, namely those essentialist claims about human nature that im-

plicitly enjoin the perfectibility of the essential quality they assert. Again, recall Derrida's assertion/prescription that persons ought to act responsibly toward one another because they are (necessarily) responsible to and for one another. Does Derrida think this assertion/prescription is illegitimate? There is some evidence to think that he does. After all, he himself notes how hard it is for speakers to resist the "metaphysical" illusion that the language they speak represents rather than constitutes reality (J. Derrida, *Positions*, trans. A. Bass [Chicago: University of Chicago Press, 1981], pp. 58–59). And because he has made much of the inherent undecidability of performance and constation in all language—especially deconstructive language—he seems to accept the *logical* verdict that all language is illegitimate and nonsensical to some degree (See, for example, the section subtitled "Beyond the Speech Act" in J. Derrida, "Psyche: Inventions of the Other," in W. Godzich and L. Waters, eds., *Reading De Man Reading* (Minneapolis: University of Minnesota Press, 1986). Whether this makes his own work an ironic exercise in self-refutation is for the reader to decide. Yet, regardless of how one resolves this issue, one thing remains abundantly clear: Derrida's apparent belief that *all* language *must* conflate performance and constation, use and mention, in an illegitimate *foundationalist* manner reveals more about the anti-hermeneutical, metaphysical cast of his own thought than it does about the representational mystifications of language. For a concise but sympathetic critique of Derrida on this point see D. Hoy, "Philosophemes," *London Review of Books* (23 November 1989).

8. Cf. J. L. Austin, *How to Do Things With Words*, 2d ed. (Cambridge: Harvard University Press, 1975), lecture 11.

9. J. Searle, "How to Derive 'Ought' from 'Is' ", in *Readings in Ethical Theory*, 2d ed., ed. by W. Sellars and J. Hospers (New York: Appleton-Century-Crofts, 1970), pp. 63–72. It might be argued that the ceteris paribus clause, which stipulates, inter alia, that Jones's obligation to keep his promise is not overriden by other obligations, conceals an evaluation, namely that regardless of what other obligations Jones has, Jones ought to keep his promise. That Searle's invocation of the ceteris paribus clause equivocates between *entitlement* (given the *fact* that no one has yet informed Jones of any overriding obligation, he is entitled to keep his promise) and *entailment* (given that no overriding obligation *could* arise *in principle*, he is compelled, logically, to keep his promise) must be conceded. So his derivation is not, as he himself claims it is, a strictly logical deduction. For our purposes, however, it suffices to note that even a weaker interpretation of Searle's derivation, namely that it explains how Jones might be weakly obligated (entitled) to keep his promise—regardless of whether he ought to or not in some unconditional sense—rebuts Derrida's objection that no obligation (however weak) follows from any constation of fact (however institutional and non-metaphysical). Cf. James Thompson and Judith Thompson, "How Not to Derive 'Ought' from 'Is' ", *Readings in Ethical Theory*, pp. 73–77.

10. There are undoubtedly strong postmodern resonances in Arendt's political philosophy, the most obvious being her antifoundationalism, privileging of plurality over sovereignty, and aesthetic conception of politics as agonistic display. But even defenders of a postmodern reading of Arendt have to acknowledge the modern—and distinctly enlightenment—mentality of *On Revolution*. For example, Dana Villa ("Beyond Good and Evil: Arendt, Nietzsche, and the Aestheticization of Action," *Political Theory* 20, May 1992), concedes that there is a tension between the agonistic, aesthetic conception of action developed in *The Human Condition* and the dialogic, deliberative model developed in *On Revolution*. However, he argues that the latter conception, especially as interpreted by Habermas, cannot account for the former in the way that the former can account for the latter (p. 279). I must demur, if only because a Nietzschean reading that places Arendt's agonistic conception of action beyond good and evil flies in the face of her own critique of evil as a failure to act and judge politically (in Arendt's opinion, Eichmann's inability to think empathetically *about* his

victims was symptomatic of his inability to think *with* them in empathetic dialogue). The same caveat applies to Villa's contention that Arendt's conception of action is largely devoid of teleological *and* instrumentalist features. Like Jon Elster ("The Market and the Forum: The Varieties of Political Theory," in J. Elster and D. Hylland, eds., *Foundations in Social Theory* [Cambridge: Cambridge University Press, 1986], pp. 103–128), I'm not sure about the accuracy of Arendt's assertion that citizens in the American town assemblies participated "neither exclusively because of duty nor, even less, to serve their own interests, but most of all because they enjoyed the discussions, the deliberations, *and the making of decisions*" (p. 119, my stress); but at least this formulation has the virtue of placing the instrumental aim of "making decisions" (presumably about the utilitarian advancement of interests) on a par with the sheer delight in agonistic self-display. In any case, Arendt herself sometimes contrasted utilitarian common sense with totalitarian ideology. In another edifying comparison of Arendt and postmodernism that explicitly addresses Derrida's and Arendt's readings of the Declaration of Independence ("Declarations of Independence: Arendt and Derrida on the Problem of Founding a Republic," *American Political Science Review* 85 [March 1991]), Bonnie Honig also seems to read Arendt as a postmodern *avant la lettre.* Although she astutely notes that Arendt grounds the authority of the Declaration in general conditions of promising, she suggests that even she had to have recourse to something *outside* of action—namely retrospective narrative—to provide for the stabilizing function of constation. This is in keeping with my view that no founding act, transcendental condition, or general norm—in short, nothing that claims to be legitimate—contains *within itself* its own absolute and final justification. Justification of any norm, even one claiming transcendental validity, is at least partly dependent on that norm's being successfully reapplied, reinterpreted, and reinvented in subsequent acts of discursive justification and narration. But this view of the matter does not seem to sit very well with Honig's contention that "in every system (every practice)" there are placeholders that enable the system, "but are illegitimate from its vantage point" (Honig, "Declarations of Independence," p. 106). If Honig is asserting that the justification of transcendental conditions, constitutive rules, regulative ideas, and the like is *partly* independent of the outcomes of the justificatory narrative practices made possible by them, then she is surely right. Such conditions, rules, and ideas *are* at least partly justified in some weak a priori sense—regardless of any actual dialogic consensus or narrative application—by purely intuitive thought experiments, in that we understand that the denial of their validity would render dialogic justification and narrative application as such meaningless. But if she is asserting that the justification of such "placeholders" is *entirely* independent of the system of practices they condition, constitute, and regulate, then she is contradicting her and Arendt's—in my opinion, correct—observation about the need to supplement the grounding of such general conditions with retrospective narrative. For it is only within dialogic and narrative practices that we discursively test and revise (reinterpret) our "private," transcendental "intuitions in a manner that accords with what Rawls calls 'wide reflective equilibrium'." I take it that Honig, who sympathizes with Derrida's and Arendt's views about the ideological violence associated with moral and political absolutes, ultimately comes down on this side as well. Yet to what extent she does remains unclear because, unlike Arendt and myself but in keeping with Derrida, she thinks the hermeneutical denial of transcendence equally *delegitimates* the "transcendental" placeholder.

11. H. Arendt, *Between Past and Present: Eight Exercises in Political Thought* (London: Penguin, 1977), p. 115.

12. For further clarification of this point see H. Blumenberg, *The Legitimacy of the Modern Age*, trans. R. Wallace (Cambridge: MIT Press, 1983), pp. 48–49; and D. Ingram, "Blumenberg and the Philosophical Grounds of Historiography," *History and Theory* vol. 29, no. 1 (1990), pp. 1–15.

13. In contrast to the postmodernists, I prefer to interpret Arendt's performative conception of action from the vantage point of Habermas's theory of communicative action, which owes much to Arendt's own distinction between legitimate power and illegitimate violence. Like Searle and Austin, Habermas notes that many (he would say *all*) speech acts combine locutionary (constative) and illocutionary (performative) meaning. In this respect, revolutionary declarations are no more "ambiguous," "confused," or "mystical" than everyday utterances of the form "I know that P," in which the validity and meaningfulness of an asserted fact P is made contingent on the future obligation of the speaker to provide warranted justification for it. Significantly, Habermas goes beyond Searle and Austin—not to mention Arendt herself—in arguing that all speech acts explicitly or implicitly raise claims to propositional truth, performative rightness (or appropriateness), and expressive sincerity (or truthfulness). By contrast, Arendt's tendency, we have seen, is to equate truth claims and moral imperatives *strictu sensu* with the purely cognitive and volitional faculties of understanding and willing, respectively, while reserving the more aesthetic functions of expression, narration, and the like to political action and historical judgment. Thus although Habermas expressly connects the validity and meaningfulness of validity claims raised in speech action to their possible "redemption" in the dialogic achievement of rational consensus, Arendt does not. For her the meaningfulness of political actions consists primarily in the expression of opinions and the rendering of interpretations—neither of which is rationally demonstrable—whereas for Habermas the exchange of opinions and the rendering of judgments are themselves meaningless unless truth or some other cognitive value is at stake. This disagreement, I submit, although significant, should not obscure the one thing they share that sets them apart from many of today's postmodernists, namely, a firm belief in the distinction between arbitrary violence, on the one hand, and legitimate power that emanates from open deliberations between free and equal persons, on the other. See J. Habermas, "Hannah Arendt's Communications Concept of Power," *Social Research* 44 (1977); *Moral Consciousness and Communicative Action*, trans. C. Lehnhardt and S. Nicholsen (Cambridge: MIT Press, 1989), esp. p. 58, and ch. 7 of my *Reason, History, and Politics* (loc. cit.).

14. Such norms are constitutive of action in a weak sense. We cannot make sense of freedom without referring to them, but failure to act in accordance with them fully—they are, after all, utopian—does not mean that we are not acting freely or responsibly. Just as one does not cease to argue by committing a fallacy, so one does not cease to deliberate by confusing one's self-interest with the interests of all. We might be better off to think of such a deep grammar as specifying a regulative ideal, so long as we are careful to distinguish it from the sorts of ordinary rules we might dispense with. For there is no other candidate besides this norm that captures our implicit understanding of what it means to act freely and rationally. Hence, any attempt to rationally disprove it would entail a kind of *performative* contradiction. If we understand them in this way, the principles underlying action straddle the performative/constative and political/philosophical boundaries in a manner that renders them partially immune to criticism. Does this immunity amount to the same sort of violent constraint associated with ideological mystification? Does it collapse *physis* (nature) and *nomos* (law) in a kind of "mystical" *jusnaturalism*, as Derrida claims all contractarian legitimations of law do ("The Force of Law: The Mystical Foundation of Authority," *Deconstruction and the Possibility of Justice*, eds. D. Cornell, M. Rosenfield, and D. G. Carlson (New York: Routledge, 1992), p. 8)—hereafter *FoL*)? I think not. For one thing, their status as historically emergent preconditions of political action does not immunize them against demands for justification (although justification in this instance would amount to showing that any attempt to persuade others to the contrary commits a performative contradiction). Nor does it immunize them against conventional interpretation and application. General and abstract rules of argumentation have only regulative force; they point us in a direction that falls somewhere short of concrete proscription and

prescription. Whatever power and authority they possess is supplemental, a function of their being interpreted in some concrete manner—which is as much a matter of politics as of anything else. That being the case, Derrida is quite right to *delimit* the legitimate scope of such supplemental political accretions, but not to deny it altogether.

15. Arendt is closer to the mark when she suggests that the long histories of despotism preceding the French and Bolshevik Revolutions—rather than any compassion for the needy—predetermined their anti-republican course. On the other hand, an assessment of the American Revolution more balanced than hers would show that its deviation from the republican course was not *simply* caused by the "rapid and constant economic growth ... of a constantly expanding private realm" (p. 252) or the absence of constitutional provisions for local forms of participatory government (such as Jefferson's "wards"). More basically, it is also traceable to a constitutional neglect of the most pressing social question at the time of the Founding: slavery.

16. According to Arendt, the complementarity obtaining between power and authority reflects the complementarity obtaining between action (the power to initiate) and judgment (the authority to retroactively redeem). The distinction between action and judgment in turn is incorporated into the constitutional separation of the legislature from the judiciary.

17. H. Arendt, *Between Past and Future*, p. 152.

18. Whether interpretation is best described as synthetic or disruptive is the main bone of contention dividing modernists like Gadamer from postmodernists like Derrida. My own attempt to split the difference between Derrida and Gadamer by way of Arendt's and Blumenberg's notion of functional reoccupation is developed in chapters 4, 6, and 8 of my *Reason, History, and Politics*.

19. The problem of historical progress that later preoccupied Hegel and later generations of revolutionaries can be situated within this context as well. On Arendt's reading, because the starving masses with whom the French revolutionaries identified were fundamentally united by an imperious need for survival, they constituted in life what Sieyès had only imagined: an irresistible force, or sovereign will. This need found successive expression in Robespierre's *marche de la révolution*, Hegel's deterministic theodicy of the modern state (*der Gang Gottes durch die Welt*), and Marx's messianic history of class struggle. The fallacy of such revolutionary world histories, Arendt observes, "consists in describing the whole realm of human action, not in terms of the actor and the agent, but from the standpoint of the spectator who watches a spectacle" (p. 52). Even if "all stories begun and enacted by men unfold their true meaning only when they have come to their end, so that it may indeed appear as though only the spectator, and not the agent, can hope to understand what actually happened in any given chain of deeds and events," it by no means follows that the spectator can place himself or herself outside of history, so as to render final verdicts about the necessary progress of history.

20. For an interpretation of American constitutional law that emphasizes the revolutionary redefinition of national identity, see B. Ackerman, *We the People. I. Foundations* (Cambridge: Harvard University Press, 1991).

21. Leaving aside the very unfinished nature of this revolution, the New Deal shared one important feature with the Civil War amendments: it began as a minor reform and became a major revolution. Part of this process involved reaching back to the Bill of Rights to invent new rights—to privacy, abortion, and so on—and to augment others, notably those political freedoms pertaining to speech, association, and religion.

11

The Political Dimension of the Public World: On Hannah Arendt's Interpretation of Martin Heidegger

Jeffrey Andrew Barash

In a speech presented to the American Society of Political Scientists in 1954 entitled "Concern with Politics in Recent European Philosophical Thought," Hannah Arendt referred to an aspect of Martin Heidegger's thought that was, in her eyes, especially pertinent to her own philosophical endeavors. As she explained:

> It lies in the nature of philosophy to deal with man in the singular, whereas politics could not even be conceived of if men did not exist in the plural. Or to put it another way: the experiences of the philosopher—insofar as he is a philosopher—are with solitude, while for man—insofar as he is political—solitude is an essential but nevertheless marginal experience. It may be—but I shall only hint at this—that Heidegger's concept of "world," which in many respects stands at the center of his philosophy, constitutes a step out of this difficulty. At any rate, because Heidegger defines human existence as being-in-the-world, he insists on giving philosophic significance to structures of everyday life that are completely incomprehensible if man is not primarily understood as being together with others.[1]

Hannah Arendt underlines here Heidegger's interpretation of human existence as being-in-the-world, in other words the characterization of human existence as inherence in a common world that is prestructured by a network of relations to things and to other people. If Arendt emphasizes this Heideggerian interpretation, it is because, as she herself indicates, it seems to present the possibility of a preliminary overcoming of what she designates as the traditional isolation of the philosopher from the common world of human affairs. And, in her own writings, Hannah Arendt seeks to surmount precisely this traditional isolation on the basis of political theory. She intends, above all, to place in question a tradition that to her mind has not sufficiently recognized the philosophical implications of political interaction in the context of a public world.

In spite of the importance she accords to Heidegger's interpretation of being-in-the-world, reflection on what she took to be this traditional relation between philosophy and politics led her to criticize Heidegger's thought. This criticism concerned not only Heidegger's official support of the Nazi regime as rector of Freiburg University from May 1933, until February 1934, but above all the absence of specifically *political* reflection in *Being and Time,* in spite of Heidegger's claim, in the framework of his analysis of being-in-the-world, to account for human existence in a *public* world. For Hannah Arendt, Heidegger's neglect of the political dimension of human existence in *Being and Time,* far from designating a simple omission in his thinking, represents one of its salient characteristics.[2] The absence of specifically political reflection in Heidegger's work signifies for Arendt a depreciation of political experience that, at the very least, bore an *indirect* relation to Heidegger's engagement in favor of the Nazis.

It is not my intention in this context to enter into the discussion on Heidegger's political activity during the Third Reich. By means of Hannah Arendt's critique of Heidegger's account of the public world, I seek rather to place Arendt's own conception of the public world in sharper relief and to determine its role in her theory of politics. I will attempt to demonstrate that Arendt, far from proposing her theory of politics as a mere supplement to the Heideggerian interpretation of being-in-the-world, places the political dimension of the public world at a far more radical level of investigation: from her point of view, indeed, the fundamental philosophical problem of *truth* cannot legitimately be addressed unless the discussion is grounded in political reflection. If the very words "public world" take on a meaning in Arendt's thought that sharply differs from Heidegger's understanding of this theme, I will attempt to illustrate that this difference, beyond a simple terminological distinction, provides an important indication for comprehending the originality of her approach to the question of truth.

In the preface to *Men in Dark Times* Hannah Arendt evokes the specific aspect of Heidegger's interpretation of the world that stands at the heart of her own critical reflection. In this preface, Arendt quotes

Heidegger's assertion in *Being and Time*, "Die Oeffentlichkeit verdunkelt alles" ("The public obscures everything"). Without indicating her own intervention, however, Arendt reformulates Heidegger's phrase—it is not clear whether intentionally or inadvertently—in terms of a paradox. She writes: "Das Licht der Oeffentlichkeit verdunkelt alles" ("The light of the public obscures everything").[3] In section 27 of *Being and Time*, nonetheless, Heidegger merely wrote: "The public obscures everything, and what has thus been covered up gets passed off as something familiar and accessible to everyone."[4]

Although Heidegger here refers to the "public," and not to the public character of the world, the chapter of *Being and Time* from which this quote is drawn is nevertheless entitled "Being-in-the-world as Being-with and Being-one's-self. The 'they;'" and the "public" clearly signifies the public character of the world. As Heidegger explains in the course of this chapter, the darkening arises essentially from publicness as a structure of being-in-the-world.

What proves to be especially pertinent for Hannah Arendt's interpretation is the specific way in which Heidegger relates publicness and the darkening it engenders to the phenomenon of the world. As all readers of *Being and Time* know, for Heidegger the phenomenon of "worldhood" (*Weltlichkeit*) is by no means equated with an external cosmos with which humans interact. Worldhood for Heidegger designates the way of being of *Dasein* itself, as the necessary precondition for any possible meaningful relation to things and to other *Dasein*. The priority of worldhood as an ontological structure of human existence expresses itself in the direct interpretability of the everyday environing and common world (*alltägliche Um- und Mitwelt*), to which *Dasein* most immediately relates and on which all comprehension of singular ontic circumstances is founded. In the context of this everyday world *Dasein* never encounters objects or individuals in the abstract, but things or other *Dasein* already engaged in a complex web of meaningful relations.

In *Being and Time* Heidegger relates this priority of the world as a coherent structure existing before any encounter with isolated individuals or singular objects to the common accessibility and openness of the everyday world, characterized above all by its continuity and its permanence: it is the everyday structure of the world that, as a way of being of *Dasein*, exists for everyone at all times. This continual openness of the everyday world constitutes an anonymous field of action, wholly indifferent to *Dasein* in its fundamental singularity—the field of action of the "they" (*das Man*)—and it is this anonymous everyday field of action that Heidegger terms the "public world" (*öffentliche Welt*).

According to Heidegger, tools, ordinary objects, and in a broader sense, pathways and streets, nature, and the environing world, as well as *Dasein* itself, existing in a web of everyday relations, may constantly be interpreted in a public light.[5] Whereas tools and ordinary objects wear out or are overtaken by progress and streets fall into disrepair, nature and the environing world continually change while death claims human individuals. What reveals itself to be the ontological kernel of the unity and continuity of the world, however, plays a particularly important role, as we will later see, in Heidegger's interpretation of truth: the world in its public, everyday dimension, accessible to everyone at each moment, which always precedes the ontic life of each individual and continues after his or her death. This durability of the public world embodies for Heidegger the anonymity of human relations, founded on total indifference to *Dasein*'s singularity, whose essential feature resides in its mortality.[6] It is this durability of the public world that comes to expression for Heidegger in the temporal permanence of the "they" ("the 'they' never dies"[7]); this permanence, at the source of the inauthentic interpretation of existence, provides *Dasein*, through the sheer durability of an anonymous, public mode of existence, with the possibility of dissimulating the finitude of its own mortal existence.

With the qualification of the public world in terms of permanence and durability, we encounter the theme of the *temporal* foundation of *Dasein*, which will prove particularly important to our present investigation. As we will see, Heidegger's analysis of the temporal structures of the public world in *Being and Time* constitutes the focus of Hannah Arendt's critical reflections concerning his interpretation of the "public" world.

In the second section of *Being and Time*, entitled "*Dasein* and Temporality," Heidegger grounds the public interpretability of the world in what he terms "public time." If in everyday existence *Dasein* utilizes tools or encounters other *Dasein* in the common, everyday world, such modes of being-in-the-world necessarily depend on the possibility of a public interpretation of *time*. Indeed the durability of the everyday world, open to everyone at each moment, presupposes for Heidegger the possibility of general access to a common measurable time. Heidegger states in *Being and Time*: "Thus when time is measured, it is made public in such a way that it is encountered on each occasion and at any time for everyone as 'now and now and now.'"[8]

Heidegger designates this measurable time, which has "for ever been rendered public" and which can be infinitely extended, as "world time" (*Weltzeit*). Given the domination of the public interpretation of time in its ordinary, everyday dimension, it is by no means accidental, for Heidegger, that this interpretation has also determined the Western idea of time at the theoretical level, from Aristotle to Kant and Hegel—and up to the present.

If for Heidegger "the public obscures everything," this is because the public world overshadows original time by means of the domination of public time. Precisely when it interprets itself in light of the durability of public time, *Dasein* is able to dissimulate the finitude of its own temporal existence and thus unburden care arising from mortal being, which is "in each case my own." This dissimulation or "looking away from finitude" (*Wegsehen von der Endlichkeit*) is at the same time the source of the idea of temporal infinity: by means of this refusal to confront finitude, "the forgetful 'representation' of the 'infinity' of public time can in the first place take hold."[9]

What concerns us in Heidegger's analysis is less the theme of temporality per se than its relation to the interpretation of truth. And most important in this regard is Heidegger's argument that the universal validity (*Allgemeingültigkeit*) of the criteria of truth arises from the generality of a public world that is accessible to everyone at each moment, and consequently, from the neglect of finite time in favor of public time.

According to *Being and Time*, the criteria of truth presupposed by the Western metaphysical tradition only serve to reinforce the everyday domination of the public interpretation of the world and of world time. This is the tradition stemming from the Platonic identification of ideas with immutability and eternity and from the Aristotelian doctrine of substance as "ousia" or permanent presence. In positing the atemporal permanence of being, it is precisely the temporal finitude of *Dasein* that these criteria either set aside or hold to be merely secondary. It is by no means accidental for Heidegger if, on the basis of this domination of the public interpretation of the world and of time, modern scientific theories of truth have adopted the criteria of "universality," even after they have abandoned all claims to metaphysical validity. The very fact that "objective" scientific truth is also "universal"—that is to say, uniformly accessible to everyone at all times—is for Heidegger the clearest testimony to the domination of the public interpretation of the world and of time. The laying bare of this tendency to dissimulate truth that is rooted in finitude provides the occasion for reflection on the idea of scientific theory, which concerns, above all, historical science, whose object is *Dasein* itself. In this regard, Heidegger writes in *Being and Time*:

> In no science are the "universal validity" of standards and the claims to "universality" which the "they" and its common sense demand less possible as criteria of "truth" than in authentic historical inquiry.[10]

We set aside in this context the question, which Heidegger himself barely examines, concerning how authentic science, in the light of the finitude of *Dasein*, might be envisioned. Although granting that even such authentic science, rooted in Dasein's being-in-the-world, can never entirely extract itself from the inauthentic dimension of existence, our question concerns the direct relation designated by Heidegger between the criteria of universal validity and inauthenticity. Must this claim to truth, valid for everyone at all times, necessarily be equated with the modes of comprehension dominated by the "they," rooted in inauthentic temporal existence? It is precisely this question that we will now examine in the perspective of Hannah Arendt's thinking.

As the starting point for the second part of this analysis, let us return to the quotation from Arendt's book *Men in Dark Times* which was referred to at the beginning. Here is the entire passage in the context of which Hannah Arendt presented her paraphrase of Heidegger's sentence "The public obscures everything:"

> In [Heidegger's] description of human existence, everything that is real or authentic is assaulted by the overwhelming power of "mere talk" that irresistibly arises out of the public realm, determining every aspect of everyday existence, anticipating and annihilating the sense or the nonsense of everything the future may bring. There is no escape, according to Heidegger, from the "incomprehensible triviality" of this common everyday world except by withdrawal from it into that solitude which philosophers since Parmenides and Plato have opposed to the political realm. We are here not concerned with the philosophical relevance of Heidegger's analyses (which, in my opinion, is undeniable) nor with the tradition of philosophic thought that stands behind them, but exclusively with certain

underlying experiences of the time and their conceptual description. In our context, the point is that the sarcastic, perverse-sounding statement, *Das Licht der Oeffentlichkeit verdunkelt alles* ("The light of the public obscures everything"), went to the very heart of the matter and actually was no more than the most succinct summing-up of existing conditions.[11]

In this passage we immediately notice how Arendt adapts Heidegger's interpretation of the public world to her own ends. Whereas for Heidegger *Dasein* always exists in a public world, and the facticity of *Dasein* presupposes its rootedness at all times in an everyday public world, Arendt relates Heidegger's analyses to "certain underlying experiences of the time" rather than to human existence per se. Heidegger conceived existence in the public world and its obscuring of truth as a mode of being of *Dasein*. We will see that Arendt transforms the meaning of Heidegger's thought. But what is the purpose of this apparently insignificant modification of Heidegger's analyses? Might it lead us to the heart of a critical reinterpretation of Heidegger's philosophy?

One might be tempted to underestimate the implications of Arendt's assertions for her own conception of the world. Arendt indeed explains that she does not wish to put forward her own judgment concerning the philosophical relevance of Heidegger's analyses, and her statement would seem to confirm rather than question Heidegger's conceptions. Does Arendt not limit the range of Heidegger's analysis to a diagnosis of the period, whereas Heidegger placed the accent on *Dasein*'s mode of being per se, beyond any determinate period? To support the correctness of this thesis, one might appeal to statements in *Being and Time* itself: according to Heidegger, even if it is impossible to completely sever one's roots in the public, everyday world, the task of *Dasein*'s authentic mode of existence is to resist the type of interpretation this world fosters, and to strive to interpret itself in the light of its finitude. Moreover, the domination of the public world is variable in its intensity, as Heidegger indicates in *Being and Time* when he writes that "the extent to which its [the 'they's'] dominion becomes compelling and explicit may change in the course of history."[12] Nonetheless, the domination of the "they" and the darkening of truth that proceeds from this domination belong to the original constitution of *Dasein* as such, independent of any consideration of its historical context. Yet here, too, Arendt would seem to agree when in the preface to *Men in Dark Times* she asserts that "dark times" hardly represent anything truly new or specifically modern.

One could not justifiably try to determine Hannah Arendt's fundamental position in regard to Heidegger on the basis of these isolated remarks, as suggestive as they may be. More decisive for her critique of Heidegger is the distance between them that reveals itself in their respective concepts of the philosophical "tradition." Whereas Heidegger defines this tradition essentially in terms of the tacit question of the finitude of *Dasein*, from Arendt's very different perspective the theme of the public world provides the touchstone for understanding this tradition from the time that Parmenides, Plato, and Aristotle took positions on this topic. For this reason we will examine the critique of Heidegger that Arendt advances in light of the philosophical tradition that she herself designates as her fundamental target.

Like Heidegger, Arendt attempts to place the modern scientific tradition in question in relation to what she takes to be the domination of a specific historical form of the philosophical concept of truth. However, whereas Heidegger as we have seen defines the tradition in relation to its claim to the temporal permanence and universal validity of the criteria of truth, Arendt's radically different interpretation of this tradition proceeds from a theme specific to her own manner of investigation: for her, the concept of truth since Plato and Aristotle gives testimony above all to the philosopher's hostility to the polis, which has traditionally predominated in the West and has given rise to a depreciation of the political realm in comparison to pure thought.[13] In her essay "Tradition and the Modern Age," which originally appeared in German in 1957 in a work entitled *Fragwürdige Traditionsbestände im politischen Denken der Gegenwart* (*Questionable Elements in Contemporary Political Thought*), Arendt describes the allegory of the cave in Plato's *Republic* as the starting point of this tradition:

> The beginning was made when, in *The Republic*'s allegory of the cave, Plato described the sphere of human affairs—all that belongs to the living together of men in a common world—in terms of darkness, confusion, and deception which those aspiring to true being must turn away from and abandon if they want to discover the clear sky of eternal ideas.[14]

Following Plato, according to Arendt, Aristotle also accepted this depreciation of the world of human affairs when he accorded a superior role to the "bios theoretikos" in relation to the "bios politikos."

During the years just after World War II, when Arendt began to search for the traces of this philosophical tradition in her contemporary context, she focused her investigation primarily on Heidegger. Her early examination of Heidegger's thought in this light led to a provocative article originally published in 1946 under the title "What Is Existenz Philosophy?" In this essay, Arendt articulated a sharp critique of Heidegger's tendency to separate the authentic task of philosophy from human affairs in the public world. For her, this tendency gives testimony to the subtle tribute Heidegger pays to the Aristotelian tradition, above all in regard to the privilege this tradition accorded to pure philosophical contemplation.[15] Be this as it may, Arendt later substantially moderated this critique and, in her 1954 talk entitled "Concern with Politics in Recent European Philosophical Thought," as mentioned earlier, she even went to the point of representing Heidegger's concept of being-in-the-world as a first step toward overcoming this tradition. Nevertheless, Arendt did not refrain in this same talk from criticizing Heidegger's thinking, above all in regard to his interpretation of the public world. In this vein she wrote:

> Thus, we find the old hostility of the philosopher toward the *polis* in Heidegger's analyses of average everyday life in terms of *das Man* (the "they," or the rule of public opinion, as opposed to the "self"), in which the public realm has the function of hiding reality and preventing even the appearance of truth.[16]

In relation to our present theme, we have emphasized that Heidegger identifies the public world primarily with an inauthentic mode of existence of *Dasein*, which continually serves to hide original truth. And it is precisely the unmitigated character of this interpretation that poses a problem: if politics can hardly dispense with a foundation in the everyday public world, how can one marshal support on the basis of *Being and Time* for a theory of the political realm that is invested with a dignity beyond mere *inauthenticity*? Granted that Heidegger allows for the possibility in *Being and Time* of an authentic human community, the ontological analysis of this authentic community is nonetheless enunciated in its distinction from a public world that would be capable of serving as an authentic ontological foundation for the political realm. And given that Heidegger's analysis of the public realm hardly accords a space for political existence or for "ontic" political activity grounded in authentic *public* being-in-the-world, it can only be of minor interest for the reconsideration and revaluation of politics in the Western tradition that constitutes Arendt's primary aim. It is thus in terms of this aim that we can comprehend the implications of her interpretation of the public world.

Sharply distinguishing her interpretation from any analysis that would derive the everyday public character of the world from *Dasein*'s quest to dissimulate its finitude, Arendt's fundamental presupposition approaches the public world from a very different perspective. In her work, the public world is above all portrayed as a symbolic, communicational space—an "interspace"[17]—that, far from arising out of the radical singularity of *Dasein*, finds its source in an original plurality whose essential signification can in no way be reduced to a finite ontology of human existence.

In her book *The Human Condition*, as in her collection of essays *Between Past and Future*, Arendt attempts to demonstrate that the "public" character of the world cannot be grasped on the basis of the mere mortality of isolated human existence. For her the durability of the public world does not stem from an inauthentic interpretation of *Dasein* in flight from its own finitude, but on the contrary designates the space itself in which human existence protects and preserves itself. In this sense the public realm designates a common world as the sphere of what Arendt terms the *vita activa*, with its different modes of work, fabrication, and action, the latter of which constitutes the authentic political domain.[18]

From Arendt's standpoint, the durability of the public world does not originate, as for Heidegger, from a mode of existence characteristic of *Dasein* per se; on the contrary, as the framework of human activity, the world proves to be essentially problematic. Its continuity is precarious, given that as a public "interspace" it is subject to historical *endangerment*. And this historical fragility of the world does not by any means correspond to the ephemerality of mortal *Dasein*. For Arendt, the disappearance of the public world does not necessarily involve the disappearance of the human beings who inhabit this world. In her essay "On Humanity in Dark Times," Arendt describes the possibility of "worldlessness," to which persecuted minorities above all are subject when "the interspace we have called world ... has simply disappeared."[19] What proves to be particularly problematic for Arendt is not the fallenness of a *Dasein* that interprets itself in terms of the public world, but rather the threat to the public world itself. For this reason she insists on the importance of sustaining the public realm through human activity.

Provided with Arendt's characterization of the public world, we are now able to reexamine more closely her rendition of Heidegger's sentence: "The light of the public obscures everything." Taken exactly, this darkening does not result, as for Heidegger, from the public dimension of the world as such, but from the *distortion* of this dimension. This darkening describes a historical phenomenon that is increasingly accentuated during the modern period. As Arendt explains in her 1959 speech, "On Humanity in Dark Times":

> The public realm has lost the power of illumination which was originally part of its very nature. More and more people in the countries of the Western world, which since the decline of the ancient world has regarded freedom from politics as one of the basic freedoms, make use of this freedom and have retreated from the world and their obligations within it. This withdrawal from the world need not harm an individual; he may even cultivate great talents to the point of genius and so by a detour be useful to the world again. But with each such retreat an almost demonstrable loss to the world takes place; what is lost is the specific and usually irreplaceable in-between which should have formed between this individual and his fellow men.[20]

Here we can appreciate the extent to which Arendt's analysis—in spite of the use of certain topics familiar to Heidegger—distinguishes itself from the basic tendency of his thinking. When Arendt claims that the darkening that overshadows the "public" dimension of the world is only meant to characterize "certain underlying experiences of the time," this is less because it inheres in the temporal and historical structure of *Dasein* per se than by virtue of its link to the historical movement of one specific epoch: that of modernity. If the main current of the Western philosophical tradition has devalued political action in the public realm, the modern darkening of the public world, as Arendt qualifies it, corresponds precisely to the culmination of this tradition in its contemporary, aporetic situation. And Heidegger's phrase "the public darkens everything" may indeed prove of particular value in the diagnosis of this situation, even if Heidegger's philosophy itself participates in the modern process of darkening of the public realm. Certainly, in Arendt's opinion, Heidegger's philosophy cannot be considered to be an ultimate "cause" of this darkening.

It is with this characterization of Arendt's interpretation of the public world that we return to our primary question: in what sense do her reflections on the public world as a framework of political action involve a specifically *philosophical* investigation concerning truth?

Before directly addressing this question, we should first dissipate a possible misunderstanding. If Arendt relates this philosophical investigation to the political domain, it is not only to advance a claim that philosophers have not sufficiently dealt with politics—in spite of the great number of political writings that belong to our philosophical tradition. The real difficulty concerns the traditional lack of comprehending the problematic relation between politics and the question of truth. For Arendt, because Heidegger's thought stems from this tradition and plays an important role in its final articulation, it is hardly surprising that the consequences of this tradition for the problem of truth appear in a particularly clear light in her interpretation of the Heideggerian conception of the public world.

In our analysis of Heidegger, we have already recalled how for him the problem of truth relates to everyday existence in the public world. If the tradition of Western metaphysics since Plato and Aristotle has generally conceived of truth in terms of eternal, immutable presence, it is because this criterion of truth, for Heidegger, expresses *Dasein*'s everyday tendency to rely on the durability of the public world as a means of dissimulating its own finitude. And according to Heidegger, this same "turning away from finitude" comes to expression precisely where the modern sciences—especially the human historical disciplines—presuppose that truth inheres in a permanent and universal standard of objectivity. Even after having abandoned the metaphysical claim to ultimate truth, it is thus this same inauthentic quest for eternity that inspires the "scientific" presupposition of the permanence of the criteria of truth.

The originality of Arendt's reflections on the problem of truth becomes apparent in her subtle distinction between "eternity" and "immortality." She establishes this distinction between the original ancient Greek conception of temporal perdurability of the public world and the eternity of truth presupposed by contemplative philosophy. In the first instance, Arendt refers to the essentially political signification of the ancient conception of speech and of action that, despite their "material futility, possess an enduring quality of their own because they create their own remembrance" and prove capable therefore of attaining immortal glory.[21] It is at the same time in relation to this capacity to endure that Arendt identifies the specific character of action insofar as it "engages in founding and preserving political bodies," which in turn "creates the condition for remembrance, that is, for history."[22] Conceived in these terms, the temporal significance of immortality consists less in avoiding mortality—which instead characterizes the contemplative thought of eternity—than in creating an earthly dwelling space for human beings in the establishment of a "public world."[23] In the creation of a framework for human plurality, the quest for immortality represents the supreme political activity. It aims at opening a field of action that, in spite of the precariousness and unpredictability typical of human affairs, endows itself with a perdurability capable of extending beyond the short life span of mortal beings. In this context, Arendt refers to the foundation of cohesion and of continuity in the public interspace constituted by the "'products' of action and speech" that she terms the "fragile web of human relationships."[24] This web overlays the tangible objects of the public world with a multiplicity of interpretations emanating from different agents. Along with these objects, the web of human relationships constitutes what Arendt terms the "reality" of this world. Far from establishing themselves in terms of fixed structures, the opening to the world depends for Arendt upon the possibility of convergence of a multiplicity of perspectives in the identification of the same objects of interest.[25] This convergence is founded on what Arendt terms "common sense:" the capacity to fit "into reality as a whole our five strictly individual senses and the strictly particular data they perceive."[26] In making accessible a common public world, common sense, according to this usage, makes it possible for our opinions to pass beyond the limits of a particular viewpoint to encompass the viewpoint of others. It permits our opinions to move beyond the horizon of purely personal interests to rise to the level of an "impartial generality."[27] At the same time, with the advent of uniform, socially conditioned behavior in an increasingly standardized mass society, there is a danger that common sense might atrophy through the loss of its capacity to illuminate a plurality of heterogeneous perspectives at the heart of the public world.[28]

With this notion of "common sense" as an opening to the public world, we reach the precise point where Arendt engages her critique of the traditional presuppositions concerning truth. Indeed if modern criteria of truth as scientific objectivity and universality have become problematic, it is not because, as for Heidegger, the ideal of the permanence of truth tacitly expresses *Dasein*'s continual tendency to avoid its own finitude. If these criteria have become problematic, this is on the contrary because the human sciences have proven increasingly incapable of orienting themselves, on the basis of common sense, in a public world that has become unstable. Far from equivalent to the criteria of universal validity, which for Heidegger express *Dasein*'s quest for eternal, immutable truth, the ability to judge according to the very criteria of objectivity and impartiality risks disappearing, for Arendt, along with the common sense in which they are grounded. Thus the problem becomes less one of the scientific ideal of universal truth that, like the common world, is supposed to be continually available to everyone, than the capacity to identify—notwithstanding all truth claims of the human sciences—the common aspect of the world that, in permitting us to place ourselves in the perspectives of others, is the source of the very possibility of attaining objective and impartial judgments.[29]

We observe here how for Arendt the political dimension of the public world does not merely represent a theoretical problem for philosophers, but evokes at its very core the original question—and that means the eminently political question—concerning truth. If Arendt continually returns to this theme in relation to the Greek polis, it is by no means due to nostalgia for antiquity, but to lay bare what she designates as the profound disparity between the traditional idea of truth and opinion—*doxa*—grounded in common sense in the framework of the public world. The fact that the criteria of impartiality and of objectivity have become problematic in the human sciences only demonstrates to what extent they have lost their original grip in public affairs. In her essay, "The Concept of History," published in *Between Past and Future*, Arendt devotes a particularly evocative passage to the idea of an original relation in Greek antiquity between the idea of impartiality and objectivity and the public world, a relation that has to her mind become increasingly problematic in the course of modern times. She writes:

> In this incessant talk the Greeks discovered that the world we have in common is usually regarded from an infinite number of different standpoints, to which correspond the most diverse points of view. In a sheer inexhaustible flow of argu-

> ments, as the Sophists presented them to the citizenry of Athens, the Greek learned to exchange his own viewpoint, his own "opinion"—the way the world appeared and opened up to him (dokei moi, "it appears to me," from which comes doxa, or "opinion")—with those of his fellow citizens. Greeks learned to *understand*—not to understand one another as individual persons, but to look upon the same world from one another's standpoint, to see the same in very different and frequently opposing aspects. The speeches in which Thucydides makes articulate the standpoints and interests of the warring parties are still a living testimony to the extraordinary degree of this objectivity.... What has obscured the modern discussion of objectivity in the historical sciences and prevented its ever touching the fundamental issues involved seems to be the fact that none of the conditions of either Homeric impartiality or Thucydidean objectivity are present in the modern age.[30]

It is at this stage of our analysis that we are able to consider the scope of Arendt's reflection concerning the Platonic origins of our philosophical tradition. Plato was the founder of this tradition for Arendt because his hostility toward the polis led to the devaluation of *doxa*, which comes to expression in a plurality of publicly supported opinions, in favor of the monolithic character of an *episteme* held to be eternally valid and shed of all traces of the public world. During the nineteenth century, the critique of metaphysical claims to truth represented an important step toward overcoming this tradition. And it is in this perspective that Heidegger's critique of the traditional criteria of truth and his attempt to remold these criteria in relation to the finitude of *Dasein* constitute a first step for Arendt toward the overcoming of the traditional idea of absolute, metaphysical truth. And this attempt to overcome the tradition falls prey to its blindness to the implications for the problem of truth of the modern fragility of the common public world.[31] Consequently, Heidegger's interpretation of truth is the clear sign, as Arendt writes in regard to a quote from Walter Benjamin characterizing contemporary philosophy in general, that the "consistence of truth ... has been lost" because truth no longer possesses those qualities that it "could acquire only through universal recognition of its validity."[32]

In her essay "Tradition and the Modern Age," Arendt notes that tradition may only reveal its full force once it seems to have been overtaken.[33] If Heidegger's interpretation of truth is to be grasped in the perspective of this tradition, it is because—if we adhere to Arendt's explanation—after renouncing all claims to eternal, absolute truth, he remained incapable of surmounting the traditional separation of philosophical truth from the polis to identify truth that might be at the same time "authentic" and rooted in the public world. Here, above all, the question of truth refers to the fundamentally political problem that the public world continually raises.

Notes

1. Hannah Arendt, "Concern with Politics in Recent European Philosophical Thought," in *Essays in Understanding (1930–54),* ed. Jerome Kohn (New York: Harcourt Brace, 1994), p. 443.

2. Ibid., p. 5; Hannah Arendt, "What Is Existential Philosophy?" (1946), translated by Robert and Rita Kimber, in *Essays in Understanding,* pp. 163–187; Hannah Arendt, "Martin Heidegger at Eighty," *New York Review of Books* vol. 17, no. 6 (21 October 1971), pp. 50–54, reprinted in Michael Murray, ed., *Heidegger and Modern Philosophy* (New Haven: Yale University Press, 1978).

3. Hannah Arendt, "Preface," *Men in Dark Times* (Harmondsworth: Penguin, 1973), p. 9.

4. Martin Heidegger, *Sein und Zeit, Gesamtausgabe,* vol. 2 (Frankfurt am Main: Klostermann, 1977), p. 127; English, *Being and Time,* translated by J. Macquarrie and E. Robinson (New York: Harper and Row, 1962). Page references are to the original Niemeyer edition of *Sein und Zeit,* which are given in the margins of both the *Gesamtausgabe* edition and the English translation. The English translation has been somewhat modified in the present article.

5. Ibid., p. 71.

6. Ibid., p. 424. We refer to *Dasein*'s radical singularity in accord with Heidegger's own statements in *Being and Time*: "When it [*Dasein*] stands before itself in this way [before the possibility of its own death], all its relations to any other *Dasein* have been undone" (p. 250); "The non-relational character of death ... singularizes (*vereinzelt*) *Dasein* unto itself" (p. 263).

7. Ibid., p. 424.

8. Ibid., p. 417.

9. Ibid., p. 424.

10. Ibid., p. 395. On this theme see J. A. Barash, *Heidegger et son siècle. Temps de l'Etre, temps de l'histoire* (Paris: Presses Universitaires de France, 1995).

11. Arendt, *Men in Dark Times,* pp. 8–9.

12. Heidegger, *Being and Time,* p. 129.

13. Hannah Arendt and Karl Jaspers, *Briefwechsel* (Munich: Piper, 1985), p. 325; Hannah Arendt, "Tradition and the Modern Age," in *Between Past and Future* (New York: Viking, 1954), p. 17.

14. Arendt, "Tradition and the Modern Age," p. 17.

15. Arendt, "What Is Existential Philosophy?" *Essays in Understanding* (1930–54), pp. 176–182.

16. Hannah Arendt, "Concern with Politics in Recent European Philosophical Thought," *Essays in Understanding (1930–54)*, pp. 432–433.

17. Hannah Arendt, "On Humanity in Dark Times: Thoughts about Lessing," in *Men in Dark Times*, p. 21.

18. Hannah Arendt, *The Human Condition* (Chicago: University of Chicago Press, 1958), pp. 7–58.

19. Arendt, "On Humanity in Dark Times: Thoughts about Lessing," p. 21.

20. Ibid., p. 12.

21. Arendt, *The Human Condition*, p. 208.

22. Ibid., pp. 8–9.

23. Ibid., pp. 17–21, 55–56.

24. Ibid., pp. 95, 175–247.

25. Ibid., pp. 57–58, 207–212.

26. Ibid., pp. 208–209.

27. I refer here to the term employed by Arendt in the essay "Truth and Politics," published in the aftermath of the controversy raised by her book *Eichmann in Jerusalem* and reprinted in *Between Past and Future* (here p. 242).

28. Hannah Arendt, "The Crisis in Education," in *Between Past and Future*, pp. 178–179; "The Crisis in Culture," in *Between Past and Future*, pp. 220–221. If this atrophy of common sense is by no means the result of a simple failure of philosophy, it nevertheless first came to expression in philosophical theories that are, for Arendt, symptomatic of what she terms the "alienation from the world." This alienation characterizes for her the relation of modern man to a world shared in common and emerges for the first time in theoretical form in Descartes' willingness to entertain the possibility of noncorrespondence between the representations of thought and real objects. Hobbes then pushed this problem to its radical extreme. Reason for Descartes, as for Hobbes, is a "calculation of consequences." This is for Arendt symptomatic of the loss of confidence in the sense thanks to which "the five animal senses are fitted into a world common to all men," underlying the conclusion that "human beings are indeed no more than animals who are able to reason, 'to reckon with consequences.'" See in this regard Arendt, *The Human Condition*, pp. 273–284. Deepening still further this "alienation from the world" marked by the modern hiatus between consciousness and world, the initial stability of Platonic ideas degenerates into the instability of values that are simply relative, "whose validity is determined not by one or many men but by society as a whole in its everchanging functional needs" (see Arendt, "Tradition and the Modern Age," p. 40).

29. Later, in her last, uncompleted work, *The Life of the Mind,* Arendt notes Heidegger's reference to the term "meaning" (Sinn) in evoking the meaning or "sense" of being. Heidegger becomes entangled here for Arendt in the metaphysical fallacy par excellence, because he fails to distinguish between "truth" and *Sinn* or "meaning," which might also be translated as "sense" in this passage; see Hannah Arendt, *The Life of the Mind* (New York: Harvest/Harcourt Brace, 1971), p. 15. Given that the theme of politics does not occupy a central role in Arendt's examination of truth in this work, it would reach beyond the scope of the present essay to discuss it in this later context.

30. Hannah Arendt, "The Concept of History," in *Between Past and Future,* pp. 51–52.

31. See in this regard Hannah Arendt, "Philosophy and Politics" (1954), *Social Research* vol. 57, no. 1 (1990), pp. 73–103. Later Arendt attempted to clarify this notion of truth in relation to politics in the essay "Truth and Politics," published in 1967. In this essay she further qualifies her idea of truth by introducing Leibniz's distinction between truths of reason, which are necessary and supposedly eternal, and factual truths, which are historical and contingent. Arendt explains that both types of truth are necessarily distinct from politics because, insofar as they require assent, they are unlike the simple opinions that animate political discussion. In its status as "truth," factual truth is not required, any more than is rational truth, to present itself as a matter of opinion or an object of political persuasion. Nonetheless, in spite of this radical distinction between truth and politics, the opinion that nourishes politics cannot remain indifferent to truth, above all to factual truth. Arendt specifies that precisely the respect for factual truth distinguishes the good opinion, capable of a measure of impartiality, from a bad opinion, which distorts the facts to the point of propagating manipulative lies. Although truth in this sense plays a fundamental role in regard to political judgment, the emergence of calculated lies and the fabrication of images by the mass media as a means of controlling mass society represents a particularly grave political danger. It is the danger of a loss of stability endowed by factual truth as a coherent network of interrelations. This loss endangers above all "the sense by which we take our bearings in the real world" "Truth and Politics," in *Between Past and Future,* p. 257).

32. Hannah Arendt, "Walter Benjamin," in *Men in Dark Times,* p. 193.

33. Arendt, "Tradition and the Modern Age," p. 26.

12

Love and Worldliness: Hannah Arendt's Reading of Saint Augustine

Ronald Beiner

Do not love the world or anything in the world. If anyone loves the world, the love of the Father is not in him.

—1 John *2:15*

As this text from the New Testament should make clear to students of *The Human Condition*, the entire thrust of Hannah Arendt's work as a political philosopher compels her to engage in a head-on confrontation with Christianity. Given that the greatest philosophical spokesman of this Christian antiworldliness is Saint Augustine, it is certainly no accident that Arendt begins her career as a philosopher with a direct engagement with Augustinian Christianity.

My enterprise in this essay is to offer a challenge to what one might call the "standard" view of Arendt's theoretical development. According to the standard view, Arendt arrived at her fundamental preoccupations as a political philosopher under the pressure of the traumatizing events of the 1930s and 1940s in Europe.[1] Admittedly, the standard view is one to which Arendt herself gives encouragement; in the preface to *Between Past and Future* she writes: "thought itself arises out of incidents of living experience and must remain bound to them as the only guideposts by which to take its bearings."[2] Nor can it be denied that her experience of, and theoretical reflection on, the evils of twentieth-century totalitarianism had a huge impact on her subsequent career as a theorist. Contrary to the standard view, however, the very fact that Arendt commences her intellectual career with a book on Saint Augustine (written and published in the 1920s—that is, antecedent to the decisive political events that are thought to have originated the concerns that define her as a political philosopher),[3] and that within that book she focuses particularly on the tension between the otherworldly demands of Christian love and the thisworldliness of social life, gives us good reason to consider tracing the fundamental structure of her philosophical concerns back to an earlier phase of her thought, prior to the politicizing trauma of Hitler and the Holocaust.

What is of course at stake in this reading of Arendt's work is the question of the autonomy of philosophical reflection vis-à-vis the contingencies of history and the biographical experiences of the philosopher. To be sure, Arendt herself, as we have noted above, saw herself as spurred to political-philosophical reflection by her experiences as a Jewish refugee, first prey to, then an escapee from, fascist Europe (and again, the horrors of Nazism and Stalinism did, unquestionably, shape profoundly her thinking about politics). But if one sees *The Human Condition* as central to Hannah Arendt's contribution as a political philosopher (as I certainly do), and if the purpose of that book is to address *universal* questions about the dignity of worldly existence, and the function of human activities, including political "words and deeds," in securing that dignity, then a dimension of philosophical questioning comes into view that transcends the contingencies of Arendt's own life and times. If so, one might then be in a position to discern limits to the historicist and biographical reading of Arendt's lifework that not only gets taken for granted by many of her leading interpreters, but even figures prominently in Arendt's own self-interpretation. In that sense, what the Augustine book may indicate is that Arendt was a political philosopher before she knew that she was one.

I

The first aspect of love that Arendt analyzes is that directed to the future: love as craving. We crave that which is, for us, a good. Possession of the good will bring us happiness or enjoyment. But to obtain the good that we crave does not give us security of love, for we no sooner possess the good than we fear its loss. This is the problem implicit in the understanding of love as craving: it is inseparable from "fear of losing."[4] "The trouble with human happiness is that it is constantly beset by fear. Not having but *safety* of possession is at stake."[5]

This applies especially to life itself. Given that mortal life is, by definition, life that constantly fears for the loss of itself, the only happy life, properly speaking, is everlasting or eternal life. It alone is free of fear; therefore the good that we crave above all is the everlastingness of life. Life as such is defined by anxiety. To love is to crave things for their own sake, but to attain what we crave is simultaneously to fear their loss; hence we can never find adequate satisfaction in earthly love. Thus love seeks not only its specific object (which is inherently insecure), but beyond that, the overcoming of fear; the ultimate goal of love is not the loved object itself but "freedom from fear."[6] But because everything desired in mortal life is, necessarily, fleeting, earthly love is in its very essence impossible to satisfy. Death casts a shadow over every mortal craving. (As Augustine puts it: "our whole life is nothing but a race towards death.")[7]

The unavoidable outcome of this dialectic of love and death is that the object of craving becomes eternity; we direct our love to that which cannot be lost. Given that all particular objects of craving are canceled out by death, the only thing that it is reasonable to crave is the very condition of being immune from death: eternity understood as fearlessness.[8] The experience of death establishes the futility of all earthly desires or cravings, and discloses a good, an object of desire, that is infinitely superior to all merely mortal goods. The only route to happiness is to crave what we cannot lose. "The right love consists in the right object."[9]

At this point, the understanding of love as craving gives rise to a disjunction between the two types of such "appetitive" love: charity (*caritas*) and cupidity (*cupiditas*). The right love, charity, is no less than the wrong love, cupidity, a kind of craving; both are rooted in desire or appetite.[10] What is all-important, then, is the *direction* of desire, whether toward the world or away from the world. What Augustine seeks is for human beings to "crave" the eternal with the same "appetite," the same intensity of feeling, with which they have always hitherto craved the things of this world.

Love as craving is the union of a subject and object, a lover and a beloved. Whether through worldly cupidity or otherworldly charity, we acknowledge our lack of self-sufficiency in desire of something outside ourselves. *What* we desire is what actually defines us (for to be free of all desire, which was the ideal of the Stoics, simply amounts to ceasing to be). "Hence, in cupidity or in charity we decide about our abode, whether we wish to belong to this world or to the world-to-come."[11] The two kinds of love represent a choice: we opt either to be citizens of this world or to be citizens of an eternal world. In choosing what to love, we choose what kind of being we are: a worldly, that is, perishable, being or an eternal, nonperishable being. We choose a home for ourselves, and thereby choose our own mode of being as inhabitants of one or the other of these two worlds.

Thus our ultimate nature, and the character of our ultimate commitments, is decided through love. Those who opt for charity over cupidity express an ultimate rejection of worldly love; they decide that love of the world cannot satisfy their most urgent longings. As Arendt quotes Augustine: "this world is for the faithful what the desert was for the people of Israel."[12] To this Arendt replies with the following challenge: "Would it not then be better to love the world in cupidity and be at home? Why should we make a desert out of this world?"[13] This is in fact what is at stake in choosing between the two kinds of love: loving the things of this world represents a determination to make oneself "at home" in it, whereas loving the eternal means that the world can never be a "home," but only a temporary abode, like a tent in the desert.

Thus Arendt's concern with "worldliness," which became a signal theme of her mature work, did not derive strictly from her political experience of the 1930s, the experience of being a stateless refugee (which she analyzed theoretically in *Origins of Totalitarianism*), for this concern was already implicit in her first philosophical writing in the 1920s. The commanding question of the Augustine book is: What drives Christians to seek to eradicate love of the world as such? The commanding question of her book *The Human Condition*, thirty years later, is: What drives moderns to exalt love of self and love of life above love of the public world? The overlap between the two inquiries is unmistakable. At the heart of both books is a preoccupation with how concern with "life" and "self" comes to prevail over concern with "the world," the site of humanity's mundane affairs. In other words, in the Augustine book Arendt was already preoccupied with the phenomenon of "world alienation" that was to become the guiding theme of *The Human Condition*.[14]

II

On Arendt's reading, man is, according to Augustine, necessarily dependent: "if he could be said to have an essential nature at all, it would be [defined by] lack of self-sufficiency."[15] In our neediness, we reach out to the world through love. But which world? The world of mundane things or the world of eternal things? In love, we decide the mode of our dependence, mundane or transmundane. The decisive question, however, is whether we depend on that which we can attain, or on that which is strictly unattainable. The former, charity, is freedom, whereas the latter, cupidity, is slavery. The reason is that being subject to desires we cannot satisfy is to be enslaved; conversely, we are liberated by a love that fulfills the object of our desires. In the contest between the two kinds of love we choose not only between two forms of being, but also between freedom and slavery.

One expression of our freedom as lovers of the eternal rather than as lovers of the world is that we treat the world as merely means to be "used," not something to be "enjoyed for its own sake" (the Latin distinction is between *uti* and *frui*).[16] Only God is loved "for His own sake."[17] Given that the world is not loved for its own sake, but merely for its utility, it becomes a kind of tool for us to manipulate in accordance with our desire. From this, Arendt draws the implication that "the world in its independent 'objectivity' has fallen into oblivion," for we no longer cherish it in itself, but simply subordinate it to our own subjective purposes.[18] All worldly concerns are viewed from a perspective located in the absolute future, a perspective that ranks charity as infinitely superior to all worldly purposes. Human existence is thereby reified into a "thing" that finds its raison d'être not within itself but outside the world (in charity directed toward transmundane purposes). This yields an "order of love" according to which our "own present existence [is] a 'thing' among things, to be fitted into the rest of what is extant."[19] Arendt refers to this as a "relativization" of the world, as well as a relativization of ourselves as individuals insofar as every individual, seen from the perspective of transmundane charity, is merely a part of the subordinated world.[20]

Having explicated the disjunction of charity and cupidity, Arendt now proceeds to uncover an essential contradiction that arises from this account of love as desire or craving. Charity demands that we forsake worldliness, or the worldly attachments that characterize cupidity. But this injunction appears to be in tension with, or to go counter to, a basic Christian principle. As Arendt puts it: this renunciation of worldliness "makes the central Christian demand, Love thy Neighbor as thyself, well-nigh impossible."[21] What is required, then, is some alternative conception of love that could serve as a basis for the maxim of loving one's neighbor. Therefore the main burden of Arendt's analysis in part 2 of the book is to articulate this other dimension of love.

If I treat myself as a manipulable thing within the order of the world, "used" and not "enjoyed for its own sake," it is not clear why treating my neighbor as I treat myself does not simply debase my neighbor in proportion as my own self and the world are themselves debased. Loving my neighbor as myself may not exalt the neighbor but indeed devalue him. The problem is, as Arendt says, "why man, existing in and anticipating the absolute future, using the world and everything in it, including his own self and his neighbor, should establish this kind of empathic relationship that is implicit in all kinds of love and is demanded of the Christian explicitly: Thou shalt love thy neighbor as thyself." As Arendt immediately points out: "There is no answer to this question in the present conceptual framework."[22] What is demanded once again is a completely different "conceptual framework" within which to make sense of Christian "neighborly love," one that lies outside the horizon of appetites and desires.[23]

According to Arendt, the conception of love as desire or craving breaks down when one realizes that the categories of use and enjoyment (*uti* and *frui*) do not apply to what is neither above nor below me (I enjoy what is above; I use what is below): "What is beside and next to me, I myself and my neighbor, is neither to be 'used' nor to be 'enjoyed.'"[24] Arendt argues that this theoretical predicament expresses a clash between Augustine's Stoic and Neoplatonic tendencies, and a radically opposed Christian demand for neighborly love ("the specifically Christian relationship with the world").[25] In Arendt's view, Augustine never quite managed to square the Stoic-Neoplatonic aspects of his thought with the requirements of orthodox Christianity. The outcome of this deep tension in his thought is a set of quite distinct concepts of love that coexist uneasily, as Arendt tries to show throughout her analysis.

In part 2 of the book Arendt considers a second aspect of humanity's essential dependency, namely humanity's dependence, as a "creature," on God as Creator. Here the emphasis shifts from "the anticipated future" to "the remembered past." Rather than projecting forward to "a transcendent, transmundane future" in the desire for an everlasting happy life, we look back in remembrance to "a transcendent, transmundane past, that is, the origin of human existence as such."[26] Without memory that allows humanity to recollect its origin, "man's existence, like the existence of the world, is utterly perishable."[27] Hence the concern with the perishable and the imperishable is no less central to part 2 than it was to part 1. In a reflection inspired by the categories of mortality and natality worked out in *The Human Condition*, Arendt adds, in one of her revisions, that just as desire corresponds to death, so remembrance corresponds to birth: "What ultimately stills the fear of death is not hope or desire but remembrance and gratitude."[28] Again, the themes both of part 1 and of part 2 arise from one and the same insight, namely, a sense of the precariousness of human existence, its utter dependence on a transmundane origin and a transmundane destination.

On the basis of the creature-Creator relationship, Arendt returns to the distinction between charity and cupidity that was central to part 1. Here the distinction is based on the idea of choosing between the world and God, between love of the world and love of the source of the world. However perishable the world may be in relation to God, it appears imperishable relative to humanity (it has "an imperishable quality"). Humanity is therefore tempted to escape its own mortality through desire directed toward the world. This is precisely the temptation of man's cupidity: "in loving [the world] for its own sake he loves the creation rather than the Creator."[29] The covetous individual forgets that the world, for all its *apparent* permanence, is no less dependent on God for its origination than humanity is. In the obviousness of our *own* mortality, we overlook the contingency of the *world* on God's will, the "creatureliness" of the world, as it were. Charity is the corrective to this illusion. In taking the world to be independent of divine origination, we attach ourselves to it, and in the same proportion detach ourselves from God. To do this, though, is in a certain manner to set ourselves up as creators of the world. Thus love of the world is inseparable from a kind of pride: we "covet" it, and to that extent are resistant to the inescapable reality of our dependence on God. Once again, love of the world means that cupidity has displaced charity. Conversely, charity signifies the recognition that the world is *not* our home, that it is a mere desert, and points us in the direction of our true home, beyond the world. This new formulation of the distinction between cupidity and charity is summed up in the following maxim that Arendt quotes from Augustine: "Love not to dwell in the building, but dwell in the Builder."[30]

Do we have our source in the world, or do we have our source in God? The former view is the expression of covetousness (*concupiscentia*) or cupidity; the latter view is the expression of charity. Only those who covet the world, those who are tempted by the illusory (because transitory) goods that it offers, can fail to see that the world itself has its source in God. Thus love of the world can only signify being oblivious to our creaturely dependence on the Creator.

When the law enjoins of us, "Thou shalt not covet," it "demands man's detachment from all created things, from the world in the broadest sense."[31] Any kind of attention to creature without reference back to Creator constitutes coveting in this sense, and "creature" here encompasses the world in its totality. To forget, even momentarily, that no creature is independent of the Creator is therefore to violate the Tenth Commandment. "No togetherness, no being at home in the world, can lessen" the urgency of this commandment.[32]

Through grace, "the creature tears itself loose from its mundane moorings, from making its home in the world."[33] With the help of grace, charity thereby secures us into Being, and rescues us from death. In charity, in the openness to grace, love conquers man's will, for "only in love can man renounce his own will."[34] "In the loving acceptance of God's love, the world has become a desert, and covetousness has thus lost its meaning."[35] And yet: "Though man's deliverance from being of the world permits him fully to understand the world as a desert again, he is no longer lost in this desert. He can live in it, because in charity he now has the 'whence,' and thus the meaning of this life."[36] (Augustine: "Howbeit, if ye would not die of thirst in this wilderness, drink charity.")[37]

The categories of mortality and natality that Arendt develops in *The Human Condition* are already implicit in the structure of the Augustine book: part I concerns the ever-present prospect of death; part 2 concerns the question of birth. The two together cover both the "whither" and the "whence" of human existence.[38] Augustine's philosophical inquiry into love, as reconstructed by Arendt, must exhibit the function of love from the perspective of both poles of human temporality. The continuity of Arendt's own reflections along these lines is shown by the fact that she relied on the categories of natality and mortality in clarifying the overall shape of the argument in one of her revisions of the manuscript: "the decisive fact determining man as a *conscious*, remembering being is birth or natality, that we have entered the world through birth, while the decisive fact determining man as a desiring being was death or mortality, the fact that we shall leave the world in death."[39] Arendt actually shared Augustine's vision of the precariousness of human temporality, and it constituted one of the major sources of impetus for her philosophical reflection. As she remarks in "Truth and Politics" (1967), the ground of her interest in the public realm is that it, "more than any other sphere of human life guarantees reality of existence to natal and mortal men—that is, to beings who know they have appeared out of non-being and will, after a short while, again disappear into it."[40]

III

We come back, once again, to the still unresolved problem of the Augustine thesis, namely, how one gives an account of neighborly love, where to love one's neighbor is to form worldly attachments that draw one away from charity and draw one toward cupidity. The question is: How can we deny the world (and ourselves) so as to avoid the sin of covetousness, and yet love our neighbor? What kind of human fellowship is possible in a world we are supposed to regard as a desert? The question ultimately comes down to this: "How, as one seized by God and detached from the world, can I still live in the world?"[41]

The initial answer that Arendt offers is that in loving the neighbor, we do not love the other as other, but simply as creature: "the other ceases to be anything but a creature of God."[42] That is to say, the neighbor "loses the import which his concrete worldly existence has" for us. Even our worst enemy is no more and no less a creature of God than our dearest friend. All such categories (friend, enemy, etc.) lose all relevance. If we take this idea seriously, we realize that "neighborly love leaves the lover himself in absolute isolation, and the world remains a desert to this isolated existence."[43] In loving the neighbor as God loves him (i.e., in respect of his creatureliness), every human yardstick is destroyed. As Arendt points out, this conception of neighborly love "fails to explain how the absolutely isolated creature can have a neighbor at all."[44] Worldly love entails distinction, choice, the privileging of *certain* human beings. But this is just what the Augustinian concept of charity rules out. We must love without distinction, without "choosing" the objects of our love. Everyone (all creatures) are equally beloved. This in fact abolishes love as we ordinarily understand it: it "means to love all men so utterly without distinctions that the world becomes a desert to the lover."[45] One does not love the *person*; one loves the creature: "I love in the other his createdness rather than what I concretely, mundanely encounter."[46] Thus Arendt concludes: "It really is not the neighbor who is loved in this neighborly love; it is love itself."[47]

As we have seen, part 2 leaves us no nearer to a resolution of the paradox with which Arendt began the book, namely, that Augustine's distinctive understanding of love as transmundane charity seems to render meaningless the traditional Christian concept of neighborly love. In fact, part 2 of the book ends with a restatement of the same paradox. The two lines of argument presented in parts 1 and 2 terminate in the same basic impasse, which, as Arendt says, leaves "neighborly love incomprehensible in its true relevance."[48] In part 3, entitled "Social Life," Arendt pursues an altogether different possibility. The problem, as it has previously been laid out, is that there can be no possible basis of community between myself and my neighbor, because the right kind of love is based not on what I might share with any particular individual but on what I share with *all* creatures (namely, our creatureliness). But in this new stage of the argument, this universal sharing is *itself* turned into a principle of community. The human community is founded on kinship deriving from our common descent from Adam. This common descent produces equality of situation: "All men share the same fate. The individual is not alone in the world; he has companions of his fate. . . . His entire life is regarded as a distinct fateful situation, the situation of mortality."[49] On this understanding, "death is never conceived as a fact of nature, but as a fateful event," the historic basis of a shared destiny.[50] In this kinship of all mortals, Augustine discovers a kind of community. To be a descendent of Adam is to be a sorry mortal, which means that I, as a mortal, am in the same boat as all others who are (by birth) as sinful as I am (i.e., all human beings). The equality of the human situation connotes: equality of sinfulness. In other words, sin supplies the basis of human community. "The sinful past is common to all, and nothing else could stabilize their social life in a community."[51] I can recognize my neighbor as my equal because we both participate in original sin, as inherited from Adam. I am unable to discriminate between different individuals as possible objects of my love because, relative to what we share (sinfulness/mortality), what distinguishes us is absolutely insignificant. "The equality of the situation . . . wipes out all distinctions."[52]

Yet this still does not explain why love of one's neighbor should be regarded as obligatory, or even desirable. Why should I love the other simply because he or she is my equal in sinfulness? Our common situation is "communion in sin."[53] What kind of community is that? All of us, as human beings, are in a sense originally "at home" in the world; the Christian vocation is to *make* ourselves strangers in this world, to "estrange" ourselves from our own native worldliness.[54] This is a challenge addressed to the whole human community, regarded as a family of descendants from Adam (which is why we are all "brothers"). The duty of love as charity is addressed to me as an individual, but it is also addressed to me as a human joined in a "communion of sin" with other humans. Because we suffer our mortality as a *common* fate (the punishment for our common sinfulness), we must address this fate in a kind of mutual solidarity, and this we can do only through charity (i.e., an experience of love that detaches us from the world and attaches us to our Creator).

On Arendt's reading of Augustine, the individual has a twofold origin: divine (creation) and human (generation). This implies, in turn, that the human being is *both* a stranger to the world (by virtue of our origin in God) *and* "at home" in the world (by virtue of our origin in historic humankind). The demand of charity is that we estrange ourselves decisively from the world that is a desert for us, but that is *also* our "home" (owing to our Adamic ancestry).[55] We both belong and do not belong to the world, and neighborly love serves to express this fundamental contradiction.

We are left with the very paradox with which we began: a form of human fellowship grounded on estrangement from the world and from all worldly attachments; a type of love that abstracts totally from the personhood of the one who is loved; a duty to neighborly love derived from the fact that the neighbor's sinfulness is equal to one's own.

Belonging or estrangement? Loving the world, or coming to view it as a desert? Being at home in the world, or "world alienation"? These are the alternatives with which Arendt grappled, not only in the book on Augustine but throughout her philosophical career.[56]

IV

Our purpose in this essay is to trace some important continuities that run from Hannah Arendt's first book to her last book. In particular, when one examines the core of Arendt's philosophical reflection, as formulated in *The Human Condition*, one can see to what extent it is governed by the problems that constitute her reading of Augustine. Labor is deprecated insofar as everything produced within the context of "man's metabolism with nature" is fated to be consumed. Work proves its superiority to labor insofar as the products that we fabricate *last*, thus composing a durable "world." And action demonstrates its philosophical advantage over work in that the immortal stories that are the reward of human deeds outlast even the world that we fabricate as the public setting for such praxis. "It is the publicity of the public realm which can absorb and make shine through the centuries whatever men may want to save from the natural ruin of time."[57] Furthermore, as I have tried to indicate elsewhere, this underlying intention is carried forward into Arendt's reflections on judging.[58]

The basic existential insight of Augustine's work is that the condition of mortality, that the things of the world do not abide but rather perish or pass away, is intolerable. The conclusion Augustine draws from this is that love of the world is futile, and must be supplanted by some other, more satisfying love of what does not pass away. In *The Human Condition*, Arendt explicates "the world" as a relatively stable dwelling-place that we fabricate in order to shelter ourselves from the flux of individual mortality; and she explicates action as the winning of an immortality in the space of publicity opened up by this enduring world. In direct response to the Augustinian argument, she holds that the activities of work and action secure, not indeed eternity, but at least a limited experience of immortality, and that therefore love of the world is *not* futile. She agrees with Augustine that we are not naturally at home in the world but contrary to Augustine, she believes that we can *make* ourselves at home in this world, which we enter as "strangers," through the immortalizing activities of world-fashioning fabrication and ever-memorable public deeds.[59] To be more precise: For Augustine, we are more "at home" in the world than we ought to be; for Arendt, we are more estranged from the world than we ought to be. One might say that the entirety of Arendt's philosophical work merely elaborates the question she had posed directly to Augustine: "Why should we make a desert out of this world?"

Notes

1. For the leading representative of what I am calling the standard view, see Elisabeth Young-Bruehl, *Hannah Arendt: For Love of the World* (New Haven: Yale University Press, 1982), which (not surprisingly for a biography) presents Arendt's political philosophy as the product (the distillation, as it were) of her life experiences.

2. Hannah Arendt, *Between Past and Future: Eight Exercises in Political Thought*, enlarged ed. (New York: Viking Press, 1968), p. 14. Cf. Arendt's statement in her famous exchange of letters with Gershom Scholem: "I came late to an understanding of Marx's importance because I was interested neither in history nor in politics when I was young." *The Jew as Pariah*, ed. Ron H. Feldman (New York: Grove Press, 1978), pp. 245–246.

3. Hannah Arendt, *Der Liebesbegriff bei Augustin: Versuch einer philosophischen interpretation* (Berlin: Julius Springer, 1929). An English translation, entitled "Love and St. Augustine: An Essay in Philosophical Interpretation," was completed by E. B. Ashton (although never published) and can be found in the collection of "Hannah Arendt Papers" deposited in the manuscript division of the Library of Congress, container 66. A large portion of the English manuscript on which I have relied (corresponding to pp. 7–53 of the German original) was substantially revised by Arendt in the early 1960s. References in subsequent notes refer first to serial numbers in the Library of Congress manuscript and then to the German original, whenever the latter corresponds to the former; a reference only to the former generally indicates a revision.

Arendt's Augustine book has, unfortunately, been almost totally neglected in the literature on Arendt's political philosophy. Young-Bruehl, at the end of her biography, does offer a "synopsis" of the Augustine dissertation. But rather than arguing that the book foreshadows some of the major themes of Arendt's later work, Young-Bruehl contends that Arendt moved decisively beyond the work on Augustine when she came to the insight, arrived at through her political experiences of the 1930s, that "pure philosophy," regarded as an autonomous pursuit, is insufficient (*Hannah Arendt*, p. 499). For one study of Arendt that makes an ambitious attempt to relate the Augustine book systematically to Arendt's more well-known later works, see Patrick Boyle, S. J., "Elusive Neighborliness: Hannah

Arendt's Interpretation of Saint Augustine," in *Amor Mundi*, ed. James W. Bernauer, S. J. (Dordrecht: Martinus Nijhoff, 1987), pp. 81–113.

4. "Love," p. 033132; *Liebesbegriff*, p. 7.

5. "Love," p. 033132.

6. "Love," p. 033133; *Liebesbegriff*, p. 9.

7. *City of God*, bk. 13, chap. 10; quoted in Hannah Arendt, *Willing* (vol. 2 of *The Life of the Mind*) (New York: Harcourt Brace Jovanovich, 1978), p. 109.

8. Cf. "Love," p. 033135; *Liebesbegriff*, pp. 10–11.

9. "Love," p. 033139; *Liebesbegriff*, p. 12.

10. "Love," pp. 033139, 033143; *Liebesbegriff*, pp. 12–13. Cf. "Love," p. 033152: "charity, like any love, must be understood as craving and is distinguished from cupidity by its object alone"; *Liebesbegriff*, p. 17.

11. "Love," p. 033143.

12. "Love," p. 033143; *Liebesbegriff*, p. 13, n. 4. The Augustinian text cited here is *Tractates on the Epistle of John*, 7, 1. Arendt also cites *Tractates on the Gospel of John*, 28, 9: "Hence before we come to the Promised Land, that is, to the eternal kingdom, we are in the desert and live in tents"; "he is in the tents who understands that he is an alien in the world; he understands that he is travelling abroad who sees himself sighing for the homeland.... What does it mean, in a wasteland? In a desert. Why in a desert? Because in this world, where one thirsts on a waterless road." *Liebesbegriff*, p. 13, n. 4, and p. 58, n. 1.

13. "Love," p. 033143; this formulation is a revision (ca. 1963). The original German version, which issues a considerably milder challenge, reads as follows: "Warum aber ist die Welt für das Suchen des Menschen die Wüste? Wie und wodurch kann der Mensch ohne jeden Anspruch an sie in seinen suchenden Fragen leben?" (*Liebesbegriff*, p. 13). Cf. *Liebesbegriff*, p. 58, on the contrast between *Heimat-patria* (home) and *Wüste-eremus* (desert). See also *Liebesbegriff*, pp. 66–67, 69–70, 90.

14. The linkage between the two works is made explicit in the following passage in *The Human Condition* (Chicago: University of Chicago Press, 1958), p. 53: "To find a bond between people strong enough to replace the world was the main political task of early Christian philosophy, and it was Augustine who proposed to found not only the Christian 'brotherhood' but all human relationships on charity.... [T]he bond of charity between people, while it is incapable of founding a public realm of its own, is quite adequate to the main Christian principle of worldlessness and is admirably fit to carry a group of essentially worldless people through the world provided only it is understood that the world itself is doomed and that every activity in it is undertaken with the proviso *quamdiu mundus durat* ('as long as the world lasts')." Cf. *Willing*, p. 92: "world-alienation ... preceded the rise of Stoic and Christian thought."

15. "Love," p. 033143 (Arendt's marginalia). Arendt tends to use male pronouns in referring to generic humanity. Where possible, I have sought to switch to genderless pronouns; but where I could not do so without tampering with her text, I have left her usage unchanged.

16. Arendt refers to this Augustinian distinction in *The Human Condition*, p. 252 n. 2; also, see *Willing*, pp. 102–103, 144.

17. "Love," p. 033166.

18. "Love," p. 033167, *Liebesbegriff*, p. 24.

19. "Love," p. 033167; *Liebesbegriff*, p. 25.

20. Ibid.

21. "Love," p. 033154.

22. "Love," pp. 033168–033169; *Liebesbegriff*, p. 26, n. 2.

23. Cf. "Love," p. 033173: "neighborly love cannot be determined as desire or craving." *Liebesbegriff*, p. 28.

24. "Love," p. 033170.

25. Ibid.

26. "Love," p. 033184.

27. "Love," p. 033187.

28. Ibid.

29. "Love," p. 03319; *Liebesbegriff*, p. 57.

30. "Love," p. 033334, n. 26; *Liebesbegriff*, p. 58, n. 1.

31. "Love," p. 033322; *Liebesbegriff*, p. 60.

32. "Love," p. 033323; *Liebesbegriff*, p. 61.

33. "Love," p. 033324; *Liebesbegriff*, p. 62.

34. "Love," p. 033331; *Liebesbegriff*, p. 67. The relationship between love and the will is discussed in Arendt's last book, *Willing*, pp. 95–96, 102–104, 122–125, 136, 143–145. Arendt's conclusion is that love alone is able to "still the will's restlessness" (p. 103). "What Love brings about is lastingness, a perdurance of which the mind otherwise seems incapable" (pp. 103–104).

35. "Love," pp. 033330–033331; *Liebesbegriff*, p. 67.

36. "Love," p. 033329; *Liebesbegriff*, p. 66.

37. "Love," p. 033338, n. 68; *Liebesbegriff*, p. 66, n. 3.

38. "Love," p. 033184.

39. "Love," p. 033187. Cf. Young-Bruehl, *Hannah Arendt*, pp. 493–494.

40. Arendt, *Between Past and Future*, p. 228.

41. "Love," p. 033345, n. 1; *Liebesbegriff*, p. 68, n. 2.

42. "Love," p. 033341; *Liebesbegriff*, p. 69.

43. Ibid.

44. Ibid.

45. "Love," p. 033343; *Liebesbegriff*, p. 70. Cf. "Love," p. 033364; *Liebesbegriff*, p. 88.

46. "Love," p. 033343; *Liebesbegriff*, p. 70.

47. "Love," p. 033345; *Liebesbegriff*, p. 72.

48. "Love," p. 033348; *Liebesbegriff*, p. 75.

49. "Love," p. 033351; *Liebesbegriff*, p. 78. Cf. "Love," p. 033363; *Liebesbegriff*, pp. 87–88.

50. "Love," p. 033360; *Liebesbegriff*, p. 85.

51. "Love," p. 033357; *Liebesbegriff*, p. 83.

52. "Love," p. 033353; *Liebesbegriff*, p. 79.

53. "Love," p. 033353; *Liebesbegriff*, p. 80.

54. Cf. "Love," p. 033357; *Liebesbegriff*, p. 83.

55. Cf. "Love," p. 033366; *Liebesbegriff*, p. 90.

56. In a lecture series on "Kant's Political Philosophy" (Chicago, fall 1964), Arendt returns to this theme of being at home or not at home in the world, in the context of a reflection on Kant's distinction between the beautiful and the sublime. Contemplation of pleasing forms makes us feel at home in the sensible world, whereas the experience of awesome formlessness gives us intimations of a supersensible world that is also our home: "if the beautiful is to show how adequate our faculties are for being at home in the world, the Sublime with its element of outrage, repellence and displeasure lets us feel a premonition of a world into which we, as we are and appear, do not fit. And yet, insofar as this displeasure indicates something beyond the sensible, it becomes the sign that we are not merely sensible beings, not only at home among appearances, but with a need (the metaphysical need) for some other home" ("Hannah Arendt Papers," Library of Congress, container 41, p. 032284). In the very next lecture, in a similar context, Arendt adverts explicitly to Augustine: ibid., pp. 032288, 032290, 032295.

57. Arendt, *The Human Condition*, p. 55.

58. Hannah Arendt, *Lectures on Kant's Political Philosophy*, ed. Ronald Beiner (Chicago: University of Chicago Press, 1982), pp. 144–156.

59. Cf. ibid., pp. 154–155.

IV

Gender and Jewishness

13

Women in Dark Times: Rahel Varnhagen, Rosa Luxemburg, Hannah Arendt, and Me

Bat-Ami Bar On

I

In this essay, I tell the story of Hannah Arendt telling the stories of two other Jewish women—Rahel Varnhagen and Rosa Luxemburg. I have engaged in my storytelling in a way that seems to resemble Arendt's engagement in the telling of hers. That is, it comes from my need to think through what Arendt would have called the condition of being Jewish, as well as Jewish identity, as my condition or identity, although in my case Jewishness is a part of an aspect of my condition or identity of which the other part is Israeli. Among the things I am is an Israeli Jew. But, not exactly, because I am an Israeli Jew who has chosen to live in exile, or the diaspora.

The choice of a diasporic life in the United States has brought me out of a world in which, due to the Jewish majority and hegemony in Israel, it is rather easy for even a secular Jew like myself to have a sense of themselves as Jewish, and into a world in which such ease is lacking, in particular when, again like me, one is without a local family. The world that surrounds me and with which my everyday life intersects is not Jewish. Most of the people at my workplaces and in my neighborhoods, as well as in the various groups and organizations to which I belong are not Jewish. The academic calendar that regulates my life is usually a calendar that recognizes the Christian high holidays—Christmas, Gregorian New Year, Easter—and little else. The shops in the towns I live in are usually open for regular business on Friday night and all day Saturday but not on Sunday. And, when it comes to holidays, for these shops, like for my academic calendar, the primary holidays are the Christian high holidays.

Not being able to take my Jewishness for granted has problematized Jewishness for me in a new way, especially given that in the context of the United States, where after World War II Judaism seems to have become more and more identified with religion, I have felt forced to mark myself religiously in order to have a public Jewish identity. Thus, I have mezuzot on my doors, a Star of David on my chain, I eat only matzo on Pesach, and although I am a vegetarian, I declare my adherence to kashrut. I am also very public about my adherence to the Jewish calendar and its holidays, most of which I mark with some kind of celebration, including, even if less obviously, the Shabbat.

But, even though I do all these religiously appearing things, doing them obscures my Israeliness, which is not merely a secular form of Judaism.[1] Moreover, I do them secularly and outside of an immediate stable community of people who also work to figure out for themselves a diasporic secular Jewishness. This makes my acts rather unintelligible; to help them be intelligible, and to continue my work, I have to turn to an imagined community. In the past few years, Arendt has become a prominent member of this community. Specifically, I find myself turning to her at this juncture of my life because she is a woman who had to come to grips with her own diasporic secular Jewishness while the Nazi Judeocide was in the making and during and following the formation of Israel in 1948, a necessarily unsettling time for Jews and a very formative history for me.

One could respond to this time like Emil Fackenheim. Yet, during this time at least some self-critical diasporic secular Jews could not uncritically follow Emil Fackenheim's six hundred fourteenth commandment, which requires denying Hitler posthumous victories through, among other things, the affirmation of a Jewish faith in a Jewish God and the normative privileging of Israel as the only concretely good outcome of secular Judaism.[2]

The Nazi Judeocide did not bring Arendt around toward a Jewish God, nor did it bring her to normatively privilege Israel, about which she was always concerned morally because of its nationalist foundations.[3] But the rise of Nazism in Germany did bring her to a pragmatic Zionism[4] and to an active learning about and connecting with her people.[5] Her research and writing about Rahel Varnhagen, née Levin, was part of Arendt's active learning about and connecting to her people, as was, I believe, her work on Rosa Luxemburg.

It was when the Nazis were rising to power that Arendt researched and completed most of the writing for her biography of Rahel Varnhagen. She began this research in 1929, when she was twenty-three years old, and she almost completed its writing by 1933, when she decided that she must leave Nazi Germany. Arendt finished the Varnhagen biography in 1938, while an exile in Paris, but it was first published only in 1958, when the Leo Baeck Institute for the Study of German-Jewish History took an interest in it.[6] Although Arendt did some early work on Rosa Luxemburg in the 1940s and early 1950s that focused on her theories of imperialism, Arendt's biographical piece on Luxemburg is a sketch written and published in 1966 as a book review of J. P. Nettl's biography of Luxemburg. This piece was included in Arendt's collection *Men in Dark Times*, which was published in 1968 when Arendt was sixty-two and already recognized as a leading intellectual in the United States, where she found refuge in 1941.[7] While not as obviously situated in relation to the Nazi Judeocide as the Varnhagen biography, the biographical piece on Luxemburg was clearly written with an eye on Germany's Nazi past; moreover, it was written just as Arendt was one-sidedly ending a struggle with the Jewish community over her most current writing about that past: *Eichmann in Jerusalem*.[8]

II

Chronologically situating Arendt's biographical work on Varnhagen and Luxemburg hints at, but does not explain, her sense of the complexity of the kind of thinking through Jewishness as a condition of Jewish identity that she took on. To understand this complexity, it is important to situate Arendt's biographical work on Varnhagen and Luxemburg in relation to her metaphorical concept of dark times.

In the preface to *Men in Dark Times*, Arendt states that her title derives from Bertolt Brecht's poem "To Posterity," which she describes as mentioning the catastrophic events of the first half of the twentieth century and the outrage and despair that accompanied them, the former because there was so much wrong and the latter because there was so little protest of and resistance to the wrong in question.[9] For her, though, Brecht's sense of dark times is too limited; borrowing from Heidegger's *Being and Time* and Sartre's *Nausea*, she goes on to articulate the metaphorical concept of dark times in terms of a kind of ethico-political betrayal. She says in words echoing her ideas from *The Human Condition*,[10] "[I]t is the function of the public realm to throw light on the affairs of men by providing a space of appearances in which they can show in deed and word, for better and worse, who they are and what they can do."[11]

She goes on to point out that the darkness of a time is the absence of this light and the result of the perversion of the public realm by the people who are entrusted with its development and maintenance—politicians, in particular, but also intellectuals, and other people who are in position to influence people. Such darkness is brought about by the deployment of a camouflaging speech, hence, a language that hides more than it discloses, like the language of propaganda or "doublespeak," thereby degrading truth and meanings.[12]

According to Arendt, Rosa Luxemburg's times were dark times. She begins her piece on Luxemburg with Luxemburg's death in 1919 rather than other points of Luxemburg's life. She seems to do this not only because she believes that it is only at the end of a life that a life can be unfolded as a story, but primarily because of the kind of death this was. It was a governmentally sanctioned murder and it consequently serves well to show both the darkness of Luxemburg's and of Arendt's own times.

The way in which Arendt tells the story of Luxemburg's death is particularly revealing. What she does is bring together events, people, and organizations that are separated from each other by time, coupling them to suggest a continuity and a repetition. Thus, she says of Luxemburg's killers, "The murderers were members of the ultra-nationalist and officially illegal *Freikorps*, a paramilitary organization from which Hitler's storm troopers were soon to recruit their most promising killers."[13] And she describes a scene in their trial as follows,

During the trial, a photograph showing Rung and his comrades celebrating the assassination in the same hotel on the following day was introduced as evidence, which caused the defendant great merriment. "Accused Rung, you must behave properly. This is no laughing matter," said the presiding judge. Forty five years later, during the Auschwitz trial in Frankfurt, a similar scene took place; the same words were spoken.[14]

Most revealing of the darkness of the times, and especially of Arendt's times, are those of Arendt's comments that couple the Weimar government of 1919 and the Bonn government of 1962. She claims about the two,

> The [Weimar] government at the time was practically in the hands of the *Freikorps*.... The Bonn government—in this as in other respects only too eager to revive the more sinister traits of the Weimar republic—let it be known that it was thanks to the *Freikorps* that Moscow had failed to incorporate all of Germany into a red Empire after the First World War and that the murder of Liebknecht and Luxemburg was entirely legal "an execution in accordance with martial law."[15]

Arendt notes that the commendation of the *Freikorps* by the Bonn government in 1962 exceeded what the Weimar government did in 1919. In the context of the times the excess is fitting with a Bonn pattern of a national unification that capitalizes on anticommunism.[16] But in 1962 anticommunism also served to divert attention from the embarrassing purge of ex-Nazis that the Bonn government engaged in from 1960 to 1962, following the Israeli abduction of Adolf Eichmann and during the preparation for his trial, the trial, verdict, execution, as well as for a short time following that.[17] How interested the Bonn government might have been in such a diversion is clear from Arendt's description of Chancellor Konrad Adenauer's braced preparation for the Eichmann trial and its predictable consequences. She says of him in *Eichmann in Jerusalem* that he "had foreseen embarrassment and voiced his apprehension that the trial would "stir up again all the horrors" and produce a new wave of anti-German feelings throughout the world.[18]

It was not only the early 1960s that, according to Arendt, were as dark as Luxemburg's times; so were the late 1960s in both Germany and the United States. The 1960s and especially the Vietnam War showed Arendt a United States exhibiting imperialist tendencies, hence, given the framework of her *Origins of Totalitarianism*, a country that had embarked on the road to totalitarianism, a road it had traveled differently in the 1950s during the McCarthy-inspired "red scare."[19] And, Arendt points out in a December 1966 letter to Jaspers that she had a feeling that, the "Germans have provisionally invented a new governmental form—the two-party dictatorship."[20]

For Arendt, a tyrannical form of government is a form of government that diminishes and even eliminates the public realm through deceit or violence, emptying citizenship and community membership of meaning because it makes them quite unpracticable, or paradoxically, practicable only oppositionally in the underground.[21] Taking the practicability of citizenship or community membership as a criterion, one can have another sense of dark times, one that is not a function of either too much wrongdoing with too little of a response or of ethico-political betrayal, but rather, a function of exclusion from a public realm that exists for others.[22] It is this sense of dark times that is gestured at by Arendt's discussion of Rahel Varnhagen, who as a woman and a Jew, born in Germany in 1771 (she died in 1833) before Jews and women were included in German civic-political life, had no public realm available to her. As Arendt notes in a letter to Jaspers in 1952 in which she responds to objections he had to her approach to Varnhagen's biography, "You are absolutely right when you say this book 'can make one feel that if a person is a Jew he cannot really live his life to the full.' And that is of course a central point."[23] Or as she points out in the biography itself, "A political struggle for equal rights might have taken the place of a personal struggle. But that was wholly unknown to this generation of Jews."[24]

Although Arendt does not make connections between her times and Varnhagen's, her times while researching and writing Varnhagen's biography were becoming as dark as Varnhagen's. It was during these times that Arendt's civic status eroded and changed from that of a German citizen with civil rights and a public realm available to her to that of a refugee and a stateless person who at various points was considered to be an enemy alien.

Arendt describes the multifaceted loss of the 1930s and 1940s Jewish refugee experience, including herself under the description, in her 1943 essay, "We Refugees."[25] She says,

> We lost our homes, which means the familiarity of daily life. We lost our occupation, which means the confidence that we are of some use in this world. We lost our language, which means the naturalness of reactions, the simplicity of gestures, the unaffected expressions of feelings. We left our relatives in the Polish

ghettos and our best friends were killed in concentration camps, and that means the rupture of our private lives.[26]

After noting that as a result of the multifaceted experience of loss undergone by the refugees they strove to have a private existence, she goes on to point out the impossibility of that, saying,

Once we could buy our food and ride in the subway without being told we were undesirable. We have become a little hysterical since newspapermen started detecting us and telling us publicly to stop being so disagreeable when shopping for milk and bread. We wonder how it can be done; we already are so damnably careful in every moment of our daily lives to avoid anybody guessing who we are, what kind of passport we have, where our birth certificates were filled out—and that Hitler did not like us. We try the best we can to fit into a world where you have to be sort of politically minded when you buy your food.[27]

Contrary to a public realm that empowers those who create and partake in it, the politicization of the refugee's private life, according to Arendt, does not empower the refugee. The refugee's situation is always precarious, a point Arendt makes succinctly when she claims in "The Stateless People" that the "whole point of giving refugees legal status is to make them deportable."[28]

Arendt's deportability was a function not merely of her refugee status but also and primarily of her status as a stateless person. Yet, Arendt would have become stateless even if she were to stay in Germany rather than leave it in 1933, as she did, given that stateless is what all German Jews became in 1935 with the passage of the Nuremberg Laws, which proclaimed that Jews were subjects rather than citizens. This was a situation that, according to Arendt, was immanent and known already in 1933. She writes,

After 1933 the fear of potential statelessness was felt by the government concerned [with the issue] mostly with regard to the Jews. To the 600,000 potential refugees in Germany and Austria, whom even the Evian Conference had recognized, could really be added the Jews of Rumania and Poland, whose situation was scarcely less precarious. Had the Polish foreign minister Beck not officially declared that Poland had one million Jews too many—which implied that at least one million Polish Jews were potentially stateless; and had the president of the Rumanian Federal Commission for Minorities, Professor Dragomir, not announced to the world: "a revision of the citizenship of all Jews in Rumania is in course of execution?" In other words native-born Rumanian Jews were regarded as naturalized citizens, and the whole world knew in the thirties that there was only a very narrow gap between being naturalized and being stateless.[29]

It was toward the end of her life that Varnhagen realized that her kind of statelessness, her kind of being excluded no matter what she tried to do to overcome her exclusion, was a mark of the Jew and inescapable.[30] For Arendt, this very same realization was an early one and with it the realization that the darkness of times resulting from her exclusion as a Jew was also inescapable. With this realization came the questions about the proper attitude in dark times and the possibility of their illumination.

III

For Arendt, though dark times may be inescapable, far-reaching, and seemingly all-encompassing, they are not unilluminable. To the contrary. Arendt even takes their illumination as something that one has a profound right to expect, probably because of her trust in human agency, whose potential she took to be a human condition.[31] Yet, according to Arendt, the illumination of dark times has to take on not an abstract theoretical form, but rather a narratival or storytelling form.[32] She says that the "illumination may well come less from theories and concepts than from the uncertain, flickering and often weak light that some men and women, in their lives and their work will kindle under all circumstances and shed over the time span given to them."[33]

Arendt believed that Luxemburg's life story illuminated her own and Arendt's dark times, of which thirteen years (1906 to 1919) were overlapping. One of the ways in which Luxemburg illuminated her own times was through a radically critical examination of the events and trends of her day and even though this examination took place in concert with others on the German Left, it was nonetheless unique because Luxemburg was never dogmatic. Her lack of dogmatism is, according to Arendt, among Luxemburg's most important qualities and she brings it into focus claiming about Luxemburg, for example, that:

> What mattered most in her view was reality, in all its wonderful and all its frightful aspects, even more than revolution itself. Her unorthodoxy was innocent, nonpolemical; she "recommended to her friends to read Marx for 'the daring of his thoughts, the refusal to take anything for granted,' rather than for the value of his conclusion."[34]

Or again:

She did not intend to spend her life in a sect, no matter how large; her commitment to revolution was primarily a moral matter, and this meant that she remained passionately engaged in public life and civil affairs, in the destinies of the world.[35]

Luxemburg's undogmatic, morally committed criticism was of word and deed. Arendt describes both with admiration. In an admiring tone she notes Luxemburg's antiwar public speaking (for which she was arrested), points out how much her political practice inspired her intellectual work, and emphasizes the extent to which her stance regarding political practice was always principled, saying of her,

[S]he refused categorically, from beginning to end, to see in the war anything but the most terrible disaster, no matter what its eventual outcome.... Moreover, it would have gone against her grain to look upon revolution as the profiteer of war and massacre.... And with respect to organization, she did not believe in a victory in which the people at large had no voice; so little, indeed, did she believe in holding power at any price that "she was more afraid of a deformed revolution than an unsuccessful one" ...[36]

While Arendt's Luxemburg shines through her dark times, Varnhagen does not. Still, she illuminates them because she is exemplary. What she exemplifies is what the condition of Jewishness did to a member of her generation and what it does in general when it has a certain configuration. Thus, Arendt says in her 1952 letter to Jaspers,

I still believe today that under the conditions of social assimilation and political emancipation the Jews could not "live." Rahel's life seems to me a proof of that precisely because she tried out everything on herself without attempting to spare herself anything and without a trace of dishonesty. What always intrigued me about her was the phenomenon of life striking her like "rain pouring down on someone without an umbrella." That's why, it seems to me, her life illustrates everything with such clarity.[37]

It would be a mistake to construe only Varnhagen as exemplifying what happens to one if she is a Jew. Luxemburg, who Arendt wanted to canonize believing that any self-respecting political science department should teach her work, remained an outsider and this may be for the very same reasons that she remained an outsider in Germany and the Left of her time, that is, because she was a Jew and because she was a woman, a point that Arendt makes stating that Luxemburg was marginalized "not only because she was and remained a Polish Jew in a country she disliked and a party she came soon to despise, but also because she was a woman."[38]

IV

Although separated in time, the situations of Varnhagen and Luxemburg shared some common elements. Nonetheless, there is an enormous difference between how they responded to those situations. Varnhagen spent most of her life using her gender in an attempt to escape her Jewishness. It is only when she seemed to have succeeded and became a member of high German society through her marriage to a non-Jewish semisuccessful social climber that she realized that she could not escape her Jewishness and that having tried to do so had bankrupted her. Arendt describes this realization using a framework for understanding the Jewish condition developed by Bernard Lazare, which she went on to develop further in much of her work on anti-Semitism.[39] She says,

> As a Jew Rahel had always stood outside, had been a pariah, and discovered at last, most unwillingly and unhappily, that entrance into society was possible only at the price of lying, of a far more generalized a lie than simple hypocrisy. She discovered that it was necessary for the parvenu—but only for him alone—to sacrifice every natural impulse, to conceal all truth, to misuse all love, not only to suppress all passion, but worse still, to convert it into a means for social climbing.[40]

Among the things that Varnhagen did in her attempt to escape her Jewishness was to disaffiliate herself from the Jewish people in general and the local Jewish world in particular. She cut herself off from lived ties with other Jews, believing that in this way she could be merely an individual. As such she could be free, which as Arendt notes, was an illusion shared by others of her generation. Arendt writes that "Jews did not even want to be emancipated as a whole; all they wanted was to escape from Jewishness, as individuals if possible. Their urge was secretly and silently to settle what seemed to them like a personal problem, a personal misfortune."[41]

Luxemburg did not separate herself from other Jews and was a member of a primarily Jewish and small oppositional friendship group.

Arendt's discussion of Luxemburg's Jewishness is done through a generalized description of this group. The sociological facts about it are that its members formed a small minority. Their families of origin were middle-class and assimilated. They were culturally oriented toward Germany and politically toward Russia and its socialism. But, otherwise, they were multilingual Europeans, something that Arendt interprets with the help of Nietzsche, agreeing with him that "position and function of the Jewish people in Europe predestined them to become the "good Europeans" *par excellence.* The Jewish middle classes of Paris and London, Berlin and Vienna, Warsaw and Moscow, were in fact neither cosmopolitan nor international. They were Europeans, something that could be said of no other group."[42]

According to Arendt, not only did Luxemburg's kind of Jewishness give her a unique social location, it also gave her a unique moral taste, which like the European social location, she shared with her group. The group took its members as equal, being contemptuous toward social and ethnic distinctions, disdaining ambition, career, and status. In addition, the members of the group expected mutual respect from each other and took the ability to trust each other for granted. And, they indeed came through for each other. Arendt points this out as follows,

> During the Russian revolution of 1905 Rosa Luxemburg was arrested in Warsaw, and her friends collected the money for bail (probably provided by the German Party). The payment was supplemented "with an unofficial threat of reprisal; if anything happened to Rosa they would retaliate with action against prominent officials." No such notion of "action" ever entered her German friends' minds either before or after the wave of political murders when the impunity of such deeds became notorious.[43]

Arendt adds to her description of Luxemburg's oppositional friendship group with her mention of Luxemburg's supportive family, to which she compares the group, though contrary to her friends, Luxemburg's family members did not share her ethico-politics. Arendt says of Luxemburg's family in a complementary tone that her "parents, brothers, sister, and niece, none of whom ever showed the slightest inclination to socialist convictions or revolutionary activities, did everything they could for her when she had to hide from the police or was in prison."[44]

Even though Arendt identifies certain features as marking Luxemburg's oppositional friendship group and family as Jewish, for Arendt,

Jewishness has no essence. According to her, Jewishness is a condition in people's lives and it is such by virtue of Judaism's long history. As a historical condition, it functions as a set of parameters that delimit but do not determine anyone's response to it. Varnhagen had her response and through it fashioned herself into the kind of Jew she was. Luxemburg's response fashioned the kind of Jew she was. They were not the same kind of Jew not merely because Jewishness was a different kind of historical condition for each of them but also, and perhaps primarily, because they inserted themselves in their respective worlds by responding to the historical condition of Jewishness differently.[45]

Of the two responses to the condition of Jewishness, Arendt seems to endorse that of Luxemburg rather than that of Varnhagen, at least until Varnhagen comes to see Jewishness as a condition that she could not escape. What for Arendt is so appealing about Luxemburg's response was her open embrace of Jewishness. Luxemburg took her Jewishness for granted yet not uncritically. This connected her to life with other Jews and yet placed her outside of the Jewish struggle for the assimilation that Varnhagen and so many other Jews have been seeking ever since assimilation seemed possible. In this respect Luxemburg was like Bernard Lazare, a conscious pariah.[46]

Arendt describes Bernard Lazare as understanding the conscious pariah as follows,

> [I]n contrast to his unemancipated brethren who accept their pariah status automatically and unconsciously, the emancipated Jew must awake to an awareness of his position and, conscious of it, become a rebel against it—the champion of an oppressed people. His fight for freedom is part and parcel of that [fight] which all the down-trodden of Europe must wage to achieve national and social liberation.[47]

The description of the conscious pariah fits Rosa Luxemburg. But, it does not fit her as well as it fits Arendt[48] who, like Luxemburg, critically embraced her Jewishness.[49] Perhaps because their times, although similarly dark, were still radically different, Arendt, in addition and contrary to Luxemburg, had to embrace her Jewishness more consciously and had to struggle passionately and principally to stay connected quite generally to the Jewish people. Even at the end of her life she was still practically involved with Jewish life, being, for example, on the editorial board of *Jewish Social Studies* and thus continuing the kind of involvement she began with her work for Jewish relief agencies while a refugee in France and the United States.

V

The more I think about Arendt's response to Jewishness as her historical condition, the more deeply moved I am by it, not merely because it offers something abstract or a model to contemplate, but also because of my sense of the depth of Arendt's feelings with regard to Jewishness. As a result, however, I find her treatment of gender to be at least perplexing. Gender, like Jewishness is, for Arendt, a historical condition.[50] Like Jewishness, then, it too can be responded to in many ways. And, in this respect too, Arendt sees Varnhagen and Luxemburg as different. According to Arendt, for Varnhagen, who wanted to be what she was not, femininity was a source of disempowerment. She was not femininely beautiful and this meant for her, "that she was entirely without weapons with which to begin the great struggle for recognition in society, for social existence, for a morsel of happiness, for security and an established position in the bourgeois world."[51]

While for Luxemburg also, femininity was limiting, she nonetheless embraced it, just as she embraced her Jewishness, and it is the way in which she was feminine that Arendt identifies as explaining her relationship with Leo Jogiches, Luxemburg's one great love, according to Arendt.[52] This relationship was marked, on the one hand, by a jealous response to his short affair with another woman and a long-term refusal to forgive him, both responses that separated them. Yet, on the other hand, the relationship was marked by a profound intellectual-political merging that made it hard to sort what was Luxemburg's and what was Jogiches'.

The ways in which Luxemburg was feminine are taken by Arendt to also explain her relationship to the women's movement of her time, a movement that she did not join or support. Arendt notes this, claiming that,

> Luxemburg's "distaste for the women's emancipation movement, to which all other women of her generation and political convictions were irresistibly drawn, was significant; in the face of suffragette equality, she might have been tempted to reply, *Vive la petite difference*.[53]

Arendt endorsed Luxemburg's avoidance of feminism. She did this though she was aware that gender was one of the concrete historical conditions of her own time, as it was one of Luxemburg's and Varnhagen's times.[54] But just as in their case, this awareness did not lead her to respond to gender in the same critically complex and searching ways in which she responded to Jewishness. Consequently, her own embrace of gender does not seem to be like her embrace of Jewishness, the embrace of a conscious pariah. And indeed, like Varnhagen and Luxemburg, she led a life that connected her mostly with men and had much fewer friendships with women (even though her friendships with women were as long and profound as those with men).

Still, Arendt might have not understood herself as embracing gender naively and a line from her piece on Isak Dinesen[55] suggests that she might have seen in the women's movement something that reminded her of Varnhagen's ways of doing things, that is, a flight. Arendt writes that according to Dinesen, "the light that illuminates the public domain is much too harsh to be flattering. She had had her experiences in this matter since her mother had been a suffragette, active in the fight for women's franchise in Denmark, and probably one of those excellent women who will never tempt a man to seduce her."[56]

Arendt was probably not motivated to write this by heteronormative anxiety, and her sentiments have been and are still echoed in feminist and queer critiques of the puritanical aspects of feminism.[57] Nevertheless, Arendt simply did not think through gender in ways that even resemble her thinking about Jewishness. She did not write much about gender, just one book review and a few comments. Moreover, although she did write about Varnhagen, Luxemburg, and Dinesen and with some sensitivity to their plight as women, most of her intellectual bonding was in nonfeminist writing about men's writing.

But why should it matter?

I believe that the slowly growing body of feminist exploration and appropriation of Arendt's works and ideas suggests that while she might have not been a feminist, there is a lot that she has to offer to feminist theorizing. At the least, she can offer feminist theoreticians a woman's voice that is given as much authority and taken as seriously and with as much respect as the men's voices that not only Arendt but most contemporary Western feminist theoreticians turn to for a dialogue.[58]

Yet, if Arendt's voice is to be taken by feminist theoreticians seriously and respectfully as an authoritative woman's voice, then Arendt's Jewishness, and specifically her intellectual and ethico-political life commitment to it, has to be understood as central to her thinking as gender is to feminist thinking. Indeed, her marginalization of gender may have resulted from the urguncy that Jewishness but not gender brought into her life. From Arendt's vantage point, the movement of the Nazis, which changed her life dramatically and endangered it by virtue of her Jewishness, might have been gender-blind enough and, therefore, de-gendering or at least decentering of gender.[59]

That this kind of traumatized de-gendering or decentering of gender is perhaps temporary could have not been obvious to Arendt. It is only now, most probably because of feminism and its centering of gender, that a centering of gender is taking place in works that examine the Nazi period and Judeocide; although some memoirs by women were published earlier, it is only now that a large enough space seems to have opened up for women's memoirs of their experiences between 1933 and 1945.[60] To Arendt's thinking what was obvious was that "From the 'disgrace' of being a Jew there is but one escape—to fight for the Jewish people as a whole."[61]

As I write, one bomb has recently exploded near the Israeli Consulate and another near the United Jewish Appeal offices in London, both following a deadly attack on a Jewish Community Center in Argentina. These events have left me feeling vulnerable as an Israeli and a Jew but not at all as a woman. Although unlike Arendt I have feminist commitments, I easily understand her trauma-captured focus. But there is more to my extension of understanding to Arendt than identificatory empathy. Working, as I have done in this essay, to understand Arendt's response to Jewishness, which seems to becomes sharper and clearer when contrasted with her perplexing response to gender, brings me back to my first steps as a feminist and how hard they were to take precisely because gender did not feel to me as a profound aspect of my identity. I think now that like Arendt, mine was then, and in some ways still is, a trauma-captured focus that decenters gender.

Notes

Acknowledgment: A version of this essay was read at the April 1994 Philosophy, Interpretation, and Culture Conference at the State University of New York at Binghamton. I would like to thank my union, the United University Professionals, for grants to help with my research, Lisa Tessman and Mary Jane Treacy for helpful discussions, and Larry May for helpful editorial comments.

1. There is a sense of Israeliness forged in contrast to both diaspora Jewishness and the Arab and particularly Palestinian environment of the Jewish-Israeli. For a discussion of Israeliness, see my "Meditations on National Identity and Friendship," *Hypatia* 9/2 (Spring 1994): 40–62.

2. See Emil L. Fackenheim, *To Mend the World: Foundations of Post-Holocaust Jewish Thought* (New York: Schocken, 1982,1989); in the introduction to the second edition, Fackenheim points out that his original formulation of the six hundred fourteenth commandment should be understood in light of the work done in *To Mend the World*, pp. xix–xv.

3. See Hannah Arendt, "Zionism Reconsidered," *Menorah Journal* 33 (August 1945): 162–196; "The Jewish State, 50 Years After, Where Have Hertzel's Politics Led?" *Commentary* 1 (May 1946): 1–8; "To Save the Jewish Homeland: There Is Still Time," *Commentary* 5 (May 1948): 398–406. For discussion of her position, see Dagmar Barnouw, *Visible Space: Hannah Arendt and the German-Jewish Experience* (Baltimore: Johns Hopkins University, 1990), pp. 72–134; Shiraz Dossa, "Hannah Arendt on Political Zionism," *Arab Studies Quarterly* 3 (Summer 1986): 219–230; and Matti Megged, "Hannah Arendt and Jewish Nationalism," in Reuben Garner, ed., *The Realm of the Humanitas: Responses to the Writings of Hannah Arendt* (New York: Peter Lang, 1990), pp. 7–18.

4. Arendt said in a 1964 interview and a 1972 conference discussion that the only group she ever belonged to was the Zionists, and this was between 1933 and 1943 and because of Hitler. See "'What Remains? The Language Remains': A Conversation with Günter Gaus," in Hannah Arendt, *Essays in Understanding: 1930–1954* (New York. Harcourt Brace and Company, 1994), pp. 11–12, and "On Hannah Arendt," in Melvyn A. Hill, ed., *Hannah Arendt: The Recovery of the Public World* (New York: St. Martin's, 1979), p. 334.

5. See Hannah Arendt and Karl Jaspers, *Correspondence: 1926–1969*, edited by Lotte Kohler and Hans Saner (German ed., 1985; English ed., San Diego, CA: Harcourt Brace and Company, 1992), p. 197, where in a letter to Jaspers, Arendt points out that she had to make the Jewish experience her own, being naive insofar as it was concerned by virtue of her familial and social background, which was that of an assimilated Jew.

6. Arendt provides some of this information in her 1956 preface to the published *Rahel Varnhagen* (London: East and West Library, 1958; New York: Harcourt Brace Jovanovich, 1974). More information about the history of the biography is scattered in Elisabeth Young-Bruehl's *Hannah Arendt: For Love of the World* (New Haven: Yale University Press, 1982), and brought together in chapter 2 of *Visible Spaces*. See also her note in a letter to Jaspers, *Correspondence*, p, 295.

7. Hannah Arendt, "A Heroine of the Revolution," *New York Review of Books* 7/5 (6 October 1966): 21–27 and "Rosa Luxemburg: 1871–1919," in *Men in Dark Times* (New York: Harcourt Brace Jovanovich, 1968), pp. 33–56.

8. Arendt's *Eichmann in Jerusalem: A Report on the Banality of Evil* was first published as a report, "A Reporter at Large: Eichmann in Jerusalem," in the February 16 and 23, March 2, 9, and 16, 1963, issues of the *New Yorker*. Its first edition was also published in 1963, and a revised and enlarged edition was published in 1965 (New York: Viking). For a description of the controversy around *Eichmann in Jerusalem*, see *For Love of the World*, pp. 328–378, and

either Dagmar Barnouw, "The Secularity of Evil: Hannah Arendt and the Eichmann Controversy," *Modern Judaism* 3 (1983): 75–94 or a version of this essay in *Visible Spaces*, pp. 223–251.

9. Arendt, *Men in Dark Times*, p. viii.

10. Hannah Arendt, *The Human Condition* (Chicago: University of Chicago Press, 1958), esp. pp. 22–78.

11. Arendt, *Men in Dark Times*, p. viii.

12. David Luban, in "Explaining Dark Times: Hannah Arendt's Theory of Theory," *Social Research* 50/1 (Spring 1983): 215–248, refers to this as the epistemological meaning of Arendt's concept of dark times (p.218), noting at the same time that the concept is value laden, a point that is acknowledged but deemphasized in discussions of Arendt's narratival "methodology." This is also a passionate concept, though Arendt does not eleborate on that.

13. Arendt, *Men in Dark Times*, p. 35.

14. Ibid.

15. Ibid.

16. See, for example, V. R. Bergahn's discussion in *Modern Germany* (Cambridge: Cambridge University Press, 1982), pp. 177–225.

17. On the importance of anticommunism to German diversion of attention away from the holocaust, see discussions of "the historians' debates" in Saul Friedlander, ed., *Probing the Limits of Representation: Nazism and the "Final Solution"* (Cambridge, MA: Harvard University Press, 1992), in particular the essay by Eric L. Santner, "History Beyond the Pleasure Principle: Some Thoughts on the Representation of Trauma," pp. 143–154. About anticommunism as a cover for anti-Semitism, hence, a more complicated sinister diversion, see Hannah Arendt, "The Seeds of a Fascist International," *Jewish Frontier* (June 1945): 12–16.

18. Arendt, *Eichmann in Jerusalem*, revised edition, p. 17.

19. See Hannah Arendt, *The Origins of Totalitarianism* (New York: Harcourt Brace and World, 1951), esp. part 2; "Lying in Politics: Reflections on the Pentagon Papers," *New York Review of Books* 17/8 (18 November 1971): 30–39; and "Europe and America: The Threat of Conformism," *Commonweal* 60/23 (24 September 1954): 607–610.

20. Arendt and Jaspers, *Correspondance*, 1926–1969, p. 663.

21. Hannah Arendt, " 'The Rights of Man' What Are They?" *Modern Review* (1949): 24–37; and "Preface: The Gap Between Past and Future," in *Between Past and Future* (New York: Viking, 1961, 1968), pp. 3–16.

22. Although not making a connection between dark times and exclusion, Frence Feher's "The Pariah and the Citizen: On Arendt's Political Theory," *Thesis Eleven* 15 (1986): 15–29 and Maurizzio Passarin d'Entréves's "Agency, Identity, and Culture: Hannah Arendt's Conception of Citizenship," *Praxis International* 9/1–2 (April–July 1989): 1–24, by focusing on practiced citizenship or community membership underscore how being deprived of that can mean dark times.

23. Arendt and Jaspers, *Correspondence*, p. 198.

24. Arendt, *Rahel Varnhagen*, 1974, p. 7.

25. Hannah Arendt, "We Refugees," *Menorah Journal* 31 (1943): 69–77.

26. Ibid., p. 69.

27. Ibid., p. 73

28. Hannah Arendt, "The Stateless People," *Contemporary Jewish Record* 8/2 (April 1945), p. 151.

29. Ibid., pp. 146–147.

30. Arendt, *Rahel Varnhagen*, 1974, p. 3.

31. See Arendt's discussions of natality in *The Human Condition*, in the chapters on "The Human Condition" (pp. 7–21) and on "Action" (pp. 175–247).

32. There is a growing interest in this particular methodological position of Arendt's. See, for example, Seyla Benhabib, "Hannah Arendt and the Redemptive Power of Narrative," *Social Research* 57/1 (Spring 1990): 167–196; Lisa J. Disch, "More Truth than Fact: Storytelling as Critical Understanding in the Writing of Hannah Arendt," *Political Theory* 21/4 (November 1993): 665–694; Eleanor Honig Skoler, *The Inbetween of Writing: Experience and Experiment in Drabble, Duras, and Arendt* (Ann Arbor: University of Michigan Press, 1993); Tobin Siebers, "The Politics of Storytelling: Hannah Arendt's *Eichmann in Jerusalem*," *Southern Humanities Review* 26/3 (Summer 1992): 201–211; Elisabeth Young-Bruehl, "Hannah Arendt's Storytelling," *Social Research* 44/1 (Spring 1977): 183–190. I believe that Arendt's position in this, as in other cases, is both similar to and different from that of Marx—similar in its rejection of abstraction as meaningless and its prioritization of the concrete, and different because it does not strive toward systematization as a means for comprehension.

33. Arendt, *Men in Dark Times*, p. ix.

34. Ibid., p. 39.

35. Ibid., p. 51.

36. Ibid., p. 53.

37. Arendt and Jaspers, *Correspondence*, p. 198.

38. Arendt, *Men in Dark Times*. pp. 44–45.

39. Arendt does not refer to Lazare in *Rahel Varnhagen* although she does in some of her other works. Both Barnouw (*Visible Spaces*, p. 38) and Young-Bruehl (*For Love of the World*, p. 121) note that Arendt became acquainted with this framework through her friendship with the German-Zionist Kurt Blumenfeld; this is also suggested by Arendt in a letter to Jaspers (*Correspondence*, p. 157). Arendt edited some of Lazare's work in 1948 for Schocken.

40. Arendt, *Rahel Varnhagen*, 1974, p. 208.

41. Ibid., p. 7.

42. Arendt, *Men in Dark Times*, p. 42.

43. Ibid., p. 47.

44. Ibid., p. 41.

45. Arendt makes this point most clearly in three of her essays: "From the Dreyfus Affair to France Today," *Jewish Social Studies* 4 (July 1942): 195–240; "The Jew as Pariah: A Hidden Tradition," *Jewish Social Studies* 6/2 (February 1944): 99–122; and "Privileged Jews," *Jewish Social Studies* 8/1 (January 1946): 3–30.

46. For the importance of the pariah for Arendt, see Feher, "The Pariah and the Citizen" and Jennifer Ring, "The Pariah as Hero," *Political Theory* 19/3 (August 1991): 413–452.

47. Arendt, "The Jew as Pariah," p. 108.

48. See Judith N. Shklar, "Hannah Arendt as Pariah," *Partisan Review* 50/1 (1983): 64–77.

49. Young-Bruehl points out Arendt's identification with Luxemburg in *For Love of the World*, as does Maria Markus in "The 'Anti-Feminism' of Hannah Arendt," *Thesis Eleven* 17 (1987), p. 82.

50. See, for example, Arendt's note in the introduction to *Rahel Varnhagen*, 1974, p. xviii, that by Varnhagen's times the modern configuration of gender relations had already taken shape. See also her 1933 book review "On the Emancipation of Women," in *Essays in Understanding*, pp. 66–68.

51. Arendt, *Rahel Varnhagen*, 1974, p. 6.

52. Arendt, *Men in Dark Times*, pp. 45–47.

53. Ibid., p. 44.

54. This is a point used to suggest that Arendt, despite what she said publicly, had feminist inclinations. See, for example, *For Love of the World*, pp. 95–97, 272–273.

55. Hannah Arendt, "Isak Dinesen, 1885–1963," in *Men in Dark Times*, pp. 95–110.

56. Ibid., p. 95.

57. The classical example is Gayle Rubin's "Thinking Sex: Notes for a Radical Theory of the Politics of Sexuality," in Carol S. Vance, ed., *Pleasure and Danger: Exploring Female Sexuality* (Boston: Routledge and Kegan Paul, 1984), pp. 267–319. For a more current discussion, see my "The Feminist 'Sexuality Debates' and the Transformation of the Political," *Hypatia* 7/4 (Fall 1992): 45–58.

58. On this point see Andrea Nye, *Philosophia: The Thought of Rosa Luxemburg, Simone Weil, and Hannah Arendt* (New York: Routledge, 1994), especially the introduction.

59. See Rey Chow, "Violence in the Other Country: China as Crisis, Spectacle, and Woman," in Chandra Talpade Mohanty, Ann Russo, and Lourdes Torres, eds., *Third*

World Women and the Politics of Feminism (Bloomington: Indiana University Press, 1991), pp. 81–100, for a discussion of the loss of the analytic category of gender as a result of trauma.

60. For early examples, see Charlotte Delbo, *None of Us Will Return* (Paris: Editions Gauthier, 1965). For current work, see Marlene E. Heinemann, *Gender and Destiny: Women Writers and the Holocaust* (New York: Greenwood Press, 1986); Carol Rittner and John K. Roth, eds., *Different Voices: Women and the Holocaust* (New York: Paragon Press, 1993); and R. Ruth Linder, *Making Stories, Making Selves: Feminist Reflections on the Holocaust* (Columbus: Ohio State University, 1993).

61. Hannah Arendt, "Portrait of a Period," *Menorah Journal* (Fall 1943), p. 314.

14

Hannah Arendt among Feminists

Elisabeth Young-Bruehl

During Hannah Arendt's last decade, until her death in 1975, feminists of the "second wave" responded to her work as Kate Millett did in *Sexual Politics*; that is, they took up her conceptualizations of such political phenomena as power and violence and employed them for the project of women's liberation. They did not ask that she be a feminist, nor assert that there is a womanly way of thinking that she should have achieved; they also did not appropriate her work for considering feminism critically. Arendt herself was certainly aware of the developing feminist movement, but she did not respond to it publicly. She did not think of herself as a feminist and she was deeply skeptical of any single-issue political movement, especially one that brought into question the distinction she drew between the private and the public.

Since Arendt's death, not particular conceptualizations, but the whole terrain of her work and of her life has been thick with feminist commentary and controversy. Panels dedicated to Arendt and feminism appear on the American programs of the political science and philosophy annual professional meetings; international conferences on the theme have been held in Italy, Germany. This year, the twentieth anniversary of her death is being marked with a collection of thirteen American feminist essays followed by an annotated bibliography citing thirty-two pieces in English and many more in German, French, Italian.[1] As my contribution to the more general collection of essays on Arendt's work that you are reading, which also marks the twentieth anniversary of her death, I would like to offer a brief overview of the feminist responses in order to raise some questions about how Hannah Arendt has become both a magnetic figure for American feminist political theorists and an exemplum of feminism's current struggle for theoretical direction.

In the first phase of post-1975 feminist writing about Hannah Arendt, which lasted until the late 1980s, Arendt's distinction between the private realm of the household and the public realm of speech and action, that is, the political realm, was lifted out of the broad range of her political theoretical concerns and targeted. Most feminists found this distinction, particularly as it was articulated in *The Human Condition*, to be a hateful legitimation of the relegation of women to the household's "separate sphere." Arendt's firm distinction seemed a kind of Victorian sexism made out of Aristotelian materials. Male citizens, Arendt seemed to be saying about the Greeks, act in public, creating and sustaining public spaces, having been given freedom from necessity and freedom to enjoy political life, to be actors, by the women and slaves and other noncitizens who performed the domestic labor and produced the offspring in households. She also seemed to be saying uncritically that this state of affairs—a politics predicated on domestic slavery—was the truly human human condition.

Actually, the household or private realm that Arendt distinguished so sharply from the public realm was characterized in *The Human Condition* in a number of different ways, and with quite different valuations. As a realm of production and necessity, it was clearly a lesser realm. But, on the other hand, it was also the realm of privacy, of intimacy, of protection from the harsh struggle of public life; a place for important prepolitical processes like the education of children, and a place for crucial extrapolitical activities like critical reflection and judging, for peacefulness to engage in the interiorized "life of the mind," the interior dialogue of thinking. As in many dimensions of Hannah Arendt's complex political theory, which is a texture of distinctions, evaluation depends on where you stand to evaluate. From the point of view of a person concerned to praise and celebrate the political realm, the household is inglorious, determined, mute. On the other hand, if the private realm should disappear or be absorbed into social and economic processes, or into the political realm itself, the conditions for tyranny or authoritarianism and, in the modern world, totalitarianism are present. Totalitarianism, a Hannah Arendt analyzed it in *The Origins of Totalitarianism*, is the form of government in which there is no action and persuasive speech in public spaces—that is, in which politics has been eliminated—and in which there is also no privacy. Even the most intimate bonds of family are corrupted or disrupted by a totalitarian regime that tries to lodge itself everywhere, driving right into the genealogies, the minds and the hearts of its subjects.

The Human Condition was, I have argued in my biography of Arendt, written under the shadow of the analysis in *The Origins of Totalitarianism*, and it offers the private/public distinction—recommends it—as a bulwark against the totalitarianizing character of the modern world. In *On Revolution*, Arendt went further and offered the distinction as a bulwark against the self-destructive, self-devouring potentialities of modern revolutions. Revolutions that focus on addressing the realm of necessity, "the social question" of how necessities are produced, supplied, distributed, or the social justice question of how different groups are employed and organized—that is, revolutions that do not focus on the political question of how a union of people is to be constituted for the possibility of continually renewing political speech and action—will be revolutions that eventually lose their meanings as new beginnings and succumb to depoliticization—sclerosis, as it were, of the political. They can become pretotalitarian.

Arendt's perspective can be compassed more generally by saying that she was trying to point out a vast modern political dilemma—a potentially or incipiently tragic dilemma. The modern industrial-technological possibilities that have been slowly changing the way in which the necessities of life are supplied and the generations raised and educated are doing two things at once: they are progressively rendering slavery—of subject peoples and of women—obsolete, and they are destroying the boundaries between household realms and public realms. Emancipation or universal citizenship for the formerly enslaved or marginalized is the great good of the modern revolutionary period; but the great danger in this period, in Arendt's estimation, is the emergence of a hybrid realm, neither private nor public, in which necessities are supplied in ways that cannot be independent of governance—they cannot be separate, unregulated—and that require laboring activity that infringes on any other form of life. So modern political theory has been organized by a deep quarrel between those who think conservatively that government, for the sake of endless increase, should be as little involved as possible in the emergent social realm and those who think liberally or socialistically that government should control this realm so that it can be made as equitable as possible, so that it can be a realm of social justice. But Hannah Arendt subscribed to none of the range of positions on this basic question, because she thought that economic processes could and should be contained and controlled by economic means, that is, administratively. Politics, for her, was something else again—not administration, but "words and deeds."

The feminists who approached Arendt's work in the 1970s, looking to her as a major political theorist and as a woman—the only European or American woman other than Rosa Luxemburg, Simone de Beauvoir, and Simone Weil who wrote philosophically about politics at the "classic" level—approached as liberationists. Their emphasis was on breaking the bonds of discrimination that kept women, despite their attained rights as citizens, in households and in the roles of domestic laborers and mothers, not on pointing to the dangers to either the private realm or the political realm of modern economic and social conditions. Their desire was to see women become fully and equally political but also free from the subordination of the household realm itself where "the personal is political." And from this point of view, of course, Arendt's emphasis—although she certainly had no trace of conservative opposition to the modern movement for equality—seemed misplaced, even perverse.

And those of this liberationist generation who criticized Hannah Arendt for ignoring what the sway of the household and the development of "the social" meant for women were certainly correct. She did not ask how the conversion of households in the process of industrialization and urbanization from productive, economic spheres into "separate spheres," not productive but only reproductive, as it were, motherhood spheres, affected women, either those pushed into the working class or those defined only by their mothering roles in households. She did not ask how "the social" shaped life in households, setting the subordination of women there more on a specifically sexual and reproductive basis, less on a laboring basis. "The personal is the *social*" was not her topic, even though she was quite aware of the social *Frauenproblem*, as a book review she wrote in 1933 makes quite clear.[2] In that review, she outlined sharply the complexities of the German situation then, noting that women had achieved many political rights but were still trapped in social contradictions as mothers and as second-class workers. But she also agreed with the socialist position, the one also taken by Rosa Luxemburg, that a "women's movement" (or a women's political party) was inappropriate because it was too abstract, too focused on specifically women's issues and not enough on the larger issues facing the working class as a whole. This position, which is of course still the position of many socialists, did not, however, inform any of Arendt's later political theorizing. Or, one might say, it did not break through her overriding concern with the household sphere as a sphere of protection against the continued expansion and extension of the social.

Her stance was, in fact, so resolute that when she applied its terms to the scene of American race relations in the 1950s, she ended up alienating another group seeking liberation. Considering the civil rights movement's school integration effort in Little Rock, Arendt objected to children being asked to do political work and to educational institutions being selected as the sites for political action, as children and schools were, in her terms, of the private, prepolitical sphere. Later, in *On Violence*, she used similar arguments against politicizing universities and specifically against "open admissions" to bring in more disadvantaged young people. For these judgments, as well as for her criticism of the 1960s Black Power movement and its debt to the theory of violence in Frantz Fanon's *The Wretched of the Earth*, which she thought implied destruction of the political realm, Arendt has been sharply criticized by African American intellectuals, most recently by a younger generation of feminists.[3]

After the early 1970s, as the American feminist movement itself evolved, the theoretical aspiration for supporting liberation as equality began to become overshadowed theoretically—if not in terms of practical politics, and if not among either socialist feminists or feminists of color—by a search for ways of addressing sexist denigrations of the particular traits that being raised by women and kept in the household sphere had inculcated in women. So-called cultural feminism or gynocentric feminism aimed to celebrate womanly virtues—womanly abilities for relationships, mothering or caretaking skills, emotional richness, and freedom from the distortions of patriarchal behavior and thought—with the hopes that achieving equality would not imply the loss of those virtues and that embracing these virtues would give the feminist movement much needed solidarity. Political participation and equality were less important theoretically to cultural feminists than the cultivation and promotion of female virtue—the triumph of these virtues was, in effect, envisioned as women's liberation. Cultural revolution superseded political revolution. Arendt's work, then, seemed to be not only underappreciative of the importance of emancipation and of the social question, but totally unappreciative of the specificities of women's lives and virtues and cultural possibilities. Arendt seemed as unconcerned with women as any patriarchalist.

Among the cultural feminists who criticized Arendt as a woman who thought like a man there was a shared—sometimes tacit, sometimes explicit—assumption that women should and naturally do think in gynocentric terms and always across the fundamental framework of sexual difference. Women's categories are FEMALE and MALE, with FEMALE being the "good" category, and all other differences being lined up with this fundamental one. PRIVATE, in this perspective, is valued as a female realm where virtues of caretaking and relationship are nurtured, and PUBLIC is a realm in which struggle and violence are corrupting, where machismo and harsh manipulation of others reign. Arendt's distinction, then, looks like a retrograde and patriarchal celebration of just this devalued masculine public space.

In most of the feminist literature on Arendt from the mid-1970s to the mid-1980s, there is a theme of castigation and lament.[4] How could a woman entertain a distinction that seemed to have no liberationist potential whatsoever, a distinction that could and did and still does serve both sexism and political conservativism more generally? How could a woman subscribe to a distinction that completely foreclosed the strong feminist insight that "the personal is political" and called for keeping the personal resolutely away from the political? In an often cited essay, the poet Adrienne Rich called Arendt's *The Human Condition* a "lofty and crippled book" and claimed that it "embodies the tragedy of a female mind nourished on male ideology."[5]

Rich's assessment can stand as a marker for the cultural feminist attitude that a next generation of feminist theorists slowly and ambivalently rejected.[6] The women of this cohort, who began to write in the mid-1980s, saw things differently when they approached Hannah Arendt's work. They could, first of all, appreciate that even though she did not consider the situation of women explicitly, she had understood quite well the special virtues that belong to people who have been denied access to the political realm, who have been kept in service or in pariahdom. But she had come upon this understanding as a Jew and as a historian of European Jewry, not as a feminist. Arendt's first book had been a biography of the Berlin salon hostess Rahel Varnhagen, and this book became a touchstone for the feminists who wanted to understand Arendt's relation to "identity politics" (as the phrase of the early 1980s went).

Different marginalized and scapegoated groups and subgroups, Arendt had shown in *Rahel Varnhagen* and in *The Origins of Totalitarianism*—where she had compared turn-of-the-century Jews to homosexuals, using Marcel Proust as her source book—have different social characters that reflect their different historical types of exclusion from politics. Further, people in such groups are often in other groups as well, their identities are plural—they are women and Jews like Rahel Varnhagen, for example—and they thus looked at the political realm from diverse perspectives. These Arendtian insights were taken up by feminists who criticized cultural feminism for overgeneralizing about women, for saying that all women—regardless of class, race, ethnicity—share the same womanly virtues. In these debates, American feminism itself became a field of controversy as women of different adjectives, often many different adjectives, struggled to determine whether they had anything culturally in common and to find ways to talk across their differences of background and purpose. They brought Arendt into the multiculturalizing moment of feminism by acknowledging that she had—for reasons that she had articulated quite self-consciously and politically—written her major works of the late 1940s and 1950s as a Jew.

"When one is attacked as a Jew," Arendt had said retrospectively in a 1964 interview., "one responds as a Jew." And then she had later, during the controversy that erupted over her *Eichmann in Jerusalem* (1963), made it just as clear that her "as a Jew" identification was not a matter of love of the Jewish people—because love, she said, was something she felt for individuals, in private; it was, rather, a matter of public, political choice. She was, thus, distancing herself from a range of ideas about identity as based on "nature" or on loving identification (of the sort implied by the phrase "woman identified woman") that cultural feminists had adopted and that cultural feminism's feminist critics described, in quite Arendtian terms, as falsifying, essentializing, and sentimental. Neither the strictly biological nor the cultural-mystical definitions of "woman" are adequate to the political complexities of being a woman and being a woman in a context, from a context with many more identity possibilities in it than FEMALE and MALE.

Second, this younger generational cohort of feminists reassessed Arendt's private/public distinction. The importance of protecting a private realm from the encroachments of the social or the political were more apparent to this group because hard-won protections of privacy, particularly the 1973 Supreme Court decision in *Roe v. Wade*, were then under assault. And, more generally, the increasing sexualization of the social realm, including the expansion of the pornography industry into new technological media, had impelled some feminists—under the theoretical leadership of Catherine McKinnon—in the direction of calling for increased regulation of the private sphere as well as of qualifications of First Amendment rights, and a deep quarrel had opened between these feminists and those who objected to the antipornography campaign's attitude toward protection of privacy. That antipornography feminists could make alliances with far right political activists who were sexist and homophobic, anti-choice on the abortion question, shocked liberal theorists into reconsidering the private/public distinction and newly appreciating its Arendtian function, that is, its function as a bulwark against totalitarianizing trends, in general and as advocated by feminists.

Third, the younger generation of theorists recontextualized Arendt's private/public distinction in the larger texture of distinctions that make up *The Human Condition.* They noticed that Arendt did not generally operate with binary concepts, that the private/public distinction is, in fact, unusual in her work and it is, further, tied to the third concept of "the social" as a hybrid modern realm, a threat to both the private and the public. Attention was turned to the fact that the main axis of distinctions in *The Human Condition* contains the troika labor, work, and action (and speech)—three modalities of activity—and that there are also six "conditions of human existence" named life, natality, mortality, earth, worldliness, and plurality. The last three of these are, respectively, the preconditions for the activities: labor is a process on and of the earth, a "metabolism of nature"; work is the fabrication of the things, the artifacts, the cultural objects, that make up the world; and action requires a plurality of human beings (as it disappears if human beings lose their distinctiveness, as they do when they live in a mass society or, more horribly, when they are reduced to the torture of concentration camp existence). Feminists who have reflected on these Arendtian categories of activity and condition have generally been more receptive to Arendt's overall approach.

But some have also tried to adapt this overall approach to feminism and its particular concerns, and for that purpose the concept of natality has often been singled out. Natality, which Arendt used to emphasize both the new beginnings of the human generations and the new beginnings represented by political action, has seemed to feminists to be the quintessential female contribution—so it is, indirectly, a celebration of motherhood—and also an antidote to the masculine imagery associated with politics as action and speech. In effect, the concept of natality has been used to make Arendt's private realm into the realm of motherhood and the font of all politics—to revalue it positively. Arendt becomes a kind of feminist, or at least not a sexist, in this expansion of the cultural feminist frame into the larger domains explored in *The Human Condition.*

But not all of the commentators who have focused on the overall approach of *The Human Condition* have tried to recoup Arendt for feminism by singling out the natality concept and extolling motherhood. Mary Dietz, for example, has noticed that *The Human Condition* presents a vast modern dilemma unfolding along with the one I highlighted above.[7] In addition to the titanic conflict between the social and the political, propelled by modern industrializing and technologizing in the domain of labor and by the instrumentalizing of life in the domain of work, Arendt noted that this same alliance of labor and work to defeat action contains an antagonism of labor and work. The industrializing and technologizing that has elevated labor and laboring people (*animal laborans* in Arendt's terms) into dominance threatens work and people who do work (*homo faber* in Arendt's terms). Laboring, processing the earth's resources into life necessities, grows like a jungle and makes fabrication, the creation of artifacts and cultural products, inefficacious, obsolete. Making furniture for the world, including the monuments and memorials that tell the stories of political action, becomes less and less possible as a consumer culture focuses on the pursuit of abundance, on nondurable goods, planned obsolescence, automation (and now telecommunications). Dietz argues that Arendt presented not the private/public distinction but *this* struggle in gendered terms—women are associated with the laboring process, men with the fabrication—and she even suggests that Arendt understood the way in which the "battle of the sexes" is played in and through these domains. Dietz also thinks that by contrasting both labor and work with action that Arendt was presenting action as beyond gendering, as a domain in which all people can be free. Action is, as Dietz puts it "beyond the phallocentric:gynocentric divide."

Looking back over the territories of these contestations and appropriations, it seems to me that there are three major questions that were raised not so much in this history as by it—questions that can be articulated by treating this history as itself an exemplum. And, specifically, I will treat it as an exemplum that has come up to the edge of possibilities for feminist reflection on Hannah Arendt's work that I would like to gesture toward—possibilities that are marked in Mary Dietz's essay with the phrase "beyond the phallocentric : gynocentric divide."

Let me start with the question raised by the cultural feminist critique of Arendt. What does it mean to claim or to believe that women think differently than men, that women's experiences—even if they have great diversity across ethnic, racial, and class groups—have a commonality that is expressed in the method or form or the content of thinking?

It seems to me that Hannah Arendt's life and work show that the cultural feminist claim that women think as women and gynocentrically, putting women at the center of their concern, is overgeneralized. I think that the most that can be said about women's thinking is that it will have a strand in it that is determined by being a woman, and that this stand may, for some women, be the major strand, whereas for others it will be subsidiary to other strands that are created from other ingredients of experience and condition. For some women, thinking will be relatively genderless—as Hannah Arendt, in *The Life of the Mind*, claimed that *all* thinking is. My differentiating conclusion could be said more succinctly in psychoanalytic terms: all thinking is on a narcissistic basis to some degree—so men think as men and androcentrically (which usually means phallocentrically), women as women and gynocentrically, to some degree. The narcissistic bases for the two sexes will always be different, to individually varying degrees. Further, women's narcissism, under conditions of sexism, will always be reactive to the oppressor's narcissism, whereas male narcissism, although it may be reactively wounded or warped by the conditions sexism produces, will not be reactive *as oppressed*. Different historical and cultural situations will promote or inhibit differently the narcissism of one sex or the other or both.

Hannah Arendt thought more as a Jew than as a woman[8]—history demanded that of her, so to speak—but the narcissistically feminine strand in her thought does not seem to me a difficult matter to identify, as it is of a piece with the insight that she said Rahel Varnhagen had come to at the end of her life about her Jewishness: she accepted, even celebrated, her Jewishness and said that she would on no account have wanted to miss what being Jewish had meant for her. Arendt often stated—most clearly in her essay on Rosa Luxemburg—that her own position on the *Frauenproblem* was, basically, *Vive la petit différence*! What this meant was: celebrate who you are in your distinctiveness, in your not-that, not-the-other, do not try to *be* or *become* the other. Plurality, the precondition of action, includes among its possibilities plurality of sex/gender identities, and this plurality, like others, should be respected.

Distinctiveness means nonconformity, which Arendt presented as preserved in thinking itself by dialogue—what she called "the dialogue between me and myself." It was not the orientation or the content of thinking that Arendt considered crucial to it, but its interactivity, its internal mobility and freedom from rigidities of ideology or received ideas. Thinking is the quintessentially human internal-mental activity, as the quintessential external activity is being political, speaking and acting, opening political spaces, and both of these activities are, in Arendt's view, more important qua activities than in the specificities of their content because it is as activities that they perpetuate themselves, renew themselves. Further, thinking's activity in the modern world, as Arendt understood it, cannot rely on tradition, much less on received ideas or ideology, because historical realities have rendered these useless, obsolete, out of touch. She imagined thinking as a process of gathering up the fragments of broken traditions and assembling them anew, in something new.

This reflection suggests a second question: How and why has sexual difference come to operate like a received idea—a fixation point—in feminism, and must it remain so? This question has been raised by historians of feminism within the last several years—it is the focus, for example, of Carol Lee Bacchi's *Same Difference: Feminism and Sexual Difference* (1990), which argues that "perceiving issues in terms of women's sameness to or difference from men" is "politically unwise," because it "diverts attention from the inadequacy of social institutions"[9] Such histories make it clear how the political contexts of Anglo-American feminism have promoted the sameness-difference focus and reinforced the alignment of feminists with either cultural feminism (stressing difference) or radical feminism (stressing future possibilities for sameness). And it is certainly appropriate psychologically to argue that the question of difference reflects the basic narcissism of men and women, both being threatened by the difference of "the other." But I think that the exemplum of feminist commentary on Hannah Arendt shows something further.

Theorists working within movements of liberation think initially from within particular experiences of oppression—nationalists from within experiences of national oppression, people of color from within experiences of racism, Jews from within experiences of anti-Semitism, women from within experiences of sexism. But the measure of their movement's longevity and vitality is the extent to which they then come to think more broadly, both in terms of others' experiences of oppression, for the sake of coalition building, and in terms of historical grasp, for the sake of freely imagining the future, imagining the future as free of repetition compulsion as possible. Arendt's work is a vivid example of how someone initially politically identified with the Jews and with Zionism pushed outward.

Arendt's political philosophy could be said to have arisen out of her reply to the anguished question that every Jew of her generation was compelled to pose by the Holocaust: Why the Jews? Her reply reached out across the nineteenth century, into the history of imperialism, the rise of "the social" as capitalism expanded relentlessly, in geographical terms and into the political realm; as European states became businesses and extended their enterprises around the world; as the modern nation states, so intolerant of their own minorities and so prejudiced against their colonials, were instituted. But her reply was also explicitly framed as a *political* reply, ultimately an analysis of a novel *form of government*, because she felt that the European Jews of her parents' and her own generation, being politically inexperienced and failing to distinguish between their social lives and their political lives, had misestimated the threat of political anti-Semitism. Specifically, they had sought social acceptance, assimilation, not realizing that this would be worth nothing unless their rights were politically and legally secured. They did not grasp that the real threat to their community lay with a political party that put itself above the law, saying "the Fuhrer's will is the law" and thereby destroying law as that which should be above all individual citizens and groups.

Arendt's analysis was, I think, historically the most rich and illuminating of any produced in response to the Holocaust. But I also think that it is not generalizable to other types and historical courses of oppression—to racism, to sexism. Each time Arendt used her framework to discuss these prejudices and their courses, she would miss important differences between them and anti-Semitism; the analogizing of the prejudices blocked her view. Her feminist critics have noted this problem again and again, but have not given it the analysis it calls for. For Arendt, all oppressed people were oppressed like the Jews. For many of her critics, all oppressed people are oppressed like women. The differences among the prejudices fall out of the theoretical picture either way.

Feminism has begun to extend its theoretical reach, but it is still tied, repetitively, to what Mary Dietz called "the phallocentric:gynocentric divide." It is tied to the categories male/female, masculine/feminine. It cannot yet see sexism as part of a much larger picture of prejudice types and a much larger set of questions about why people need prejudices, what functions they serve. When the frame is broadened in this way, a third question appears on its horizon. The conclusion that extrapolating from one experience of prejudice and discrimination to another, analogizing the prejudices, is problematic has only been drawn on the basis of realizations that victim groups' self-understandings are not being taken into account—black women's feeling that racism, not sexism, is their main problem, for example. But the problem of analogizing the prejudices and the experiences of victim groups has not been clearly formulated theoretically. What is there in the specificity of sexism as a prejudice—held by individuals and vastly institutionalized—that distinguishes it from anti-Semitism, from racism, and that distinguishes the experience of its victims? What is it that makes the private/public distinction so central to feminist theory, whereas it is not central to current Zionism, to black pride or Afrocentricity, to other forms of single-group (defensive) self-assertion?

The key to pursuing this question, it seems to me, is an initial admission that not all prejudiced people are prejudiced alike—there is no such creature as "the prejudiced personality" and no single psychic or social dynamic underlying all prejudices. I would argue—on the basis of psychoanalytic characterology—that there exist fundamentally different character types, each of which uses a particular type of prejudice as part of its defensive structure, as what might be called its social mechanism of defense. The major character types seem to me to be three in number, and I will call them in clinical shorthand obsessional, hysterical, and narcissistic as I sketch them.[10]

The rigidly, conformistically structured obsessional type, commonly quite paranoid, is suited to hold prejudices against groups construed as international commercial conspiracies of infiltrating, dirty or polluting secret agents who can burrow into the obsessional's fortressed self. All such groups—especially immigrant commercial groups—are "Jewish." Hysterical people, volatile, chameleonic, theatrical, and so typically divided or split psychically into an eroticized self and a chaste self, are prejudiced against groups construed as hypersexual and threatening "from below" against the bulwarks of civilization and the natural hierarchies of human society. Narcissists, arrogant and unempathic, who imagine themselves as their own living standards of measurement, finally, are prejudiced against groups construed as sexually other, threatening to the coherence of narcissistic bodily and mental ideals and transgressive of gender identities, and in need of rigorous control to keep them from asserting their otherness, to keep them in the role of mirrors, enhancing to the narcissist's sense of self.

A model like this, even sketched in such quick strokes, without theoretical rationale, can raise important questions about the ways in which anti-Semitism—the prejudice Arendt dissected so brilliantly—and sexism—the one she could hardly see—differ in terms of their service as psychic defenses. But this kind of distinction making can also run along more political theoretical lines—less psychological, more Arendtian. The main danger of sexism—or rather the phenomenon that marks its dangerous ascendancy—is not collapse of the private/public distinction. This was the danger of anti-Semitism as it grew into totalitarianism, which entailed a complete erasure of privacy, even of the privacy of peoples' thoughts. Such a collapse, as I implied before, could, given the material precondition of drastic socioeconomic decline, very well follow upon sustained, progressive erosions of First Amendment rights such as those being mounted now, with which antipornography feminists are unfortunately associated. But this kind of arena, fundamentally antistate, is really an arena made for people whose prejudices resemble anti-Semitism, obsessional people who see infiltrating conspiracies everywhere, who fear penetration of the fortresses of their defenses by polluting agents. The main danger of sexism, by contrast, is complete separation of private and public and assignment of women to the private, an extrapolitical realm where law does not reach, rights cannot be secured, only the master's will orders life. Essentially, such a domain has historically functioned as an arena for the control of reproduction, either by permitting men to insist that males are really the agents of reproduction or by permitting them control over the bodies of women.[11]

For the sake of further comparison, it is important to note that neither separation of the private and the public nor collapse of the distinction has been central to the theorizing of victims of white racism. Neither the New World descendants of African slaves nor the descendants of colonialized Africans think in these categories. They have been oppressed by people who have thought of them as servants—as naturally fitted for being servants—in households and in larger entities imagined as vast households, societal households, national households, indeed, imagined as what Hannah Arendt called "the social." Their oppressors' main psychological need is for male and female servants who care for them, support them, give them inside or alongside their households a second family, which can be the quasi-familial object of their desires while at the same time being not family, not being incestuous parental or sibling objects of desire. Racist ruling elites and less successful racists imagining themselves as elites are *patrons*, no matter what the size of their real or imaginary, rural or urban estates. Racism is most dangerous when this expansionary vision of households with natural servants is strongest, so the liberationist rhetoric of racism's victims focuses on fighting free of the master's house—whether that be a single family dwelling or a nation.

The analytical categories that different victim groups need and find to present the nature of their oppression and to organize their resistances and rebellions are not the same, and should not be. Feminists who recognize this stand at the edge of a complex theoretical problem of integrating perspectives, both for political coalition building and for taking into account the complex experiences of people who are multiply victimized—Jewish women, black women, for examples—and people who are suited to be victims for any type of prejudiced person—homosexuals, for example, who can be targeted for their "Jewish" qualities, for their hypersexuality, or for the threat they pose to gender identity. The future of feminist theory, I think, lies in these territories.

I do not think that Hannah Arendt's political theorizing is going to be very helpful in this project—although it has been and will continue to be crucial for understanding anti-Semitism in itself and as the ideological centerpiece of Nazi totalitarianism. But, on the other hand, the encounter that the current generation of feminist political theorists has had with Arendt's work has certainly helped dislodge the feminist theoretical fixation on the question of sexual difference and the single-minded view of the private/public distinction as in every way—for every group—a distinction to be overcome. The encounter with Arendt has helped feminism in this direction because she would not fit into the feminist frameworks with which she had been approached. In her intellectual greatness, Arendt has had her greatest value to feminism, I think, precisely because feminists have said clearly "*she* was not one of us" and proceeded from there to an examination not of her but *of feminism* in light of her life and work.

Notes

1. Bonnie Honig, ed., *Feminist Interpretations of Hannah Arendt* (State Park: Pennsylvania State University Press, 1995).

2. See "On the Emancipation of Women" in *Arendt: Essays in Understanding 1930–1954*, ed. J. Kohn (New York: Harcourt, 1994).

3. An unilluminating example is Anne Norton's badly argued tract "Heart of Darkness: Africa and African Americans in the Writings of Hannah Arendt," in Honig, ed., *Feminist Interpretations of Hannah Arendt.*

4. There are exceptions to this generalization. For example, Nancy Harstock in *Money, Sex and Power* (New York: Longman, 1983), writing from a socialist point of view, who cites Arendt as a theorist writing out of female experience toward a concept of power as potentiality rather than as domination, the more masculine conceptualization.

5. Adrienne Rich, *On Lies, Secrets and Silence: Selected Prose 1966–1978* (New York: Norton, 1979), pp. 211–212; this passage was, then, quoted again and again in feminist writings on Arendt.

6. For example, a reassessment from the late 1980s: Maria Markus, "The 'Anti-Feminism' of Hannah Arendt," in G. Kaplan and C. Kessler, eds., *Hannah Arendt: Thinking, Judging, Freedom* (Sydney: Allen and Unwin, 1989).

7. Mary Dietz, "Feminist Receptions of Hannah Arendt," in Honig, ed., *Feminist Interpretations of Hannah Arendt.*

8. In *Hannah Arendt: For Love of the World,* I stressed Arendt's Jewishness and gave little attention to her life as a woman—as little as she gave it herself or as was reflected in her literary estate, as little as she gave to Rahel Varnhagen in her biography, which stressed Varnhagen's Jewishness, not her life as a woman. In keeping with the spirit prevailing in 1970s feminism, this approach was criticized by Elizabeth Minnich, "Friendship Between Women: The Act of Feminist Biography," *Feminist Studies* 11/2 (summer 1985), pp. 287–305, although Minnich praised Arendt's own biographical method as relational and "feminist." I find Minnich's position narrow, almost sectarian, because to me it seems to prescribe that biographers should fit their subject's lives to a feminist agenda rather than respecting the way a woman lived her life and understood herself. In retrospect, however, I wish that I had devoted a longer passage to exploring why Arendt was not interested in feminism (in the Germany of her youth or later in America) and why she did not analyze—especially in privacy of her correspondences—her own position as a woman. She reacted strongly when she thought she had been treated as an exception or token woman, on the model of "the exception Jew" she had often written about (see *Hannah Arendt*, p. 272), but she ignored what might be called the ordinary sexism of everyday life. I think the key to this silence is her strict distinction between social anti-Semitism and the truly dangerous political anti-Semitism, and her assumption that social anti-Semitism can and ought to be ignored as inconsequential—personally hurtful, but politically inconsequential. The following statement, which she wrote shortly after the war, makes the point starkly, and it can be extrapolated to social sexism: "It should be borne in mind that whether a person does or does not like Jews is of little interest. If, however, somebody maintains "we fought this war for the Jews," then his statement assumes importance. The person who declares "the Jews want to dominate the world" is clearly an antisemite; the same is not necessarily true for

people who prefer not to share a hotel with Jews, or even declare that Jews are greedy." (See also note 11.)

9. Carol Lee Bacchi, *Same Difference* (Sydney: Allen and Unwin, 1990), p. ix.

10. I have set out a history of psychoanalytic characterology and a rationale for this statement in my *Creative Characters* (New York: Routledge, 1991) and in a forthcoming work, *The Anatomy of Prejudices* (Cambridge: Harvard University Press, 1996).

11. To continue the line of thought in note 8, I would speculate that one of the key reasons why Hannah Arendt did not focus her attention on sexism is that she never had to confront personally the complexities of combining motherhood with an intellectual public life. She could also stress the private side of child rearing and insist on the prepolitical nature of education without having been challenged as a parent by the grey zone where private and public meet—the zone she encountered in the Little Rock dispute.

15

Ethics in Many Different Voices

Annette C. Baier

What difference do the increasing numbers of women philosophers make to the way ethics gets thought about in philosophy seminars, at philosophy conferences, and in the philosophy books and the articles now being published? They are making many differences. The new voices that are joining the debate are interestingly various. We should no more expect agreement in views, in method, and in style among women who write on ethics, of course, than we expect to find agreement among male moral philosophers. There are as big and important disagreements between, say, Judith Jarvis Thomson and Catherine McKinnon, or Mary Daly and Simone Weil, as there are between Aquinas and Hobbes, or Hume and Kant. Some women moral philosophers dislike being perceived as *women* philosophers, whereas others glory in being so perceived; some call themselves "feminist," some refuse that label, and some of us welcome it when others apply it, while having felt no need to proclaim it for ourselves.

It is dangerous to make suggestions about what difference women are making to the ethics getting done in philosophy departments, because any generalization will be disputed by some women. Male observers down the centuries have seen women as a quarrelsome lot, given to mutual hair pulling and jealous spite as well as to maternal solicitude and gentle soothing of the hurt feelings of others. We have shown ourselves capable of pandering to male fantasies as well as of having our own alternative fantasies. In philosophy seminars, as in the boudoir, some will prove protective of fragile male egos, others will fulfill the worst male nightmares of the castrating woman by putting some teeth into their philosophical grip on male moral theories. Some try gentleness where the style of debate has been aggressive cut and slash. Others try new modes of slashing, and yet others alternate their styles in disconcerting ways, or simply display that postmenopausal rise in assertiveness that should be no surprise, but often does disconcert those who suffer assaults from feisty old women who had been meeker and more diplomatic when younger. Some women focus on women's issues, such as abortion, others avoid those and prefer to rethink the issues that concern men as closely as they do women, issues such as environmental protection, health care, civil disobedience. Some do theory, some engage in antitheory campaigns. Whatever else we are doing, we are helping to diversify the philosophical scene.

Those who undoubtedly altered the moral philosophy agenda include some women whose academic home base was not philosophy but literature, law, politics, theology. (The revolt of the nuns is a significant and still reverberating social event.) Mary Daly from theology, Catherine McKinnon from law, Adrienne Rich from literature, Hannah Arendt, Judith Shklar, and Carole Pateman from political science have voiced challenges that moral philosophers today can scarcely ignore. Women who were or are not academics—such as Virginia Woolf, Rebecca West, Doris Lessing, Nadine Gordimer, and Alice Walker—are altering our sense of the moral issues, as are former academics such as Iris Murdoch. When we look beyond writing in English, at least to Europe (and I am not knowledgeable enough to look to Asia, South and Central America, or Africa), there is of course the voice of Simone de Beauvoir to be taken into account. *The Second Sex*[1] continues to provoke both men and women, and certainly provokes many feminists. Other women writing in French, such as Hélène Cixous, Luce Irigaray, and Julia Kristeva, are also increasingly impinging on our Anglo-American consciousness.

There are a few English-speaking and English-writing women philosophers whose writings have had great impact of a less agenda-altering sort on the Anglo-American philosophical profession. Judith Jarvis Thomson's article on abortion must be among the most frequently cited twentieth-century English-language publications in ethics. But, like most influential articles, it did not exactly change the agenda—rather it carried a certain style of thinking about this issue, one already popular among men who wrote about it, to its logical conclusion. Some regard it as a *reductio ad absurdum* of that approach, but there is no evidence that it was intended that way, and considerable evidence that it was not. Philippa Foot's work in ethics is very influential, especially among those favoring the "virtues" approach to ethics, but of course this is a very old approach, one favored by those notorious spokesmen for patriarchal values, Aristotle and Aquinas. (No feminist with any sense of etymology is likely to select the word "virtue" for whatever sort of moral excellence she is endorsing, but we have not settled on a better word.) Susan Wolf's "Moral Saints" has become a classic, but there were earlier papers by men, such as Michael Stocker's "The Schizophrenia of Modern Moral Philosophy," which had started the train of thought that Wolf developed so memorably.

There are very many self-styled feminist philosophers, exhibiting a great variety of approaches and opinions. Sandra Bartky, Seyla Benhabib, Claudia Card, Marilyn Friedman, Marilyn Frye, Virginia Held, Alison Jaggar, Maria Lugones, Linda Nicholson, Nel Noddings, Martha Nussbaum, Susan Moller Okin, Sara Ruddick, Elizabeth Spelman, Iris Young, and hearteningly many others are doing ethics in a self-consciously feminist manner. These feminists do not all welcome the idea that the different voice with which they speak on ethical issues is one that puts more emphasis on "care" than on "justice." Some feminist critics of influential theories of justice, such as John Rawls's theory, fault it for its less than adequately acknowledged assumption that someone or ones are caring for the young who are expected to develop a sense of justice in a loving home, be ready to go out into the world to maintain just public institutions, or to reform unjust ones; others, such as Susan Moller Okin, locate the fault not so much in the accepted parasitism of the virtue of justice on maternal or at least parental love and care as in the lack of attention to the justice of the family as an institution. Some are continuing the fight for justice for women; others are seeing a need for more than justice. These different feminist lines of thought are best seen as complementary and mutually supportive rather than as mutually opposed. But there are some real disagreements among self-styled feminists when it comes to the details of what would count as justice within the family, and who should be socialized to be willing to take care of whom. The influence of traditional patriarchal religions is not automatically canceled by the rise of a feminist consciousness, and so we should expect all degrees of radicalism among those who call themselves feminists, all degrees of determination to distance ourselves from the old oppressors, ranging from lesbian separatism, through resolute spinsterhood, and a rethinking and reform of the roles and priority of careers of wife and husband within a heterosexual marriage, to a willingness to continue as before to "love, honor, and obey" a male lord and master, as long as the service is voluntary, and as long as there is no male conspiracy to restrict all women to the role of devoted wife and mother. There are all sorts of feminists, of all sorts of political persuasion.

A question that bears looking into is just when in their careers our more radical self-styled feminist moral philosophers began so styling themselves, when they began to make feminist philosophy their area of specialization. I have here listed the women who made it to some security in the academic system, and I would not like to bet much on the chances of success of more than one or two of all the many bold young women philosophers who are trying to get tenure by their explicitly feminist written work. For they are engaged in exposing the sexist bias of our society, our academic establishment, and so of most of those who will decide their own academic fate. These women are bold; they may be rash. How many tenured women philosophers who write in provocatively feminist ways wrote this way, or wrote mainly this way, before they had tenure? Maybe I stand out as conspicuously cowardly, but I certainly did not. It was not until I had a secure base that I published anything about the position of women. As far as public statements went, I in effect ignored that issue until it was relatively safe for me to speak about it. I admire the courage of my younger colleagues, but such courage will not topple a patriarchal academic establishment that can so easily evict them from its halls. It can easily do so, as long as the senior faculty who are making the tenure decisions can tell themselves, with perfect correctness, that they cannot judge the merits of this sort of philosophy (especially when it is cooperative), and that there is no one whose views they already respect who can judge it and who also judges the candidate's work to be of the quality required for tenure. While such a situation prevails, it will remain professionally suicidal for untenured women philosophers to specialize in feminist philosophy, and perhaps dangerous for them even to pursue their feminist interests openly. Unless some tenured philosophers make it their business to become knowledgeable about feminist philosophy, it will be a no-win situation for younger feminist philosophers.

One way that women are certainly changing the profession of ethics is by presenting the professions, including the profession of academic philosophy and ethics, with some acute problems of professional ethics. We are enlarging the subject matter for problem-oriented ethics. It is also clear that there is a lot more attention being paid to the old topic of pornography, and that sexual harassment is joining rape on the normal agenda for applied ethics. Women's voices on those topics are obviously essential for informed debate. Yet they were just as essential for the debate on abortion, which for long enough proceeded contentedly without it, at both Supreme Court and philosophical levels. Even when women did join the philosophical debate, the ones whose voices were listened to most respectfully, on both sides, were those whose views chimed in best with men's way of reasoning on this topic. So we had good Catholic women arguing against abortion and good liberal women arguing for it, each lot saying just what their respective male teachers and lovers would want them to say. We are only recently getting the views of the independent-minded women philosophers who are mothers, the views of single mothers, of lesbians, and of others who are both experience-informed enough about pregnancy and its early termination and liberated enough from male indoctrination to have the best credentials for deliberation on this matter. The philosophical debate on abortion is really just beginning to get going, as it at last gets taken over by those who know what they are talking about.

As to what more general difference has been made by the different way that Anglo-American women philosophers have approached topics in ethics, before and after tenure decisions, there are probably at least as many different answers as the different women whose voices have been heard, and as many as the phases of their articulate philosophical lives. One fairly pervasive difference that I perceive is a greater realism, a reluctance to do "ideal" ethical theory, an insistence on looking for a version of ethics that applies to us now, in the conditions we actually find ourselves in, oppressed or beginning to be liberated, few or increasingly many in the tenured ranks, on the hospital rounds, on the advisory boards, and on the policy-setting councils. We find this real-world emphasis in relatively theoretical writings, such as Virginia Held's *Rights and Goods*,[2] in Cora Diamond's essays on the "realistic spirit" in philosophy,[3] and in the writings of the many women who are choosing to do "applied ethics."

Along with this realism goes a greater emphasis than before on what we could call the ethics of timing. In *The Realm of Rights*[4] Thomson has an interesting discussion of when an invitation lapses, how long the right given in an accepted invitation can be taken to last. Is it fanciful to see it as typically a woman's preoccupation to care about timing and timeliness, indeed to be very interested in ways of dividing up and managing time? Women, because of the rhythm of their biological lives, have had to make themselves think about the precise timing of what they do and what they promise, and relate that appropriately to the timing of what their bodies do. They have to think about ways of undoing what was regrettably done, and of fixing the future so that regrets may be minimized.

I shall now turn to one woman philosopher whose thoughts about our attitudes to time present and time past had considerable impact on me—indeed reading her book *The Human Condition*[5] divides my philosophical past into its purely analytic early period and its more eclectic later period. I refer of course to Hannah Arendt. There was a woman who really knew what she was talking about when she spoke of resistance or nonresistance to evil regimes, when she spoke about civil disobedience or about forgiveness. In *The Human Condition* she chooses two human actions as the quintessentially human ones: forgiving a past wrong (unfixing the fixed past), and promising a future benefit (fixing the unfixed future). Concern with past evils and future avoidance of evils is a common human concern, and it would be absurd to suggest that male moralists had not thought about forgiveness or about ways of securing the future. But it took Arendt to couple contract, that favorite moral device of the secular male theorists, with forgiveness, which had been more or less left to the theologians. Arendt writes, "The two faculties belong together in so far as one of them, forgiving, serves to undo the deeds of the past, whose 'sins' hang like Damocles' sword over every new generation; and the other, binding oneself through promises, serves to set up in the ocean of uncertainty, which the future is by definition, islands of security without which not even continuity, let alone durability of any kind, would be possible in the relationships between men" (p. 237). She means "between human agents," of course, not "between *men*," but part of what makes *The Human Condition* the interesting work that it is is the odd mix of Arendt's originality and her deference to the ideas and the terminology of her teacher and lover, Martin Heidegger,[6] of her teacher and friend, Karl Jaspers, and of the sexist tradition of Hegel and Marx that she is transcending. Her book is about the active life, about various conditions of laboring, working, and acting together, about escape from "the darkness of each man's lonely heart" (p. 237). There is little explicit discussion of women's hearts, or women's work, except in the early chapter "The Public and Private Realm," where (pp. 47–48, n. 38; pp. 72–73) it is noted that women's relegation to the private realm went with the belief that their task was "to with their bodies minister to the needs of life" (Aristotle, *Politics*, 1254b25). Arendt refers to "the odd notion of a division of labor between the sexes, which is even considered by some writers to be the most original one. It presumes as its single subject mankind, the human species, which has divided its labors among men and women" (p. 48, n. 38). Odd indeed, to take women to be a subdivision of mankind, laboring for it, in or out of the home. But Arendt, after this subversive note, continues to speak of "man" and "men," as those whose powers of action she is analyzing. Their redemptive action possibilities are located, however, in the combined miracles of forgiveness and promise that come together in what Arendt terms "natality." "The miracle that saves the world, the realm of human affairs, from its normal, 'natural' ruin is ultimately the fact of natality, in which the faculty of action is ontologically rooted.... 'A child has been born unto us'" (p. 247). Appropriating Nietzsche's Zarathustra as much as the New Testament's Jesus of Nazareth, Isak Dinesen as much as Dante, Arendt plunders the Western cultural tradition to get a version of human agency *(praxis)* in relation to human work *(poesis)* and human labor, a version that makes women's labor in childbirth the bringer of redemption, in the birth of a new person whose life story will be a fresh one, a bringer of hope. Action, Arendt believes (with Dante), discloses the agent, and is intended to do so. Individual agents' lives are "enacted stories," unique narratives, produced by action "with or without intention as naturally as fabrication produces tangible things" (p. 184).[7] Arendt's self-disclosure in writing *The Human Condition* can be seen as an act of forgiveness to a tradition that had endorsed and enforced that odd notion that women's labor is for men. It is also a fulfilled promise of better thinking, an act of faith in the possibility of better conditions for women's action and of less tragic narratives with women as heroines.

As far as I am aware, Arendt never called herself a feminist, and probably would not have wanted to be so called. From her youth in Germany she had opposed the separation of women's issues from more encompassing political concerns. (In 1931 she reviewed Alice Ruhle-Gerstel's *Das Frauen-problem der Gegenwart.*[8]) Her biographer, Elisabeth Young-Bruehl, writes that she urged younger women to independence, "but always, always with a qualification: for women, her maxim was *Viva la petite différence.*"[9] In an interview at the time of her Christian Gauss Lectures at Princeton in 1953, she said, "I am not disturbed at all about being a woman professor, ... because I am quite used to being a woman,"[10] a rather splendid statement. She did not want to be seen as an "exception woman," anymore than as an "exception Jew," but of course in 1953 the press was not in error in seeing it as exceptional for a woman to be a professor at Princeton. During a discussion of "women's liberation" by the editorial board of the *American Scholar* in 1972, Arendt is reported to have written a note to Hiram Haydn, commenting, "The real question to ask is, what will we lose if we win?"[11] She clearly valued what she feared we might lose, and was not only used to being a woman but gloried in it, even in conditions of inequality where a married woman's options seemed to be as Ruhle-Gerstel saw them—becoming either housekeepers, princesses, or demonesses.[12] It now seems to me time for those of us who do call ourselves feminists to draw freely on whatever philosophical resources nourish our enterprises, to be feminist in a large and generously appropriative sense, not a narrow sectarian one. Now that we are winning we can afford to disagree about what loss our win entailed, and whether it must be permanent.

Arendt's work certainly nourished my philosophical soul. She led me to reread Hegel, to read Heidegger, and certainly to reconceive what "action-theory" might become. Among other twentieth-century books in that genre, hers cries out with the voice of a prophet. The term "action-theory" itself invites reflection, but few of its analytic practitioners reflect, as Arendt does, on the exact links between theory and action, on how various sorts of thinking can transform action, on how thinking and theorizing are themselves actions that are as self-disclosing as any other.

As the current rage for "applied ethics" in the health professions, in business, in engineering, and in scientific research can be expected to revivify ethical theory, so attention to these various sorts of professional action would revivify our moribund analytical action theory, a field where things are still more or less where they were when I opted out twenty years ago—at best a matter of cooperative house painting, at worst one of solitary agents vainly willing to move their missing limbs. Arendt-type action, such as civil disobedience, emigration, proclamation, let alone pardoning and forgiving wrongs, has yet to make it into the discussions of the self-styled action theorists. (Even those who do ethics and social philosophy as well as action theory can choose, in their action-theoretical guise, to discuss housecleaning, not voting or political protest. Anscombe had "bringing down the regime" in her analysis, but her followers have tended to stick with the pumping.)

"For everything there is a season, and a time for every matter under heaven," but since Solomon's time not much has been said about the ethics of good timing. Nor is it easy to say anything general and more helpful than Solomon's pronouncements. Although Arendt's discussion of the twin miracle workers, forgiving and promising, forces our attention on the relation between our backward-looking surveys of action and efforts at wiping of our copybooks and our forward-looking agreements and solemn signings, she does not in *The Human Condition* discuss the question of how agents decide when is the time to give their word or to forgive broken words and other wrongs.[13] But in her more political works we do get more such attention,[14] and it is a natural follow-up to an account of action that put such emphasis on these two cycle-breaking acts, forgiving and promising, without which "we would be doomed to swing forever in the ever-recurring cycle of becoming" (p. 246). Forgiving is of definite past offenses or debts, which are taken to have been as it were recorded in some doomsday book, complete with date and details. Their remission is also a definite dated act, as it were a crossing-out in the record book, signed and dated. A promise similarly is an act that fixes some aspect or aspects of a limited future, a time future to the time of the promise. Often we promise to do something by a certain day or hour, and even when we promise mutual devotion "till death do us part," death does end the period that was fixed by the promise. Without calendars, there could be no promising of our normal sort, and where clocks are rare or rarely used, promises are interpreted more flexibly. In New Zealand we have the phrase "Maori time," which means Pakeha (European) time, give or take an hour or so. ("We are to meet at noon, Maori time.") Without any rough measures of time, the "pro" element in promising would become simply a future tense marker, and promises would be indistinguishable from totally vague hopes or predictions. "We will overcome" is not a promise, precisely because of its lack of temporal precision.

With forgiving, the need for time specifications is not so obvious, given the religious near-monopoly on that concept and the promiscuous scope of Christian forgiveness. It is typically *all* one's sins, as an undifferentiated bunch, that get forgiven by divine pardoners (although there is that mysterious unforgivable sin, against the Holy Spirit, that has to be sifted out, so maybe some sin-by-sin count does actually have to go on). Human forgivers are selective—typically they forgive particular specifiable doings or omissions. To announce, "I forgive you for any wrongs you have done me, and forgive you in advance for any you may do me," is to debase the moral currency, just as senseless an act as to say, "I promise you that you could count on me, for all our past, and can count on me, in whatever way you wish, in the future." Promises must be for the future, and must be selective as to what aspect of that future they purport to fix. Forgiveness must be of the past, and of selected wrongs within it. The selection is the hard bit. Arendt writes, "the moment that promises lose their character as isolated islands of certainty in an ocean of uncertainty, that is, when this faculty is misused to cover the whole ground of the future and to map out a path secured in all directions, they lose their binding power and the whole enterprise becomes self-defeating" (p. 244). Many of us who have inveighed against contractarianism in ethics have merely repeated Arendt's point, at greater length and with less eloquence.

It may reasonably be objected[15] that my claim that promises typically mention dates or time periods ignores promises of the form "I will never do *x* again"—the sort of commitment given by those trying to turn away from bad habits, from excessive drinking, smoking, drug taking, or by those entering monasteries. Such promises or vows do seem to be for an open-ended future, and could be made by members of a precalendar culture. Vows of allegiance to superiors, vows of abstinence of various sorts, divide time simply into the prevow and the postvow periods. But "vow," not "promise," is the right word for these acts. They are typically made to some higher-than-human power, to God or one's country. Vows are indeed taken and sometimes honored. It was not vows that Arendt chose to focus on but promises, which "depend on plurality, on the presence and acting of others, for no one . . . can feel bound by a promise made only to himself" (p. 237). It is an important fact about the human person that she can be multiple, play many roles, and play roles before her other personae, but Arendt is surely right that promises lose their grip once the promisee is oneself, one's conscience, or the divine spokesperson within. Our ability to talk to ourselves can be a redemptive power,[16] but the speech acts we can perform to ourselves do seem of a limited variety, compared with the ways in which we can speak to others. We can tell ourselves stories, ask and answer questions, propose courses of action then criticize and reject them, encourage, flatter, mock, and denigrate ourselves. But promising to ourselves, like lying to ourselves, seems ruled out, except for those who are seen to *suffer* from multiple personality disorders or who alter their status within the time between the promise and its expected performance.[17]

The biblical notion of a covenant between God and Israel, which might reasonably be taken to serve the identity-establishing function for a whole people rather well, was a very special sort of commitment, both in the open-ended time that it covered and in the sort of parties it involved—a divine being and the father of a people. Arendt's discussion of the covenant made by Abraham with God is distinctly ironical. "Abraham, the man from Ur, whose whole story, as the Bible tells it, shows such a passionate drive toward making covenants that it is as though he departed from his country for no other reason than to try out the power of mutual promise in the wilderness of the world, until eventually God himself agreed to make a Covenant with him" (pp. 243, 244). Such a "covenant" with God, until it acquires human witnesses and public recognition,[18] is no different, on Abraham's part, from cases of "promising enacted in solitude or isolation," and so "without reality . . . no more than a role played before one's self" (p. 237). The covenant as described in Genesis 17 is an "everlasting" one, binding not just Abraham but his seed ("Thy seed after thee in their generations"). Ordinary promises are neither everlasting nor taken to bind the promisor's seed.

(Hume relies heavily on this fact in his arguments against a social contract theory of political obligation.) A covenant of the sort that the nation of Israel took itself to have with its God can indeed serve to confer distinctive identity both on nationals of that nation and on the God in question ("the God of Israel"), but "promise" is the wrong term for the sort of identity-establishing tie for a whole people that the biblical covenant instituted.

Arendt claims that our identity over time is confirmed by those others who recognize the one who fulfills a promise as the same person who gave it, and that this confirmation of identity is needed, if we are not to "be condemned to wander helplessly and without direction in the darkness of each man's lonely heart" (p. 237). This is a strong claim. One might think that a recorded lifetime resolve would be the simplest way to give direction to the aimless wanderer, providing at least as good an identity-marker as that conferred by a series of promises to different people to do differing things by a series of deadlines. (I often have felt torn into pieces by the different promises I have given.) Arendt's "promise" may need overtones of an ongoing "covenant" to do the job that she gives it, that is, to structure a life over a long period.

In a television interview in 1964 she told how, when as a child in Königsberg she encountered anti-Semitism in her playmates and schoolmates, her mother instructed her to defend herself, and if a schoolteacher made anti-Semitic remarks, "to stand up immediately, to leave the class, go home."[19] This policy of standing up and leaving anti-Semitic company seems to have been followed by Arendt throughout her life. She and her mother left Nazi Germany in 1933 (over the Erzegebirge Mountains, into Czechoslovakia), and she eventually made her "home" with other emigrants from Europe in New York. Her last years in Germany were spent working on her study of Rahel Varnhagen (born as Rahel Levin in 1771). She subtitled this book "The Life of a Jewess" and referred to Rahel as "my closest friend, although she has been dead for some one hundred years."[20] She also wrote a newspaper article entitled "The Jewish Question," and publicly criticized those who (like Adorno and Heidegger) were cooperating with the Nazis. She certainly "stood up" before "walking out" of the country that had become "nicht für meiner Mutters Tochter."[21] Such clear self-identification involved neither covenants nor promises, simply a consistent line of action and proclamation. (Her "Mutt," as she calls her mother in her letters to Jaspers, seems to have been a splendidly devoted and loyal mother. When both mother and daughter were arrested by the Nazis in 1933 and interrogated separately, Martha Arendt was asked what her daughter Hannah had been doing in her regular visits to the Prussian National Library, where she had in fact been researching anti-Semitic literature for the German Zionist Organization. The mother replied that she did not know, but she knew that, whatever it was, it was right for her daughter to do it, and she herself would have done the same. The Nazis released her after one day, having the sense to realize that she was interrogation-proof.[22])

Do we really need witnesses and records to give us reassurance of who we are? Do we need receipts to reassure us that we are the same persons as the ones who entered into the sale as a buyer? Do we need some "well done, good and faithful servant," to be sure that we are the same ones who entered into that service? Arendt, when she makes her claim about the role of promises, is writing about the active life, the life of labor, work, and action, about the bringing into existence of the means of subsistence, of artifacts, of narratives or commitments, of meaningful lives such as her own. If our service is mere labor, which another laborer or a relay team of laborers could have done as well as one and the same person, then there may be no signature, as it were, left on the outcome of our labor, on the field that is ploughed or the house that is cleaned. But if we have made something or built something—a pot, say, or a church—then we may leave our signature on the base of the pot, or our face carved into the door lintel. Even if we do not, the work may exhibit our distinctive personal style and so not be just what any other potter or architect (or team of them) could as easily have come up with. Our work is not fungible, in the way that our labor is. But the work of our hands and minds, like our labor, is alienable and can have a price put on it. What Arendt calls our actions, by contrast, are inalienable. Their distinctive style, if indeed they have that, results not in any salable product but in a unique life story, a succession of words and deeds bounded by birth and death, a sequence of commitments and refusals to commit oneself, of forgivings and refusals to forgive, and of words and deeds in reaction to others' actions, and to their deaths and births. For women, that life story may include the births that they commit themselves to or refuse to commit themselves to, that is, to childbirths or abortions. Like any other outcome of human action (in Arendt's rich sense), the child who is born because of the mother's decision to carry to term will be unique, with its own life story and distinctive character, not merely a continuation of that of any parental agent. Action typically results in new possibilities for action, but not so typically in new actors. Only when nations, religions, or other collective agents are intentionally brought into being do we get any other human action that is at all like intentionally giving birth to a new human person.

Yet as Arendt emphasized when discussing the traditional place of women in the private sphere, giving birth is often not free action, but coerced "labor" for others. As long as there is no individual control and no individual choice, then labor and childbirth are for the species' survival, not for any laborer's or labor-owner's survival or satisfaction. As long as the initiative, the control, and the choice rest with men rather than with woman, then the labor and birth will be less than the mother's action. Arendt gives a central role to the idea of natality, and she views it as having a closer connection with action than with the idea of labor, or with the work that must "provide and preserve the world for ... the constant influx of newcomers who are born into the world as strangers" (p. 9). This is because "the new beginning inherent in birth can make itself felt in the world only because the newcomer possesses the capacity of beginning something anew, that is, of acting" (p. 9). Of course, as she later notes when discussing Marx's concept of labor power (p. 88), the newcomer can also be seen merely as a replacement of labor power, rather than as one capable of acting. If the child is consigned to factory labor or (if she is a female) simply to reproducing her mother's unchosen procreative labor, then nothing new will have been begun, merely the old cycle continued. Birth will be paired with unchosen death, as correlative happenings that preserve a sort of species status quo not only at the biological level but also at the socioeconomic level. Births sustain a more or less steady labor force for the creation and procreation of salable goods and labor. Yet despite these all too often actualized possibilities for birth, it still retains its power to symbolize the new start, the hope of new and better directions. Hence Arendt can write "since action is the political activity par excellence, natality, and not mortality, may be the central category of political, as distinguished from metaphysical, thought" (p. 9). Heidegger had made mortality a central category of metaphysical thought. Arendt is balancing his act by a move that totally transforms it.[23] Natality for us today is a fairly central topic of political debate, if not so central a category of metaphysical[24] or political theory. The Hegelian "truth" of Arendt's political thought may be found not in contemporary political theory so much as in the debate over *Roe v. Wade* and in the confrontations outside abortion clinics.

Arendt's prophetic powers, or should one say her thought initiatives, extend to the metaphysical as well as to the political. The final section of *The Human Condition* is devoted to various reversals in the "modern age," and one of these is the "reversal of the hierarchical order between the *vita contemplativa* and the *vita activa*" (p. 289). She introduces this theme by a discussion of René Descartes' method of doubt and of Copernicus's and Galileo's "alienation" of the earth, their "dislocation" of it, from their imaginary Archimedean point beyond it. She quotes Copernicus's words about "the virile man standing in the sun ... overlooking the planets" and seeing the earth move with them. Descartes' doubt and his thoughts about himself as a thinker, as much as his analytical-geometrical physics, are taken as expressions of this alienation of the familiar world brought about by the new science. Whitehead is quoted as likening the new sciences' beginnings in the discovery of the telescope and in Galileo's use of it to "a babe ... born in a manger,"[25] a great thing happening with little stir. Arendt adds: "Like the birth in a manger, which spelled not the end of antiquity but the beginning of something so unexpectedly and unpredictably new that neither hope nor fear could have anticipated it, these first tentative glances into the universe through an instrument, at once adjusted to human senses and destined to uncover what definitely and forever must lie beyond them, set the stage for an entirely new world" (pp. 257–258). The inquiring and imaginative mind too can give birth to inventions and ideas that break cycles and introduce new directions. It is not merely in social philosophy but in physics and metaphysics that the category of natality provides a favorite metaphor for what the innovative thinker aspires to. (David Hume mourned the apparent fate of his *Treatise of Human Nature*,[26] fallen "deadborn from the press.")

In the final part of *The Human Condition*, Arendt treats thinking, including the sort of earth-shifting thinking that Galileo and Descartes did, as activity, properly seen as part of the *vita activa*. (She continued her exploration of thinking in her 1973 Gifford Lectures, published as *The Life of the Mind.*[27]) The Cartesian doubt and exploration of subjectivity, as much as the telescope-using and technology-linked thinking of modern scientists, involved the "removal of the Archimedean point into the mind of man" (p. 285). They involved mental labor, the making of books, and self-revealing or self-concealing action. Although Descartes called his metaphysical masterpiece *Meditations*, which may suggest contemplative stillness, and in the course of the *First Meditation* contrasted his thought with action in order to excuse the dangerousness of his strategy of radical doubt, his own language there was certainly the language of action. In the first paragraph he reports a resolve; he keeps making new resolves, and he says he will stick "stubbornly" to them; he complains of how arduous he finds his chosen path; he gives his mind a rest from its tough new sense-distrusting discipline for the duration of his discussion of the piece of wax; he celebrates the near divine freedom of his will in the *Fourth Meditation*; he takes himself to be made in the image of a self-expressive powerful creative God. Although earlier (after hearing of Galileo's fate), he had announced that he would go forth masked, his masks are mere veils, his writings acts of self-expression. His ethics, put forward in the *Passions of the Soul* under the thin mask of a gift of requested advice to the spiritually troubled and mentally sharp Princess Elizabeth of Bohemia, exalt that generosity of mind that, disdaining both jealousy of competitors and fear of human enemies, indulges its own desire for truth and enjoys its love or willing union with the God-or-universe that it is trying better to understand.

A recent interesting philosophical phenomenon in this country is the number of women working on Descartes' writings, including his writings on ethics. Maybe this phenomenon is no more significant than that of the number of women Kant interpreters, but whereas the women Kantians prefer to stay off the topic of Kant's relations with women, women (such as Ann W. MacKenzie,[28] Margaret Atherton,[29] Ruth Mattern,[30] and Eileen O'Neill[31]) who are working on Descartes' thought can turn without defensiveness to those (mostly royal and aristocratic) women who took up his ideas and carried them further, who engaged with him in his strenuous pseudomeditative labor, work, and action.[32] Perhaps Descartes appeals to women[33] not just because of the refreshing disdain of deontology in his ethics and the engaging directness and apparent simplicity of his metaphysical moves but also for his very doubleness—he is both solitary meditator and impassioned correspondent, both self-protective mask wearer and reckless intellectual exhibitionist. His books ended on the Index, but he led the church an entertaining dance for years before the full irony of his dedication of the *Meditations* became apparent to the professors of theology to whom they were offered.

As Naomi Scheman sees Ludwig Wittgenstein as a philosopher of the cultural margin[34] who, precisely for that reason, has a special appeal to rebellious women, so one can see René Descartes as an inspiring rebel. He tried ways of subverting his culture from within, wearing the masks of orthodoxy while busy replacing the foundations and rebuilding the edifice of belief. His quite astonishing attempt, or pretended attempt, to persuade the church that he had an intellectually superior account of how, in the Eucharist, bread could become flesh and wine blood is, for its sheer effrontery, one of the high points of European intellectual and cultural history, a moment of supreme intellectual intoxication and divinely willful joie de vivre. When a century later Hume offers the believers in religious miracles the thought that they have a continuing confirmation of the occurrence of miracles in their own ability to sustain belief in the miracles on which their religious faith is grounded,[35] when he ends his *Dialogues on Natural Religion* with Philo's switch to humble pietism, we get echoes of this philosophical playfulness, this daring dance on the edge of cultural abysses that may be typical of our greatest thinkers.[36]

In his *Discourse on the Method*[37] Descartes told us how he resolved to avoid making promises, which would have bound him to others and restricted his freedom, but how he had made and intended to keep this and other resolves. To get out of any forests he might seem lost in, he would walk as best he could in a straight line, pursuing his research strategy wherever it took him. It took him far, and he did, until near the end, avoid commitments to other people. He did not marry his daughter's mother, and he preferred to live as a resident alien in the relatively tolerant Netherlands to living as a presumptively loyal citizen in France. He showed devoted concern for the Princess Elizabeth of Bohemia and was a faithful correspondent to her, but all without any formal promises. His commitment to serve Queen Christina of Sweden did restrict his freedom, turning him from his straight scientific and philosophical path back toward the musical interests with which he had begun. His ties to her proved to be lethal, so he may have been wiser in his initial stubborn resolves than in his later capitulations to sociability and personal commitment. At any rate his life serves as a challenge to Arendt's thesis that, without promises to others, and without others' recognition of our later promise-fulfilling selves as identical with the earlier promise-making selves, we would lose ourselves. In the privacy of his study Descartes made resolves, including the resolve not to give promises, and then he published his resolves in the vernacular to the reading public. He did not seem to lose himself in the darkness of his doubtlessly lonely heart, and his actions of self-revelation (and also of sometimes judicious, sometimes playful self-concealment) are a standing challenge to those of us who live less dangerously. They are also a salutary challenge to those of us who criticize modern variants of individualism, since he is both an unparalleled individualist and the philosopher who celebrated love as the central ethical fact; both a despiser of tradition and the founder of a new tradition; both the solitary thinker and the energetic correspondent and dedicated friend.

I have in these ruminations exhibited two undeniable facts about women who write about ethics—that they often see fit to discuss the writings of nonfeminists and of men, and that they are usually interested in more than ethics. For ethics refuses to stay neatly in the bounds of, say, the personal as contrasted with the political, or the practical as contrasted with the theoretical. Moral psychology spills over into metaphysics, as moral commitment does into political action. Descartes' philosophy of mind is scarcely separable from his ethics. In *The Human Condition* Arendt merges philosophy of action, ethics, politics, and history of science, and this was one reason why I found her so stimulating, and why I chose to focus here on that book of hers. And a striking feature of that book is the way that she rakes up and transforms the ideas of male thinkers from Aristotle to Marx, from Augustine[38] to Heidegger. Feminists could well take up and emend her ideas.[39] We women whose voices are joining those of others in contemporary ethics will often choose to try to transfigure old ideas, to divest them of their antifeminist or excessively masculinist aspects, to indulge in a bit of philosophical transvestitism, as well as to try out androgyny, and to invent new styles. Ethics is a polyphonic art form, in which the echoes of the old voices contribute to the quality of the sound of all the new voices.

Notes

1. Simone de Beauvoir, *The Second Sex* (New York: Vintage Books, 1974, 1952; Bantam Books, 1961).

2. Virginia Held, *Rights and Goods: Justifying Social Action* (New York: Free Press; London: Collier Macmillan, 1984).

3. Cora Diamond, *The Realistic Spirit: Wittgenstein, Philosophy, and the Mind* (Cambridge: MIT Press, 1991).

4. Judith Jarvis Thomson, *The Realm of Rights* (Cambridge: Harvard University Press, 1990), especially chapter 14. For an earlier discussion of the ethics of timing by Thomson, see her "The Time of a Killing," *Journal of Philosophy*, 68 (1971): 115–132.

5. Hannah Arendt, *The Human Condition* (Chicago: University of Chicago Press, 1958). Page references in the text, unless otherwise indicated, are to this work.

6. She went at age nineteen to Marburg, studied philosophy, became Heidegger's lover, then at the end of one year transferred to Freiburg to study with Husserl, then to Heidelberg. She wrote *Die Schatten* as a sort of record of her relationship with Heidegger, which continued intermittently during her student years.

7. See Seyla Benhabib, "Hannah Arendt and the Redemptive Power of Narrative," *Social Research* 57 (Spring 1990), for an exploration of Arendt's emphasis on narrative, not just in *The Human Condition* but also in other works, especially *The Life of the Mind* (New York: Harcourt Brace Jovanovich, 1978).

8. Alice Ruhle-Gerstel, *Das Frauen-problem der Gegenwart*, reviewed by Hannah Arendt, *Die Gesellshaft* 10 (1932): 177–179.

9. Elisabeth Young-Bruehl, *Hannah Arendt: For Love of the World* (New Haven: Yale University Press, 1982) p. 238.

10. Ibid., p. 273.

11. Ibid., p. 513, n. 54.

12. Ibid., p. 96.

13. Did she forgive Heidegger when she met him again after the war? And for what exactly? In her letter to Jaspers shortly before that meeting she sounds very condemnatory of his "dishonesty." After their meeting in Freiburg in 1950, she described Heidegger's demeanor to a friend as like a "begossener Pudel" (Young-Bruehl, *Arendt*, pp. 246, 514, n. 81). His tail was between his legs not for his Nazi activities, which had led to the break in their relationship in about 1930 (ibid., p. 69), but for wrongs against her personally, presumably at least the secrecy he had imposed on their affair. At any rate the form his penitence took was to make, to his wife Elfriede Heidegger-Petri, a belated declaration of the fact that Arendt had been the passion of his life and the inspiration of his work. This news was not well received (ibid., pp. 247, 514, n. 83). Jaspers's ironic words are apt: "poor Heidegger." Arendt had written to Jaspers, in the letter discussing Heidegger's habitual dishonesty (and his "quite awful babbling lectures on Nietzsche"), that what Jaspers saw as

Heidegger's "impurity" she would call "a lack of character.... At the same time, he lives in depths and with a passionateness that one can't easily forget." *Hannah Arendt and Karl Jaspers Correspondence*, ed. Lotte Kohler and Hans Saner (New York: Harcourt Brace Jovanovich, 1992), p. 142, letter 93, Hannah Arendt to Karl Jaspers, 29 September 1949. She did not forget him. Did she forgive him his cold reaction to her gift of *Vita Activa* (her German version of *The Human Condition*)? He had not acknowledged the gift, and when Arendt was in Freiburg in 1960, he not only ignored her presence but pressured his disciple Eugen Fink to refuse an invitation to a reception given in her honor. (*Correspondence*, p. 447, letter 293, Hannah Arendt to Karl and Gertrud Jaspers, 6 August 1961.) Her explanation to Jaspers of Heidegger's change of attitude to her, while it is generous in assuming some blame herself, is not notable for any forgiving note: "Last winter I sent him one of my books, the *Vita Activa*, for the first time. I know that he finds it intolerable that my name appears in public, that I write books, etc. All my life I've pulled the wool over his eyes, so to speak, always acted as if none of that existed and as if I couldn't count to three, unless it was in the interpretation of his own works. Then he was always very pleased when it turned out that I could count to three and sometimes even to four. Then I suddenly felt that this deception was becoming just too boring, and so I got a rap on the nose. (*Correspondence*, p. 457, letter 297, Hannah Arendt to Gertrud and Karl Jaspers, 1 November 1961.) Jaspers replied that Heidegger must have been long aware that she had become a famous author, and that "the only thing that is new is that he received a book directly from you—and then such a reaction!" (*Correspondence*, pp. 459–460, letter 298, Karl Jaspers to Hannah Arendt, 6 November 1961.)

14. For a very comprehensive and helpful study of Arendt as a political philosopher, see Margaret Canovan, *Hannah Arendt: A Reinterpretation of Her Political Thought* (New York: Cambridge University Press, 1992).

15. Walter Sinnott-Armstrong, in conversation, made this objection.

16. I have only recently come to realize that part of what I like so much about New York City is the number of people a pedestrian encounters there who are unabashedly talking aloud to themselves.

17. An interesting case occurs when a promise is made by a person in some special capacity, say, as provost, to a group, say, a department of which the now ex-provost becomes chair. Then her successor in the provost's chair could break that promise, to herself as departmental representative, so the promise that one person made is broken to that very person, in another role. Thanks to Paul Benacerraf for alerting me to this real possibility.

18. Spinoza, in chapters 8 and 12 of his *Theological Political Treatise*, discusses the renewals of the covenant made by Moses and Joshua, and implicitly raises questions about the criteria of identity for such a covenant, which apparently was interrupted by periods of idolatry and desecration of the ark of the covenant, an ark eventually lost track of. With mock innocence he writes, "I find it strange that Scripture tells us nothing of what became of the Ark of the Covenant." *Tractatus Theologico-Politicus*, trans. Samuel Shirley and E. J. Brill (Leiden: København, 1989).

19. Young-Bruehl, *Arendt*, pp. 11–12.

20. Ibid., p. 56.

21. Ibid., p. xv.

22. Ibid., p. 106.

23. That, perhaps, was what he found unforgivable, once he got to read his former student-mistress's book, when in 1960 she forced it on him.

24. See my presidential address, "A Naturalist View of Persons," delivered before the Eighty-Seventh Annual Eastern Division Meeting of the American Philosophical Association in Boston, Mass., December 29, 1990, *Proceedings and Addresses of the American Philosophical Association* 65 (November 1991): 5–17.

25. Alfred North Whitehead, *Science and the Modern World* (New York: Macmillan, 1960), p. 12, quoted by Arendt in *The Human Condition* at p. 257.

26. David Hume, *A Treatise of Human Nature*, ed. L. A. Selby-Bigge and P. H. Nidditch (Oxford: Clarendon Press, 1978).

27. Hannah Arendt, *The Life of the Mind* (New York: Harcourt Brace Jovanovich, 1978).

28. Ann W. MacKenzie, "Descartes on Life and Sense," *Canadian Journal of Philosophy*, 19 (1989): 163–192.

29. Margaret Atherton, "Cartesian Reason and Gendered Reason," in *A Mind of One's Own*, ed. Louise B. Anthony and Charlotte Witt (Boulder, CO: Westview Press, 1992), pp. 19–34.

30. Ruth Mattern, "Descartes' Correspondence with Elizabeth: Concerning the Union and Distinction of Mind and Body," in *Descartes: Critical Interpretative Essays*, ed. Michael Hacker (Baltimore: Johns Hopkins University Press, 1978).

31. Eileen O'Neill, "Mind and Mechanism: An Examination of Some Mind-Body Problems in Descartes' Philosophy" (Ph.D. dissertation, Princeton University, 1983), and "Mind-Body Interaction and Metaphysical Consistency: A Defense of Descartes," *Journal of the History of Philosophy* 25 (1987): 227–245.

32. See Erica Harth, *Cartesian Women: Versions and Subversions of Rational Discourse in the Old Regime* (Ithaca, NY: Cornell University Press, 1992).

33. Naomi Scheman, in "Though This Be Method Yet There Is Madness in It: Paranoia and Liberal Epistemology" (in Anthony and Witt, eds., *A Mind of One's Own*, pp. 145–170), allows that Descartes has had appeal for feminist women, despite his emphasis on the supposed need for control of the passions by a somewhat dictatorial reason. See p. 167, n. 15.

34. Naomi Scheman, "Closets, Margins, and Forms of Life," in *Companion on Wittgenstein*, ed. Hans Sluga and David Stern (New York: Cambridge University Press, forthcoming).

35. This Humean move repeats one that Cicero makes in *De Natura Deorum*, where Balbus suggests that the most providential thing of all is the human propensity to believe in providence.

36. Some read Kant as equally daring in his *Religion within the Limits of Reason Alone*, trans. Louis Infield (New York: Harper Torchbooks, 1963). I am grateful to Onora O'Neill for her suggestion that this work, especially given Kant's reference at p. 123 to the Bible as "das Buch, was einmal da ist" ("that book which happens to be there"), should be read as a

conscious continuation of the sort of biblical interpretation that Spinoza gave in his *Theological Political Treatise*, an interpretation that offered the pious a way of accepting much of what their Holy Scriptures contained while at the same time effectively undermining any claim that might be made for the foundational nature of religious doctrines for moral or other knowledge.

37. René Descartes, *Discourse on the Method of Rightly Conducting One's Reason and Seeking Truth in the Sciences*, ed. C. Adam and P. Tannery (Paris: Vrin CNRS, 1964–1976), VI, 24–25; *The Philosophical Writings of Descartes*, trans. John Cottingham, Robert Stoothoff, and Dugald Murdoch (New York: Cambridge University Press, 1985), I, 123.

38. Arendt's doctoral dissertation was on Augustine's views about love. It was published in Germany in 1929: *Der Liebesbegriffe bei Augustin: Versuch einer Philosophischen Interpretation* (Berlin: Springer-Verlag, 1929). It was translated into English in 1966 by E. B. Ashton, entitled "Love and Saint Augustine: An Essay in Philosophical Translation" (manuscript).

39. Seyla Benhabib seems to be doing just this. See her "Judgment and the Moral Foundations of Politics in Arendt's Thought," *Political Theory* 16 (Feb. 1988): 29–51; "Hannah Arendt and the Redemptive Power of Narrative," *Social Research* 57 (Spring 1990): 167–196; and "The Reluctant Modernism of Hannah Arendt" (manuscript).

Appendix: A Bibliography of Writings in English about Hannah Arendt

Johann A. Klaassen and Angela Klaassen

Abel, Lionel. "The Aesthetics of Evil: Hannah Arendt on Eichmann and the Jews." *Partisan Review* 30 (1963): 211–230.

Adams, Carole. "Hannah Arendt and the Historian: Nazism and the New Order." In *Hannah Arendt: Thinking, Judging, Freedom*, edited by Gisela T. Kaplan and Clive Kessler. Sydney: Unwin Hyman, 1989.

Adamson, Walter. "Beyond 'Reform or Revolution': Notes on Political Education in Gramsci, Habermas and Arendt." *Theory and Society* 6 (1978): 429–460.

Alford, C. Fred. "The Organization of Evil." *Political Psychology* 11 (1990): 5–27.

Allardyce, Gilbert. Review of *Hannah Arendt: For Love of the World*, by Elisabeth Young-Bruehl. *American History Review* 88 (1983): 75.

Allen, Wayne. "Hannah Arendt: Existential Phenomenology and Political Freedom." *Philosophy and Social Criticism* 9 (1982): 169–190.

Allen, Wayne. "'Homo Aristocus': Hannah Arendt's Elites." *Idealistic Studies* 13 (1983): 226–239.

Allen, Wayne. "Hannah Arendt and the Politics of Evil." *Ideal Studies* 21 (1991): 97–105.

Allen, Wayne. "Hannah Arendt and the Ideological Structure of Totalitarianism." *Man World* 26 (1993): 115–129.

Allen, William S. Commentary on "Hannah Arendt in Jerusalem: The Controversy Revisited," by Walter Laqueur. In *Western Society After the Holocaust*, edited by Lyman H. Letgers. Boulder, CO: Westview Press, 1983.

Anders, Laura. "Desire and Receptivity." *Continental Philosophy* 15 (1993): 1–3.

Arnold, G.L. "Three Critics of Totalitarianism." *Twentieth Century* 150 (July 1951): 23–24.

Aron, Raymond. "The Essence of Totalitarianism According to Hannah Arendt." Translated by Marc Le Pain and Daniel Mahoney. *Partisan Review* 60 (1993): 366–376.

Asahina, Robert. "Who Was That Mass Man, Anyway?" *Harper's* 265, no. 1588 (1982): 70–74.

Bakan, Mildred. "Hannah Arendt's Concepts of Work and Labor." In *Hannah Arendt: The Recovery of the Public World*, edited by Melvyn Hill. New York: St. Martin's Press, 1979.

Bakan, Mildred. "Hannah Arendt's Critical Appropriation of Heidegger's Thought as Political Philosophy." In *Descriptions*, edited by Don Ihde and Hugh Silverman. Albany: State University of New York Press, 1985.

Bakan, Mildred. "Arendt and Heidegger: The Episodic Intertwining of Life and Work." *Philosophy and Social Criticism* 12 (1987): 71–98.

Bakhale, S.W. "Hannah Arendt on Civil Disobedience." *Indian Philosophical Quarterly* 13 (1986): 261–269.

Balcomb, A. O. "Theology and Transition in South Africa—Hannah Arendt's *On Revolution* Revisited." *Journal of Theology for Southern Africa* 83 (1993): 32–45.

Bar-on, A. Zvie. "Measuring Responsibility." In *Collective Responsibility*, edited by Larry May and Stacey Hoffman. Savage, MD: Rowman and Littlefield, 1991.

Barnard, F. Mechner. "Infinity and Finality: Hannah Arendt on Politics and Truth." *Canadian Journal of Political and Social Theory* 1 (1977): 29–57.

Barnouw, Dagmar. "The Secularity of Evil: Hannah Arendt and the Eichmann Controversy." *Modern Judaism* 3 (1983): 75–94.

Barnouw, Dagmar. "Speech Regained: Hannah Arendt and the American Revolution." *Clio* 15 (1986): 137–152.

Barnouw, Dagmar. *Visible Spaces: Hannah Arendt and the German-Jewish Experience.* Baltimore: Johns Hopkins University Press, 1990.

Baron, J. "Hannah Arendt: Personal Reflections." *Response* 12 (1980): 58–63.

Barrett, William. *The Truants: Adventures among the Intellectuals.* Garden City, NY: Anchor, 1983.

Beatty, Joseph. "Thinking and Moral Considerations: Socrates and Arendt's Eichmann." In *Hannah Arendt: Critical Essays*, edited by Lewis P. Hinchman and Sandra K. Hinchman. Albany: State University of New York Press, 1994.

Beiner, Ronald. "Hannah Arendt on Capitalism and Socialism." *Government and Opposition* 25 (1980): 359–370.

Beiner, Ronald. "Hannah Arendt on Judging." In *Lectures on Kant's Political Philosophy* by Hannah Arendt. Chicago: University of Chicago Press, 1982.

Beiner, Ronald. *Political Judgment.* Chicago: University of Chicago Press, 1983, pp. 12–19.

Beiner, Ronald. "Action, Natality, and Citizenship: Hannah Arendt's Concept of Freedom." In *Conceptions of Liberty in Political Philosophy*, edited by Z. Pelczynski and J. Gray. London: Athlone Press, 1984.

Beiner, Ronald. *Hannah Arendt: Lectures on Kant's Political Philosophy*. Chicago: University of Chicago Press, 1989.

Beiner, Ronald. "Hannah Arendt and Leo Strauss: the Uncommenced Dialogue." *Political Theory* 18 (1990): 238–254.

Beiner, Ronald. "Judging in a World of Appearances: A Commentary on Hannah Arendt's Unwritten Finale." In *Hannah Arendt: Critical Essays*, edited by Lewis P. Hinchman and Sandra K. Hinchman. Albany: State University of New York Press, 1994.

Bell, Daniel. "The Alphabet of Justice." *Partisan Review* 30 (1963): 417–429.

Bell, Daniel. "The Alphabet of Justice: On 'Eichmann in Jerusalem'." In *The Winding Passage: Essays and Sociological Journeys, 1960–1980*. Cambridge: Abt Books, 1980.

Benhabib, Seyla. *Situating the Self: Gender, Community, and Postmodernism in Contemporary Ethics*. New York: Routledge, 1992.

Benhabib, Seyla. "Feminist Theory and Hannah Arendt's Concept of Public Space." *History of the Human Sciences* [Great Britain] 6 (1993): 97–114.

Benhabib, Seyla. "Hannah Arendt and the Redemptive Power of Narrative." In *Hannah Arendt: Critical Essays*, edited by Lewis P. Hinchman and Sandra K. Hinchman. Albany: State University of New York Press, 1994.

Benton, Sarah. Review of *Hannah Arendt: A Reinterpretation of Her Political Thought*, by Margaret Canovan. *New Statesman and Society* 5 (23 October 1992): 45–46.

Bernasconi, Robert. "Habermas and Arendt on the Philosopher's 'Error': Tracking the Diabiological in Heidegger." *Graduate Faculty Philosophy Journal* (1991): 3–24.

Bernauer, James. "On Reading and Mis-reading Hannah Arendt." *Philosophy and Social Criticism* 11 (1985): 1–34.

Bernauer, James. "The Faith of Hannah Arendt: *Amor Mundi* and its Critique-Assimilation of Religious Experience." In *Amor Mundi: Explorations in the Thought of Hannah Arendt*, edited by James Bernauer. Boston: Martinus Nijhoff, 1987.

Bernstein, Richard J. "Hannah Arendt: The Ambiguities of Theory and Practice." In *Political Theory and Praxis*, edited by Terence Ball. Minneapolis: University of Minnesota Press, 1977.

Bernstein, Richard J. "The Meaning of Public Life." In *Religion and American Public Life: Interpretations and Explorations*, edited by Robin W. Lovin. New York: Paulist Press, 1986.

Bernstein, Richard J. *Philosophical Profiles*. Philadelphia: University of Philadelphia Press, 1986.

Bernstein, Richard J. "Rethinking the Social and Political." *Graduate Faculty Philosophy Journal* 11 (1986): 111–130.

Bernstein, Richard J. "Judging—the Actor and the Spectator." In *The Realm of Humanitas: Responses to the Writings of Hannah Arendt.* New York: Lang, 1990.

Bernstein, Richard J. Review of *Hannah Arendt's Philosophy of Natality*, by Patricia Bowen-Moore. *Review of Metaphysics* 45 (1991): 393–394.

Best, Geoffrey. Review of *Hannah Arendt: Politics, Conscience, Evil*, by George Kateb. *Times Literary Supplement* 4247 (24 August 1984): 946.

Bettelheim, Bruno. "Eichmann: The System, the Victims." In *Surviving and Other Essays.* New York: Alfred A. Knopf, 1979.

Betz, Joseph M. "An Introduction to the Thought of Hannah Arendt." *Transactions of the Peirce Society* 28 (1992): 379–422.

Biskowski, Lawrence J. "Practical Foundations for Political Judgment: Arendt on Action and World." *The Journal of Politics* 55 (1993): 867–887.

Bittman, Michael. "Totalitarianism: The Career of a Concept." In *Hannah Arendt: Thinking, Judging, Freedom*, edited by Gisela T. Kaplan and Clive Kessler. Sydney: Unwin Hyman, 1989.

Botstein, Leon. "Hannah Arendt." Commentary on "Hannah Arendt: Opposing Views" by Martin Jay. *Partisan Review* 45 (1978): 368–380.

Botstein, Leon. "Hannah Arendt: The Jewish Question." *The New Republic* 179 (21 October 1978): 32–37.

Botstein, Leon. "The Jew as Pariah: Hannah Arendt's Political Philosophy." *Dialectical Anthropology* 8 (1983): 47–73.

Botstein, Leon. "Liberating the Pariah: Politics, the Jews, and Hannah Arendt." *Salmagundi* 60 (1983): 73–106.

Botstein, Leon. Review of *Hannah Arendt: For Love of the World*, by Elisabeth Young-Bruehl. *Journal of Modern History* 57 (1985): 335–338.

Bottomore, Tom. "Is There a Totalitarian View of Human Nature?" *Social Research* 40 (1973): 428–442.

Bowen-Moore, Patricia. "Natality, *Amor Mundi* and Nuclearism in the Thought of Hannah Arendt." In *Amor Mundi: Explorations in the Thought of Hannah Arendt*, edited by James Bernauer. Boston: Martinus Nijhoff, 1987.

Bowen-Moore, Patricia. *Hannah Arendt's Philosophy of Natality.* New York: St. Martin's Press, 1989.

Boyle, Patrick. "Elusive Neighborliness: Hannah Arendt's Interpretation of St. Augustine." In *Amor Mundi: Explorations in the Thought of Hannah Arendt*, edited by James Bernauer. Boston: Martinus Nijhoff, 1987.

Bradshaw, Leah. *Acting and Thinking: The Political Thought of Hannah Arendt.* Toronto: University of Toronto Press, 1989.

Bradshaw, Leah. Review of *Public Realm and Public Self: The Political Theory of Hannah Arendt*, by Shiraz Dossa. *Canadian Journal of Political Science* 22 (1989): 908–909.

Branch, Taylor. "America's Errant Philosopher." *The Washington Monthly* 15 (1983): 49–57.

Brand, Arie. "The 'Colonization of the Lifeworld' and the Disappearance of Politics—Arendt and Habermas." *Thesis Eleven* 13 (1986): 39–53.

Breton, Albert, and Ronald Wintrobe. "The Bureaucracy of Murder Revisited." *Journal of Political Economy* 94 (1986): 905–926.

Brown, Wendy. *Manhood and Politics.* Totowa, NJ: Rowman and Littlefield, 1988.

Burke, John Francis. "Voegelin, Heidegger, and Arendt: Two's Company, Three's a Crowd?" *The Social Science Journal* 30 (1993): 83–97.

Burns, Robert P. "A Lawyer's Truth: Notes for a Moral Philosophy of Litigation Practice." *Journal of Law and Religion* 3 (1985): 229–276.

Burns, Robert. "Hannah Arendt's Constitutional Thought." In *Amor Mundi: Explorations in the Thought of Hannah Arendt*, edited by James Bernauer. Boston: Martinus Nijhoff, 1987.

Burrowes, Robert. "Totalitarianism: The Revised Standard Version." *World Politics* 21 (1969): 272–294.

Bush, Clive. *Halfway to Revolution: Investigation and Crisis in the work of Henry Adams, William James, and Gertrude Stein.* New Haven: Yale University Press, 1991.

Cannon, Dale. "Toward the Recovery of Common Sense in a Post-Critical Intellectual Ethos." *Tradition and Discovery* 19 (1992–1993): 5–15.

Canovan, Margaret. *The Political Thought of Hannah Arendt.* London: Dent and Sons, 1974.

Canovan, Margaret. "The Contradictions of Hannah Arendt's Political Thought." *Political Theory* 6 (1978): 5–26.

Canovan, Margaret. "On Levin's 'On *Animal Laborans* and *Homo Politicus* in Hannah Arendt'." *Political Theory* 8 (1980): 403–405.

Canovan, Margaret. "Chesterton and Hannah Arendt." *The Chesterton Review* 7 (1981): 139–153.

Canovan, Margaret. "Arendt, Rousseau, and Human Plurality in Politics." *Journal of Politics* 45 (1983): 286–302.

Canovan, Margaret. "A Case of Distorted Communication: A Note on Habermas and Arendt." *Political Theory* 11 (1983): 105–116.

Canovan, Margaret. "On Pitkin, 'Justice'." *Political Theory* 10 (1983): 464–468.

Canovan, Margaret. "Hannah Arendt on Ideology in Totalitarianism." In *The Structure of Modern Ideology*, edited by Noel O'Sullivan. Aldershot: Edward Elgar, 1989.

Canovan, Margaret. "Socrates or Heidegger? Hannah Arendt's Reflections on Philosophy and Politics." *Social Research* 57 (1990): 135–165.

Canovan, Margaret. *Hannah Arendt: A Reinterpretation of Her Political Thought.* New York: Cambridge University Press, 1992.

Canovan, Margaret. "Politics as Culture: Hannah Arendt and the Public Realm." In *Hannah Arendt: Critical Essays*, edited by Lewis P. Hinchman and Sandra K. Hinchman. Albany: State University of New York Press, 1994.

Carlebach, J. "Cosmopolitan or—Pariah?" *Jewish Spectator* 44 (1979): 15–16.

Castoriadis, Cornelius. "The Destinies of Totalitarianism." *Salmagundi* 60 (1983): 107–122.

Clarke, Barry. "Beyond 'The Banality of Evil'." *British Journal of Political Science* 10 (1980): 417–439.

Clarke, James P. "Social Justice and Political Freedom: Revisiting Hannah Arendt's Conception of Need." *Philosophy and Social Criticism* 19 (1993): 333–347.

Clarke, James P. "A Kantian Theory of Political Judgment: Arendt and Lyotard." *Philosophy Today* 38 (1994): 135–148.

Cooper, Barry. "Action into Nature: Hannah Arendt's Reflections on Technology." In *Democratic Theory and Technological Society*, edited by Richard B. Day, Ronald Beiner, and Joseph Masciulli. Armonk, NY: M. E. Sharpe, 1988.

Cooper, Barry. *Action into Nature: An Essay on the Meaning of Technology.* Notre Dame, IN: University of Notre Dame Press, 1991.

Cooper, Leroy. "Hannah Arendt's Political Philosophy: An Interpretation." *Review of Politics* 38 (1976): 145–176.

Cornell, Drucilla L. "Gender Hierarchy, Equality, and the Possibility of Democracy." *American Imago* 48 (1991): 247–263.

Coser, Lewis A. Review of *Hannah Arendt: For Love of the World*, by Elisabeth Young-Bruehl. *Political Science Quarterly* 97 (1982–1983): 735–737.

Coughlin, Ellen. "The Contradictory Legacy of Hannah Arendt." *The Chronicle of Higher Education* 25, no. 3 (1982): 27–28.

Craig, Gordon A. "Letters on Dark Times." Review of *Hannah Arendt, Karl Jaspers: Correspondence, 1926–1969*, edited by Lotte Kohler and Hans Saner. *New York Review of Books* 40 (13 May 1993): 10–14.

Cranston, Maurice. "Hannah Arendt, Personally." *Encounter* 46 (1976): 54–56.

Cranston, Maurice. "Hannah Arendt, Personally: Light on the Life of a Philosopher." *Encounter* 59 (1982): 54–60.

Crick, Bernard. "On Rereading *The Origins of Totalitarianism.*" In *Hannah Arendt: The Recovery of the Public World*, edited by Melvyn Hill. New York: St. Martin's Press, 1979.

Crick, Bernard. "Hannah Arendt: Hedgehog or Fox?" *Listener* 107 (1982): 6–7.

Crick, Bernard. "Hannah Arendt's Political Philosophy." In *Proceedings of "History, Ethics, Politics": A Conference Based on the Work of Hannah Arendt*, edited by Robert Boyers. New York: Empire State College, 1982.

Crunden, Robert M. Review of *Hannah Arendt: For Love of the World*, by Elisabeth Young-Bruehl. *Indian Journal of American Studies* 14 (1984): 135–144.

Cutting-Gray, Joanne. "Hannah Arendt's *Rahel Varnhagen*." *Philosophy and Literature* 15 (1991): 229–245.

Cutting-Gray, Joanne. "Hannah Arendt, Feminism, and the Politics of Alterity: 'What Will We Lose if We Win?'" *Hypatia* 8 (1993): 35–54.

Dalin, David G. "The Jewish Historiography of Hannah Arendt." *Conservative Judaism* 40 (1988): 47–58.

Dallmayr. Fred. "Public or Private Freedom? Response to Kateb." *Social Research* 54 (1987): 617–628.

Dannhauser, Werner. "Hannah Arendt and the Jews." *Commentary* 67 (1979): 70–72.

Delzell, Charles F. Review of *Into the Dark: Hannah Arendt and Totalitarianism*, by Stephen J. Whitfield. *South Atlantic Quarterly* 80 (1981): 478–479.

Denneny, Michael. "The Privilege of Ourselves: Hannah Arendt on Judgment." In *Hannah Arendt: The Recovery of the Public World*, edited by Melvyn Hill. New York: St. Martin's Press, 1979.

Dietz, Mary J. "Citizenship with a Feminist Face: The Problem with Maternal Thinking." *Political Theory* 13 (1985): 19–37.

Dietz, Mary J. Review of *Public Realm and Public Self: The Political Theory of Hannah Arendt*, by Shiraz Dossa, and *Acting and Thinking: The Political Thought of Hannah Arendt*, by Leah Bradshaw. *American Political Science Review* 85 (1991): 259–260.

Dietz, Mary J. "Hannah Arendt and Feminist Politics." In *Hannah Arendt: Critical Essays*, edited by Lewis P. Hinchman and Sandra K. Hinchman. Albany: State University of New York Press, 1994.

Diner, Dan. "Historical Experience and Cognition: Perspectives on National Socialism." *History and Memory* 2 (1990): 84–110.

Disch, Lisa J. "More Truth Than Fact: Storytelling as Critical Understanding in the Writings of Hannah Arendt." *Political Theory* 21 (1993): 665–694.

Disch, Lisa J. *Hannah Arendt and the Limits of Philosophy*. Ithaca, NY: Cornell University Press, 1994.

Disch, Lisa J. Review of *Political Theory and the Displacement of Politics*, by Bonnie Honig. *Political Theory* 22 (1994): 176–179.

Donat, Alexander. "Revisionist History of the Jewish Catastrophe: An Empiric Examination." *Judaism* 12 (1963): 416–435.

Dossa, Shiraz. "Human Status and Politics: Hannah Arendt on the Holocaust." *Canadian Journal of Political Science* 13 (1980): 309–323.

Dossa, Shiraz. "Hannah Arendt on Billy Budd and Robespierre: The Public Realm and the Private Self." *Philosophy and Social Criticism* 9 (1982): 307–318.

Dossa, Shiraz. "Hannah Arendt on Eichmann: the Public, the Private and the Evil." *The Review of Politics* 46 (1984): 163–182.

Dossa, Shiraz. Review of *Hannah Arendt: Politics, Conscience, Evil*, by George Kateb. *Canadian Journal of Political Science* 17 (1984): 839–840.

Dossa, Shiraz. "Lethal Fantasy: Hannah Arendt on Political Zionism." *Arab Studies Quarterly* 8 (1986): 219–230.

Dossa, Shiraz. *The Public Realm and the Public Self: The Political Theory of Hannah Arendt.* Waterloo, Ontario: Wilfrid Laurier University Press, 1989.

Dossa, Shiraz. "Hannah Arendt's Political Theory: Ethics and Enemies." *History of European Ideas* 13 (1991): 385–398.

Dostal, Robert. "Judging Human Action: Arendt's Appropriation of Kant." *Review of Metaphysics* 37 (1984): 725–755.

Draenos, San Spyros. "Thinking Without a Ground: Hannah Arendt and the Contemporary Situation of the Understanding." In *Hannah Arendt: The Recovery of the Public World*, edited by Melvyn Hill. New York: St. Martin's Press, 1979.

Draenos, San Spyros. "The Totalitarian Theme in Horkheimer and Arendt." *Salmagundi* 56 (1982): 155–169.

Dunne, Joseph. *Back to the Rough Ground.* Notre Dame, IN: University of Notre Dame Press, 1993.

Elbaz, Freema. "Hope, Attentiveness, and Caring for Difference: The Moral Voice in Teaching." *Teaching and Teacher Education* 8 (1992): 421–432.

Elevitch, Bernard. "Hannah Arendt's Testimony." *The Massachusetts Review* 20 (1979): 369–376.

Ellis, Mark H. "Critical Thought and Messianic Trust: Reflections on a Jewish Theology of Liberation." *Ecumenical Review* 42 (1990): 35–47.

Elshtain, Jean B. "Reflections on War and Political Discourse: Realism, Just War, and Feminism in a Nuclear Age." *Political Theory* 13 (1985): 39–57.

Elshtain, Jean B. "Reflections on War and Political Discourse: Realism, Just War, and Feminism in a Nuclear Age." In *Nuclear Weapons and the Future of Humanity*, edited by Avner Cohen. Totowa, NJ: Rowman and Allanheld.

Elshtain, Jean B. *Meditations on Modern Political Thought: Masculine/Feminine Themes from Luther to Arendt.* New York: Praeger Books, 1986.

Elshtain, Jean B. "Hannah Arendt's French Revolution." *Salmagundi* 84 (1989): 203–213.

Elshtain, Jean B. "Political Children." *Criterion* 33 (1994): 2–15.

Elshtain, Jean B. Review of *Essays in Understanding* by Hannah Arendt and edited by Jerome Kohn. *First Things* 47 (1994): 49–52.

Endelman, Todd. "Disraeli's Jewishness Reconsidered." *Modern Judaism* 5 (1985): 109–123.

Everett, William. "Ecclesiology and Political Authority: A Dialogue with Hannah Arendt." *Encounter* 36 (1975): 25–36.

Ezorsky, Gertrude. "Hannah Arendt Against the Facts." *New Politics* 2 (1963): 53–73.

Ezorsky, Gertrude. "Hannah Arendt's View of Totalitarianism and the Holocaust." *The Philosophical Forum* 16 (1984–1985): 53–73.

Fairchild, David. "Revolution and Cause: An Investigation of an Explanatory Concept." *New Scholasticism* 50 (1976): 277–292.

Farganis, Sondra. "The Chosen People: The Historical Formation of Identity." In *Hannah Arendt: Thinking, Judging, Freedom*, edited by Gisela Kaplan and Clive Kessler. Sydney: Unwin Hyman, 1989.

Feher, Ferenc. "The Pariah and the Citizen (On Arendt's Political Theory)." *Thesis Eleven* 15 (1986): 15–29.

Feher, Ferenc. "Freedom and the Social Question: Hannah Arendt's Theory of Revolution." *Philosophy and Social Criticism* 12 (1987): 1–30.

Feldman, Ron. "Introduction: The Jew as Pariah: The Case of Hannah Arendt." In *The Jew as Pariah: Jewish Identity and Politics in the Modern Age*, edited by Ron Feldman. New York: Grove Press, 1978.

Flynn, Bernard. "The Question of an Ontology of the Political: Arendt, Merleau-Ponty, Lefort". *International Studies in Philosophy* 16 (1984): 1–24.

Flynn, Bernard. "Arendt's Appropriation of Kant's Theory of Judgment." *Journal of the British Society for Phenomenology* 19 (1988): 128–140.

Flynn, Bernard. "The Places of the Work of Art in Arendt's Philosophy." *Philosophy and Social Criticism* 17 (1991): 217–228.

Forester, John. "Hannah Arendt and Critical Theory: A Critical Response." Commentary on "Hannah Arendt and the Problem of Critical Theory" by Gerald Heather and Matthew Stolz. *Journal of Politics* 43 (1981): 196–202.

Frampton, Kenneth. "The Status of Man and the Status of His Objects: A Reading of *The Human Condition*." In *Hannah Arendt: The Recovery of the Public World*, edited by Melvyn Hill. New York: St. Martin's Press, 1979.

Frankel, S. Herbert. "The Riddle of Hannah Arendt." *Journal of Jewish Studies* 34 (1983): 93–100.

Fruchter, Norman. "Arendt's Eichmann and Jewish Identity." In *For a New America: Essays in History and Politics from 'Studies on the Left', 1959–1967*, edited by James Weinstein and David Eakins. New York: Random House, 1970.

Fuss, Peter. "Conscience." *Ethics* 74 (1964): 111–120.

Fuss, Peter. "Hannah Arendt's Conception of Political Community." In *Hannah Arendt: The Recovery of the Public World*, edited by Melvyn Hill. New York: St. Martin's Press, 1979.

Galston, William A. Review of *Lectures on Kant's Political Philosophy*, by Hannah Arendt. *Journal of Politics* 46 (1984): 304–306.

Garner, Reuben. "Authority, Authoritarianism, and Education." In *The Realm of Humanitas: Responses to the Writings of Hannah Arendt*. New York: Lang, 1990.

Gellner, E. "Accounting for the Horror." *Times Literary Supplement* 4140 (6 August 1982): 843–845.

Gendre, Michael. "Transcendence and Judgment in Arendt's Phenomenology of Action." *Philosophy and Social Criticism* 18 (1992): 29–50.

Glazer, Nathan. "Hannah Arendt's America." *Commentary* 60 (1975): 61–67.

Gordon, Haim. "Peacemaking in Action." In *Education for Peace: Testimonies from World Religions*, edited by Haim Gordon and Leonard Grob. Maryknoll, NY: Orbis Books, 1987.

Gottsegen, Michael G. *The Political Thought of Hannah Arendt*. Albany: State University of New York Press, 1994.

Grafstein, Robert. "Political Freedom and Political Action." *Western Political Quarterly* 39 (1986): 464–479.

Gray, Glenn. "The Winds of Thought." *Social Research* 44 (1977): 44–61.

Gray, Glenn. "The Abyss of Freedom—and Hannah Arendt." In *Hannah Arendt: The Recovery of the Public World*, edited by Melvyn Hill. New York: St. Martin's Press, 1979.

Gray, Sherry. "Hannah Arendt and the Solitariness of Thinking." *Philosophy Today* 25 (1981): 121–130.

Greene, Maxine. "Cognition and Consciousness: Humanities and the Elementary School Teacher." *Philosophic Exchange* 1 (1973): 43–62.

Gregor, Mary J. Review of *Lectures on Kant's Political Philosophy*, by Hannah Arendt. *Review of Metaphysics* 37 (1983): 102–104.

Gunn, Giles. "Moral Order in Modern Literature and Criticism: The Challenge of the 'New New Criticism'." *Journal of the American Academy of Religion Thematic Studies* 49 (1983): 45–59.

Gunnell, John. *Political Theory: Tradition and Interpretation.* Cambridge: Winthrop, 1979.

Gutman, Emanuel. "Dr. Hannah Arendt and the Whole Truth." *Political Studies* 12 (1964): 372–376.

Habermas, Jürgen. *Philosophical-Political Profiles.* Translated by Frederick G. Lawrence. Cambridge: MIT Press, 1983.

Habermas, Jürgen. "Hannah Arendt's Communications Concept of Power." In *Hannah Arendt: Critical Essays*, edited by Lewis P. Hinchman and Sandra K. Hinchman. Albany: State University of New York Press, 1994.

Hansen, Phillip Birger. *Hannah Arendt: Politics, History and Citizenship.* Stanford, CA: Stanford University Press, 1993.

Hartsock, Nancy. *Money, Sex, and Power: Toward a Feminist Historical Materialism.* New York: Longman, 1983.

Hauerwas, Stanley. "Eschatology and Nuclear Disarmament." *NICM Journal* 8 (1983): 7–16.

Heather, Gerald, and Matthew Stolz. "Hannah Arendt and the Problem of Critical Theory." *Journal of Politics* 41 (1979): 2–22.

Heather, Gerald and Matthew Stolz. "Reply." Response to "Hannah Arendt and Critical Theory: A Critical Response" by John Forester. *Journal of Politics* 43 (1981): 203–207.

Heller, Agnes. "Hannah Arendt and the *Vita Contemplativa.*" In *Hannah Arendt: Thinking, Judging, Freedom*, edited by Gisela T. Kaplan and Clive Kessler. Sydney: Unwin Hyman, 1989.

Heller, Agnes. "An Imaginary Preface to the 1984 Edition of Hannah Arendt's *The Origins of Totalitarianism.*" In *The Public Real: Essays on Discursive Types in Political Philosophy*, edited by Reiner Schürmann. Albany: State University of New York Press, 1989.

Heller, Erich. "Hannah Arendt as a Critic of Literature." *Social Research* 44 (1977): 147–159.

Heller, Wlodzimierz. "The Public and the Private in Hannah Arendt's Political Philosophy." In *Social System, Rationality, and Revolution*, edited by Leszek Nowak. Amsterdam: Rodopi, 1993.

Helm, Thomas E. "Enchantment and the Banality of Evil." *Religion in Life* 49 (1980): 81–95.

Hersch, Charles. Review of *Hannah Arendt's Philosophy of Natality*, by Patricia Bowen-Moore. *Review of Politics* 52 (1990): 643–645.

Hertz, Deborah. "Hannah Arendt's *Rahel Varnhagen.*" In *German Women in the Nineteenth Century: A Social History*, edited by John Fout. New York: Holmes and Meier, 1984.

Hill, Melvyn. "The Fictions of Mankind and the Stories of Men." In *Hannah Arendt: The Recovery of the Public World*, edited by Melvyn Hill. New York: St. Martin's Press, 1979.

Hinchman, Lewis P. and Sandra K. Hinchman. "In Heidegger's Shadow: Hannah Arendt's Phenomenological Humanism." *Review of Politics* 46 (1984): 183–211.

Hinchman, Lewis P., and Sandra K. Hinchman. Review of *Acting and Thinking: The Political Thought of Hannah Arendt*, by Leah Bradshaw. *Canadian Journal of Political Science* 22 (1989): 906–908.

Hinchman, Lewis P., and Sandra K. Hinchman. "Existentialism Politicized: Arendt's Debt to Jaspers." In *Hannah Arendt: Critical Essays*, edited by Lewis P. Hinchman and Sandra K. Hinchman. Albany: State University of New York Press, 1994.

Hinchman, Sandra K. "Common Sense and Political Barbarism in the Theory of Hannah Arendt." *Polity* 17 (1984): 317–339.

Hinchman, Sandra K. Review of *Hannah Arendt: Politics, Conscience, Evil*, by George Kateb. *Journal of Politics* 46 (1984): 1268–1271.

Hinchman, Sandra K. Review of *Hannah Arendt: Politics, Conscience, Evil*, by George Kateb. *Journal of Politics* 47 (1985): 1293–1295.

Hobsbawm, Eric. *Revolutionaries: Contemporary Essays*. New York: Pantheon Books, 1973.

Hollinger, David A. Review of *Into the Dark: Hannah Arendt and Totalitarianism*, by Stephen J. Whitfield. *Journal of American History* 68 (1981): 444–445.

Honahan, Iseult. "Hannah Arendt's Concept of Freedom." *Irish Philosophical Journal* 4 (1987): 41–63.

Honahan, Iseult. "Arendt and Benjamin on the Promises of History: A Network of Possibilities or One Apocalyptic Moment?" *Clio* 19 (1990): 311–330.

Honeywell, J. "Revolution: Its Potentialities and Its Degradations." *Ethics* 80 (1970): 251–265.

Honig, Bonnie. "Arendt, Identity, and Difference." *Political Theory* 16 (1988): 77–98.

Honig, Bonnie. Review of *Public Realm and Public Self: The Political Theory of Hannah Arendt*, by Shiraz Dossa. *Political Theory* 18 (1990): 320–323.

Honig, Bonnie. "Declarations of Independence: Arendt and Derrida on the Problem of Founding a Republic." *American Political Science Review* 85 (1991): 97–113.

Honig, Bonnie. "Toward an Agonistic Feminism: Hannah Arendt and the Politics of Identity." In *Feminists Theorize the Political*, edited by Judith Butler and Joan Scott. New York: Routledge, 1992.

Honig, Bonnie. *Political Theory and the Displacement of Politics*. Ithaca, NY: Cornell University Press, 1993.

Honig, Bonnie. "The Politics of Agonism: A Critical Response to 'Beyond Good and Evil . . .' by Dana Villa." *Political Theory* 21 (1993): 528–533.

Honneth, Axel, and Mitchell Ash. "Work and Instrumental Action: On the Normative Basis of Critical Theory." *Thesis Eleven* 5/6 (1982): 162–184.

Honneth, Axel, and Mitchell Ash. "Work and Instrumental Action." *Acta Sociologica* 28 (1985): 55–61.

Howe, Irving. "*The New Yorker* and Hannah Arendt." *Commentary* 36 (1963): 318–319.

Huchingson, James E. "Earthstruck: a Reflection on *The Home Planet*, edited by Kelvin W. Kelley, and 'The Conquest of Space and the Stature of Man' by Hannah Arendt." *Zygon* 25 (1990): 357–362.

Hughes, H. Stuart. *The Sea Change: The Migration of Social Thought, 1930–1965*. New York: Harper and Row, 1975.

Ingram, David. "The Postmodern Kantianism of Arendt and Lyotard." In *Judging Lyotard*, edited by Andrew Benjamin. New York: Routledge, 1992.

Isaac, Jeffrey C. "Arendt, Camus, and Postmodern Politics". *Praxis International* 9 (1989): 48–71.

Isaac, Jeffrey C. "At the Margins: Jewish Identity and Politics in the Thought of Hannah Arendt." *Tikkun* 5 (1990): 23–26, 86–92.

Isaac, Jeffrey C. *Arendt, Camus, and Modern Rebellion*. New Haven: Yale University Press, 1992.

Isaac, Jeffrey C. "Situating Hannah Arendt on Action and Politics." *Political Theory* 21 (1993): 534–540.

Jackson, Michael. "The Responsibility of Judgement and the Judgement of Responsibility." In *Hannah Arendt: Thinking, Judging, Freedom*, edited by Gisela T. Kaplan and Clive Kessler. Sydney: Unwin Hyman, 1989.

Jacobitti, Suzanne. "Hannah Arendt and the Will." *Political Theory* 16 (1988): 53–76.

Jacobitti, Suzanne. "Individualism and Political Community: Arendt and Tocqueville on the Current Debate in Liberalism." *Polity* 23 (1991): 585–604.

Jacobitti, Suzanne. "The Public, the Private, the Moral: Hannah Arendt and Political Morality." *International Political Science Review* 12 (1991): 281ff.

Jacobson, Norman. "Parable and Paradox: In Response to Arendt's *On Revolution*." *Salmagundi* 60 (1983): 123–139.

Jasinski, James. "(Re)constituting Community Through Narrative Argument: *Eros* and *Philia* in *The Big Chill*." *The Quarterly Journal of Speech* 79 (1993): 467–486.

Jay, Martin. "Hannah Arendt: Opposing Views." *Partisan Review* 45 (1978): 348–368.

Jay, Martin. *Permanent Exiles: Essays on the Intellectual Migration from Germany to America*. New York: Columbia University Press, 1986.

Jay, Martin. "Women in the Dark Ages: Agnes Heller and Hannah Arendt." In *The Social Philosophy of Agnes Heller*, edited by John Burnheim. Atlanta: Rodopi, 1994.

Jegstrup, Elsebet. "Spontaneous Action: The Rescue of the Danish Jews from Hannah Arendt's Perspective." *Humboldt Journal of Social Relations* 13 (1986): 260–284.

Jha, Hetukar. "Legitimacy and Political Violence." *Journal of Social and Economic Studies* 1 (1984): 365–372.

Johnson, G. "Wetharryngton: Scholia on Hannah Arendt." *American Scholar* 33 (1964): 202–210.

Jonas, Hans. "Hannah Arendt 1906–1975." *Social Research* 43 (1976): 3–5.

Jonas, Hans. "Acting, Knowing, Thinking: Gleanings from Hannah Arendt's Philosophical Work." *Social Research* 44 (1977): 25–43.

Jones, N. S. Carey. "Democracy, Dictatorships, and Totalitarianism." *Political Studies* 17 (1969): 79–86.

Jung, Hwa Yol and Petae Jung. "Toward a New Humanism: The Politics of Civility in a 'No-Growth' Society." *Man and World* 9 (1976): 283–306.

Jung, L. Shannon. "Beyond Narcissism: Review of Cristopher Lasch's *The Culture of Narcissism* (1979)." *Religion in Life* 49 (1980): 211–220.

Justman, Stewart. "Hannah Arendt and the Idea of Disclosure." *Philosophy and Social Criticism* 4 (1981): 407–423.

Kalla, Sarala. "Hannah Arendt on Civil Disobedience." *Indian Philosophical Quarterly* 13 (1986): 261–269.

Kaplan, Gisela T. "Hannah Arendt: The Life of a Jewish Woman." In *Hannah Arendt: Thinking, Judging, Freedom*, edited by Gisela T. Kaplan and Clive Kessler. Sydney: Unwin Hyman, 1989.

Kaplan, Gisela T. *Contemporary Western European Feminism.* New York: New York University, 1992.

Karmis, Dmitri. Review of *Une femme de pensée, Hannah Arendt*, by Genevieve Even-Granboulan. *Canadian Journal of Political Science* 24 (1991): 886–889.

Kateb, George. "Freedom and Worldliness in the Thought of Hannah Arendt." *Political Theory* 5 (1977): 141–182.

Kateb, George. "Dismantling Philosophy." *The American Scholar* 47 (1978): 118–126.

Kateb, George. *Hannah Arendt: Politics, Conscience, Evil.* Totowa, NJ: Rowman and Allanheld, 1984.

Kateb, George. "Death and Politics: Hannah Arendt's Reflections on the American Constitution." *Social Research* 54 (1987): 605–616.

Kateb, George. "Arendt and Representative Democracy." In *The Realm of Humanitas: Responses to the Writings of Hannah Arendt.* New York: Lang, 1990.

Kazin, Alfred. "Uprooted Writers." In *Contemporaries: From the 19th Century to the Present.* New York: Horizon Press, 1982.

Kazin, Alfred. "The European Writers in Exile." In *The Muses Flee Hitler: Cultural Transfer and Adaptation, 1930–1945,* edited by Jarrell Jackman and Carla Borden. Washington, DC: Smithsonian Institute Press, 1983.

Keenan, Alan. "Promises, Promises: The Abyss of Freedom and the Loss of the Political in the Work of Hannah Arendt." *Political Theory* 22 (1994): 297–322.

Kessler, Clive. "The Politics of Jewish Identity: Arendt and Zionism." In *Hannah Arendt: Thinking, Judging, Freedom,* edited by Gisela T. Kaplan and Clive Kessler. Sydney: Unwin Hyman, 1989.

King, Richard. "Endings and Beginnings: Politics in Arendt's Early Thought." *Political Theory* 12 (1984): 235–251.

Klawiter, Maren. "Using Arendt and Heidegger to Consider Feminist Thinking on Women and Reproduction/Infertility Technologies." *Hypatia* (1990) 65–89.

Knauer, James. "Motive and Goal in Hannah Arendt's Concept of Political Action." *American Political Science Review* 74 (1980): 721–733.

Knauer, James. Review of *Into the Dark: Hannah Arendt and Totalitarianism,* by Stephen J. Whitfield. *American Political Science Review* 75 (1981): 755–756.

Knauer, James. "On Canovan, 'Pitkin, Arendt, and Justice'." *Political Theory* 11 (1983): 451–454.

Knauer, James. "Re-thinking Arendt's 'Vita Activa': Towards a Theory of Democratic Praxis." *Praxis International* 5 (1985): 185–194.

Knauer, James. "Hannah Arendt on Judgment, Philosophy and Praxis." *International Studies in Philosophy* 21 (1989): 71–83.

Kohn, Jerome. "Thinking/Acting." *Social Research* 57 (1990): 105–134.

Kotler, Milton. "Biblical Faith and Political Life." *Dialog* 16 (1977): 25–30.

Krieger, Leonard. "The Historical Hannah Arendt." *Journal of Modern History* 48 (1976): 672–684.

Lambert, Jean. *The Human Action of Forgiving: A Critical Application of the Metaphysics of Alfred North Whitehead.* Lanham, MD: University Press of America, 1965.

Lane, Ann. "The Feminism of Hannah Arendt." *Democracy* 3 (1983): 107–117.

Lang, Berel. "Hannah Arendt and the Politics of Evil." In *Hannah Arendt: Critical Essays,* edited by Lewis P. Hinchman and Sandra K. Hinchman. Albany: State University of New York Press, 1994.

Laqueur, Walter. "Footnotes to the Holocaust." In *The Jew as Pariah: Jewish Identity and Politics in the Modern Age,* edited by Ron Feldman. New York: Grove Press, 1978.

Laqueur, Walter. "A Reply to Hannah Arendt." In *The Jew as Pariah: Jewish Identity and Politics in the Modern Age*, edited by Ron Feldman. New York: Grove Press, 1978.

Laqueur, Walter. "Re-reading Hannah Arendt." *Encounter* 52 (1979): 73–79.

Laqueur, Walter. "Hannah Arendt in Jerusalem: The Controversy Revisited." In *Western Society After the Holocaust*, edited by Lyman H. Letgers. Boulder, CO: Westview Press, 1983.

Lasch, Christopher. "Introduction" to special issue on Arendt. *Salmagundi* 60 (1983): iv–xvi.

LeFort, Claude. *Democracy and Political Theory*. Translated by David Macey. Minneapolis, University of Minnesota Press, 1988.

Levin, Martin. "On *Animal Laborans* and *Homo Politicus* in Hannah Arendt: A Note." *Political Theory* 7 (1979): 521–531.

Lichtheim, George. "Two Revolutions." In *The Concept of Ideology and Other Essays*. New York: Random House, 1967.

Litke, Robert F. "Why Domination Defeats Us: A Hobbesian Analysis." In *On the Eve of the 21st Century*, edited by William C. Gay. Lanham, MD: Rowman and Littlefield, 1994.

Lowell, Robert. "On Hannah Arendt." *New York Review of Books* (13 May 1976): 6.

Luban, David. "On Habermas on Arendt on Power." *Philosophy and Social Criticism* 6 (1979): 79–95.

Luban, David. "Explaining Dark Times: Hannah Arendt's Theory of Theory." In *Hannah Arendt: Critical Essays*, edited by Lewis P. Hinchman and Sandra K. Hinchman. Albany: State University of New York Press, 1994.

Lustigman, Mike. "The Fifth Business: The Business of Surviving in Extremity." *The Human Context* 7 (1975): 426–440.

Macauley, David. "Out of Place and Outer Space: Hannah Arendt on Earth Alienation." *Capitalism, Nature, Socialism* 3 (1992): 19–45.

MacCannell, Juliet Flower. "Facing Fascism: A Feminine Politics of *Jouissance*." *Topoi* 12 (1993): 137–151.

MacDonald, Dwight. "Arguments." *Partisan Review* 2 (1964): 262–269.

Macdonald, H. Malcolm. Review of *Lectures on Kant's Political Philosophy*, by Hannah Arendt. *Social Science Quarterly* 64 (1983): 914–915.

MacIntyre, Alasdair. "Hannah Arendt as Thinker." *Commonweal* 109 (1982): 471–472.

Major, Robert. "A Reading of Hannah Arendt's 'Unusual' Distinction between Labor and Work." In *Hannah Arendt: The Recovery of the Public World*, edited by Melvyn Hill. New York: St. Martin's Press, 1979.

Maletz, Donald J. Review of *Lectures on Kant's Political Philosophy*, by Hannah Arendt. *American Political Science Review* 78 (1984): 277–278.

Margolis, Joseph. "Prospects for a Theory of Radical History." *Monist* (1991): 268–292.

Markus, Maria. "The 'Anti-Feminism' of Hannah Arendt." In *Hannah Arendt: Thinking, Judging, Freedom*, edited by Gisela T. Kaplan and Clive Kessler. Sydney: Unwin Hyman, 1989.

May, Derwent. *Hannah Arendt.* New York: Penguin, 1986.

May, Larry. "On Conscience". *American Philosophical Quarterly* 20 (1983): 57–67.

May, William E. "*Animal Laborans* and *Homo Faber*: Reflections on a Theology of Work." *Thomist* 36 (1972): 626–644.

Mayer, Robert. "Hannah Arendt, National Socialism and the Project of Foundation." *Review of Politics* 47 (1991): 469–487.

Mayer, Robert. "Hannah Arendt, Leninism, and the Disappearance of Authority." *Polity* 24 (1992): 399ff.

McBride, William L. "What is the Value of Thinking?" Review of *Hannah Arendt: For Love of the World* by Elisabeth Young-Bruehl. *Yale Law Journal* 92 (1982): 396.

McBride, William L. Review of *Hannah Arendt and the Search for a New Political Philosophy*, by Bhikhu Parekh. *Review of Politics* 46 (1984): 141–142.

McCarthy, Mary. *On the Contrary.* New York: Farrar, Straus, and Cudahy, 1961.

McCarthy, Mary. "The Hue and Cry." *Partisan Review* 31 (1964): 82–94.

McCarthy, Mary. "Discussion." *Partisan Review* 31 (1964): 253–283.

McCarthy, Mary. "Correction." *Partisan Review* 31 (1964): 478.

McCarthy, Mary. "Saying Good-by to Hannah." *New York Review of Books* (22 January 1976): 8–11.

McCarthy, Mary. "Hannah Arendt and Politics." *Partisan Review* 51 and 52 (1985): 729–738.

McKenna, George. "On Hannah Arendt; Politics: As It Is, Was, Might Be." In *The Legacy of the German Refugee Intellectuals*, edited by Robert Boyers. New York: Schocken Books, 1972.

McKenna, George. "Bannisterless Politics: Hannah Arendt and Her Children." *History of Political Thought* 5 (1984): 333–360.

Megged, Matti. "Hannah Arendt and Jewish Nationalism." In *Proceedings of "History, Ethics, Politics": A Conference Based on the Work of Hannah Arendt*, edited by Robert Boyers. New York: Empire State College, 1982.

Milchman, Alan. "Hannah Arendt and the Etiology of the Desk Killer: The Holocaust as Portent." *History of European Ideas* 14 (1992): 213–226.

Miller, James. "The Pathos of Novelty: Hannah Arendt's Image of Freedom in the Modern World." In *Hannah Arendt: The Recovery of the Public World*, edited by Melvyn Hill. New York: St. Martin's Press, 1979.

Minnich, Elizabeth K. "Hannah Arendt: Thinking as We Are." In *Between Women*, edited by Carol Ascher, Louise De Salvo, and Sara Ruddick. Boston: Beacon Press, 1984.

Minnich, Elizabeth K. "Friendship Between Women: The Act of Feminist Biography". Review of *Hannah Arendt: For Love of the World*, by Elisabeth Young-Bruehl. *Feminist Studies* 11 (1985): 287–305.

Minnich, Elizabeth K. "To Judge in Freedom: Hannah Arendt on the Relation of Thinking and Morality." In *Hannah Arendt: Thinking, Judging, Freedom*, edited by Gisela T. Kaplan and Clive Kessler. Sydney: Unwin Hyman, 1989.

Moehle, Natalia. *The Dimensions of Evil and of Transcendence: A Sociological Perspective.* Washington, DC: University Press of America, 1978.

Moors, Kent. "Modernity and Human Initiative: The Structure of Hannah Arendt's *Life of the Mind.*" *Political Science Reviewer* 10 (1980): 189–230.

Morganthau, Hans. "Hannah Arendt 1906–1975." *Political Theory* 4 (1976): 5ff.

Morganthau, Hans. "Hannah Arendt on Totalitarianism and Democracy." *Social Research* 44 (1977): 127–131.

Moruzzi, Norma C. "Re-placing the Margin: (Non)Representations of Colonialism in Hannah Arendt's *The Origins of Totalitarianism.*" *Tulsa Studies in Women's Literature* 10 (1991): 109–120.

Muller, Sharon. "The Origins of *Eichmann in Jerusalem*: Hannah Arendt's Interpretation of Jewish History." *Jewish Social Studies* 43 (1981): 237–254.

Nash, Henry. "The Bureaucratization of Homicide." *The Bulletin of Atomic Scientists* 36 (1980): 22–27.

Nelson, John. "Politics and Truth: Arendt's Problematic." *American Journal of Political Science* 22 (1978): 270–301.

Neyer, Joseph. "The Condition of Man and the State of the Jews." *Midstream* 26 (1980): 57–60.

Nichols, R. "Rebels, Beginners, and Buffoons: Politics as Action." In *Political Theory and Praxis: New Perspectives*, edited by Terence Ball. Minneapolis: University of Minnesota Press, 1977.

Nielsen, Richard. "Toward an Action Philosophy for Managers Based on Arendt and Tillich." *Journal of Business Ethics* 3 (1984): 153–162.

Nisbet, Robert. "Hannah Arendt and the American Revolution." *Social Research* 44 (1977): 63–79.

Nordquist, Joan. *Hannah Arendt.* Santa Cruz, CA: Reference and Research Services, 1989.

Nye, Andrea. *Philosophia: The Thought of Rosa Luxemburg, Simone Weil, and Hannah Arendt.* New York, Routledge, 1994.

O'Brien, Mary. *The Politics of Reproduction.* Boston: Routledge and Kegan Paul, 1981.

O'Neil, John. "Violence, Technology, and the Body Politic." In *Reason and Violence: Philosophical Investigations*, edited by Sherman Stanage. Totowa, NJ: Rowman and Littlefield, 1975.

O'Sullivan, Noel. "Politics, Totalitarianism and Freedom: The Political Thought of Hannah Arendt." *Political Studies* 21 (1973): 183–198.

O'Sullivan, Noel. "Hannah Arendt: Hellenic Nostalgia and Industrial Society." In *Contemporary Political Philosophers*, edited by Anthony de Crespigny and Kenneth Minogue. New York: Dodd, Mead and Company, 1975.

Parekh, Bhikhu C. "Hannah Arendt's Critique of Marx." In *Hannah Arendt: The Recovery of the Public World*, edited by Melvyn Hill. New York: St. Martin's Press, 1979.

Parekh, Bhikhu C. *Hannah Arendt and the Search for a New Political Philosophy*. Atlantic Highlands, NJ: Humanities Press International, 1981.

Parekh, Bhikhu. C. *Contemporary Political Thinkers*. Baltimore: Johns Hopkins University Press, 1982.

Passerin d'Entrèves, Maurizio. "Agency, Identity and Culture: Hannah Arendt's Conception of Citizenship." *Praxis International* 9 (1989): 1–24.

Passerin d'Entrèves, Maurizio. "Freedom, Plurality, Solidarity: Hannah Arendt's Theory of Action." *Philosophy and Social Criticism* 15 (1989): 317–350.

Passerin d'Entrèves, Maurizio. *The Political Philosophy of Hannah Arendt*. London; New York: Routledge, 1994.

Peters, Richard. "Dark Illumination." *The Nation* 187 (4 October 1958): 196–197.

Phelan, Shane. Review of *Meditations on Modern Political Thought: Masculine/Feminine Themes from Luther to Arendt*, by Jean B. Elshtain. *Women and Politics* 9 (1989): 110ff.

Phillips, William. "Hannah Arendt and Lionel Trilling." *Partisan Review* 43 (1977): 9–11.

Phillips, William. "Four Portraits." *Partisan Review* 50 (1983): 537–543.

Pickens, Donald K. Review of *Hannah Arendt: For Love of the World*, by Elisabeth Young-Bruehl. *History: Review of New Books* 11 (1983): 130–131.

Pietz, William. "The 'Post-Colonialism' of Cold War Discourse." *Social Text* 19–20 (1988): 55–75.

Pitkin, Hanna Fenichel. "Are Freedom and Liberty Twins?" *Political Theory* 16 (1988): 533–552.

Pitkin, Hanna Fenichel. "Justice: On Relating Private and Public." In *Hannah Arendt: Critical Essays*, edited by Lewis P. Hinchman and Sandra K. Hinchman. Albany: State University of New York Press, 1994.

Podhoretz, Norman. "Hannah Arendt on Eichmann: A Study in the Perversity of Brilliance." *Commentary* 36 (1963): 201–208.

Power, M. Susan. Review of *Human Nature Under Fire: The Political Philosophy of Hannah Arendt*, by Gordon J. Tolle. *American Political Science Review* 78 (1984): 587–588.

Presbey, Gail M. "Hannah Arendt on Nonviolence and Political Action." In *Nonviolence: Social and Psychological Issues*, edited by Vinod K. Kool. Lanham, MD: University Press of America, 1993.

Quinton, Anthony. "Culture and Expertise." *Listener* 83 (1970): 348–349.

Raffel, S. "Health and Life." *Theoretical Medicine* 6 (1985): 153–164.

Reck, Andrew. "Metaphysics and Authority." *Cogito* 1 (1983): 1–13.

Redfield, James. "The Sense of Crisis." In *New Views on the Nature of Man*, edited by J. Platt. Chicago: University Press, 1965.

Reshaur, Ken. "Concepts of Solidarity in the Political Theory of Hannah Arendt." *Canadian Journal of Political Science* 25 (1992): 723–736.

Richardson, William. "Contemplation in Action." In *The Public Realm: Essays on Discursive Types in Political Philosophy*, edited by Reiner Schürmann. Albany, NY: State University of New York Press, 1989.

Ricoeur, Paul. "Action, Story and History." *Salmagundi* 60 (1983): 60–72.

Ricoeur, Paul. "Action, Story, and History—On Rereading *The Human Condition*." In *The Realm of Humanitas: Responses to the Writings of Hannah Arendt*. New York: Lang, 1990.

Rieff, Philip. "The Theology of Politics: Reflections on Totalitarianism as the Burden of Our Time." *Journal of Religion* 32 (1952): 119–126.

Riesman, David. "The Path to Total Terror." *Commentary* 11 (1951): 392–398.

Riley, Patrick. "On DeLue's Review of Arendt's *Lectures on Kant's Political Philosophy*." *Political Theory* 12 (1984): 435–439.

Riley, Patrick. "Hannah Arendt on Kant, Truth and Politics." In *Essays on Kant's Political Philosophy*, edited by Howard Lloyd Williams. Chicago: University of Chicago Press, 1992.

Ring, Jennifer. "On Needing Both Marx and Arendt: Alienation and the Flight from Inwardness." *Political Theory* 17 (1989): 432–448.

Ring, Jennifer. *Modern Political Theory and Contemporary Feminism: A Dialectical Analysis*. Albany: State University of New York Press, 1991.

Ring, Jennifer. "The Pariah as Hero: Hannah Arendt's Political Actor." *Political Theory* 19 (1991): 433–452.

Roach, Timothy. "Enspirited Words and Deeds: Christian Metaphors Implicit in Arendt's Concept of Personal Action." In *Amor Mundi: Explorations in the Thought of Hannah Arendt*, edited by James Bernauer. Boston: Martinus Nijhoff, 1987.

Robinson, Jacob. *And the Crooked Shall Be Made Straight: The Eichmann Trial, The Jewish Catastrophe, and Hannah Arendt's Narrative*. New York: Macmillan, 1965.

Rogozinski, Jacob. "Hell on Earth: Hannah Arendt in the Face of Hitler." Translated by Peter Dews. *Philosophy Today* 37 (1993): 257–274.

Roman, Joel. "Thinking Politics without a Philosophy of History: Arendt and Merleau-Ponty." Translated by Stephen Michaelman. *Philosophy and Social Criticism* 15 (1989): 403–422.

Rosenfield, Lawrence W. "Hannah Arendt's Legacy." *Quarterly Journal of Speech* 70 (1984): 90–96.

Rosenthal, Abigail. *A Good Look at Evil*. Philadelphia: Temple University Press, 1987.

Rostenstreich, Nathan. "Introspection Without Insight." *Midstream* 26 (1980): 47–53.

Rostenstreich, Nathan. "Can Evil Be Banal?" *Philosophical Forum* 16 (1984): 50–62.

Roth, Michael S. "The Ironist's Cage." *Political Theory* 19 (1991): 419–432.

Rubenstein, Richard L. "The Philosopher and the Jews: The Case of Martin Heidegger." *Modern Judaism* 9 (1989): 179–196.

Rubenstein, Richard L. "Totalitarianism and Population Superfluity." In *The Realm of Humanitas: Responses to the Writings of Hannah Arendt*. New York: Lang, 1990.

Rubinoff, Lionel. "The Dialectic of Work and Labour in the Ontology of Man." *Humanitas* 7 (1971): 147–176.

Rumscheidt, H. Martin. "Voices from Prison: Boethius and Bonhoeffer." *Studies in Religion/Sciences Réligieuses* 10 (1981): 463–471.

Ryan, A. "A Thinker of Our Time." *New Society* (10 June 1982): 434–435.

Schoenbaum, David. Commentary on "Hannah Arendt in Jerusalem: The Controversy Revisited," by Walter Laqueur. In *Western Society After the Holocaust*, edited by Lyman H. Letgers. Boulder, CO: Westview Press, 1983.

Scholem, Gershom. "*Eichmann in Jerusalem*: An Exchange of Letters [with Hannah Arendt]." In *The Jew as Pariah: Jewish Identity and Politics in the Modern Age*, edited by Ron Feldman. New York: Grove Press, 1978.

Schwartz, Benjamin. "The Religion of Politics: Reflections on the Thought of Hannah Arendt." *Dissent* 17 (1970): 144–161.

Schwartz, Joseph M. "Arendt's Politics: The Elusive Search for Substance." *Praxis International* 9 (1989): 25–47.

Schweder, Richard. "Dialogue Amid the Deluge." *New York Times Book Review* (20 September 1992): 1, 53–54.

Scott, Joanna Vecchiarelli. "'A Detour Through Pietism': Hannah Arendt on St. Augustine's Philosophy of Freedom." *Polity* 20 (1988): 394ff.

Scully, Edgar. "Aquinas' State: A Tyrranical Household Writ Large?" *Science et Esprit* 33 (1981): 379–393.

Seery, John E. "Floating Balloons: An Essay on Nonviolent Theory, Irony, and the Anti-Nuclear Movement." *Soundings* 70 (1987): 355–377.

Shanks, Andrew. *Hegel's Political Theology.* Cambridge: Cambridge University Press, 1992.

Sharp, Gene. *Social Power and Political Freedom.* Boston: Porter Sargent, 1980.

Shklar, Judith. "Hannah Arendt's Triumph." *The New Republic* (27 December 1975): 8–10.

Shklar, Judith. "Rethinking the Past." *Social Research* 44 (1977): 80–90.

Shklar, Judith. "Hannah Arendt as Pariah." *Partisan Review* 50 (1983): 64–77.

Siebers, Tobin. "Kant and the Origins of Totalitarianism." *Philosophy and Literature* 15 (1991): 19–39.

Siebers, Tobin. "The Politics of Storytelling: Hannah Arendt's *Eichmann in Jerusalem.*" *Southern Humanities Review* 26 (1992): 201–211.

Simon, Ernest. "Revisionist History of the Jewish Catastrophe: A Textual Examination." *Judaism* 12 (1963): 387–415.

Sitton, John. "Hannah Arendt's Argument for Council Democracy." In *Hannah Arendt: Critical Essays*, edited by Lewis P. Hinchman and Sandra K. Hinchman. Albany: State University of New York Press, 1994. Originally published in *Polity* 20 (1981): 80–100.

Skoller, Eleanor Honig. *The In-between of Writing: Experience and Experiment in Drabble, Duras, and Arendt.* Ann Arbor: University of Michigan Press, 1993.

Smith, Steven B. Review of *Lectures on Kant's Political Philosophy*, by Hannah Arendt. *Ethics* 94 (1984): 531–534.

Smith, Steven B. Review of *Hannah Arendt: Politics, Conscience, Evil*, by George Kateb. *Ethics* 95 (1985): 362–364.

Snauwaert, Dale T. "Reclaiming the Lost Treasure: Deliberation and Strong Democratic Education." *Educational Theory* 42 (1992): 351–367.

Sollers, Werner. "Of Mules and Mares in a Land of Difference: Or, Quadrupeds All?" *American Quarterly* 42 (1990): 167–190.

Sontheimer, K. "Hannah Arendt." *Political Studies* 24 (1976): 192–194.

Spitz, David. "Politics and the Realms of Being." *Dissent* 6 (1959): 56–65.

Spitz, David. "The Politics of Segregation." In *Essays on the Liberal Idea of Freedom.* Phoenix: University of Arizona Press, 1964.

Springborg, Patricia. "Arendt, Republicanism, and Patriarchalism." *History of Political Thought* 10 (1989): 499–523.

Stanley, John L. "The Uncertain Hobbesian: Ellul's Dialogue with the Sovereign and the Tradition of French Politics." In *Jacques Ellul: Interpretive Essays*, edited by Clifford G. Christians and Jay M. Van Hook. Urbana: University of Chicago Press, 1981.

Stanley, John L. "Is Totalitarianism a New Phenomenon? Reflections on Hannah Arendt's *Origins of Totalitarianism.*" In *Hannah Arendt: Critical Essays*, edited by Lewis P. Hinchman and Sandra K. Hinchman. Albany: State University of New York Press, 1994.

Staub, Ervin. *Roots of Evil: The Origins of Genocide and Other Group Violence.* New York: Cambridge University Press, 1989.

Steinberger, Peter. "Hannah Arendt on Judgment." *American Journal of Political Science* 34 (1990): 803–821.

Stern, Peter and Jean Yarbrough. "Hannah Arendt." *American Scholar* 47 (1978): 371–381.

Sternberger, Dolf. "The Sunken City: Hannah Arendt's Idea of Politics." *Social Research* 44 (1977): 132–146.

Stillman, Peter. "Freedom as Participation: The Revolutionary Theories of Hegel and Arendt." *American Behavioral Scientist* 20 (1977): 477–479.

Stolz, Matthew F. Review of *Hannah Arendt: For Love of the World*, by Elisabeth Young-Bruehl. *American Political Science Review* 77 (1983): 552–553.

Stolz, Matthew F. Review of *Hannah Arendt: Politics, Conscience, Evil*, by George Kateb. *American Political Science Review* 79 (1985): 283–284.

Stortz, Martha E. "Beyond Justice: Friendship in the City." *Word and World* 14 (1994): 409–418.

Suchting, W. A. "Marx and Hannah Arendt's *The Human Condition.*" *Ethics* 73 (1962–1963): 47–55.

Sullivan, Robert R. "Public Authority, Technology, Speech and Language." *Polity* 14 (1982): 585–602.

Syrkin, Marie. "Hannah Arendt: The Clothes of the Empress." *Dissent* 4 (1963): 344–352.

Tamineaux, Jacques. "Phenomenology and the Problem of Action." *Philosophy and Social Criticism* 11 (1986): 207–219.

Tartakower, A. "Self-Hate of Hannah Arendt." *World Jewry* 6 (1963): 8–9.

Taylor, Allen. Review of *Hannah Arendt: Politics, Conscience, Evil*, by George Kateb. *Review of Metaphysics* 38 (1985): 645–647.

Thalberg, Irving. "Socialization and Autonomous Behavior." *Tulane Studies in Philosophy* 28 (1979): 21–37.

Thompson, Kenneth W. "Power, Force, and Diplomacy." *Review of Politics* 43 (1981): 410–435.

Thompson, Kirk. "Constitutional Theory and Political Action." *Journal of Politics* 31 (1969): 655–681.

Tijmes, Pieter. "The Archimedean Point and Eccentricity: Hannah Arendt's Philosophy of Science and Technology." *Inquiry* 35 (1992): 389–406.

Tlaba, Gabriel. *Politics and Freedom: Human Will and Action in the Thought of Hannah Arendt.* Lanham, MD: University Press of America, 1987.

Tolle, Gordon. *Human Nature Under Fire: The Political Philosophy of Hannah Arendt.* Washington, DC: University Press of America, 1982.

Tolle, Gordon. Review of *Hannah Arendt: Politics, Conscience, Evil,* by George Kateb. *Review of Politics* 47 (1985): 309–312.

Tumin, Melvin. "Pie in the Sky . . ." *Dissent* 6 (1959): 65–71.

Udovicki, Jasminka. "The Uses of Freedom and the Human Condition." *Praxis International* 3 (1983): 54–61.

Villa, Dana. "Beyond Good and Evil: Arendt, Nietzsche, and the Aestheticization of Political Action." *Political Theory* 29 (1992): 274–308.

Villa, Dana. "Postmodernism and the Public Sphere." *American Political Science Review* 86 (1992): 712–721.

Voegelin, Eric. "The Origins of Totalitarianism." *Review of Politics* 15 (1953): 68–76.

Vollrath, Ernst. "Hannah Arendt and the Method of Political Thinking." *Social Research* 44 (1977): 160–182.

Wadler, Neal S. Review of *Hannah Arendt: For Love of the World,* by Elisabeth Young-Bruehl. *The Historian* 46 (1983): 111–112.

Wainwright, Eric. "The *Vita Activa* of Hannah Arendt." *Politikon* 16 (1989): 22ff.

Wald, Alan M. "Radical Evil." *Reviews in American History* 9 (1981): 260–265.

Wald, Alan M. Review of *Into the Dark: Hannah Arendt and Totalitarianism,* by Stephen J. Whitfield. *Reviews in American History* 9 (1981): 260–265.

Wanker, William Paul. *"Nous" and "Logos": Philosophical Foundations of Hannah Arendt's Political Theory.* Hamden CT: Garland, 1991.

Washington, Johnny. *Alain Locke and Philosophy: A Quest for Cultural Pluralism.* Westport, CT: Greenwood Press, 1986.

Washington, Johnny. "An Outline of an Economic Ethics for Developing Countries." *Journal of Social Philosophy* 25 (1994): 110–116.

Watson, David. "Hannah Arendt and the American Republic." *Transactions of the Peirce Society* 28 (1992): 423–465.

Weiss-Rosmarin, T. "Hannah Arendt as a Topic." *Jewish Spectator* 29 (1964): 4–5.

Weissberg, Liliane. "Stepping Out: The Writing of Difference in Rahel Varnhagen's Letters." In *Anti-Semitism in Times of Crisis,* edited by Sander L. Gilman and Steven T. Katz. New York: New York University Press, 1991.

West, Thomas. *Nature, Community, and Will: A Study in Literary and Social Thought.* Columbia: University of Missouri Press, 1976.

Whiteside, Kerry H. "Hannah Arendt and Ecological Ethics." *Environmental Ethics* 16 (1994): 339–358.

Whitfield, Stephen J. *Into the Dark: Hannah Arendt and Totalitarianism.* Philadelphia: Temple University Press, 1980.

Whitfield, Stephen J. "Hannah Arendt and the Banality of Evil." *History Teacher* 14 (1981): 469–478.

Whitfield, Stephen J. "Hannah Arendt and Apocalypse." *Michigan Quarterly Review* 26 (1987): 445–458.

Wieseltier. Leon. "Hannah Arendt's History of the Jews." In *Proceedings of "History, Ethics, Politics": A Conference Based on the Work of Hannah Arendt,* edited by Robert Boyers. New York: Empire State College, 1982.

Winant, Terry. "The Feminist Standpoint: A Matter of Language." *Hypatia* 2 (1987): 123–148.

Winter, Gibson. "The Challenge of Nuclearism [response to critics of 'Hope for the Earth']." *Religion and Intellectual Life* 1 (1984): 137–145.

Winter, Gibson. "Hope for the Earth: A Hermeneutic of Nuclearism." *Religion and Intellectual Life* 1 (1984): 5–29.

Winters, Francis X. "The Banality of Virtue: Reflection on Hannah Arendt's Reinterpretation of Political Ethics." In *Amor Mundi: Explorations in the Thought of Hannah Arendt,* edited by James Bernauer. Boston: Martinus Nijhoff, 1987.

Wobbe, Theresa. "Hannah Arendt." In *Against Patriarchal Thinking: Proceedings of the VIth Symposium of the International Association of Women Philosophers.* Amsterdam: VU University Press, 1992.

Wolff, Kurt. "On the Significance of Hannah Arendt's *The Human Condition* for Sociology." *Inquiry* 4 (1961): 67–106.

Wolin, Sheldon. "Hannah Arendt and the Ordinance of Time." *Social Research* 44 (1977): 91–105.

Wolin, Sheldon. "Paradigms and Political Theories." In *Politics and Experience: Essays Presented to Michael Oakeshott,* edited by P. King and Bhikhu Parekh. Cambridge: Cambridge University Press, 1978.

Wolin, Sheldon. "Stopping to Think." *New York Review of Books* 25, no. 16 (1978): 16–21.

Wolin, Sheldon. "Democracy and the Political." In *The Realm of Humanitas: Responses to the Writings of Hannah Arendt.* New York: Lang, 1990.

Wolin, Sheldon. "Hannah Arendt: Democracy and the Political." In *Hannah Arendt: Critical Essays,* edited by Lewis P. Hinchman and Sandra K. Hinchman. Albany: State University of New York Press, 1994.

Woolf, Robert Paul. "Notes for Materialist Analysis of the Public and Private Realms." *Graduate Faculty Philosophy Journal* 9 (1982): 135–150.

Woolfolk, Alan. "Hannah Arendt: The Burden of Anticreedal Culture." *Human Studies* 10 (1987): 247–261.

Yaeger, P. "Hannah Arendt and the Banality of Evil." *History Teacher* 14 (1981): 469–478.

Yaeger, P. "The Animality of the Letter." In *Honey-Mad Women: Emancipatory Strategies in Women's Writing*. New York: Columbia University Press, 1988.

Yarbrough, Jean, and Peter Stern. "Hannah Arendt." *American Scholar* 47 (1978): 371–381.

Yarbrough, Jean, and Peter Stern. "*Vita Activa* and *Vita Contemplativa*: Reflections on Hannah Arendt's Political Thought in *The Life of the Mind*." *Review of Politics* 43 (1981): 323–354.

Young, Iris M. *Justice and the Politics of Difference*. Princeton: Princeton University Press, 1990.

Young-Bruehl, Elisabeth. "Hannah Arendt's Storytelling." *Social Research* 44 (1977): 183–190.

Young-Bruehl, Elisabeth. "A Chronological Bibliography of the Works of Hannah Arendt." In *Hannah Arendt: The Recovery of the Public World*, edited by Melvyn Hill. New York: St. Martin's Press, 1979.

Young-Bruehl, Elisabeth. "From the Pariah's Point of View: Reflections on Hannah Arendt's Life and Work." In *Hannah Arendt: The Recovery of the Public World*, edited by Melvyn Hill. New York: St. Martin's Press, 1979.

Young-Bruehl, Elisabeth. "Accuracy on Arendt." Commentary on J. Baron, "Hannah Arendt: Personal Reflections." *Response* 12 (1981): 90–91.

Young-Bruehl, Elisabeth. *Hannah Arendt: For Love of the World*. New Haven: Yale University Press, 1982.

Young-Bruehl, Elisabeth. "Cosmopolitan History." *Review of International Philosophy* 37 (1983): 440–459.

Young-Bruehl, Elisabeth. "Reflections on Hannah Arendt's *The Life of the Mind*." In *Hannah Arendt: Critical Essays*, edited by Lewis P. Hinchman and Sandra K. Hinchman. Albany: State University of New York Press, 1994.

Zagorski, Paul W. Review of *Human Nature Under Fire: The Political Philosophy of Hannah Arendt*, by Gordon J. Tolle. *Midwest Quarterly* 27 (1986): 260–263.

Index

Index

Studies in Contemporary German Social Thought

Thomas McCarthy, General Editor

Theodor W. Adorno, *Against Epistemology: A Metacritique*
Theodor W. Adorno, *Hegel: Three Studies*
Theodor W. Adorno, *Prisms*
Karl-Otto Apel, *Understanding and Explanation: A Transcendental-Pragmatic Perspective*
Seyla Benhabib, Wolfgang Bonß, and John McCole, editors, *On Max Horkheimer: New Perspectives*
Seyla Benhabib and Fred Dallmayr, editors, *The Communicative Ethics Controversy*
Richard J. Bernstein, editor, *Habermas and Modernity*
Ernst Bloch, *Natural Law and Human Dignity*
Ernst Bloch, *The Principle of Hope*
Ernst Bloch, *The Utopian Function of Art and Literature: Selected Essays*
Hans Blumenberg, *The Genesis of the Copernican World*
Hans Blumenberg, *The Legitimacy of the Modern Age*
Hans Blumenberg, *Work on Myth*
Susan Buck-Morss, *The Dialectics of Seeing: Walter Benjamin and the* Arcades Project
Craig Calhoun, editor, *Habermas and the Public Sphere*
Jean Cohen and Andrew Arato, *Civil Society and Political Theory*
Maeve Cooke, *Language and Reason: A Study of Habermas's Pragmatics*
Helmut Dubiel, *Theory and Politics: Studies in the Development of Critical Theory*
John Forester, editor, *Critical Theory and Public Life*
David Frisby, *Fragments of Modernity: Theories of Modernity in the Work of Simmel, Kracauer and Benjamin*
Hans-Georg Gadamer, *Philosophical Apprenticeships*
Hans-Georg Gadamer, *Reason in the Age of Science*
Jürgen Habermas, *Between Facts and Norms: Contributions to a Discourse Theory of Law and Democracy*
Jürgen Habermas, *Justification and Application: Remarks on Discourse Ethics*
Jürgen Habermas, *On the Logic of the Social Sciences*
Jürgen Habermas, *Moral Consciousness and Communicative Action*
Jürgen Habermas, *The New Conservatism: Cultural Criticism and the Historians' Debate*
Jürgen Habermas, *The Philosophical Discourse of Modernity: Twelve Lectures*
Jürgen Habermas, *Philosophical-Political Profiles*
Jürgen Habermas, *Postmetaphysical Thinking: Philosophical Essays*
Jürgen Habermas, *The Structural Transformation of the Public Sphere: An Inquiry into a Category of Bourgeois Society*
Jürgen Habermas, editor, *Observations on "The Spiritual Situation of the Age"*
Axel Honneth, *The Critique of Power: Reflective Stages in a Critical Social Theory*
Axel Honneth and Hans Joas, editors, *Communicative Action: Essays on Jürgen Habermas's* The Theory of Communicative Action
Axel Honneth, Thomas McCarthy, Claus Offe, and Albrecht Wellmer, editors, *Cultural-Political Interventions in the Unfinished Project of Enlightenment*
Axel Honneth, Thomas McCarthy, Claus Offe, and Albrecht Wellmer, editors, *Philosophical Interventions in the Unfinished Project of Enlightenment*
Max Horkheimer, *Between Philosophy and Social Science: Selected Early Writings*
Hans Joas, *G. H. Mead: A Contemporary Re-examination of His Thought*
Michael Kelly, editor, *Critique and Power: Recasting the Foucault/Habermas Debate*
Reinhart Koselleck, *Critique and Crisis: Enlightenment and the Pathogenesis of Modern Society*
Reinhart Koselleck, *Futures Past: On the Semantics of Historical Time*

Harry Liebersohn, *Fate and Utopia in German Sociology, 1887–1923*
Herbert Marcuse, *Hegel's Ontology and the Theory of Historicity*
Larry May and Jerome Kohn, editors, *Hannah Arendt: Twenty Years Later*
Pierre Missac, *Walter Benjamin's Passages*
Gil G. Noam and Thomas E. Wren, editors, *The Moral Self*
Guy Oakes, Weber and Rickert: *Concept Formation in the Cultural Sciences*
Claus Offe, *Contradictions of the Welfare State*
Claus Offe, *Disorganized Capitalism: Contemporary Transformations of Work and Politics*
Helmut Peukert, *Science, Action, and Fundamental Theology: Toward a Theology of Communicative Action*
Joachim Ritter, *Hegel and the French Revolution: Essays on the Philosophy of Right*
William E. Scheuerman, *Between the Norm and the Exception: The Frankfurt School and the Rule of Law*
Alfred Schmidt, *History and Structure: An Essay on Hegelian-Marxist and Structuralist Theories of History*
Dennis Schmidt, *The Ubiquity of the Finite: Hegel, Heidegger, and the Entitlements of Philosophy*
Carl Schmitt, *The Crisis of Parliamentary Democracy*
Carl Schmitt, *Political Romanticism*
Carl Schmitt, *Political Theology: Four Chapters on the Concept of Sovereignty*
Gary Smith, editor, *On Walter Benjamin: Critical Essays and Recollections*
Michael Theunissen, *The Other: Studies in the Social Ontology of Husserl, Heidegger, Sartre, and Buber*
Ernst Tugendhat, *Self-Consciousness and Self-Determination*
Georgia Warnke, *Justice and Interpretation*
Mark Warren, *Nietzsche and Political Thought*
Albrecht Wellmer, *The Persistence of Modernity: Essays on Aesthetics, Ethics, and Postmodernism*
Joel Whitebook, *Perversion and Utopia: A Study in Psychoanalysis and Critical Theory*
Rolf Wiggershaus, *The Frankfurt School: Its History, Theories, and Political Significance*
Thomas E. Wren, editor, *The Moral Domain: Essays in the Ongoing Discussion between Philosophy and the Social Sciences*
Lambert Zuidervaart, *Adorno's Aesthetic Theory: The Redemption of Illusion*